PEARSON

Foundations and Pre-calculus
Mathematics 10

PREPARATION AND PRACTICE BOOK

Jack Hope
Delcy Rolheiser
David Sufrin

PEARSON

Pearson Canada Inc.
26 Prince Andrew Place
Don Mills, ON M3C 2T8
Customer Service: 1-800-361-6128

ISBN: 978-0-321-61066-9

Publisher: Mike Czukar
Research and Communications Manager: Craig Featherstone
Publishing Team:
Claire Burnett
Lesley Haynes
Alison Rieger
Enid Haley
Ioana Gagea
Lynne Gulliver
Cheri Westra
Carolyn Sebestyen
Jane Schell
Karen Alley
Judy Wilson
Design and Art Direction: David Cheung
Composition: Lapiz Digital Services, India
Vice-President, Publishing: Mark Cobham

2 3 4 5 — WC — 14 13 12 11 10
Printed and bound in Canada

Contents

About *Foundations and Pre-calculus Mathematics 10* Preparation and Practice Book

Welcome to *Foundations and Pre-calculus Mathematics 10*.
This *Preparation and Practice Book* offers ways to support your success this year.

For the main lessons of *Foundations and Pre-calculus Mathematics 10*,
this workbook gives you:

- *Skill Builder pages*

  - Each topic identifies a prerequisite skill or concept you will need in that lesson.

  - Each topic starts with a quick review and short example.

  - General rules are highlighted to help you find them more easily.

  - Try the **Check** questions to see whether you're ready to move on.

- *Matching lessons for the ones in your Student Book*

  - General rules are highlighted to help you find them more easily.

  - *Examples* show you what you need to know and be able to do.

  - For each Example, **Check** lets you try a question on your own before moving on.

  - *Practice* questions help you put it all together during the lesson.

- *Step-by-step support*

  - Most questions break down the steps to follow for a complete solution.

For each chapter of *Foundations and Pre-calculus Mathematics 10*, you'll find:

- an opening page that tells you **What You'll Learn** and
  Why It's Important, as well as an expanded list of **Key Words**

- two **Checkpoints** of review pages at appropriate intervals

- a **Chapter Puzzle** for fun and reinforcement

- a **Chapter Study Guide** to summarize key ideas

- **Chapter Review** pages to help you see what you remember

You can check your work as you go. The **Answers** section, starting on page 431,
gives final numerical answers for **Check** and **Practice** questions.

978-0-321-61066-9 Copyright © 2011 Pearson Canada Inc. **v**

Measurement

What You'll Learn

- Convert measurements in imperial units.

- Convert measurements between SI units and imperial units.

- Find surface areas and volumes of:
  prisms
  pyramids
  cylinders
  cones
  spheres

Why It's Important

Imperial units are used by:

- construction workers, to order, measure, and cut building materials

- graphic designers, to label products and containers that are sold in both the United States and Canada

Surface area and volume are used by:

- interior designers, to find the amount of material needed to cover furniture, paint walls, or make drapes and blinds

- farmers, to find the storage space in a silo or bin

Key Words

imperial units	prism
referent	pyramid
SI units	cylinder
slant height	cone
lateral area	sphere

▶ 1.1 Skill Builder

Converting between Mixed Numbers and Improper Fractions

To write the mixed number $4\frac{5}{6}$ as an improper fraction:

$$4\frac{5}{6} = 4 + \frac{5}{6}$$

$$4\frac{5}{6} = \frac{24}{6} + \frac{5}{6}$$

$$4\frac{5}{6} = \frac{29}{6}$$

A quick way is to think:
$$4\frac{5}{6} = \frac{4 \times 6 + 5}{6} = \frac{29}{6}$$

To write the improper fraction $\frac{29}{6}$ as a mixed number:

Think: How many times does 6 go into 29?

6 goes into 24 four times.

So, 6 goes into 29 four times, with remainder 5.

We write: $\frac{29}{6} = 4\frac{5}{6}$

Check

1. Write each mixed number as an improper fraction.

a) $4\frac{1}{2} = 4 + \underline{\quad}$

$4\frac{1}{2} = \frac{8}{2} + \underline{\quad}$

$4\frac{1}{2} = \underline{\quad}$

b) $7\frac{3}{4} = 7 + \underline{\quad}$

$7\frac{3}{4} = \frac{28}{4} + \underline{\quad}$

$7\frac{3}{4} = \underline{\quad}$

c) $5\frac{7}{12} = \underline{\quad} + \underline{\quad}$

$5\frac{7}{12} = \underline{\quad} + \underline{\quad}$

$5\frac{7}{12} = \underline{\quad}$

2. Write each improper fraction as a mixed number.

a) $\frac{13}{5} = \frac{10}{5} + \underline{\quad}$

$\frac{13}{5} = 2 + \underline{\quad}$

$\frac{13}{5} = \underline{\quad}$

b) $\frac{37}{8} = \underline{\quad} + \frac{5}{8}$

$\frac{37}{8} = \underline{\quad} + \underline{\quad}$

$\frac{37}{8} = \underline{\quad}$

c) $\frac{83}{12} = \underline{\quad} + \underline{\quad}$

$\frac{83}{12} = \underline{\quad} + \underline{\quad}$

$\frac{83}{12} = \underline{\quad}$

1.1 Imperial Measures of Length

FOCUS Find referents for imperial units.

Some imperial units are: the inch, the foot, the yard, and the mile
We can use a personal referent to estimate a length. For example:

Unit	Referent
Inch (in.)	Thumb length
Foot (ft.)	Foot length
Yard (yd.)	Arm span
Mile (mi.)	Distance walked in 20 min

The thumb length, foot length, and arm span are **referents**.
Each referent is an approximate measure for an imperial unit.

Example 1 | Estimating Lengths Using Imperial Units

Describe how you would estimate the width of your locker.

Solution

The most appropriate imperial unit is the inch.
I use the width of my hand as a referent. It is about 4 in. across.

I line up one hand with one edge of the locker.
I count how many times I place my hands, one next to the other, to go from one edge
of the locker to the other.
I multiply the number of hands by 4, to get the approximate width of my locker in inches.

Check

1. Describe how you would estimate the length of a driveway.
The most appropriate imperial unit is: _____
The referent is: _____

Here are some relationships between imperial units:

1 ft. = 12 in.

1 yd. = 3 ft.   1 yd. = 36 in.

1 mi. = 1760 yd.   1 mi. = 5280 ft.

To convert 4 ft. to inches, think:

1 ft. = 12 in.

So, 4 ft. = 4 × 12 in.

4 ft. = 48 in.

Example 2 | Converting between Imperial Units

Convert:

a) 5 mi. to yards

b) 100 in. to feet and inches

Solution

a) 1 mi. = 1760 yd.

So, multiply by 1760 to convert miles to yards.

5 mi. = 5 × 1760 yd.

5 mi. = 8800 yd.

> *It takes more smaller units to measure the same length, so the number should be greater.*

b) 12 in. = 1 ft.

So, divide by 12 to convert inches to feet.

100 in. = (100 ÷ 12) ft., or

$100 \text{ in.} = \frac{100}{12} \text{ ft.}$

Write the improper fraction as a mixed number.

$100 \text{ in.} = 8\frac{4}{12} \text{ ft.}$

Write $\frac{4}{12}$ ft. as 4 in.

100 in. = 8 ft. 4 in.

> *It takes fewer larger units to measure the same length, so the number should be less.*

Check

1. Convert:

a) 14 ft. to inches

1 ft. = _____ in.

14 ft. = 14 × _____

14 ft. = _____

b) 14 ft. to yards and feet

_____ ft. = 1 yd.

14 ft. = (14 ÷ _____) yd.

14 ft. = _____ yd.

14 ft. = _____ yd.

14 ft. = _____ yd. _____ ft.

Example 3 | Solving a Problem Involving Conversions

Alex purchased 7 yd. of ribbon to trim some napkins. The ribbon is sewn around a napkin, which is 14 in. wide and 16 in. long. How many napkins can Alex trim with this ribbon?

Solution

Write the measurements in the same units.

Convert 7 yd. to inches.

1 yd. = 36 in.

So, 7 yd. = 7 × 36 in.

  7 yd. = 252 in.

Find the perimeter of each napkin.

Perimeter = 2 × 16 in. + 2 × 14 in.

Perimeter = 32 in. + 28 in.

Perimeter = 60 in.

The number of napkins that can be trimmed is:

$\frac{252 \text{ in.}}{60 \text{ in.}} = 4.2$

Alex can trim 4 napkins with this ribbon.

> It's often easier to change to the smaller unit.

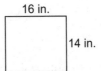

16 in.

14 in.

Check

1. One of Eric's steps is 18 in. long. How many steps would he take to walk 1 mi.?

Convert miles to yards, then inches:

1 mi. = _____ yd.

1 yd. = _____ in.

1760 yd. = _____ × _____

1760 yd. = _____

> Write the measurements in the same units.

The number of steps is: _____

Eric would take _____ steps to walk 1 mi.

1. To estimate the width of the classroom:

    a) Which is the most appropriate imperial unit? Why?

    _____

    b) Which referent could you use?

    _____

2. To estimate the greatest width of a maple leaf:

    a) Which is the most appropriate imperial unit? Why?

    _____

    b) Which referent could you use?

    _____

3. To estimate the length of your friend's shadow:

    a) Which is the most appropriate imperial unit? Why?

    _____

    b) Which referent could you use?

    _____

4. a) Convert yards to feet.

    1 yd. = _____ ft.
    2 yd. = _____
    3 yd. = _____
    4 yd. = _____
    5 yd. = _____

    b) Convert feet to inches.

    1 ft. = _____ in.
    2 ft. = _____
    3 ft. = _____
    4 ft. = _____
    5 ft. = _____

5. Convert:

    a) 8 ft. to inches
    1 ft. = _____
    8 ft. = 8 × _____
    8 ft. = _____

    b) 235 yd. to feet
    1 yd. = _____
    235 yd. = _____ × _____
    235 yd. = _____

    c) 6 mi. to yards
    1 mi. = _____
    6 mi. = _____
    6 mi. = _____

6. Convert:

a) 72 in. to feet

_____ in. = 1 ft.

72 in. = (72 ÷ _____) ft.

72 in. = _____

b) 87 ft. to yards

_____ ft. = 1 yd.

87 ft. = (_____ ÷ _____) yd.

87 ft. = _____

c) 288 in. to yards

_____ in. = 1 yd.

288 in. = (_____) yd.

288 in. = _____

7. Convert:

a) 67 in. to feet and inches

_____ in. = 1 ft.

67 in. = (67 ÷ _____) ft., or

67 in. = $\dfrac{}{\rule{1cm}{0.4pt}}$ ft.

67 in. = $\dfrac{}{\rule{1cm}{0.4pt}}$ ft.

67 in. = _____ ft. _____ in.

b) 418 ft. to yards and feet

_____ ft. = 1 yd.

418 ft. = (_____ ÷ _____) yd., or

418 ft. = $\dfrac{}{\rule{1cm}{0.4pt}}$ yd.

418 ft. = $\dfrac{}{\rule{1cm}{0.4pt}}$ yd.

418 ft. = _____ yd. _____ ft.

c) 2148 in. to yards and feet

12 in. = _____ ft.

2148 in. = (_____ ÷ _____) ft., or

2148 in. = $\dfrac{}{\rule{1.2cm}{0.4pt}}$ ft.

2148 in. = _____ ft.

_____ ft. = 1 yd.

_____ ft. = (_____ ÷ _____) yd., or

_____ ft. = $\dfrac{}{\rule{1cm}{0.4pt}}$ yd.

_____ ft. = $\dfrac{}{\rule{1cm}{0.4pt}}$ yd.

2148 in. = _____ yd. _____ ft.

8. Convert:

a) 7 ft. 5 in. to inches

1 ft. = _____ in.

7 ft. = _____ × _____

7 ft. = _____

Add _____

7 ft. 5 in. = _____ + _____

7 ft. 5 in. = _____

b) 9 yd. 1 ft. to feet

1 yd. = _____ ft.

9 yd. = _____ × _____

9 yd. = _____

Add _____

9 yd. 1 ft. = _____ + _____

9 yd. 1 ft. = _____

c) 11 yd. 2 ft. to inches

   1 yd. = _____

   11 yd. = _____ × _____

   11 yd. = _____

   1 ft. = _____ in.

   2 ft. = _____ × _____

   2 ft. = _____

   Add the inches.

   11 yd. 2 ft. = _____ + _____

   11 yd. 2 ft. = _____

d) 3 mi. 128 yd. to feet

   1 mi. = _____ ft.

   3 mi. = _____ × _____

   3 mi. = _____

   1 yd. = _____ ft.

   128 yd. = _____

   128 yd. = _____

   Add the feet.

   3 mi. 128 yd. = _____ + _____

   3 mi. 128 yd. = _____

9. Sue wants to fence part of her yard. She measures the perimeter as 44 yd. What is the perimeter in feet? 1 yd. = 3 ft.

The perimeter is _____

10. A dog trainer advises that, when walking a dog on a city street, the walker should allow the dog 42 in. of leash. Greg bought a retractable leash that extends $5\frac{1}{2}$ yd. Greg follows the trainer's advice. What length of the leash, in inches, is not used?

Write $5\frac{1}{2}$ as an improper fraction: _____

Convert _____ yd. to inches.

Find the difference between the two measures.

_____ of the leash is not used.

11. A mural is 3 yd. long and 2 yd. wide. It has a border that is made with sections that are 48 in. long. How many sections were needed to make the border?

_____ were needed to make the border.

▶ 1.2 Math Lab: Measuring Length and Distance

FOCUS Measure lengths and distances.

Work with a partner.

The materials you need are listed on page 14 of the Student Text.

Part A

Choose one object and sketch it below.

Use referents. Estimate all linear measures, in imperial units and SI units.

Record these measures on the sketch.

Repeat for two more objects.

Object 1:	Referent for imperial unit: Referent for SI unit:
Object 2:	Referent for imperial unit: Referent for SI unit:
Object 3:	Referent for imperial unit: Referent for SI unit:

For each object, justify your choice of units.

Object 1: _____

_____

Object 2: _____

Object 3: _____

_____

Part B

Sketch each object in the spaces below.
Use imperial units and SI units to measure the lengths you estimated.
Record these measures on each sketch.

Object 1:	Measuring instrument for imperial units:
	Measuring instrument for SI units:
Object 2:	Measuring instrument for imperial units:
	Measuring instrument for SI units:
Object 3:	Measuring instrument for imperial units:
	Measuring instrument for SI units:

List the measures that were hard to find.

_____

Describe how you found these measures.

_____

_____

_____

 978-0-321-61066-9 Copyright © 2011 Pearson Canada Inc.

1. Which of these items is best for measuring each object below:
calipers, ruler, yard stick, measuring tape, or string?

a) the thickness of 50 sheets of paper: _____

b) the length of a frog: _____

c) the length of a bus : _____

d) the distance around a can of juice: _____

2. Which of these imperial units would you use to measure each item
in question 1: inch, foot, yard, or mile?

a) the thickness of 50 sheets of paper: _____

b) the length of a frog: _____

c) the length of a bus : _____

d) the distance around a can of juice: _____

3. For each object below:
- Describe how you would measure it.
- Include the measuring device and the imperial unit.

a) the length of your foot

b) the width of a computer screen

c) the perimeter of the top of a large garbage can

d) the distance between your classroom door and the next classroom door

▶ 1.3 Skill Builder

Converting between Metric Units of Length

1 m = 100 cm	1 m = 1000 mm
1 cm = 10 mm	1 cm = 0.01 m
1 mm = 0.1 cm	1 mm = 0.001 m

To convert 12 m to centimetres:

Start with 1 m = 100 cm

Then, 12 m = 12 × 100 cm

So, 12 m = 1200 cm

Mark a decimal point after 12. To multiply by 100, move the decimal point 2 places to the right. Use zeros as place holders.

To convert 372 mm to centimetres:

Start with 1 mm = 0.1 cm

Then, 372 mm = 372 × 0.1 cm

So, 372 mm = 37.2 cm

Mark a decimal point after 372. To multiply by 0.1, move the decimal point 1 place to the left.

Check

1. Convert each measurement to centimetres.

a) 7 m = _____ × 100 cm

7 m = _____

b) 33 m = _____ × _____

33 m = _____

c) 45 mm = _____ × 0.1 cm

45 mm = _____

d) 6 mm = _____ × _____

6 mm = _____

2. Convert each measurement to millimetres.

a) 9 cm = _____ × 10 mm

9 cm = _____

b) 89 cm = _____ × _____

89 cm = _____

c) 3 m = _____ × 1000 mm

3 m = _____

d) 38 m = _____ × _____

38 m = _____

3. Convert each measurement to metres.

a) 800 cm = _____ × 0.01 m

800 cm = _____

b) 27 cm = _____ × _____

27 cm = _____

c) 9000 mm = _____ × 0.001 m

9000 mm = _____

d) 235 mm = _____ × _____

235 mm = _____

 978-0-321-61066-9

1.3 Relating SI and Imperial Units

FOCUS Convert between SI units and imperial units.

Use this table to convert a measure in imperial units to SI units.

Imperial Units to SI Units
1 in. ≐ 2.5 cm
1 ft. ≐ 30 cm 1 ft. ≐ 0.3 m
1 yd. ≐ 90 cm 1 yd. ≐ 0.9 m
1 mi. ≐ 1.6 km

"SI units" is another name for metric units.

Example 1 — Converting from Imperial Units to SI Units

Convert:

a) 17 ft. to metres

b) 5 mi. to kilometres

Solution

a) From the table,
   1 ft. ≐ 0.3 m
   So, 17 ft. ≐ 17 × 0.3 m
      17 ft. ≐ 5.1 m

b) From the table,
   1 mi. ≐ 1.6 km
   So, 5 mi. ≐ 5 × 1.6 km
      5 mi. ≐ 8 km

Check

1. Convert:

a) 2 yd. to centimetres
   1 yd. ≐ _____
   2 yd. ≐ 2 × _____
   2 yd. ≐ _____

b) 4 ft. to centimetres
   1 ft. ≐ _____
   4 ft. ≐ _____ × _____
   4 ft. ≐ _____

c) 13 in. to centimetres
   1 in. ≐ _____
   13 in. ≐ _____ × _____
   13 in. ≐ _____

d) 87 yd. to metres
   1 yd. ≐ _____
   87 yd. ≐ _____ × _____
   87 yd. ≐ _____

Use this table to convert a measure in SI units to imperial units.

SI Units to Imperial Units
$1 \text{ mm} \doteq \dfrac{4}{100}$ in.
$1 \text{ cm} \doteq \dfrac{4}{10}$ in.
$1 \text{ m} \doteq 39$ in. $1 \text{ m} \doteq 3\dfrac{1}{4}$ ft.
$1 \text{ km} \doteq \dfrac{6}{10}$ mi.

Remember that imperial units are written as fractions, not decimals.

Example 2 Converting from SI Units to Imperial Units

Convert:

a) 16 cm to inches

b) 58 m to feet

Solution

a) From the table,

$1 \text{ cm} \doteq \dfrac{4}{10}$ in.

So, $16 \text{ cm} \doteq 16 \times \dfrac{4}{10}$ in.

$16 \text{ cm} \doteq \dfrac{16}{1} \times \dfrac{4}{10}$ in. Multiply the numerators. Multiply the denominators.

$16 \text{ cm} \doteq \dfrac{64}{10}$, or $\dfrac{32}{5}$ in. Write as a mixed number.

$16 \text{ cm} \doteq 6\dfrac{2}{5}$ in.

b) From the table,

$1 \text{ m} \doteq 3\dfrac{1}{4}$ ft.

So, $58 \text{ m} \doteq 58 \times 3\dfrac{1}{4}$ ft. Write the mixed number as an improper fraction.

$58 \text{ m} \doteq \dfrac{58}{1} \times \dfrac{13}{4}$ ft.

$58 \text{ m} \doteq \dfrac{754}{4}$, or $\dfrac{377}{2}$ ft. Write as a mixed number.

$58 \text{ m} \doteq 188\dfrac{1}{2}$ ft.

Check

1. Convert:

a) 94 m to inches

1 m ≐ _____

So, 94 m ≐ _____ × _____

94 m ≐ _____

b) 183 km to miles

1 km ≐ _____

So, 183 km ≐ _____

183 km ≐ _____

183 km ≐ _____

You may need to do more than one conversion to solve a problem.

| Example 3 | Problem Solving with Conversions |

The school librarian needs to reach a shelf that is 1.7 m above the floor. The librarian can only reach to 5 ft. 11 in. from the floor. Will the librarian be able to reach the shelf? Justify the answer.

Solution

First, find how high the librarian can reach in inches.

1 ft. = 12 in.

So, 5 ft. = 5 × 12 in.

    5 ft. = 60 in.

And, 5 ft. 11 in. = 60 in. + 11 in.

            = 71 in.

> You can also solve the problem by converting 1.7 m to inches.

Convert the measurement in inches to centimetres.

1 in. ≐ 2.5 cm

So, 71 in. ≐ 71 × 2.5 cm

    71 in. ≐ 177.5 cm

Convert the measurement in centimetres to metres.

100 cm = 1 m

So, 177.5 cm = $\frac{177.5}{100}$ m

    177.5 cm = 1.775 m

The librarian can reach 1.775 m high.

The shelf is 1.7 m high.

So, the librarian can reach the shelf.

Check

1. A truck driver wants to park her 3.25-m high truck in a storage shed that is 11 ft. 6 in. high. Will the truck fit in the shed? Justify your answer.

Convert the height of the storage shed to inches.

1 ft. = _____ in.

11 ft. = 11 × _____ in.

11 ft. = _____

11 ft. 6 in. = _____ + 6 in.

= _____

Convert inches to centimetres.

1 in. ≐ _____ cm

_____ in. ≐ _____ × _____ cm

_____ ≐ _____

Convert centimetres to metres.

_____ cm = 1 m

$$\underline{\hspace{2cm}} \text{ cm} = \frac{\overline{\hspace{2cm}}}{100} \text{ m}$$

_____ cm = _____ m

Since the height of the truck is 3.25 m and the height of the shed is _____, the truck will _____.

Practice

1. Convert:

a) 24 yd. to centimetres

1 yd. ≐ _____ cm

24 yd. ≐ 24 × _____

24 yd. ≐ _____

b) 5 in. to centimetres

1 in. ≐ _____ cm

5 in. ≐ _____ × _____

5 in. ≐ _____

c) 8 ft. to metres

1 ft. ≐ _____

8 ft. ≐ _____ × _____

8 ft. ≐ _____

d) 7 mi. to kilometres

1 mi. ≐ _____

7 mi. ≐ _____

7 mi. ≐ _____

 978-0-321-61066-9

2. Convert:

a) 12 m to inches

1 m ≐ _____ in.

12 m ≐ 12 × _____

12 m ≐ _____

Don't forget to write the fractions in simplest form.

b) 7 km to miles

1 km ≐ _____ mi.

7 km ≐ _____ × _____

7 km ≐ _____

7 km ≐ _____

c) 276 mm to inches

1 mm ≐ _____

276 mm ≐ 276 × _____

276 mm ≐ _____

276 mm ≐ _____

d) 86 cm to inches

1 cm ≐ _____

86 cm ≐ _____ × _____

86 cm ≐ _____

86 cm ≐ _____

Use the table on page 14.

3. Convert:

a) 4 ft. 9 in. to millimetres
Convert feet to inches first.

1 ft. = _____

4 ft. = _____ × _____

4 ft. = _____

4 ft. 9 in. = _____ + 9 in.

4 ft. 9 in. = _____

Convert inches to millimetres.

1 in. ≐ _____ cm

1 in. ≐ _____ mm

_____ in. ≐ _____ mm

_____ ≐ _____

4 ft. 9 in. ≐ _____

b) 3 yd. 2 ft. to centimetres
Convert yards to feet first.

1 yd. = _____

3 yd. = _____ × _____

3 yd. = _____

3 yd. 2 ft. = _____ + _____

3 yd. 2 ft. = _____

Convert feet to centimetres.

1 ft. ≐ _____

_____ ft. ≐ _____ cm

_____ ≐ _____

3 yd. 2 ft. ≐ _____

4. Tammy drove 85 km to a camp site.

Todd drove 52 mi. to meet Tammy at the camp site.

Who drove farther? Justify your answer.

Convert miles to _____.

1 mi. ≐ _____

52 mi. ≐ _____

52 mi. ≐ _____

Since _____ is _____ than _____, _____ drove farther.

5. To qualify for the school volleyball try-outs, Rick needs to be able to jump and touch a line on a wall that is 8 ft. 2 in. off the ground. In his workouts, Rick jumped 243 cm. Will he qualify for the try-outs? Justify your answer.

Convert feet to inches.

Convert inches to centimetres.

Since _____ is _____ than _____, Rick _____ qualify.

6. The cross-country running team is preparing for a meet. Katy ran 18 laps around the 400-yd. track and Ben ran 7.5 km. Who ran farther? Justify your answer.

Since Katy ran approximately _____ and Ben ran _____,
_____ ran farther.

 978-0-321-61066-9

CHECKPOINT 1

Can you...

- estimate a length using a referent?
- convert between imperial units?
- convert between SI units and imperial units?

1.1 **1. a)** To estimate the length of a semi-truck and trailer
  i) Which is the most appropriate imperial unit? Why?

  _____

  ii) Which referent could you use?

  _____

b) To estimate the width of your text book:
  i) Which is the most appropriate imperial unit? Why?

  _____

  ii) Which referent could you use?

  _____

2. Describe how you would estimate:

a) the distance from your classroom to the school's office
The most appropriate imperial unit is: _____
The referent is: _____

b) the length of a pencil
The most appropriate imperial unit is: _____
The referent is: _____

3. Convert:

a) 99 in. to feet and inches

_____ in. = 1 ft.

99 in. = (99 ÷ _____) ft., or

99 in. = _____ ft.

99 in. = _____ ft.

99 in. = _____ ft. _____ in.

b) 4 yd. 2 ft. to inches

1 yd. = _____ in.

4 yd. = _____ × _____

4 yd. = _____

1 ft. = _____ in.

2 ft. = _____ × _____

2 ft. = _____

Add the inches.

4 yd. 2 ft. = _____ + _____

4 yd. 2 ft. = _____

4. Two students measured a set for a school play. One student said it was 3 yd. 2 ft. wide. The other student said it was 132 in. wide. Are the students' measurements the same? Show your work.

_____, the measurements _____ the same.

1.2 **5. a)** Which of these imperial units is best for measuring each item below: inch, foot, yard, or mile?

i) the width of your bedroom: _____

ii) the length of your longest finger: _____

b) Which of these SI units is best for measuring each item below: millimetre, centimetre, metre, kilometre?

i) the distance between your house and school: _____

ii) the width of a pencil: _____

 978-0-321-61066-9

6. Describe one method to measure the circumference of a marker pen. Identify the unit and measuring device you would use.

1.3 **7.** Convert:

a) 16 ft. to metres

1 ft. $\doteq$ _____ m

16 ft. $\doteq$ 16 $\times$ _____ m

16 ft. $\doteq$ _____

b) 27 mi. to kilometres

1 mi. $\doteq$ _____ km

27 mi. $\doteq$ _____ $\times$ _____ km

27 mi. $\doteq$ _____

c) 44 mm to inches

1 mm $\doteq$ _____ in.

44 mm $\doteq$ _____ $\times$ _____ in.

44 mm $\doteq$ _____ in.

44 mm $\doteq$ _____

d) 840 cm to yards and feet

_____ cm $\doteq$ 1 ft.

840 cm $\doteq$ (_____ $\div$ _____) ft., or

840 cm $\doteq$ _____ ft.

840 cm $\doteq$ _____ ft.

_____ ft. = 1 yd.

_____ ft. = _____ yd.

_____ ft. = _____ yd.

840 cm $\doteq$ _____ yd. _____ ft.

8. Nina ran an 8-km race for charity. What is this distance in miles and yards?

8 km is approximately _____.

▶ 1.4 Skill Builder

The Pythagorean Theorem

In a right triangle with hypotenuse length c and leg lengths a and b,
$$c^2 = a^2 + b^2$$

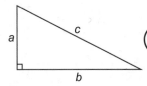

The hypotenuse is the side opposite the right angle.

In the right triangle below, to find the value of a to the nearest tenth of a centimetre:

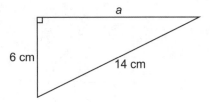

6 cm

14 cm

Use:

$c^2 = a^2 + b^2$ Substitute: $c = 14$ and $b = 6$

$14^2 = a^2 + 6^2$ Simplify.

$196 = a^2 + 36$ Solve for a^2.

$a^2 = 196 - 36$

$a^2 = 160$ Solve for a.

$a = \sqrt{160}$

$a = 12.6491...$

a is about 12.6 cm.

Check

1. Find the value of c, to the nearest tenth of a centimetre.

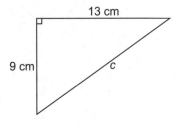

13 cm

9 cm

c

Use: $c^2 = a^2 + b^2$ Substitute: $a =$ _____ and $b =$ _____

$c^2 =$ _____ + _____

$c^2 =$ _____ + _____

$c^2 =$ _____

$c =$ _____

$c =$ _____

c is about: _____

1.4 Surface Areas of Right Pyramids and Right Cones

Find the surface areas of pyramids and cones.

The surface area of a pyramid is:
Area of base + area of triangular faces

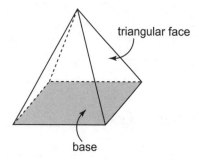

Example 1 | Finding the Surface Area of a Square Pyramid

A square pyramid has a base with side length 4 ft. Each triangular face has height 5 ft. Find the surface area of the pyramid.

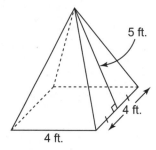

*The height of a triangular face is the **slant height** of a square pyramid.*

Solution

The base of the pyramid is a square, so the area of the base is:

$4 \times 4 = 16$

There are 4 triangular faces.

Each face has base 4 ft. and height 5 ft.

The area of each face is:

$$\frac{1}{2} \times \text{base} \times \text{height} = \frac{1}{2} \times 4 \times 5$$
$$= 10$$

The area of all 4 faces is: $4 \times 10 = 40$

The surface area of the pyramid is: $16 + 40 = 56$

The surface area of the pyramid is 56 square feet.

Check

1. Find the surface area of this square pyramid.

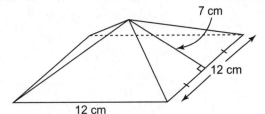

Area of the base is: _____ × _____ = _____

Area of each triangular face is: $\frac{1}{2}$ × _____ × _____ = _____

Area of all 4 faces is: 4 × _____ = _____

The surface area of the pyramid is: _____ + _____ = _____

The surface area of the pyramid is: _____ cm²

| Example 2 | Finding the Surface Area of a Rectangular Pyramid |

Find the surface area of this rectangular pyramid.

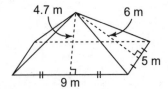

Solution

The base of the pyramid is a rectangle, so the area of the base is: $9 \times 5 = 45$

There are 2 triangular faces with base 9 m and height 4.7 m.

The area of each face is: $\frac{1}{2} \times$ base $\times$ height $= \frac{1}{2} \times 9 \times 4.7$

$$= 21.15$$

> Opposite triangular faces are congruent.

There are 2 triangular faces with base 5 m and height 6 m.

The area of each face is: $\frac{1}{2} \times$ base $\times$ height $= \frac{1}{2} \times 5 \times 6$

$$= 15$$

The area of all 4 faces is: $(2 \times 21.15) + (2 \times 15) = 72.3$

The surface area of the pyramid is: $45 + 72.3 = 117.3$

The surface area of the pyramid is 117.3 m².

Check

1. Find the surface area of this rectangular pyramid.

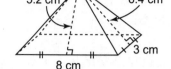

The base of the pyramid is a _____ ,
so the area of the base is: _____
There are 2 triangular faces with base _____
and height _____ .
The area of each face is:

$\frac{1}{2}$ × base × height =

_____

= _____

There are 2 triangular faces with base _____ and height _____ .
The area of each face is:

$\frac{1}{2}$ × base × height =

_____

= _____

The area of all 4 faces is: _____ + _____ = _____
The surface area of the pyramid is: _____ + _____ = _____
The surface area of the pyramid is: _____

Sometimes we must find the slant height of an object before we can calculate its surface area.

Example 3 | Finding the Surface Area of a Pyramid Given Its Height

Find the surface area of this square pyramid, to the nearest square inch.

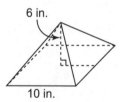

6 in.

10 in.

Solution

Sketch a triangle that shows the height of the pyramid and the slant height.

6 in. s

5 in.

The base of this triangle is: $\frac{1}{2}$ × 10 in. = 5 in.

Let the slant height be s inches.

Use the Pythagorean Theorem to find the slant height, s.

$s^2 = 6^2 + 5^2$ Simplify.

$s^2 = 36 + 25$

$s^2 = 61$

$s = \sqrt{61}$

The slant height is $\sqrt{61}$ in.

Now find the surface area of the pyramid.

The area of the base is: $10 \times 10 = 100$

The area of the 4 faces is:

$4 \times \dfrac{1}{2} \times$ base $\times$ height $= 2 \times$ base $\times$ slant height

$\qquad\qquad\qquad\qquad\qquad = 2 \times 10 \times \sqrt{61}$

$\qquad\qquad\qquad\qquad\qquad = 20 \times \sqrt{61}$

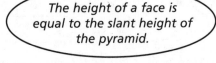

The height of a face is equal to the slant height of the pyramid.

The surface area of the pyramid is: $100 + 20 \times \sqrt{61} = 256.2049\ldots$

The surface area of the pyramid is about 256 square inches.

Check

1. Find the surface area of this square pyramid, to the nearest square yard.

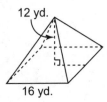

12 yd.

16 yd.

This triangle shows the height of the pyramid and its slant height, s.
The base of the pyramid has length 16 yd.

12 yd. s

8 yd.

So, the base of this triangle is: $\dfrac{1}{2} \times$ 16 yd. $=$ 8 yd.

Use the Pythagorean Theorem to find the slant height.

$s^2 =$ _____ $+$ _____   Simplify.

$s^2 =$ _____

$s^2 =$ _____

$s =$ _____

The slant height is: _____

For the surface area of the pyramid:

Area of the base is: _____

Area of the 4 faces is:

$$4 \times \frac{1}{2} \times \text{base} \times \text{height} = 2 \times \text{base} \times \text{slant height}$$

$$= \text{_____}$$

$$= \text{_____}$$

The surface area of the pyramid is: _____ = _____

The surface area of the pyramid is about: _____

The surface area, *SA*, of a cone is: Lateral area + base area

For a cone with slant height *s* and base radius *r*:

$$SA = \pi rs + \pi r^2$$

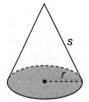

Example 4 | Finding the Surface Area of a Cone

Find the surface area of this cone, to the nearest square millimetre.

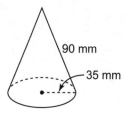

90 mm

35 mm

Solution

Use the formula:

$$SA = \pi rs + \pi r^2 \qquad \text{Substitute: } r = 35 \text{ and } s = 90$$

$$SA = \pi(35)(90) + \pi(35)^2$$

$$SA = 13\ 744.4678\ldots$$

The surface area is about 13 744 mm².

Check

1. Find the surface area of this cone, to the nearest square foot.

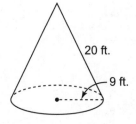

20 ft.

9 ft.

$$SA = \pi rs + \pi r^2 \qquad \text{Substitute: _____}$$

$$SA = \text{_____} + \text{_____}$$

$$SA = \text{_____}$$

The surface area is about: _____

1. Find the surface area of each object, to the nearest square unit.

a) a square pyramid

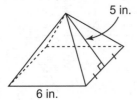

5 in.

6 in.

Area of the base is: _____

Area of each triangular face is: $\frac{1}{2} \times$ _____ $\times$ _____ = _____

Area of all 4 faces is: 4 $\times$ _____ = _____

The surface area of the pyramid is:

_____ + _____ = _____

The surface area of the pyramid is:

_____ square inches

b) a cone

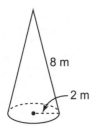

8 m

2 m

$SA = \pi rs + \pi r^2$

$SA =$ _____ + _____

$SA =$ _____

The surface area is about: _____

c) a rectangular pyramid

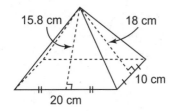

15.8 cm   18 cm

10 cm

20 cm

The base of the pyramid is a _____,

so the area of the base is: _____

Two triangular faces have:

base _____ and height _____

Area of the 2 faces is:

$2 \times \frac{1}{2} \times$ base $\times$ height = _____

= _____

Two triangular faces have:

base _____ and height _____

The area of the 2 faces is:

$2 \times \frac{1}{2} \times$ base $\times$ height = _____

= _____

The surface area of the pyramid is:

_____ + _____ + _____ = _____

The surface area of the pyramid is: _____

2. A triangular pyramid has 4 congruent faces. Find its surface area.

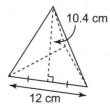
10.4 cm

12 cm

Four triangular faces have: base _____ and height _____

The area of the 4 faces is:

$4 \times \dfrac{1}{2} \times$ base $\times$ height = _____

= _____

The surface area of the pyramid is: _____

3. Find the slant height of this cone, to the nearest tenth of a unit.

10 yd.

7 yd.

Label this triangle to show the height and slant height of the cone.
Let the slant height be *s* yards.

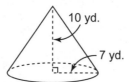

Use the Pythagorean Theorem to find the slant height.

$s^2 =$ _____ + _____
$s^2 =$ _____ + _____
$s^2 =$ _____
$s =$ _____
$s =$ _____

Remember to write an imperial measure as a fraction.

The slant height is about:

_____

4. A wooden square pyramid is to be painted. The side length of the base is 8 cm and the height of the pyramid is 6 cm. To the nearest square centimetre, what is the area that will be painted?

The painted area is the surface area of the pyramid.
The slant height is: *s* centimetres.
Use the Pythagorean Theorem to find the slant height.

$s^2 =$ _____

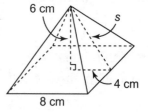
6 cm
s
4 cm
8 cm

$s =$ _____
The slant height is: _____

The area of the base is: _____

The area of the 4 faces is:

$4 \times \dfrac{1}{2} \times$ base $\times$ height = 2 $\times$ base $\times$ slant height

= _____

= _____

The surface area of the pyramid is: _____ + _____ = _____

The surface area of the pyramid is about: _____

978-0-321-61066-9 Copyright © 2011 Pearson Canada Inc. **29**

5. A cone-shaped hat is to be made with radius 5 in. and height 12 in. To the nearest square inch, how much material will be needed for the hat?

The amount of material is the lateral surface area of the cone.

12 in.

s

5 in.

Use the _____ to find the slant height, s.

$s^2 = $ _____

The hat is a cone with no base.

$s = $ _____
The slant height is: _____

Use the formula for the lateral surface area of a cone.

$SA = \pi r s$ Substitute: _____

$SA = $ _____

$SA = $ _____

The surface area is about: _____
About _____ of material will be needed.

6. This triangular pyramid has 4 congruent faces. The surface area of this pyramid is 250 square inches. Find its slant height, to the nearest tenth of an inch.

s

12 in.

The slant height is: s inches
Use the formula to write an expression for the surface area.

$SA = $
_____

This expression is equal to: _____
Write an equation, then solve for s.

The slant height is about:

_____

▶ 1.5 Skill Builder

Volume of a Prism

To find the volume, V, of a prism, use this formula:
V = base area × height

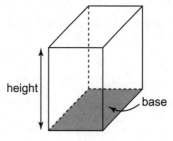

height
base

To find the volume, V, of this triangular prism:
The base is a triangle.
So, the area of the base is: $\frac{1}{2} \times 8 \times 5 = 20$

V = base area × height
$V = 20 \times 12$
$V = 240$
The volume of the prism is 240 cm³.

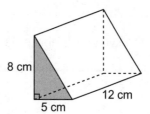

8 cm
5 cm
12 cm

Check

1. Find the volume of this rectangular prism.

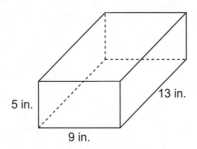

5 in.
9 in.
13 in.

The base is a _____.
So, the area of the base is: _____

V = base area × height
$V =$ _____
$V =$ _____
The volume of the prism is: _____

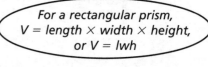

For a rectangular prism,
$V = length \times width \times height,$
or $V = lwh$

2. Find the volume of this triangular prism.

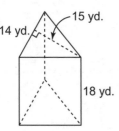

14 yd.
15 yd.
18 yd.

The base is a _____.

So, the area of the base is:
_____

$V =$ _____
$V =$ _____
$V =$ _____
The volume of the prism is: _____

Volume of a Cylinder

The volume, V, of a cylinder is: base area $\times$ height
The base of a cylinder is a circle.
So, for a cylinder with base radius r and height h:
$V = \pi r^2 h$

To find the volume, V, of this cylinder:
Use the formula:

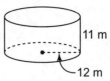

$V = \pi r^2 h$ Substitute: $r = 12$ and $h = 11$
$V = \pi \times 12^2 \times 11$
$V = 4976.2827\ldots$
The volume of the cylinder is about 4976 m^3.

Check

1. Find the volume of each cylinder, to the nearest tenth of a cubic unit.

a)

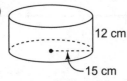

$V = \pi r^2 h$ Substitute: $r =$ _____ and $h =$ _____
$V =$ _____
$V =$ _____
The volume of the cylinder is about: _____

b)

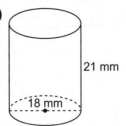

The diameter of the cylinder is: _____
So, its radius is: _____
$V =$ _____   Substitute: _____
$V =$ _____
$V =$ _____
The volume of the cylinder is about: _____

▶ 1.5 Volumes of Right Pyramids and Right Cones

FOCUS Find the volumes of pyramids and cones.

When a prism and a pyramid have the same base and the same height, the volume of the pyramid is $\frac{1}{3}$ the volume of the prism.

Volume, V, of a pyramid is: $V = \frac{1}{3} \times$ base area $\times$ height

For a rectangular pyramid, $V = \frac{1}{3}lwh$

Example 1	Finding the Volume of a Rectangular Pyramid

Find the volume of this rectangular pyramid.

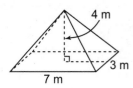

Solution

Use the formula:

$V = \frac{1}{3}lwh$ Substitute: $l = 7$, $w = 3$, and $h = 4$

$V = \frac{1}{3} \times 7 \times 3 \times 4$

$V = 28$

The volume is 28 m³.

Check

1. Find the volume of this square pyramid.

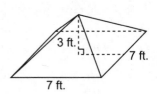

Use the formula:

$V = \frac{1}{3}lwh$ Substitute: _____

$V =$ _____

$V =$ _____

The volume is: _____

When a cylinder and a cone have the same base and the same height, the volume of the cone is $\frac{1}{3}$ the volume of the cylinder.

Volume, V, of a cone is: $V = \frac{1}{3}\pi r^2 h$

Example 2 | Finding the Volume of a Cone

Find the volume of this cone, to the nearest tenth of a cubic centimetre.

3 cm
6 cm

Solution

Use the formula:

$V = \frac{1}{3}\pi r^2 h$ Substitute: $r = 3$ and $h = 6$

$V = \frac{1}{3} \times \pi \times 3^2 \times 6$

$V = 56.5486...$

The volume is about 56.5 cm³.

Check

1. Find the volume of this cone, to the nearest tenth of a cubic metre.

2 m
3 m

Use the formula:

$V = \frac{1}{3}\pi r^2 h$ Substitute: _____

$V =$

_____

$V =$ _____

The volume is about: _____

 978-0-321-61066-9

When the slant height of a pyramid or cone is given, we find the height before calculating the volume.

Example 3 | Finding the Volume of a Cone Given Its Slant Height

A cone has radius 7 in. and slant height 17 in.
Find the volume of the cone, to the nearest cubic inch.

Solution

Sketch a diagram. Let the height be h inches.
Use the Pythagorean Theorem to find h.

$17^2 = h^2 + 7^2$ Simplify.

$289 = h^2 + 49$ Solve for h^2.

$h^2 = 289 - 49$

$h^2 = 240$ Solve for h.

$h = \sqrt{240}$

Use this value of h in the formula for the volume.

$V = \frac{1}{3}\pi r^2 h$ Substitute: $r = 7$ and $h = \sqrt{240}$

$V = \frac{1}{3} \times \pi \times 7^2 \times \sqrt{240}$

$V = 794.9326\ldots$

The volume is about 795 cubic inches.

Check

1. Find the volume of this cone, to the nearest cubic yard.

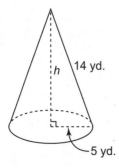

Use the Pythagorean Theorem to find h.

$14^2 = $ _____ + _____

$h = $ _____

Use this value of h in the formula for the volume.

$V = \frac{1}{3}\pi r^2 h$ Substitute: _____

$V = $ _____

$V = $ _____

The volume is about: _____

We can use a volume measure to find an unknown measure.

Example 4 | Finding the Height of a Pyramid

A rectangular pyramid can hold 1250 cubic feet of water.
The base of the pyramid is 15 ft. by 10 ft.
What is the height of the pyramid?

Solution

Let the height of the pyramid be h feet.

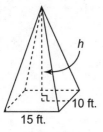

Use the formula for the volume of a rectangular pyramid:

$$V = \frac{1}{3}lwh$$ Substitute: $V = 1250$, $l = 15$, and $w = 10$

$$1250 = \frac{1}{3} \times 15 \times 10 \times h$$ Simplify.

$$1250 = 50h$$ Divide each side by 50.

$$h = \frac{1250}{50}$$

$$h = 25$$

The pyramid is 25 ft. high.

Check

1. This cone can hold 870 cm³ of sand. What is the height of the cone, to the nearest tenth of a centimetre?

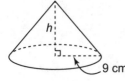

Use the formula for the volume of a cone:

$$V = \frac{1}{3}\pi r^2 h$$ Substitute: _____

$h = $ _____

Remember to use brackets when you divide by the denominator.

The height of the cone is about: _____

1. Find the volume of each pyramid.

a) a square pyramid

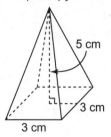

Use the formula:

$V = \frac{1}{3}lwh$ Substitute: _____

$V =$ _____

$V =$ _____
The volume is: _____

b) a rectangular pyramid

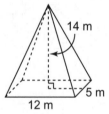

Use the formula:

$V =$ _____   Substitute: _____

$V =$ _____

$V =$ _____
The volume is: _____

2. Find the volume of this cone, to the nearest cubic foot.

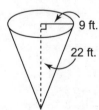

Use the formula:

$V = \frac{1}{3}\pi r^2 h$ Substitute: _____

$V =$ _____

$V =$ _____

The volume is about: _____

3. Find the volume of this square pyramid, to the nearest cubic inch.

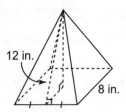

12 in. 8 in.

Label a triangle to show the height and slant height of the pyramid.

Let the height be h inches.

The base of the triangle is: $\frac{1}{2} \times$ _____ = _____

Use the Pythagorean Theorem to find h.

$12^2 =$ _____ + _____

$h =$ _____

Use this value of h in the formula for the volume.

$V = \frac{1}{3}lwh$ Substitute: _____

$V =$ _____

The volume is about: _____

4. Find the volume of this cone, to the nearest cubic inch.
Label this triangle to show the height and slant height of the cone.

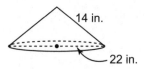

14 in.

22 in.

Let the height be h inches.
Use the Pythagorean Theorem to find h.

$h =$ _____

Use this value of h in the formula for the volume.

$V = \frac{1}{3}\pi r^2 h$

$V =$ _____

$V =$ _____

The volume is about: _____

5. The base of a square prism has side length 8 cm; its height is 12 cm.
The base of a square pyramid has side length 12 cm; its height is 17 cm.
Which object has the greater volume?

The volume of the prism is: The volume of the pyramid is:

The volume of the prism is: _____

                                     The volume of the pyramid is: _____

The _____ has the greater volume.

6. Both a cylinder and a cone have volume 1525 cubic inches and base radius 7 in.
Find the height of each object, to the nearest tenth of an inch.

Let the height of the cylinder be h inches.
To find h, use the formula for the volume of a cylinder.

h
7 in.

The height of the cylinder is about: _____

Let the height of the cone be H inches.

To find H, use the formula for the volume of a cone.

H
7 in.

The height of the cone is about: _____

▶ 1.6 Surface Area and Volume of a Sphere

FOCUS Find the surface area and volume of a sphere.

To find the surface area of a sphere, use this formula:
$SA = 4\pi r^2$

To find the surface area of a hemisphere, use this formula:
$SA = 3\pi r^2$

Example 1 | Finding the Surface Area of a Sphere

A glass sphere has radius 25 cm. What is the surface area of the sphere, to the nearest square centimetre?

Solution

Use the formula:

$SA = 4\pi r^2$ Substitute: $r = 25$

$SA = 4 \times \pi \times 25^2$

$SA = 7853.9816...$

The surface area of the sphere is about 7854 cm².

Check

1. Find the surface area of each object, to the nearest square unit.

a)

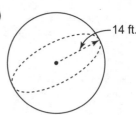
14 ft.

Use the formula:

$SA = 4\pi r^2$ Substitute: _____

$SA =$ _____

$SA =$ _____

The surface area is about: _____

b)

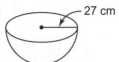
27 cm

Use the formula:

$SA = 3\pi r^2$ Substitute: _____

$SA =$ _____

$SA =$ _____

The surface area of the hemisphere is about: _____

To find the volume of a sphere, use this formula:

$V = \frac{4}{3}\pi r^3$

To find the volume of a hemisphere, use this formula:

$V = \frac{2}{3}\pi r^3$

Example 2 | Finding the Volume of a Sphere

A sphere has diameter 8 yd. What is the volume of the sphere, to the nearest cubic yard?

Solution

Radius is: $\frac{1}{2} \times 8$ yd. $= 4$ yd.

Use the formula:

$V = \frac{4}{3}\pi r^3$ Substitute: $r = 4$

$V = \frac{4}{3} \times \pi \times 4^3$

The radius is one-half the diameter.

$V = 268.0825\ldots$

The volume of the sphere is about 268 cubic yards.

Check

1. Find the volume of each object, to the nearest cubic unit.

a)

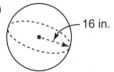

16 in.

Use the formula:

$V = \frac{4}{3}\pi r^3$ Substitute: _____

$V = $ _____

$V = $ _____

The volume of the sphere is about: _____

b)

14 mm

Radius is:

_____

Use the formula:

$V = \frac{2}{3}\pi r^3$ Substitute: _____

$V = $ _____

$V = $ _____

The volume of the hemisphere is about: _____

If the surface area of a sphere or hemisphere is known, we can find its radius.

Example 3 | Finding the Radius of a Sphere

A globe has surface area 2735 cm^2. Find the radius of the globe, to the nearest tenth of a centimetre.

Solution

Use the formula:

$SA = 4\pi r^2$ Substitute: $SA = 2735$

$2735 = 4\pi r^2$ Solve for r^2. Divide each side by 4π.

$r^2 = \dfrac{2735}{4\pi}$ Solve for r. Take the square root of each side.

$r = \sqrt{\dfrac{2735}{4\pi}}$

$r = 14.7527...$

Remember to use brackets in the denominator. Input: $\sqrt{\dfrac{2735}{(4\pi)}}$

The radius of the globe is about 14.8 cm.

Check

1. A sphere has surface area 3567 m^2. What is the radius of the sphere, to the nearest tenth of a metre?

Use the formula:

$SA = 4\pi r^2$ Substitute: _____

$r^2 =$ _____

$r =$ _____

$r =$ _____

The radius of the sphere is about: _____

1. Find the surface area of each object, to the nearest square unit.

a)

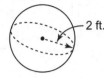
— 2 ft.

Use the formula:

$SA = 4\pi r^2$ Substitute: _____

$SA = $ _____

$SA = $ _____

The surface area is about: _____

b)

17 cm

Radius:

_____

Use the formula:

$SA = $ _____   Substitute: _____

$SA = $ _____

$SA = $ _____

The surface area is about: _____

c)

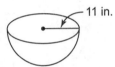
— 11 in.

Use the formula:

$SA = 3\pi r^2$ Substitute: _____

$SA = $ _____

$SA = $ _____

The surface area is about: _____

d)

5 m

Radius:

_____

Use the formula:

$SA = $ _____   Substitute: _____

$SA = $ _____

$SA = $ _____

The surface area is about: _____

2. Find the volume of each object in question 1.
Give the answers to the nearest cubic unit.

a) Use the formula:

$V = \dfrac{4}{3}\pi r^3$ Substitute: _____

$V = $

_____

$V = $ _____

The volume is about: _____

b) Use the formula:

$V = $ _____   Substitute: _____

$V = $ _____

$V = $ _____

The volume is about: _____

c) Use the formula:

$V = \dfrac{2}{3}\pi r^3$ Substitute: _____

$V = $ _____

$V = $ _____

The volume is about: _____

d) Use the formula:

$V = $ _____   Substitute: _____

$V = $ _____

$V = $ _____

The volume is about: _____

3. A solid cork ball is covered in gold plating. It has diameter 14 cm.

a) To the nearest tenth of a square centimetre, what is the area of gold plating?
Find the surface area of the ball.

Radius: _____

$SA = 4\pi r^2$

$SA = $ _____

$SA = $ _____

The area of gold plating is about: _____

b) To the nearest cubic centimetre, what is the volume of cork?
Find the volume of the ball.

Radius: _____

$V = \dfrac{4}{3}\pi r^3$

$V = $ _____

$V = $ _____

The volume of cork is about: _____

4. A ball has a surface area of 28 square inches.
Find the radius of the ball, to the nearest tenth of an inch.

Let the radius of the ball be r inches.
Use the formula:

$SA =$ _____   Substitute: $SA =$ _____
                         Solve for r.

$r^2 =$ _____

$r =$ _____

$r =$ _____

The radius of the ball is about: _____

5. A disco ball is covered in 9 square feet of silver foil. To the nearest inch,
what is the diameter of the ball?

Let the radius of the ball be r feet.
Use the formula:

$SA =$ _____   Substitute: $SA =$ _____
                         Solve for r.

Assume a disco ball approximates a sphere.

$r^2 =$ _____

$r =$ _____

$r =$ _____

Diameter: $2 \times$ _____ ft. = _____ ft.

Convert feet to inches:

_____ ft. = _____ $\times$ 12 in.

1 ft. = 12 in.

= _____

The diameter of the ball is about: _____

CHECKPOINT 2

Can you...

- find the height or slant height of an object using the Pythagorean Theorem?
- find the surface areas of pyramids, cones, and spheres?
- find the volumes of pyramids, cones, and spheres?

1.4 **1.** Find the surface area of each object.

a) a square pyramid

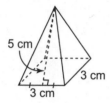

The base of the pyramid is a _____, so the base area is: _____ × _____ = _____

Area of each triangular face: $\frac{1}{2}$ × _____ × _____ = _____

Area of all 4 faces: 4 × _____ = _____

Surface area of the pyramid: _____ + _____ = _____
The surface area of the pyramid is: _____

b) a rectangular pyramid

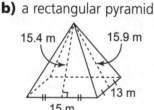

The base of the pyramid is a _____, so the base area is: _____ = _____

Two triangular faces have base _____ and height _____.
Area of these 2 faces is:

$2 \times \frac{1}{2} \times$ base × height =

_____

= _____

Two triangular faces have base _____ and height _____.
Area of these 2 faces is:

$2 \times \frac{1}{2} \times$ base × height =

_____

= _____

Surface area of the pyramid: _____ + _____ + _____ = _____
The surface area of the pyramid is: _____

2. Find the surface area of this cone, to the nearest square foot.

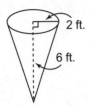

Label this triangle to show the height and slant height of the cone.
Let the slant height be *s* feet.

Use the Pythagorean Theorem to find the slant height.

$s^2 =$ _____ + _____   Simplify.

$s^2 =$ _____ + _____

$s^2 =$ _____

$s =$ _____

The slant height is: _____

Use the formula for the surface area of a cone.

$SA =$ _____   Substitute: _____

$SA =$ _____

$SA =$ _____

The surface area is about: _____

1.5 **3.** Find the volume of this cone, to the nearest cubic inch.

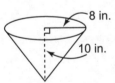

Use the formula for the volume of a cone.

$V =$ _____   Substitute: _____
      _____

$V =$
      _____

$V =$ _____

The volume is about: _____

4. A glass paperweight has the shape of a square pyramid. Alex measured the edge of the base as 3 in. and the slant height as 4 in. What is the volume of the paperweight, to the nearest cubic inch?

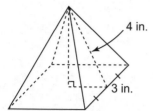

Label this triangle to show the height and slant height of the pyramid.

Let the height be h inches.

Use the Pythagorean Theorem to find h.

Solve for h.

$h =$ _____

Substitute this value of h in the formula for the volume.

$V = \frac{1}{3}lwh$ Substitute: _____

$V =$ _____

$V =$ _____

The volume is about: _____

1.6 **5.** Find the surface area of each object, to the nearest tenth of a square unit.

a) a sphere

Radius: _____

Use the formula:

$SA =$ _____   Substitute: _____

$SA =$ _____

$SA =$ _____

The surface area is about: _____

b) a hemisphere

8 in.

Radius: _____

Use the formula:

SA = _____   Substitute: _____

SA = _____

SA = _____

The surface area is about: _____

6. To the nearest cubic unit, find the volume of each object in question 5.

a) Use the formula for the volume of a sphere:

V = _____   Substitute: _____
    _____

V =
    _____

V = _____
The volume is about: _____

b) Use the formula for the volume of a hemisphere:

V = _____   Substitute: _____
    _____

V =
    _____

V = _____
The volume is about: _____

▶ 1.7 Skill Builder

Surface Area of a Prism

The surface area, *SA*, of a prism, is:
SA = sum of the areas of all the faces

The surface area of a rectangular prism is:
$SA = 2(lw + lh + wh)$

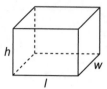

To find the surface area of this rectangular prism:

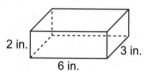

2 in.   3 in.
6 in.

Use:
$SA = 2(lw + lh + wh)$ Substitute: $l = 6$, $w = 3$, and $h = 2$
$SA = 2(6 \times 3 + 6 \times 2 + 3 \times 2)$ Use the order of operations.
$SA = 2(18 + 12 + 6)$
$SA = 2(36)$
$SA = 72$
The surface area of the prism is 72 square inches.

Check

1. Find the surface area of this cube.

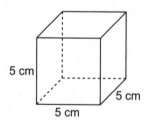

5 cm
5 cm
5 cm

Use:
$SA = 2(lw + lh + wh)$ Substitute: _____
$SA = $ _____
$SA = $ _____
$SA = $ _____
$SA = $ _____
The surface area of the cube is: _____

Surface Area of a Cylinder

The surface area, *SA*, of a cylinder, is:
SA = Area of the 2 bases + Area of curved surface

The surface area of this cylinder is:
$SA = 2\pi r^2 + 2\pi rh$

To find the surface area of this cylinder:

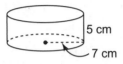

5 cm
7 cm

Use:
$SA = 2\pi r^2 + 2\pi rh$ Substitute: $r = 7$ and $h = 5$
$SA = 2\pi(7)^2 + 2\pi(7)(5)$
$SA = 527.7875...$
The surface area of the cylinder is about 528 cm².

Check

1. Find the surface area of each cylinder, to the nearest square unit.

a)

6 ft.
3 ft.

Use:
$SA = 2\pi r^2 + 2\pi rh$ Substitute: _____

$SA =$ _____

$SA =$ _____

The surface area is about: _____

b)

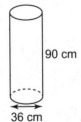

90 cm

36 cm

Radius:

_____

Use:

$SA =$ _____   Substitute: _____

$SA =$ _____

$SA =$ _____

The surface area is about: _____

1.7 Solving Problems Involving Objects

FOCUS Find the surface areas and volumes of composite objects.

The formulas for surface area and volume are summarized in this chart:

Object	Surface Area Formula	Volume Formula
Prism	SA = Area of two bases + area of faces	V = (Base area)(height)
Rectangular prism	$SA = 2(lw + lh + wh)$	$V = lwh$
Cube	$SA = 6s^2$	$V = s^3$
Pyramid	SA = Area of base + area of faces	$V = \frac{1}{3}$(Base area)(height)
Rectangular pyramid	SA = Area of base + 2(Area of one triangular face) + 2(Area of different triangular face)	$V = \frac{1}{3}lwh$
Cylinder	$SA = 2\pi r^2 + 2\pi rh$	$V = \pi r^2 h$
Cone	$SA = \pi rs + \pi r^2$	$V = \frac{1}{3}\pi r^2 h$
Sphere	$SA = 4\pi r^2$	$V = \frac{4}{3}\pi r^3$
Hemisphere	$SA = 3\pi r^2$	$V = \frac{2}{3}\pi r^3$

To find the volume of a composite object, add the volumes of the objects that make up the composite object.

A composite object is made from 2 or more objects.

Example 1 | Finding the Volume of a Composite Object

Find the volume of this composite object, to the nearest tenth of a cubic centimetre.

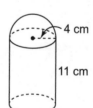

4 cm

11 cm

Solution

The composite object is a hemisphere on a cylinder.
Find the volume of each separate object.

Volume of the hemisphere:

$V = \frac{2}{3}\pi r^3$

Substitute: $r = 4$

$V = \frac{2}{3}\pi(4)^3$

$V = 134.0412...$

Volume of cylinder:

$V = \pi r^2 h$

Substitute:

$r = 4$ and $h = 11$

$V = \pi(4)^2(11)$

$V = 552.9203...$

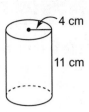

Add the volumes of the hemisphere and the cylinder.

Total volume is: $134.0412... + 552.9203... = 686.9615...$

The volume of the composite object is about 687.0 cm^3.

Check

1. Find the volume of this composite object.

The composite object is a rectangular pyramid on a rectangular prism.

Find the volume of each separate object.

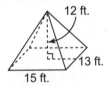

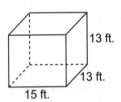

Volume of the rectangular pyramid:

$V = \frac{1}{3}lwh$

Substitute: $l = $ _____, $w = $ _____, $h = $ _____

$V = $ _____

$V = $ _____

Volume of the rectangular prism:

$V = lwh$

Substitute: $l = $ _____, $w = $ _____, $h = $ _____

$V = $ _____

$V = $ _____

Add the volumes.

Total volume is: _____ + _____ = _____

The volume of the composite object is: _____

To find the surface area of a composite object, add the areas of all exposed surfaces.

978-0-321-61066-9 Copyright © 2011 Pearson Canada Inc. **53**

Example 2 | **Finding the Surface Area of a Composite Object**

Find the surface area of this composite object.

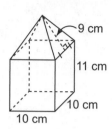

9 cm

11 cm

10 cm

10 cm

Solution

The composite object is a square pyramid on a square prism.
Find the area of the exposed surfaces of each separate object.

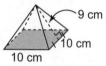

9 cm

10 cm

10 cm

*The shaded regions are **not** included in the surface area.*

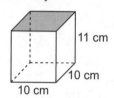

11 cm

10 cm

10 cm

Surface area of the square pyramid
is: area of 4 triangular faces

Area of 1 face is: $\frac{1}{2} \times 10 \times 9 = 45$

Area of 4 faces is: $4 \times 45 = 180$

Surface area of the square prism is:
area of 4 rectangular faces + area of base
Area of 1 face is: $10 \times 11 = 110$
Area of 4 faces is: $4 \times 110 = 440$
Area of base is: $10 \times 10 = 100$
Surface area is: $440 + 100 = 540$

Add the surface areas.
Total surface area is: $180 + 540 = 720$
The surface area of the composite object is 720 cm².

Check

1. Find the surface area of this composite object,
to the nearest square centimetre.

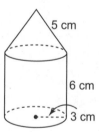

5 cm

6 cm

3 cm

The composite object is: _____
Find the surface area of each separate object.

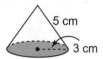

5 cm

3 cm

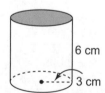

6 cm

3 cm

Surface area of the: _____

$SA = \pi rs$

Substitute: $r =$ _____ and $s =$ _____

$SA =$ _____

$SA =$ _____

Surface area of the: _____

$SA = 2\pi rh + \pi r^2$

Substitute: $r =$ _____ and $h =$ _____

$SA =$ _____

$SA =$ _____

Total surface area is: _____ + _____ = _____

The surface area is about: _____

---

1. This composite object is a triangular prism on a rectangular prism.
The base of the triangular prism is an equilateral triangle.
Find the surface area of this object.

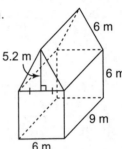

Find the area of the exposed surfaces of each separate object.

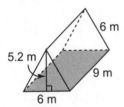

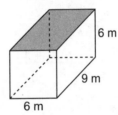

Surface area of: _____

is the area of _____ triangular faces +
the area of _____ rectangular faces

Area of 1 triangular face is:

_____ = _____

Area of _____ triangular faces is:

_____ × _____ = _____

Area of 1 rectangular face is:

_____ × _____ = _____

Area of _____ rectangular faces is:

_____ = _____

Surface area of: _____

is: _____ + _____ = _____

Add the surface areas.

Total surface area is: _____ + _____ = _____

The surface area is: _____

Surface area of: _____

is the area of _____ square faces +
the area of _____ rectangular faces

Area of 1 square face is:

_____ = _____

Area of _____ square faces is:

_____ × _____ = _____

Area of 1 rectangular face is:

_____ × _____ = _____

Area of _____ rectangular faces is:

_____ = _____

Surface area of: _____

is: _____ + _____ = _____

2. Determine the volume of each composite object, to the nearest cubic unit.

a) a rectangular prism on a cylinder

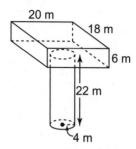

Find the volume of each separate object.

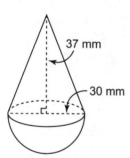

Volume of the rectangular prism:

$V =$ _____

Substitute: _____

$V =$ _____

$V =$ _____

Add the volumes.

Total volume is: _____ + _____ = _____

The volume is about: _____

Volume of the cylinder:

$V =$ _____

Substitute: _____

$V =$ _____

$V =$ _____

b) a cone on a hemisphere

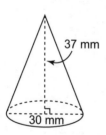

Find the volume of each separate object.

Radius: _____

Volume of the cone:

$V =$

_____

Substitute: _____

$V =$

_____

$V =$ _____

Add the volumes.

Total volume is: _____ + _____ = _____

The volume is about: _____

Volume of the hemisphere:

$V =$

_____

Substitute: _____

$V =$

_____

$V =$ _____

3. A sphere of flavoured ice is served in a cylinder-shaped paper cup. The cup has diameter 6 cm and height 10 cm. The sphere has the same diameter as the cup. To the nearest cubic centimetre, how much space is left inside the cup? (Hint: One-half of the sphere is below the rim of the cup.)

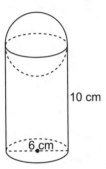

10 cm

6 cm

Volume of space = Volume of _____ − volume of _____

Radius: _____

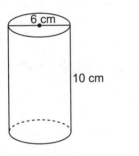

6 cm

10 cm

Volume of: _____

$V = \pi r^2 h$

Substitute: _____

$V =$ _____

$V =$ _____

Subtract the volumes.

Volume of space is: _____ − _____ = _____

There is about _____ of space in the cup.

6 cm

Volume of: _____

$V = \dfrac{2}{3}\pi r^3$

Substitute: _____

$V =$

_____

$V =$ _____

4. A tent has the shape of a square pyramid on top of a cube, as shown. To the nearest square foot, find the amount of material needed to make the tent.

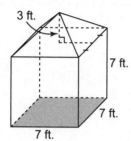

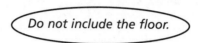
Do not include the floor.

Find the area of the exposed surfaces of each separate object.

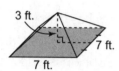

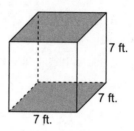

Surface area of square pyramid
is the area of _____ triangular faces.

Find the slant height of the pyramid.
Let s represent the slant height.

Use the Pythagorean Theorem.
$s^2 =$ _____ + _____
$s^2 =$ _____
$s =$ _____

Area of 1 triangular face is:
_____

Area of _____ triangular faces is:

_____ = _____

Surface area of cube
is the area of _____ square faces.
Area of 1 square face is:
_____ = _____
Area of _____ square faces is:
_____ = _____

Add the surface areas.
Total surface area is:
_____ + _____ = _____
The amount of material needed is about: _____

Figure It Out

To simplify this expression: $[(AB) \div E]^C + D$, you need to find the value of each letter.

Calculate the surface area and volume of each object below on another sheet of paper. Write each measure to the nearest whole unit. Record your answers below, then answer the questions that follow.

A.

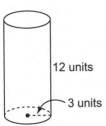

12 units

3 units

SA ≐ _____
V ≐ _____

B.

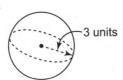

3 units

SA ≐ _____
V ≐ _____

C.

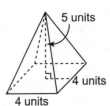

5 units

4 units

4 units

SA ≐ _____
V ≐ _____

D.

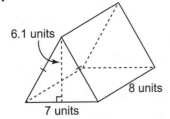

6.1 units

8 units

7 units

SA ≐ _____
V ≐ _____

E.

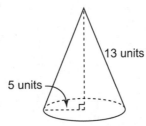

13 units

5 units

SA ≐ _____
V ≐ _____

Answer these questions with the letter that represents the object.

Which object has its volume and surface area differ by 40? _____ = 1

Which object has a volume of 314? _____ = 2

Which object has the least volume? _____ = 3

Which object has the second to least volume? _____ = 4

Which object has the greatest difference in its volume and surface area? _____ = 5

Substitute the number that corresponds to each letter in the expression below, then simplify.

$[(AB) \div E]^C + D =$

The solution is: _____

Skill	Description	Example
Convert between units in the imperial system.	Use the relationships between the units.	Convert: 19 yd. to feet 1 yd. = 3 ft. 19 yd. = 19 × 3 ft. 19 yd. = 57 ft.
Convert between units in the imperial system and the SI system.	Use the relationships between the systems.	Convert: 37 mi. to kilometres 1 mi. ≐ 1.6 km 37 mi. ≐ 37 × 1.6 km 37 mi. ≐ 59.2 km
Find the slant height or height of a cone.	Use the Pythagorean Theorem.	To the nearest centimetre, find the height of this cone. $26^2 = 14^2 + h^2$ $h^2 = 26^2 - 14^2$ $h = \sqrt{26^2 - 14^2}$ $h = 21.9089\ldots$ The height is about 22 cm.
Find the surface areas of pyramids, prisms, cones, cylinders, and spheres.	For a pyramid or a prism, add the area of the base or bases to the area of the faces. For a cone or a cylinder, add the area of the base or bases to the curved surface area. Surface area of a sphere is: $4\pi(\text{radius})^2$	To the nearest square foot, find the surface area of a cylinder with radius 3 ft. and height 9 ft. $SA = 2\pi r^2 + 2\pi rh$ $SA = 2\pi(3)^2 + 2\pi(3)(9)$ $SA = 226.1946\ldots$ The surface area is about 226 square feet.
Find the volumes of prisms, cylinders, pyramids, cones, and spheres.	Volume of a prism and a cylinder is: (base area)(height) Volume of a pyramid and a cone is: $\frac{1}{3}$(base area)(height) Volume of a sphere is: $\frac{4}{3}\pi(\text{radius})^3$	To the nearest cubic inch, find the volume of a cylinder with radius 2 in. and height 8 in. $V = \pi r^2 h$ $V = \pi(2)^2(8)$ $V = 100.5309\ldots$ The volume is about 101 cubic inches.

Chapter 1 Review

1.1 **1.** Which imperial unit is best to measure each item below:
mile, yard, foot, or inch?

a) the distance between your locker and the front door of the school: _____

b) the width of a house: _____

c) the distance around a pop can: _____

2. Convert:

a) 84 ft. to yards
_____ ft. = 1 yd.
84 ft. = (_____ ÷ _____) yd., or

84 ft. =   yd.
_____

84 ft. = _____

b) 9 ft. 7 in. to inches
1 ft. = _____ in.
9 ft. = _____ × _____ in.

9 ft. = _____

Add the inches.
9 ft. 7 in. = _____ + _____
9 ft. 7 in. = _____

See page 6 of the Student Text for a conversion chart.

1.2 **3.** For each object below:
- Describe how you measure it.
- Include the measuring device.
- State the imperial unit.
- State the SI unit.

a) the greatest distance around a fish bowl
Imperial unit: _____
SI unit: _____
Measuring device: _____

b) the width of your kitchen floor
Imperial unit: _____
SI unit: _____
Measuring device: _____

4. Convert:

a) 17 yd. to metres

1 yd. ≐ _____ m

17 yd. ≐ 17 × _____

17 yd. ≐ _____

b) 68 mi. to kilometres

1 mi. ≐ _____ km

68 mi. ≐ _____ × _____

68 mi. ≐ _____

> See page 13 for a conversion chart.

5. Ryan drove 19 km to watch a lacrosse game. Julie drove 11 mi. to see the same game. Who drove farther?

Ryan drove: _____

Convert Julie's distance to kilometres.

1 mi. ≐ _____

11 mi. ≐ _____ × _____

11 mi. ≐ _____

Since _____ is greater than _____, _____ drove farther.

6. Find the surface area of each object, to the nearest square unit.

a) a right cone

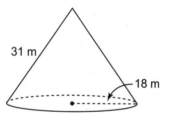

31 m

18 m

For a cone:

$SA = \pi$_____ $+ \pi$_____

Substitute: $r =$ _____ and $s =$ _____

$SA = \pi$_____ $+ \pi$_____

$SA =$ _____

The surface area is about: _____

> See page 27 for the formula for the surface area of a cone.

b) a square pyramid

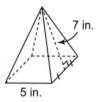

7 in.

5 in.

For a square pyramid:

Area of base is: _____

Area of each triangular face is: $\frac{1}{2} \times$ _____ $\times$ _____ $=$ _____

Area of all 4 faces is: 4 × _____ $=$ _____

The surface area of the pyramid is: _____ $+$ _____ $=$ _____

The surface area is: _____

7. Find the surface area of this rectangular pyramid.

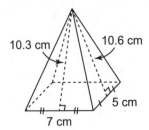

10.3 cm   10.6 cm

5 cm

7 cm

For a rectangular pyramid:
SA = area of rectangular base + area of each triangular face

The surface area of the pyramid is: _____.

8. Is the surface area of this cone less than 500 square inches?

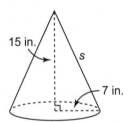

15 in.

s

7 in.

Find the slant height, s.
Use the Pythagorean Theorem.

$s^2 =$ _____ + _____

$s^2 =$ _____

$s =$ _____

Find the surface area:

$SA =$ _____ + _____

Substitute: _____ = _____ and _____ = _____

The surface area of the cone is about: _____

The surface area of the cone is _____ than 500 square inches.

9. Find the volume of this rectangular pyramid, to the nearest cubic centimetre.

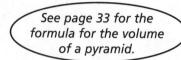

8 cm

5 cm

11 cm

See page 33 for the formula for the volume of a pyramid.

For a rectangular pyramid:

$V = $ _____

Substitute: _____ = _____, _____ = _____, _____ = _____

$V = $ _____

$V = $ _____

The volume is about: _____

10. A bowl of sugar was knocked over. The spilled sugar formed this cone. How much sugar was in the pile?

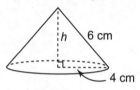

h 6 cm

4 cm

Use the Pythagorean Theorem to find h.

_____ = $h^2 + $ _____

$h^2 = $ _____

$h^2 = $ _____

$h = $ _____

Find the volume:

$V = $ _____

Substitute: _____ = _____ and _____ = _____

$V = $ _____

$V = $ _____

See page 34 for the formula for the volume of a cone.

There was about _____ of sugar in the pile.

1.6 **11.** Find the surface area and volume of each object. Give the answers to the nearest whole number of units.

a) a sphere

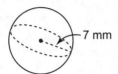

See pages 40 and 41 for the formulas for a sphere.

For a sphere:

SA = _____   Substitute: ____ = ____

SA = _____

SA = _____

The surface area is about: _____

V =

_____

Substitute: ____ = ____

V =

_____

V = _____

The volume is about: _____

b) a hemisphere

Radius is: _____

For a hemisphere:

SA = _____   Substitute: ____ = ____

SA = _____

SA = _____

The surface area is about: _____

V =

_____

Substitute: ____ = ___

V =

_____

V = _____

The volume is about: _____

1.7 **12.** A garden shed has the shape of a square pyramid on top of a square prism. Both the pyramid and the prism have base side length 8 ft. The prism is 6 ft. high and the pyramid is 3 ft. high.

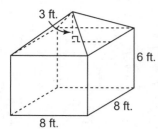

a) Find the surface area of the shed. Do not include the base of the shed.

Let the slant height of the pyramid be *s* feet.

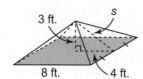   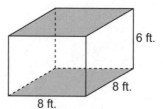

Surface area of square pyramid is the area of _____ triangular faces.

Find the slant height of the pyramid. Use the Pythagorean Theorem.

$s^2 =$ _____

Surface area of square prism is the area of _____ rectangular faces.

Area of 1 rectangular face is:

_____ = _____

Area of _____ rectangular faces is:

_____ = _____

s = _____

Area of 1 triangular face is: _____ = _____

Area of _____ triangular faces is: _____ = _____

Add the surface areas.

Total surface area is: _____ + _____ = _____

The surface area of the shed is: _____

b) How much space is inside the shed?

Find the volume of the shed.

Volume of square pyramid:

$V =$
_____

Substitute: _____

$V =$
_____

$V =$ _____

Volume of square prism:

$V =$ _____

Substitute: _____

$V =$ _____

$V =$ _____

Total volume is: _____ + _____ = _____

There is _____ of space in the shed.

Trigonometry

What You'll Learn

- Determine the measure of an acute angle in a right triangle using the lengths of two sides.

- Determine the length of a side in a right triangle using the length of another side and the measure of an acute angle.

- Solve problems that involve one or more right triangles.

Why It's Important

Trigonometric ratios are used by:

- surveyors, to determine the distance across a river or a very busy street

- pilots, to determine flight paths and measure crosswinds

- forestry technicians, to calculate the heights of trees

Key Words

tangent ratio

angle of inclination

indirect measurement

sine ratio

cosine ratio

angle of elevation

angle of depression

▶ 2.1 Skill Builder

Similar Triangles

Similar triangles have:
- the measures of matching angles equal
- the ratios of matching sides equal

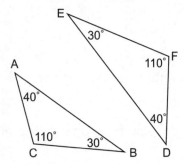

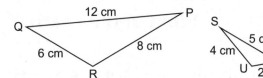

These triangles are similar because matching angles are equal.

$\angle A = \angle D = 40°$

$\angle B = \angle E = 30°$

$\angle C = \angle F = 110°$

These triangles are not similar because the ratios of matching sides are different.

$\dfrac{PQ}{ST} = \dfrac{12}{5} = 2.4$

$\dfrac{QR}{TU} = \dfrac{6}{2} = 3$

$\dfrac{RP}{US} = \dfrac{8}{4} = 2$

Compare the longest sides, compare the shortest sides, then compare the third pair of sides.

Check

1. Are the triangles in each pair similar?

a)

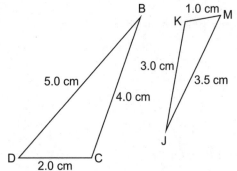

Compare the ratios of matching sides.

$\dfrac{DB}{\rule{1.5cm}{0.4pt}} = \dfrac{\rule{1.5cm}{0.4pt}}{\rule{1.5cm}{0.4pt}} = \rule{1.5cm}{0.4pt}$

$\dfrac{CD}{\rule{1.5cm}{0.4pt}} = \dfrac{\rule{1.5cm}{0.4pt}}{\rule{1.5cm}{0.4pt}} = \rule{1.5cm}{0.4pt}$

$\dfrac{BC}{\rule{1.5cm}{0.4pt}} = \dfrac{\rule{1.5cm}{0.4pt}}{\rule{1.5cm}{0.4pt}} = \rule{1.5cm}{0.4pt}$

The triangles _____ similar.

b)

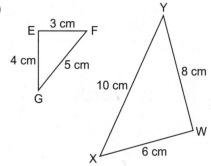

Compare the ratios of matching sides.

$\dfrac{\rule{1.5cm}{0.4pt}}{\rule{1.5cm}{0.4pt}} = \dfrac{\rule{1.5cm}{0.4pt}}{\rule{1.5cm}{0.4pt}} = \rule{1.5cm}{0.4pt}$

$\dfrac{\rule{1.5cm}{0.4pt}}{\rule{1.5cm}{0.4pt}} = \dfrac{\rule{1.5cm}{0.4pt}}{\rule{1.5cm}{0.4pt}} = \rule{1.5cm}{0.4pt}$

$\dfrac{\rule{1.5cm}{0.4pt}}{\rule{1.5cm}{0.4pt}} = \dfrac{\rule{1.5cm}{0.4pt}}{\rule{1.5cm}{0.4pt}} = \rule{1.5cm}{0.4pt}$

The triangles _____ similar.

2.1 The Tangent Ratio

FOCUS Use the tangent ratio to find an angle measure.

The Tangent Ratio

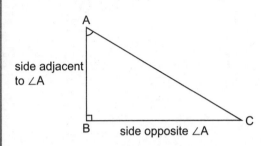

side adjacent to ∠A

side opposite ∠A

*An **acute angle** is less than 90°.*

If ∠A is an acute angle in a right triangle, then $\tan A = \dfrac{\text{length of side opposite } \angle A}{\text{length of side adjacent to } \angle A}$

Example 1 | Finding the Tangent Ratio

Find the tangent ratio for ∠G.

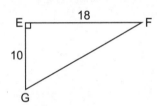

18

10

Solution

Draw an arc at ∠G.
The side opposite ∠G is EF.
The side adjacent to ∠G is GE.

$\tan G = \dfrac{\text{length of side opposite } \angle G}{\text{length of side adjacent to } \angle G}$

$\tan G = \dfrac{EF}{GE}$ Substitute: EF = 18 and GE = 10

$\tan G = \dfrac{18}{10}$

$\tan G = 1.8$

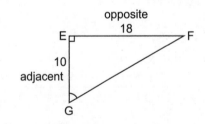

opposite
18
10
adjacent

The side opposite the right angle is always the hypotenuse.

$Tan = \dfrac{opp}{adj}$

Check

1. a) Find tan P.

The side opposite ∠P is __10__ .

The side adjacent to ∠P is __8__ .

$\tan P = \dfrac{\text{length of side} \underline{\hspace{2cm}} \angle P}{\text{length of side} \underline{\hspace{2cm}} \angle P}$

$\tan P = \dfrac{}{\underline{\hspace{1.5cm}}}$

$\tan P = \dfrac{}{\underline{\hspace{1.5cm}}}$

$\tan P = \underline{\hspace{1.5cm}}$

b) Find tan Q.

The side opposite ∠Q is _____ .

The side adjacent to ∠Q is _____ .

$\tan Q = \underline{\hspace{5cm}}$

$\tan Q = \dfrac{}{\underline{\hspace{1.5cm}}}$

$\tan Q = \dfrac{}{\underline{\hspace{1.5cm}}}$

$\tan Q = \underline{\hspace{1.5cm}}$

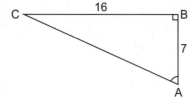

To find the measure of an angle, use the $\tan^{-1}$ key on a scientific calculator.

Example 2 — Using the Tangent Ratio to Find the Measure of an Angle

Find the measure of ∠A to the nearest degree.

16
C — B
7
A

Solution

The side opposite ∠A is BC.

The side adjacent to ∠A is AB.

$\tan A = \dfrac{\text{length of side opposite } \angle A}{\text{length of side adjacent to } \angle A}$

$\tan A = \dfrac{BC}{AB}$ Substitute: BC = 16 and AB = 7

$\tan A = \dfrac{16}{7}$

If you are using a different calculator, consult the user's manual.

To find ∠A using a TI-30XIIS calculator, enter:

[2nd] [TAN] [1] [6] [÷] [7] [)] [ENTER]

tan⁻¹(16/7)
66.37062227

∠A ≐ 66°

Check

1. Find the measure of each indicated angle to the nearest degree.

a) ∠F

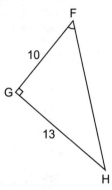

The side opposite ∠F is _____.

The side adjacent to ∠F is _____.

$$\tan F = \frac{\text{length of side } \underline{\hspace{2cm}} \angle F}{\text{length of side } \underline{\hspace{2cm}} \angle F}$$

$\tan F = \underline{\hspace{3cm}}$

$\tan F = \underline{\hspace{3cm}}$

∠F = tan⁻¹ $\underline{\hspace{2cm}}$ Use a calculator.

∠F ≐ $\underline{\hspace{2cm}}$

b) ∠E

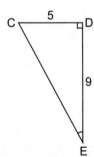

The side opposite ∠E is _____.

The side adjacent to ∠E is _____.

$\tan E = \underline{\hspace{5cm}}$

$\tan E = \underline{\hspace{3cm}}$

$\tan E = \underline{\hspace{3cm}}$

∠E = tan⁻¹$\underline{\hspace{3cm}}$

∠E ≐ $\underline{\hspace{2cm}}$

Example 3 **Using the Tangent Ratio to Find an Angle of Inclination**

A guy wire is fastened to a cell-phone tower 8.5 m above the ground. The wire is anchored to the ground 14.0 m from the base of the tower. What angle, to the nearest degree, does the wire make with the ground?

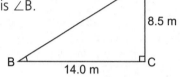

The angle the wire makes with the ground is called the angle of inclination.

Solution

Draw a diagram.
The angle the wire makes with the ground is ∠B.
To find ∠B, use the tangent ratio.

Assume the tower is perpendicular to the ground.

$$\tan B = \frac{\text{length of side opposite } \angle B}{\text{length of side adjacent to } \angle B}$$

The side opposite ∠B is CA.
The side adjacent to ∠B is BC.

$$\tan B = \frac{CA}{BC}$$

Substitute: CA = 8.5 and BC = 14.0

$$\tan B = \frac{8.5}{14.0}$$

Use a calculator.

$$\angle B \doteq 31°$$

The angle between the ground and the wire is about 31°.

Check

1. A ladder leans against a house. The top of the ladder is 2.4 m above the ground. Its base is 0.9 m from the wall. What angle, to the nearest degree, does the ladder make with the ground?

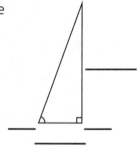

Label the given triangle FGH.
Label G where the ladder meets the ground.
Label F where it meets the wall.
We want to find the measure of ∠G.

The side opposite ∠G is _____.

The side adjacent to ∠G is _____.

$$\tan G = \underline{\hspace{3cm}}$$

$\tan G = \frac{opposite}{adjacent}$

$$\tan G = \underline{\hspace{3cm}}$$

$$\angle G \doteq \underline{\hspace{3cm}}$$

The angle between the ground and the ladder is about _____.

1. Label the hypotenuse, opposite, and adjacent sides of each right triangle in relation to the given angle.

a) ∠H

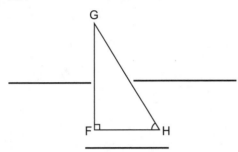

b) ∠P

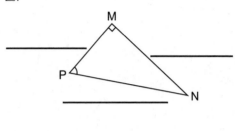

2. Find the tangent ratio for each indicated angle. Leave the ratio in fraction form.

a)

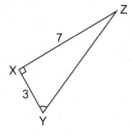

The side opposite ∠Y is _____.
The side adjacent to ∠Y is _____.

$$\tan Y = \frac{\text{length of side _____ } \angle Y}{\text{length of side _____ } \angle Y}$$

tan Y = _____

tan Y = _____

b)

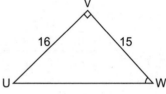

The side opposite ∠W is _____.
The side adjacent to ∠W is _____.

tan W = _____

tan W = _____

tan W = _____

3. Find the measure of ∠A for each value of tan A. Give your answer to the nearest degree.

a) tan A = 0.5

∠A = tan⁻¹(_____) Use a calculator.

∠A ≐ _____

b) tan A = $\frac{5}{6}$

∠A = _____

∠A ≐ _____

4. Find the measure of ∠B to the nearest degree.

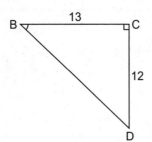

The side opposite ∠B is _____.

The side adjacent to ∠B is _____.

$$\tan B = \frac{\text{length of side} \underline{\hspace{2cm}}}{\text{length of side} \underline{\hspace{2cm}}}$$

tan B = _____

tan B = _____

∠B ≐ _____

5. A telephone pole is supported by a wire, as shown.
What angle, to the nearest degree, does the wire make with the ground?

We want to find the measure of ∠N.
Use the tangent ratio.

$$\tan \underline{\hspace{1.5cm}} = \frac{\text{length of side} \underline{\hspace{2cm}}}{\text{length of side} \underline{\hspace{2cm}}}$$

tan _____ = _____

tan _____ = _____

∠_____ ≐ _____

The angle between the ground and the wire is about _____.

6. Victor is building a wheelchair ramp to an entranceway that is 3 m above the sidewalk. The ramp will cover a horizontal distance of 50 m. What angle, to the nearest degree, will the ramp make with the ground?

R
3 m⌐_____Q
S   50 m

The angle between the ground and the ramp is about _____.

 978-0-321-61066-9

2.2 Skill Builder

Solving Equations

Inverse operations "undo" each other's results.
Multiplication and division are inverse operations.
We can use inverse operations to solve some equations.

To solve $\frac{a}{5} = 4$:

$$\frac{a}{5} = 4$$

$$5 \times \frac{a}{5} = 5 \times 4$$

$$a = 20$$

Undo the division.
Multiply each side by 5.

To solve $\frac{36}{b} = 9$:

$$b \times \frac{36}{b} = b \times 9$$

$$36 = 9b$$

Undo the division.
Multiply each side by b.

Recall: $b \times 9 = 9b$

$$\frac{36}{9} = \frac{9b}{9}$$

$$4 = b$$

Undo the multiplication.
Divide each side by 9.

Check

1. Solve each equation.

a) $\frac{a}{7} = 5$

Multiply each side by _____.

$$\underline{\hspace{1cm}} \times \frac{a}{7} = \underline{\hspace{1cm}} \times 5$$

$$a = \underline{\hspace{1cm}}$$

b) $9 = \frac{c}{8}$

Multiply each side by _____.

$$\underline{\hspace{1cm}} = c$$

c) $13 = \frac{156}{f}$

Multiply each side by _____.

$$\underline{\hspace{1cm}} \times 13 = \underline{\hspace{1cm}} \times \frac{156}{f}$$

$$\underline{\hspace{1cm}} = \underline{\hspace{1cm}}$$

Divide each side by _____.

$$\underline{\hspace{1cm}} = \underline{\hspace{1cm}}$$

$$\underline{\hspace{1cm}} = \underline{\hspace{1cm}}$$

d) $\frac{15}{b} = 6$

$$\underline{\hspace{1cm}} = b$$

2.2 Using the Tangent Ratio to Calculate Lengths

FOCUS Use the tangent ratio to calculate lengths.

When we know the measure of an acute angle and the length of a leg of a
right triangle, we can use the tangent ratio to find the length of the other leg.

Example 1 | Finding the Length of an Opposite Side

Find the length of BC to the nearest tenth of a centimetre.

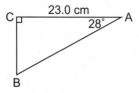

Solution

We know the measure of ∠A.
BC is the side opposite ∠A.
CA is the side adjacent to ∠A.
Use the tangent ratio to write an equation.

$$\tan A = \frac{\text{length of side opposite } \angle A}{\text{length of side adjacent to } \angle A}$$

$$\tan A = \frac{BC}{CA}$$

Substitute: ∠A = 28° and CA = 23

$$\tan 28° = \frac{BC}{23}$$

Solve the equation for BC.
Multiply each side by 23.

$$23 \times \tan 28° = 23 \times \frac{BC}{23}$$

$$23 \tan 28° = BC$$

Use a calculator. Enter: ⟨2⟩⟨3⟩⟨×⟩⟨TAN⟩⟨2⟩⟨8⟩⟨)⟩⟨ENTER⟩

$$BC = 12.2293...$$

```
23*tan(28)
              12.22931693
```

BC is about 12.2 cm long.

Check

---

1. Find the length of each indicated side to the nearest tenth of a centimetre.

a) Side ED

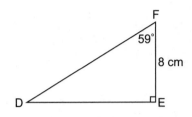

The given angle is ∠F.

_____ is the side opposite ∠F.

_____ is the side adjacent to ∠F.

$$\tan F = \frac{\text{side} \rule{3cm}{0.4pt}}{\text{side} \rule{3cm}{0.4pt}}$$

tan F = _____

tan _____ = _____

Solve the equation for DE.

Multiply each side by _____ .

_____ × tan _____ = _____ × _____

_____ × tan _____ = _____

DE = _____

DE is about _____ long.

b) Side HJ

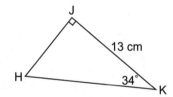

The given angle is _____ .

_____ is the side opposite _____ .

_____ is the side adjacent to _____ .

tan _____ = _____

tan _____ = _____

tan _____ = _____

HJ is about _____ long.

Example 2 | **Finding the Length of an Adjacent Side**

Find the length of PQ to the nearest tenth of a centimetre.

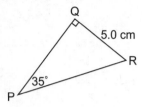

Solution

Use the tangent ratio to write an equation.

$$\tan P = \frac{\text{side opposite } \angle P}{\text{side adjacent to } \angle P}$$

> *We know $\angle P = 35°$.*
> *QR is opposite $\angle P$.*
> *PQ is adjacent $\angle P$.*

$$\tan P = \frac{QR}{PQ}$$ Substitute: QR = 5 and $\angle P = 35°$

$$\tan 35° = \frac{5}{PQ}$$

Solve the equation for PQ.

Multiply each side by PQ.

$$PQ \times \tan 35° = PQ \times \frac{5}{PQ}$$

$$PQ \tan 35° = 5$$ Divide each side by tan 35°.

$$\frac{PQ \tan 35°}{\tan 35°} = \frac{5}{\tan 35°}$$

$$PQ = \frac{5}{\tan 35°}$$ Use a calculator.

$$PQ = 7.1407...$$

So, PQ is about 7.1 cm long.

Check

1. Find the length of TU to the nearest tenth of a centimetre.

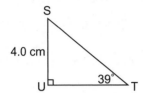

The given angle is ∠T.

_____ is the side opposite ∠T.

_____ is the side adjacent to ∠T.

$$\tan T = \frac{\text{side} \underline{\hspace{3cm}}}{\text{side} \underline{\hspace{2.5cm}}}$$

tan T = _____   Substitute: _____ and _____

tan _____ = _____   Multiply each side by _____.

_____ × tan _____ = _____ × _____

_____ × tan _____ = _____   Divide each side by _____.

$$\frac{\underline{\hspace{1cm}} \tan \underline{\hspace{1cm}}}{\underline{\hspace{2cm}}} = \frac{}{\underline{\hspace{2cm}}}$$

TU = _____   Use a calculator.

TU = _____

TU is about _____ long.

Example 3 | Using the Tangent Ratio to Solve a Problem

A wire supports a flagpole. The angle between the wire and the level ground is 73°. The wire is anchored to the ground 10 m from the base of the pole. How high up the pole does the wire reach? Give the answer to the nearest tenth of a metre.

Solution

Sketch and label a diagram.
Assume the flagpole meets the ground at a right angle.

The given angle is ∠A. We want to find the length of BC.

$$\tan A = \frac{\text{side opposite } \angle A}{\text{side adjacent to } \angle A}$$

> BC is opposite ∠A.
> CA is adjacent to ∠A.

$$\tan A = \frac{BC}{CA}$$ Substitute: ∠A = 73° and CA = 10
Solve the equation for BC.

$$\tan 73° = \frac{BC}{10}$$ Multiply each side by 10.

$$10 \tan 73° = BC$$ Use a calculator.

$$BC = 32.7085...$$

The wire reaches the flagpole at a height of about 32.7 m.

Check

1. A ladder leans on a wall, as shown. How far up the wall does the ladder reach? Give your answer to the nearest tenth of a metre.

The given angle is ∠F.
We want to find the length of _____.

$$\tan F = \frac{\text{side} \rule{3cm}{0.4pt}}{\text{side} \rule{2cm}{0.4pt}}$$

$\tan F = \rule{2cm}{0.4pt}$ Substitute: $\rule{2cm}{0.4pt}$ and $\rule{2cm}{0.4pt}$

$\tan \rule{2cm}{0.4pt} = \rule{2cm}{0.4pt}$ Multiply each side by $\rule{2cm}{0.4pt}$.

$\rule{2cm}{0.4pt} \tan \rule{2cm}{0.4pt} = \rule{2cm}{0.4pt}$

$DE = \rule{3cm}{0.4pt}$

The ladder reaches the wall at a height of about $\rule{3cm}{0.4pt}$.

Practice

1. Find the length of the side opposite the given angle to the nearest tenth of a centimetre.

a)

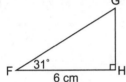

The given angle is ∠F.
The side opposite ∠F is $\rule{2cm}{0.4pt}$.
The side adjacent to ∠F is $\rule{2cm}{0.4pt}$.

$$\tan F = \frac{\text{side} \rule{3cm}{0.4pt}}{\text{side} \rule{3cm}{0.4pt}}$$

$\tan F = \rule{2.5cm}{0.4pt}$

$\tan \rule{1.5cm}{0.4pt} = \rule{2cm}{0.4pt}$

$\rule{1.5cm}{0.4pt} \times \tan \rule{1.5cm}{0.4pt} = \rule{3cm}{0.4pt}$

$\rule{1.5cm}{0.4pt} \tan \rule{1.5cm}{0.4pt} = \rule{2cm}{0.4pt}$

$GH = \rule{3cm}{0.4pt}$

GH is about $\rule{3cm}{0.4pt}$ long.

b)

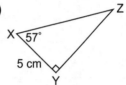

The given angle is ∠$\rule{2cm}{0.4pt}$.
The side opposite ∠$\rule{2cm}{0.4pt}$ is $\rule{2cm}{0.4pt}$.
The side adjacent to ∠$\rule{2cm}{0.4pt}$ is $\rule{2cm}{0.4pt}$.

$$\tan \rule{2cm}{0.4pt} = \frac{\text{side} \rule{3cm}{0.4pt}}{\text{side} \rule{3cm}{0.4pt}}$$

$\rule{2cm}{0.4pt}$ is about $\rule{3cm}{0.4pt}$ long.

2. Find the length of CD to the nearest tenth of a centimetre.

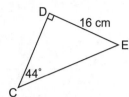

The given angle is ∠C.

The side opposite ∠C is _____.

The side adjacent to ∠C is _____.

$$\tan C = \frac{\text{side} \underline{\hspace{3cm}}}{\text{side} \underline{\hspace{2.5cm}}}$$

$$\tan C = \underline{\hspace{1.5cm}}$$

$$\tan \underline{\hspace{1.5cm}} = \underline{\hspace{1.5cm}}$$

Multiply each side by _____.

Divide each side by _____.

CD is about _____ long.

3. Find the length of the indicated side to the nearest tenth of a centimetre.

a) Side PQ

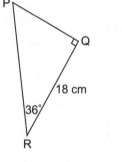

$$\tan R = \frac{\text{opposite}}{\text{adjacent}}$$

$$\tan \underline{\hspace{1.5cm}} = \underline{\hspace{1.5cm}}$$

b) Side UV

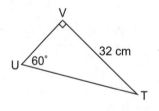

$$\tan \underline{\hspace{1.5cm}} = \underline{\hspace{2.5cm}}$$

$$\tan \underline{\hspace{1.5cm}} = \underline{\hspace{1.5cm}}$$

UV is about _____ long.

PQ is about _____ long.

4. This diagram shows an awning over the window of a house. Find the height of the awning, GH, to the nearest tenth of a metre.

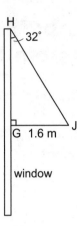

tan H = _____

_____

The height of the awning is about _____.

5. A rope supports a tent. The angle between the rope and the level ground is 59°. The rope is attached to the ground 1.2 m from the base of the tent. At what height above the ground is the rope attached to the tent? Give your answer to the nearest tenth of a metre.

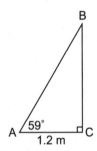

The rope is attached to the tent at a height of about _____.

2.3 Math Lab: Measuring an Inaccessible Height

FOCUS Determine a height that cannot be measured directly.

When we find a length or an angle without using a measuring instrument, we are using **indirect measurement.**

Try This

Work with a partner.

Follow the instructions in Part A on Student Text page 85 to make a clinometer.

The materials you need are listed on Student Text page 84.

Record all your measurements on the diagram below.

Choose a tall object; for example, a tree or a flagpole.

Object: _____

Mark a point on the ground.

Measure the distance to the base of the object.

One person stands at the point. He holds the clinometer, then looks at the top of the object through the straw. The other person records the angle shown by the thread on the protractor. Then that person measures the height of the eyes above the ground of the person holding the clinometer.

Subtract the clinometer angle from 90°.

This is the angle of inclination of the straw.

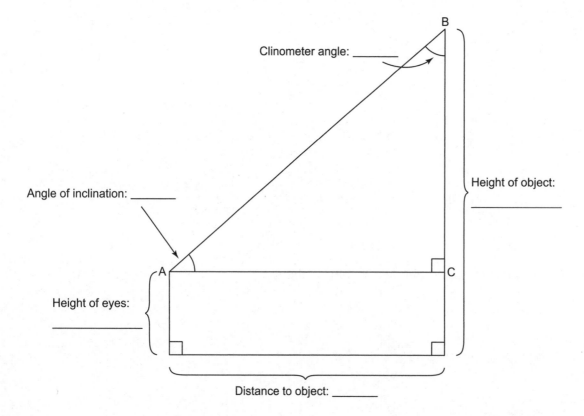

Use the tangent ratio to calculate the length of BC:

$$\tan A = \frac{BC}{AC}$$

$$\tan \underline{\hspace{1cm}} = \frac{BC}{\underline{\hspace{2cm}}}$$

$$BC = \underline{\hspace{1cm}} \times \tan \underline{\hspace{1cm}}$$

$$BC \doteq \underline{\hspace{1cm}}$$

Height of object = length of BC + height of eyes above the ground

Height of object = _____ + _____

Height of object = _____

Change places with your partner.

Repeat the activity.

Does the height of your eyes affect the measurements? Explain.

_____

_____

_____

Does the height of your eyes affect the final result? Explain.

_____

_____

_____

Practice

1. Which angle of inclination does each clinometer measure?

a)

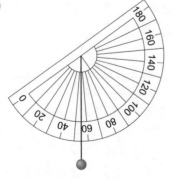

Angle of inclination

= 90° − angle on clinometer

= 90° − _____

= _____

b)

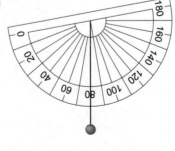

Angle of inclination

= 90° − _____

= _____

2. Use the information in the diagram to find the height of the flagpole to the nearest tenth of a metre.

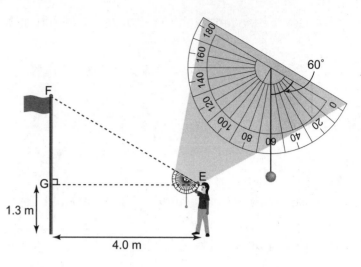

Angle on clinometer: _____
Angle of inclination: 90° − _____ = _____
So, ∠E = _____

$$\tan E = \frac{\text{opposite}}{\text{adjacent}}$$

tan _____ = _____

tan _____ = _____

FG = _____

So, height of flagpole = _____ + height of eyes above ground

= _____ + _____

= _____

The height of the flagpole is about _____.

3. Use the information in the diagram to find the height of the tree to the nearest tenth of a metre.

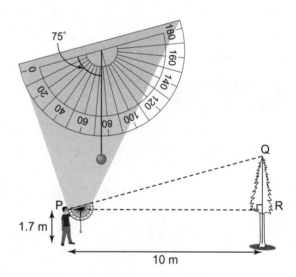

This diagram is not drawn to scale.

∠P is: 90° − _____ = _____

tan P = _____

tan _____ = _____

QR = _____

So, height of tree = _____

= _____

The height of the tree is about _____.

 978-0-321-61066-9 Copyright © 2011 Pearson Canada Inc.

 CHECKPOINT 1

Can you...

- use the tangent ratio to find an angle measure?
- use the tangent ratio to calculate a length?
- use the tangent ratio to solve a problem?

2.1 **1.** Find the tangent ratio for each indicated angle. Leave the ratio in fraction form.

a)

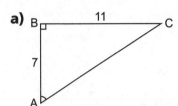

The side opposite ∠A is _____.

The side adjacent to ∠A is _____.

$$\tan A = \frac{\text{side} \underline{\hspace{3cm}}}{\text{side} \underline{\hspace{2.5cm}}}$$

$\tan A = \underline{\hspace{1.5cm}}$

$\tan A = \underline{\hspace{1.5cm}}$

b)

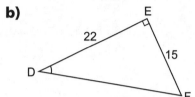

$\tan D = $ _____

$\tan D = \underline{\hspace{1cm}}$

$\tan D = \underline{\hspace{1cm}}$

2. Find the measure of each indicated angle to the nearest degree.

a)

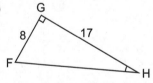

The side opposite ∠H is _____.

The side adjacent to ∠H is _____.

$$\tan H = \frac{\text{side} \underline{\hspace{3cm}}}{\text{side} \underline{\hspace{2.5cm}}}$$

$\tan H = \underline{\hspace{1.5cm}}$

$\tan H = \underline{\hspace{1.5cm}}$

$\angle H = \tan^{-1} \underline{\hspace{1.5cm}}$

$\angle H \doteq \underline{\hspace{1.5cm}}$

b)

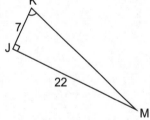

$\tan \underline{\hspace{1cm}} = $ _____

$\tan \underline{\hspace{1cm}} = \underline{\hspace{1cm}}$

$\tan \underline{\hspace{1cm}} = \underline{\hspace{1cm}}$

$\angle \underline{\hspace{1cm}} = \tan^{-1} \underline{\hspace{1.5cm}}$

$\angle \underline{\hspace{1cm}} \doteq \underline{\hspace{1.5cm}}$

978-0-321-61066-9 Copyright © 2011 Pearson Canada Inc.

3. Find the length of each indicated side to the nearest tenth of a centimetre.

a) Side ST

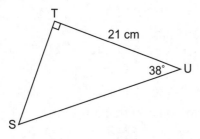

b) Side PQ

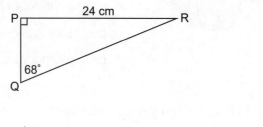

tan _____ = _____

$$\tan U = \frac{\text{side} \underline{\hspace{3cm}}}{\text{side} \underline{\hspace{2cm}}}$$

tan U = _____

tan _____ = _____

ST = _____

ST is about _____ long.

PQ is about _____ long.

4. Margy is building a support brace to reach the top of a wall, as shown. How far from the wall should the brace be anchored to the ground? Give your answer to the nearest tenth of a metre.

We want to find the length of AB.

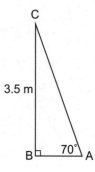

The brace should be anchored to the ground about _____ from the wall.

▶ 2.4 Skill Builder

Sum of the Angles in a Triangle

In any triangle, the sum of the
angle measures is 180°.

So, to find an unknown angle measure:

• start with 180°

• subtract the known measures

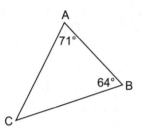

$\angle C = 180° - 71° - 64°$

$\angle C = 45°$

In any right triangle, the sum of the
measures of the acute angles is 90°.

So, to find the measure of an acute angle:

• start with 90°

• subtract the known acute angle

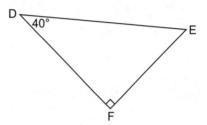

$\angle E = 90° - 40°$

$\angle E = 50°$

Check

1. Find the measure of the third angle.

a)

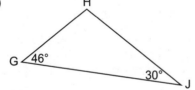

$\angle H = 180° - \underline{\hspace{2cm}} - \underline{\hspace{2cm}}$

$\angle H = \underline{\hspace{2cm}}$

b)

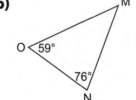

$\angle M = \underline{\hspace{3cm}}$

$\angle M = \underline{\hspace{1.5cm}}$

2. Find the measure of the third angle.

a)

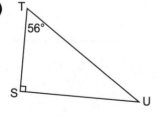

$\angle U = 90° - \underline{\hspace{2cm}}$

$\angle U = \underline{\hspace{2cm}}$

b)

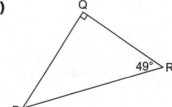

$\angle P = \underline{\hspace{3cm}}$

$\angle P = \underline{\hspace{1.5cm}}$

▶ 2.4 The Sine and Cosine Ratios

FOCUS Use the sine and cosine ratios to determine angle measures.

The Sine and Cosine Ratios

In a right triangle, if ∠A is an acute angle, then

$$\sin A = \frac{\text{length of side opposite } \angle A}{\text{length of hypotenuse}}$$

$$\cos A = \frac{\text{length of side adjacent to } \angle A}{\text{length of hypotenuse}}$$

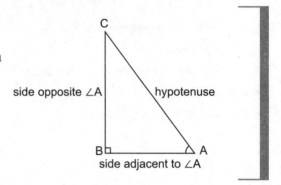

Example 1 | **Finding the Sine and Cosine of an Angle**

Find sin B and cos B to the nearest hundredth.

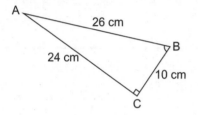

> *The nearest hundredth means two decimal places.*

Solution

AC is the side opposite ∠B.
AB is the hypotenuse.

$$\sin B = \frac{\text{length of side opposite } \angle B}{\text{length of hypotenuse}}$$

$\sin B = \dfrac{AC}{AB}$ Substitute: AC = 24 and AB = 26

$\sin B = \dfrac{24}{26}$

$\sin B = 0.9230\ldots$

$\sin B \doteq 0.92$

BC is the side adjacent to ∠B.
AB is the hypotenuse.

$$\cos B = \frac{\text{length of side adjacent to } \angle B}{\text{length of hypotenuse}}$$

$\cos B = \dfrac{BC}{AB}$ Substitute: BC = 10 and AB = 26

$\cos B = \dfrac{10}{26}$

$\cos B = 0.3846\ldots$

$\cos B \doteq 0.38$

Check

1. Find sin D and cos D to the nearest hundredth.

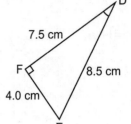

$$\sin D = \frac{\text{side opposite } \angle D}{\text{hypotenuse}}$$

$$\cos D = \frac{\text{side adjacent to } \angle D}{\text{hypotenuse}}$$

sin D = _____

cos D = _____

sin D = _____

cos D = _____

sin D = _____

cos D = _____

sin D $\doteq$ _____

cos D $\doteq$ _____

To find the measure of an angle, use the $\sin^{-1}$ or $\cos^{-1}$ key on a scientific calculator.

Example 2 | **Using the Sine or Cosine Ratio to Find the Measure of an Angle**

Find the measures of $\angle B$ and $\angle D$
to the nearest degree.

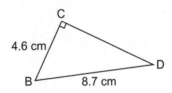

Solution

Find the measure of $\angle B$ first.
BC is adjacent to $\angle B$. BD is the hypotenuse.
So, use the cosine ratio to write an equation.

> We could use the sine ratio to find the measure of $\angle D$ first.

$$\cos B = \frac{\text{side adjacent to } \angle B}{\text{hypotenuse}}$$

$$\cos B = \frac{BC}{BD}$$ Substitute: BC = 4.6 and BD = 8.7

$$\cos B = \frac{4.6}{8.7}$$

To find $\angle B$ using a TI-30XIIS calculator, enter:

[2nd] [COS] [4] [.] [6] [÷] [8] [.] [7] [)] [ENTER]

$\angle B \doteq 58°$

Since the sum of the acute angles in a right triangle is 90°,

$$\angle D = 90° - \angle B$$

So, $\angle D \doteq 90° - 58°$

$$\angle D \doteq 32°$$

> Since the measure of $\angle B$ is an estimate, so is the measure of $\angle D$.

Check

1. Find the measure of each acute angle to the nearest degree.

a)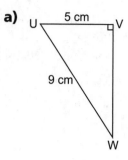

Find the measure of ∠U first.

UV is the _____ ∠U.

UW is the _____.

So, use the cosine ratio to write an equation.

$$\cos U = \underline{\hspace{4cm}}$$

$$\cos U = \underline{\hspace{2cm}}$$

$$\cos U = \underline{\hspace{2cm}}$$

$$\angle U = \cos^{-1} \underline{\hspace{2cm}}$$

$$\angle U \doteq \underline{\hspace{2cm}}$$

So, ∠W = 90° − ∠U

$$\angle W \doteq 90° - \underline{\hspace{2cm}}$$

$$\angle W \doteq \underline{\hspace{2cm}}$$

b)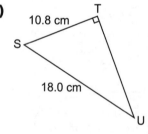

Find the measure of ∠U first.

ST is the _____.

SU is the _____.

So, use the _____ ratio to write an equation.

$$\underline{\hspace{2cm}} U = \underline{\hspace{4cm}}$$

$$\underline{\hspace{2cm}} U = \underline{\hspace{2cm}}$$

$$\underline{\hspace{2cm}} U = \underline{\hspace{2cm}}$$

$$\angle U = \sin^{-1} \underline{\hspace{2cm}}$$

$$\angle U \doteq \underline{\hspace{2cm}}$$

So, ∠S = 90° − _____

$$\angle S \doteq 90° - \underline{\hspace{2cm}}$$

$$\angle S \doteq \underline{\hspace{2cm}}$$

 978-0-321-61066-9

Example 3 | **Using Sine or Cosine to Solve a Problem**

A storm caused a 15.3-m hydro pole to lean over. The top of the pole is now 12.0 m above the ground. What angle does the pole make with the ground? Give the answer to the nearest degree.

Solution

Draw a diagram. AC represents the pole.

The pole meets the ground at A.

BC is the side opposite ∠A. AC is the hypotenuse.

So, use the sine ratio to find ∠A.

$$\sin A = \frac{\text{side opposite } \angle A}{\text{hypotenuse}}$$

$\sin A = \dfrac{BC}{AC}$ Substitute: BC = 12.0 and AC = 15.3

$\sin A = \dfrac{12.0}{15.3}$ Use a calculator.

$\angle A \doteq 52°$

So, the hydro pole makes an angle of about 52° with the ground.

Assume the ground is horizontal.

Check

1. A ladder leans on a wall as shown.
   What angle does the ladder make with the ground?
   Give your answer to the nearest degree.
   We want to find the measure of ∠D.
   DF is _____.
   DE is _____.
   So, use the _____ ratio to find ∠D.

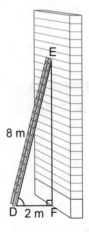

8 m

D 2 m F

Assume the ground is horizontal.

_____ D = _____

_____ D = _____   Substitute: _____ and _____

_____ D = _____

∠D ≐ _____   So, the ladder makes an angle of about _____
with the ground.

2. The string of a kite is 160 m long. The string is anchored to the
ground. The kite is 148 m high. What angle does the string make
with the ground? Give your answer to the nearest degree.

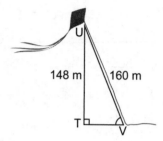

We want to find the measure of ∠V.

TU is the _____.
UV is the _____.
So, use the _____ ratio to write an equation.

The angle the string makes with the ground is about _____.

Practice

1. Fill in the blanks.

a)

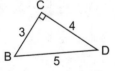

The side opposite ∠B is _____.
The side adjacent to ∠B is _____.
The hypotenuse is _____.

b)

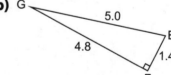

The side opposite ∠B is _____.
The side adjacent to ∠B is _____.
The hypotenuse is _____.

2. For each triangle in question 1, find sin B and cos B as decimals.

a) $\sin B = \dfrac{\text{side} \underline{\hspace{2cm}} \angle B}{\text{hypotenuse}}$ $\qquad$ $\cos B = \dfrac{\text{side} \underline{\hspace{2cm}} \angle B}{\text{hypotenuse}}$

$\sin B =$ _____ $\qquad\qquad\qquad$ $\cos B =$ _____

$\sin B =$ _____ $\qquad\qquad\qquad$ $\cos B =$ _____

$\sin B =$ _____ $\qquad\qquad\qquad$ $\cos B =$ _____

b) $\sin B =$ _____ $\qquad\qquad$ $\cos B =$ _____

$\sin B =$ _____ $\qquad\qquad\qquad\qquad$ $\cos B =$ _____

3. Find the measure of each indicated angle to the nearest degree.

a)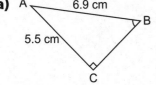

b)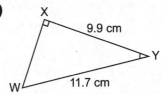

AC is the _____. $\qquad$ XY is the _____.

AB is the _____. $\qquad$ WY is the _____.

So, use the _____ ratio. $\qquad$ So, use the _____ ratio.

$\angle B \doteq$ _____ $\qquad\qquad\qquad\qquad$ $\angle Y \doteq$ _____

4. A firefighter rests a 15.6-m ladder against a building, as shown.
What angle does the ladder make with the ground?
Give your answer to the nearest degree.

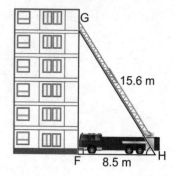

We want to find the measure of ∠H.
FH is the _____.
GH is the _____.
So, use the _____ ratio.

_____ H = _____

_____ H = _____

_____ H = _____

∠H ≐ _____

The angle the ladder makes with the ground is about _____.

5. A loading ramp is 4.5 m long. The top of the ramp has height 1.6 m.
What angle does the ramp make with the ground?
Give your answer to the nearest degree.

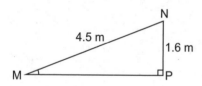

The angle the ramp makes with the ground is about _____.

2.5 Using the Sine and Cosine Ratios to Calculate Lengths

Use the sine and cosine ratios to determine lengths.

To use the sine or cosine ratio to find the length of a leg, we need to know:
- the measure of an acute angle, and
- the length of the hypotenuse

Example 1 | **Using the Sine or Cosine Ratio to Find the Length of a Leg**

Find the length of RS to the nearest tenth of a metre.

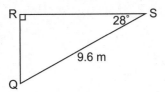

Solution

The measure of ∠S is known.
RS is the side adjacent to ∠S.
QS is the hypotenuse.
So, use the cosine ratio.

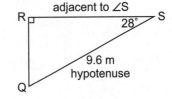

$$\cos S = \frac{\text{side adjacent to } \angle S}{\text{hypotenuse}}$$

$$\cos S = \frac{RS}{QS}$$ Substitute: ∠S = 28° and QS = 9.6

$$\cos 28° = \frac{RS}{9.6}$$ Multiply both sides by 9.6.

$$9.6 \times \cos 28° = 9.6 \times \frac{RS}{9.6}$$

$$9.6 \cos 28° = RS$$ Use a calculator.

$$RS = 8.4762\ldots$$

RS is about 8.5 m long.

Check

1. Find the length of each indicated side to the nearest tenth of a centimetre.

a) AC

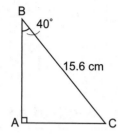

The measure of ∠B is known.

AC is the _____.

BC is the _____.

So, use the _____ ratio.

$$\text{_____} B = \frac{\text{side}\text{_____}}{\text{hypotenuse}}$$

$$\text{_____} B = \frac{\text{\_\_\_}}{BC}$$

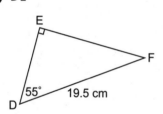

$$AC = \text{_____}$$

AC is about _____ long.

b) DE

The measure of ∠_____ is known.

DE is the _____.

DF is the _____.

So, use the _____ ratio.

DE is about _____ long.

To use the sine or cosine ratio to find the length of the hypotenuse, we need to know:
• the measure of an acute angle, and
• the length of one leg

Example 2 | Using the Sine or Cosine Ratio to Find the Length of the Hypotenuse

Find the length of the hypotenuse to the nearest tenth of a centimetre.

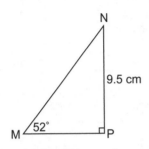

The hypotenuse is the side opposite the right angle.

Solution

The measure of ∠M is known.
NP is the side opposite ∠M.
MN is the hypotenuse.
So, use the sine ratio to write an equation.

$$\sin M = \frac{\text{side opposite } \angle M}{\text{hypotenuse}}$$

$$\sin M = \frac{NP}{MN} \qquad \text{Substitute: } \angle M = 52° \text{ and } NP = 9.5$$

$$\sin 52° = \frac{9.5}{MN} \qquad \text{Multiply both sides by MN.}$$

$$MN \sin 52° = 9.5 \qquad \text{Divide both sides by } \sin 52°.$$

$$\frac{MN \sin 52°}{\sin 52°} = \frac{9.5}{\sin 52°}$$

$$MN = \frac{9.5}{\sin 52°} \qquad \text{Use a calculator.}$$

$$MN = 12.0556...$$

MN is about 12.1 cm long.

Check

1. Find the length of each hypotenuse to the nearest tenth of a centimetre.

a)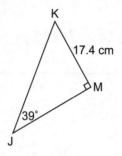

The measure of ∠J is known.
The side opposite ∠J is: _____
The hypotenuse is: _____
Use the sine ratio.

sin J = $\dfrac{\text{side} _____}{_____}$

sin J = $\dfrac{_____}{}$

sin ____ = _____

____ sin ____ = _____

JK = _____

JK = _____

JK is about _____ long.

b)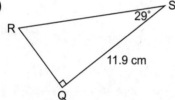

The measure of ∠_____ is known.
QS is the side _____.
RS is the _____.
So, use the _____ ratio.

RS = _____
RS is about _____ long.

Example 3 | **Using Sine or Cosine to Solve a Problem**

A surveyor makes the measurements shown in the diagram to find the distance between two observation towers on opposite sides of a river. How far apart are the towers? Give the answer to the nearest metre.

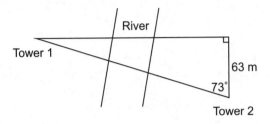

Solution

The distance between the towers is the hypotenuse, AC.

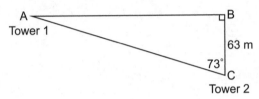

The measure of ∠C is known.
BC is the side adjacent to ∠C.
AC is the hypotenuse.
So, use the cosine ratio.

$$\cos C = \frac{\text{side adjacent to } \angle C}{\text{hypotenuse}}$$

$$\cos C = \frac{BC}{AC} \qquad \text{Substitute: } \angle C = 73° \text{ and } BC = 63$$

$$\cos 73° = \frac{63}{AC} \qquad \text{Multiply both sides by AC.}$$

$$AC \times \cos 73° = 63 \qquad \text{Divide both sides by } \cos 73°.$$

$$AC = \frac{63}{\cos 73°} \qquad \text{Use a calculator.}$$

$$AC = 215.4791...$$

The distance between the towers is about 215 m.

Check

1. Sam and Sofia are building a wooden ramp for skateboarding. The height of the ramp is 0.75 m. The ramp makes an angle of 8° with the ground. What length of plywood do Sam and Sofia need for the top of the ramp? Give your answer to the nearest tenth of a metre.

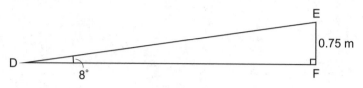

$sin\ D = \dfrac{opposite}{hypotenuse}$

We want to find the length of DE.
The measure of ∠D is known.
The side opposite ∠D is: _____
The hypotenuse is: _____
So, use the sine ratio.

$sin\ D =$ _____

sin ____ = _____

____ sin ____ = ____

Substitute: _____

Multiply both sides by _____.

Divide both sides by _____.

DE = _____

Sam and Sofia need about _____ of plywood.

Practice

1. Which ratio would you use to find each length?

a) XY

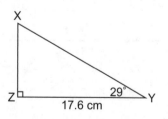

The measure of ∠_____ is known.
YZ is the side _____.
XY is the _____.
So, use the _____ ratio.

b) ST

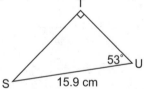

The measure of ∠_____ is known.
ST is the side _____.
SU is the _____.
So, use the _____ ratio.

2. Find the length of each indicated side to the nearest tenth of a centimetre.

a) VW

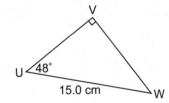

The measure of ∠_____ is known.
The side opposite ∠_____ is _____.
The hypotenuse is _____.
So, use the _____ ratio.

$$\sin \underline{\hspace{1cm}} = \frac{\text{side} \underline{\hspace{2cm}}}{\text{hypotenuse}}$$

$$\sin \underline{\hspace{1cm}} = \underline{\hspace{2cm}}$$

$$\sin \underline{\hspace{1cm}} = \underline{\hspace{2cm}}$$

$$\underline{\hspace{1cm}} \sin \underline{\hspace{1cm}} = \underline{\hspace{1cm}}$$

$$VW = \underline{\hspace{2cm}}$$

VW is about _____ long.

b) QR

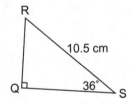

The measure of ∠_____ is known.
QR is the _____.
RS is the _____.
So, use the _____ ratio.

QR is about _____ long.

3. Find the length of side PM to the nearest tenth of a metre.

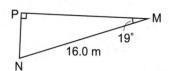

The measure of ∠_____ is known.

PM is the side _____.

MN is the _____.

So, use the _____ ratio.

PM is about _____ long.

4. Find the length of each hypotenuse to the nearest tenth of a centimetre.

a)

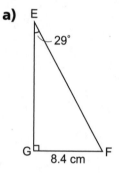

The measure of ∠_____ is known.

The side opposite ∠_____ is: _____

The hypotenuse is: _____

So, use the sine ratio.

$$\sin \underline{\hspace{1cm}} = \frac{\text{opposite}}{\text{hypotenuse}}$$

$$\sin \underline{\hspace{1cm}} = \underline{\hspace{1.5cm}}$$

$$\sin \underline{\hspace{1cm}} = \underline{\hspace{1.5cm}}$$

$$\underline{\hspace{1cm}} \sin \underline{\hspace{1cm}} = \underline{\hspace{0.8cm}}$$

$$EF = \underline{\hspace{2cm}}$$

$$EF = \underline{\hspace{2cm}}$$

EF is about _____ long.

b)

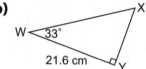

The measure of ∠_____ is known.

WY is the side _____.

WX is the _____.

So, use the _____ ratio.

$$WX = \underline{\hspace{2cm}}$$

WX is about _____ long.

5. A straight slide in a playground makes an angle of 28° with the ground. The slide covers a horizontal distance of 4.5 m. How long is the slide? Give your answer to the nearest tenth of a metre.

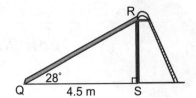

The measure of ∠Q is known.
The side adjacent to ∠Q is: _____
The hypotenuse is: _____
So, use the _____ ratio.

QR = _____

The slide is about _____ long.

6. A 15-m support cable joins the top of a telephone pole to a point on the ground. The cable makes an angle of 32° with the ground. Find the height of the pole to the nearest tenth of a metre.

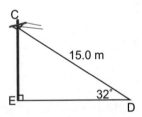

The height of the pole is about _____.

CHECKPOINT 2

Can you...

- use the sine or cosine ratio to find an angle measure?
- use the sine or cosine ratio to calculate a length?
- use the sine or cosine ratio to solve a problem?

2.4 **1.** Find sin A and cos A to the nearest hundredth.

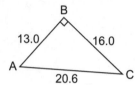

sin A = _____

cos A = _____

sin A = _____

cos A = _____

sin A = _____

cos A = _____

sin A = _____

cos A = _____

sin A ≐ _____

cos A ≐ _____

2. Find the measure of each indicated angle to the nearest degree.

a)

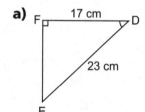

FD is the _____.

DE is the _____.

So, use the _____ ratio.

_____ D = _____

_____ D = _____

_____ D = _____

∠D ≐ _____

b)

G   13.4 cm   H

5.9 cm

J

GJ is the _____.

GH is the _____.

So, use the _____ ratio.

_____ H = _____

_____ H = _____

_____ H = _____

∠H ≐ _____

 978-0-321-61066-9

3. Find the length of each indicated side to the nearest tenth of a centimetre.

a) PR

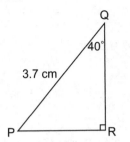

The measure of ∠_____ is known.
The side opposite ∠_____ is _____.
The hypotenuse is _____.
So, use the _____ ratio.

PR is about _____ long.

b) ST

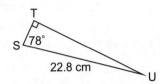

The measure of ∠_____ is known.
ST is the side _____.
SU is the _____.
So, use the _____ ratio.

ST is about _____ long.

4. Find the length of the hypotenuse
to the nearest tenth of a centimetre.

The measure of ∠W is known.
The side opposite ∠W is: _____
The hypotenuse is: _____
Use the sine ratio.

$$\sin W = \frac{}{}$$

$$\sin \text{\_\_\_\_\_} = \text{\_\_\_\_\_}$$

$$\text{\_\_\_\_\_} \sin \text{\_\_\_\_\_} = \text{\_\_\_\_\_}$$

Multiply both sides by _____.

Divide both sides by _____.

WY is about _____ long.

2.6 Applying the Trigonometric Ratios

FOCUS Use trigonometric ratios to solve a right triangle.

When we **solve a triangle**, we find the measures of all the angles and the lengths of all the sides.
To do this we use any of the sine, cosine, and tangent ratios.

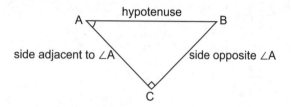

We can use the acronym
SOH-CAH-TOA
to help us remember
these ratios.

$$\sin A = \frac{\text{opposite}}{\text{hypotenuse}} \qquad \cos A = \frac{\text{adjacent}}{\text{hypotenuse}} \qquad \tan A = \frac{\text{opposite}}{\text{adjacent}}$$

Example 1 | Finding the Measures of All Angles

Find all unknown angle measures to the nearest degree.

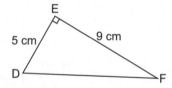

Solution

Find the measure of ∠D.
EF is the side opposite ∠D.
DE is the side adjacent to ∠D.
So, use the tangent ratio.

We could have used the
tangent ratio to find ∠F.

$$\tan D = \frac{\text{opposite}}{\text{adjacent}}$$

$$\tan D = \frac{EF}{DE} \qquad \text{Substitute: EF = 9 and DE = 5}$$

$$\tan D = \frac{9}{5}$$

∠D ≐ 61°

The acute angles in a right triangle have a sum of 90°.
So, ∠F = 90° − ∠D
∠F ≐ 90° − 61°
∠F ≐ 29°

Check

1. Find all unknown angle measures to the nearest degree.

a)

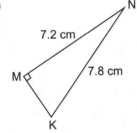

Find the measure of ∠G.

HJ is the side _____.

GH is the side _____.

So, use the _____ ratio.

> We could use the tangent ratio to check the measure of ∠J.

_____ G = _____

_____ G = _____

_____ G = _____

∠G ≐ _____

The acute angles have a sum of 90°.

So, ∠J = 90° − _____

∠J ≐ 90° − _____

∠J ≐ _____

b)

Find the measure of ∠K.

MN is the side _____ ∠K.

NK is the _____.

So, use the _____ ratio.

> We could use the cosine ratio to check the measure of ∠N.

_____ K = _____

_____ K = _____

_____ K = _____

∠K ≐ _____

The acute angles have a sum of 90°.

So, ∠N = 90° − _____

∠N ≐ 90° − _____

∠N ≐ _____

Example 2 | **Finding the Lengths of All Sides**

Find all unknown side lengths to the nearest tenth of a metre.

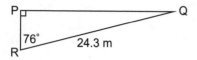

Solution

Find the length of PR.
PR is the side adjacent to ∠R.
QR is the hypotenuse.
So, use the cosine ratio.

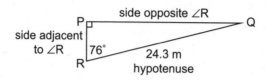

$$\cos R = \frac{\text{adjacent}}{\text{hypotenuse}}$$

$$\cos R = \frac{PR}{QR}$$ Substitute: ∠R = 76° and QR = 24.3

$$\cos 76° = \frac{PR}{24.3}$$ Multiply both sides by 24.3.

24.3 cos 76° = PR

          PR = 5.8787...

PR is about 5.9 m long.

Find the length of PQ.
PQ is the side opposite ∠R.
QR is the hypotenuse.
So, use the sine ratio.

$$\sin R = \frac{\text{opposite}}{\text{hypotenuse}}$$

$$\sin R = \frac{PQ}{QR}$$ Substitute: ∠R = 76° and QR = 24.3

$$\sin 76° = \frac{PQ}{24.3}$$ Multiply both sides by 24.3.

24.3 sin 76° = PQ

          PQ = 23.5781...

PQ is about 23.6 m long.

> We could use the
> Pythagorean Theorem to
> check the side lengths.

Check

1. Find all unknown side lengths to the nearest tenth of a metre.

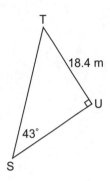

Find the length of ST.

TU is the side _____ ∠S.

ST is the _____.

So, use the _____ ratio.

_____ S = _____

_____ S = _____

ST = _____

ST is about _____ long.

Find the length of SU.

TU is the side _____ ∠S.

SU is the side _____ ∠S.

So, use the _____ ratio.

_____ S = _____

_____ S = _____

SU = _____

SU is about _____ long.

Example 3 | **Solving a Triangle**

Solve this triangle.
Give angle measures to the nearest degree.
Give side lengths to the nearest tenth of a centimetre.

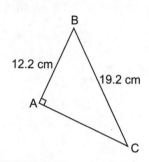

Solution

Find the measure of ∠B.
AB is the side adjacent to ∠B.
BC is the hypotenuse.
So, use the cosine ratio.

> *We know the lengths of two sides.*

$$\cos B = \frac{\text{adjacent}}{\text{hypotenuse}}$$

$$\cos B = \frac{AB}{BC}$$ Substitute: AB = 12.2 and BC = 19.2

$$\cos B = \frac{12.2}{19.2}$$

$$\angle B \doteq 51°$$

The acute angles in a right triangle have a sum of 90°.
So, ∠C = 90° − ∠B

$$\angle C \doteq 90° − 51°$$

$$\angle C \doteq 39°$$

Find the length of AC.
Use the Pythagorean Theorem to find AC.

$$AC^2 = BC^2 − AB^2$$

$$AC^2 = 19.2^2 − 12.2^2$$

$$AC^2 = 219.8$$

$$AC = \sqrt{219.8}$$

$$AC = 14.8256…$$

AC is about 14.8 cm long.

> *We could have used the sine ratio and the exact measure of ∠B to find AC.*

 978-0-321-61066-9

Check

1. Solve this triangle. Give side lengths to the nearest tenth of a centimetre.

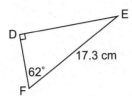

17.3 cm

62°

We know the length of one side and the measure of one acute angle.

The acute angles have a sum of _____.

So, ∠E = _____ − _____

∠E = _____ − _____

∠E = _____

Find the length of DF.

DF is the side _____ ∠F.

EF is the _____.

So, use the _____ ratio.

_____ F = _____

_____ F = _____

DF is about _____ long.

Find the length of DE.

DE is the side _____ ∠F.

EF is the _____.

So, use the _____ ratio.

_____ F = _____

_____ F = _____

DE is about _____ long.

Practice

1. Which ratio would you use to find the measure of each angle?

a) ∠P

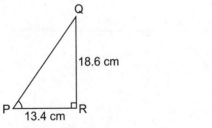

18.6 cm

13.4 cm

QR is the side _____.

PR is the side _____.

So, use the _____ ratio.

b) ∠E

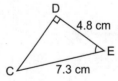

4.8 cm

7.3 cm

Remember the acronym SOH–CAH–TOA.

DE is the _____.

CE is the _____.

So, use the _____ ratio.

2. Which ratio would you use to find the length of each indicated side?

a) GH

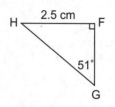

HF is the _____.

GH is the _____.

So, use the _____ ratio.

b) MN

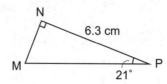

MN is the _____.

NP is the _____.

So, use the _____ ratio.

3. Find all unknown angle measures to the nearest degree.

a)

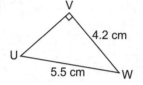

Find the measure of ∠U.

_____ U = _____

_____ U = _____

_____ U = _____

∠U ≐ _____

The acute angles have a sum of 90°.

So, ∠W = 90° − _____

∠W ≐ 90° − _____

∠W ≐ _____

b)

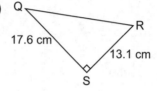

Find the measure of ∠Q.

_____ Q = _____

_____ Q = _____

_____ Q = _____

∠Q ≐ _____

The acute angles have a sum of 90°.

So, ∠R = _____

∠R ≐ _____

∠R ≐ _____

4. Find all unknown side lengths to the nearest tenth of a centimetre.

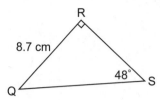

Find the length of QS.

_____ S = _____

_____ S = _____

Find the length of RS.

_____ S = _____

_____ S = _____

QS is about _____ long.

RS is about _____ long.

5. Solve this triangle. Give angle measures to the nearest degree. Give side lengths to the nearest tenth of a centimetre.

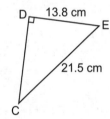

Find the measure of ∠E.

_____ E = _____

_____ E = _____

_____ E = _____

∠E ≐ _____

The acute angles have a sum of 90°.

So, ∠C = 90° − _____

∠C ≐ 90° − _____

∠C ≐ _____

Find the length of CD.
Use the Pythagorean Theorem.

CD is about _____ long.

6. The base of a ladder is on level ground 1.9 m from a wall. The ladder leans against the wall. The angle between the ladder and the ground is 65°.

a) How far up the wall does the ladder reach?

b) How long is the ladder?

Give your answers to the nearest tenth of a metre.

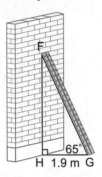

a)

The ladder reaches the wall at a height of about _____.

b)

The ladder is about _____ long.

2.7 Solving Problems Involving More than One Right Triangle

FOCUS Use trigonometric ratios to solve problems that involve more than one right triangle.

When a problem involves more than one right triangle, we can use information from one triangle to solve the other triangle.

Example 1 | Solving a Problem with Two Triangles

Find the length of BC to the nearest tenth of a centimetre.

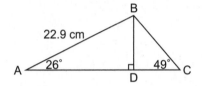

> To solve a right triangle we must know:
> • the lengths of two sides, or
> • the length of one side and the measure of one acute angle

Solution

First use $\triangle$ABD to find the length of BD.

$$\sin A = \frac{\text{opposite}}{\text{hypotenuse}}$$

$$\sin A = \frac{BD}{AB}$$

$$\sin 26° = \frac{BD}{22.9}$$

$$22.9 \sin 26° = BD$$

$$BD = 10.0386\ldots$$ Do not clear the calculator screen.

> Side BD is common to both triangles.

In $\triangle$BCD, find the length of BC.

$$\sin C = \frac{\text{opposite}}{\text{hypotenuse}}$$

$$\sin C = \frac{BD}{BC}$$

$$\sin 49° = \frac{10.0386\ldots}{BC}$$

$$BC \sin 49° = 10.0386\ldots$$

$$BC = \frac{10.0386\ldots}{\sin 49°}$$

$$BC = 13.3014\ldots$$

BC is about 13.3 cm long.

Check

1. Find the measure of ∠F to the nearest degree.

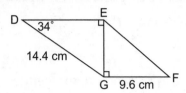

Use △DEG to find the length of EG.
Use the sine ratio.

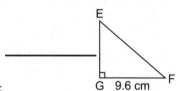

> Side EG is common to both triangles.

sin D = _____

sin D = _____

sin _____ = _____

EG = _____ .

In △EFG, use the _____ ratio to find ∠F.

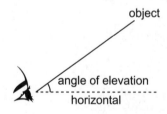

The measure of ∠F is about _____.

The **angle of elevation** is the angle between the horizontal and a person's line of sight to an object above.

object

angle of elevation

horizontal

 978-0-321-61066-9 Copyright © 2011 Pearson Canada Inc.

Example 2 | Solving a Problem Involving Angle of Elevation

Jason is lying on the ground midway between two trees, 100 m apart.
The angles of elevation of the tops of the trees are 13° and 18°. How much taller is one tree than the other? Give the answer to the nearest tenth of a metre.

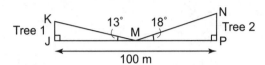

Solution

Jason is midway between the trees.

So, the distance from Jason to the base of each tree is: $\dfrac{100 \text{ m}}{2} = 50$ m

Use △JKM to find the length of JK.

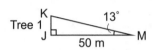

$$\tan M = \dfrac{\text{opposite}}{\text{adjacent}}$$

$$\tan M = \dfrac{JK}{JM}$$

$$\tan 13° = \dfrac{JK}{50}$$

$$50 \tan 13° = JK$$

$$JK = 11.5434...$$

We know ∠M = 13°.
JK is opposite ∠M.
JM is adjacent to ∠M.
Use the tangent ratio.

Substitute: ∠M = 13° and JM = 50

Use △MNP to find the length of NP.

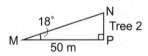

$$\tan M = \dfrac{\text{opposite}}{\text{adjacent}}$$

$$\tan M = \dfrac{NP}{MP}$$

$$\tan 18° = \dfrac{NP}{50}$$

$$50 \tan 18° = NP$$

$$NP = 16.2459...$$

We know ∠M = 18°.
NP is opposite ∠M.
MP is adjacent to ∠M.
Use the tangent ratio.

Substitute: ∠M = 18° and MP = 50

To find how much taller one tree is than the other, subtract:
16.2459... m − 11.5434... m = 4.7025... m
One tree is about 4.7 m taller than the other.

Check

1. The angle of elevation of the top of a tree, T, is 27°. From the same point on the ground, the angle of elevation of a hawk, H, flying directly above the tree is 43°. The tree is 12.7 m tall. How high is the hawk above the ground? Give your answer to the nearest tenth of a metre.

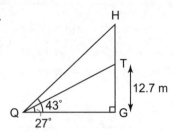

We want to find the length of HG.
Use △QTG to find the length of QG.
Use the tangent ratio.

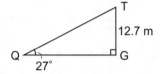

tan Q = _____

tan Q = _____   Substitute: _____ and _____

tan _____ = _____

QG = _____

In △QHG, use the tangent ratio to find HG.

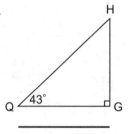

HG = _____

The hawk is about _____ above the ground.

The **angle of depression** is the angle between the horizontal and a person's line of sight to an object below.

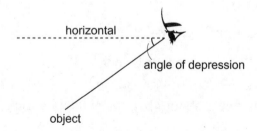

Example 3 | **Solving a Problem Involving Angle of Depression**

From a small plane, V, the angle of depression of a sailboat is 21°.
The angle of depression of a ferry on the other side of the plane is 52°.
The plane is flying at an altitude of 1650 m.
How far apart are the boats, to the nearest metre?

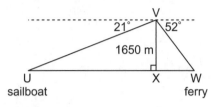

Solution

We want to find the length of UW.
The angle of depression of the sailboat is 21°.
So, in △UVX, ∠V = 90° − 21°, or 69°.

Use △UVX to find the length of UX.

$$\tan V = \frac{\text{opposite}}{\text{adjacent}}$$

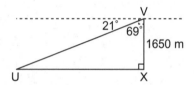

$$\tan V = \frac{UX}{VX}$$ Substitute: ∠V = 69° and VX = 1650

> We know ∠V = 69°.
> UX is opposite ∠V.
> VX is adjacent to ∠V.
> So, use the tangent ratio.

$$\tan 69° = \frac{UX}{1650}$$

1650 tan 69° = UX

UX = 4298.3969…

The angle of depression of the ferry is 52°.
So, ∠V in △VWX is: 90° − 52°, or 38°.

Use △VWX to find the length of WX.

$$\tan V = \frac{\text{opposite}}{\text{adjacent}}$$

$$\tan V = \frac{WX}{VX}$$ Substitute: ∠V = 38° and VX = 1650

> We know ∠V = 38°.
> WX is opposite ∠V.
> VX is adjacent to ∠V.
> So, use the tangent ratio.

$$\tan 38° = \frac{WX}{1650}$$

1650 tan 38° = WX

WX = 1289.1212…

To find the distance between the boats, add:
4298.3969… m + 1289.1212… m = 5587.5182… m
The boats are about 5588 m apart.

Check

1. This diagram shows a falcon, F, on a tree, with a squirrel, S, and a chipmunk, C, on the ground. From the falcon, the angles of depression of the animals are 36° and 47°. How far apart are the animals on the ground to the nearest tenth of a metre?

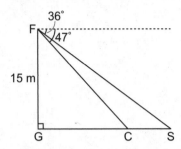

We want to find the length of CS.

CS = GS − GC

The angle of depression of the squirrel is _____.

So, ∠F in △FSG is: 90° − _____, or _____.

Use △FSG to find the length of GS.

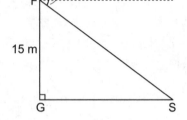

tan ____ = _____

tan ____ = _____

tan ____ = _____

GS = _____

The angle of depression of the chipmunk is _____.

So, ∠F in △FCG is: 90° − _____, or _____.

Use △FCG to find the length of GC.

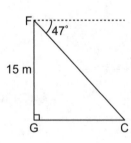

GC = _____

To find the distance between the animals, subtract:

_____ − _____ = _____

The animals on the ground are about _____ apart.

1. Find the measure of ∠C to the nearest degree.

Use △ABD to find the length of BD.

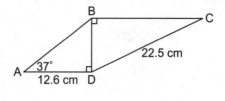

Use the tangent ratio.

tan A = _____

tan A = _____

tan _____ = _____

BD = _____

In △BCD, use the _____ ratio to find ∠C.

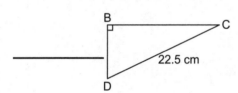

The measure of ∠C is about _____.

2. Two guy wires support a flagpole, FH. The first wire is 11.2 m long and has an angle of inclination of 39°. The second wire has an angle of inclination of 47°. How tall is the flagpole to the nearest tenth of a metre?

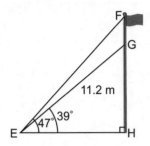

Recall that the angle the wire makes with the ground is called the **angle of inclination**.

We want to find the length of FH.
Use △EGH to find the length of EH.
Use the cosine ratio.

cos E = _____

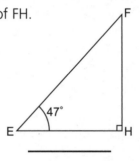

11.2 m

Side EH is common to both triangles.

cos E = _____

cos _____ = _____

EH = _____

In △EFH, use the _____ ratio to find the length of FH.

47°

FH = _____

The flagpole is about _____ tall.

3. A mountain climber is on top of a mountain that is 680 m high. The angles of depression of two points on opposite sides of the mountain are 48° and 32°. How long would a tunnel be that runs between the two points? Give your answer to the nearest metre.

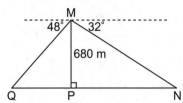

We want to find the length of QN.

The angle of depression of point Q is _____.

So, ∠M in △PQM is: 90° − _____, or _____.

Use △PQM to find the length of PQ.
Use the _____ ratio.

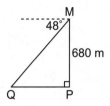

PQ = _____

The angle of depression of point N is _____.
So, ∠M in △PMN is: 90° − _____, or _____.

Use △PMN to find the length of PN.
Use the _____ ratio.

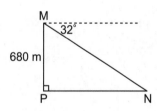

NP = _____

The length of the tunnel is: _____ = _____ + _____

QN = _____

The tunnel would be about _____ long.

Angle Mania!

A. Find the angles of inclination of the diagonals shown.
Assume the squares have side length 1 unit.

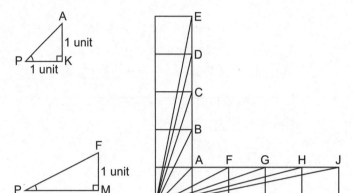

B. How many squares would be needed on the vertical rectangle for a diagonal to have an angle of inclination greater than:

- 80°?
- 85°?
- 88°?
- 89°?

C. How many squares would be needed on the horizontal rectangle for a diagonal to have an angle of inclination less than:

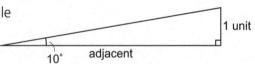

- 10°?

- 5°?

- 2°?

- 1°?

Skill	Description	Example
Find a trigonometric ratio.	In $\triangle ABC$, $\sin A = \dfrac{\text{opposite}}{\text{hypotenuse}}$ $\cos A = \dfrac{\text{adjacent}}{\text{hypotenuse}}$ $\tan A = \dfrac{\text{opposite}}{\text{adjacent}}$	$\sin A = \dfrac{\text{opposite}}{\text{hypotenuse}}$ $\sin A = \dfrac{BC}{AB}$ $\sin A = \dfrac{6}{10}$, or 0.6
Find the measure of an angle.	To find the measure of an acute angle in a right triangle: **1.** Use the given lengths to write a trigonometric ratio. **2.** Use the inverse function on a scientific calculator to find the measure of the angle.	To find the measure of $\angle B$ in $\triangle ABC$ above: $\tan B = \dfrac{\text{opposite}}{\text{adjacent}}$ $\tan B = \dfrac{AC}{BC}$ $\tan B = \dfrac{8}{6}$ $\angle B = \tan^{-1}\left(\dfrac{8}{6}\right)$ $\angle B \doteq 53°$
Find the length of a side.	To find the length of a side in a right triangle: **1.** Use the measure of an angle and the length of a related side to write an equation using a trigonometric ratio. **2.** Solve the equation.	To find the length of EF in $\triangle DEF$: $\cos E = \dfrac{\text{adjacent}}{\text{hypotenuse}}$ $\cos E = \dfrac{DE}{EF}$ $\cos 64° = \dfrac{3.0}{EF}$ $EF \cos 64° = 3.0$ $EF = \dfrac{3.0}{\cos 64°}$ $EF = 6.8435\ldots$ $EF \doteq 6.8$ cm

2.1 **1.** Find the measure of ∠P to the nearest degree.

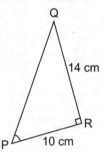

tan P = _____

tan P = _____

tan P = _____

∠P ≐ _____

2.2 **2.** Find the length of TU to the nearest tenth of a centimetre.

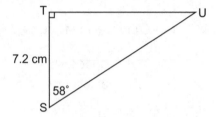

tan S = _____

tan S = _____

tan _____ = _____

TU = _____

TU is about _____ long.

3. A flagpole casts a shadow that is 25 m long when the angle between the sun's rays and the ground is 40°. What is the height of the flagpole to the nearest metre?

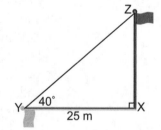

_____ is the side opposite ∠Y.

_____ is the side adjacent to ∠Y.

tan Y = _____

tan Y = _____

ZX = _____

The flagpole is about _____ high.

2.3 **4.** Use the information in the diagram to find the height of the tower of a wind turbine observed with a drinking-straw clinometer. Give the answer to the nearest tenth of a metre.

$\angle A = 90° -$ _____, or _____
Side opposite $\angle A$: _____
Side adjacent to $\angle A$: _____

tan A = _____

tan _____ = _____

BC = _____

So, height of tower = _____ + _____

= _____

The height of the tower is about _____.

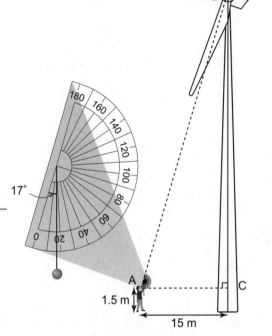

17°

1.5 m

15 m

This diagram is not drawn to scale.

2.4 **5.** Find the measure of each indicated angle to the nearest degree.

a)

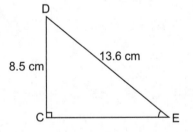

D

13.6 cm

8.5 cm

C   E

CD is the _____.
DE is the _____.
So, use the _____ ratio.

$\angle E \doteq$ _____

b)

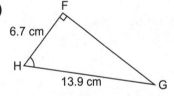

F

6.7 cm

H

13.9 cm   G

HF is the _____.
GH is the _____.
So, use the _____ ratio.

$\angle H \doteq$ _____

6. A 2.8-m ladder is leaning against a barn, as shown. What angle does the ladder make with the barn? Give your answer to the nearest degree.

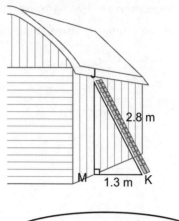

We want to find the measure of ∠_____.
KM is the _____.
JK is the _____.
So, use the _____ ratio.

Assume the ground is horizontal.

∠J ≐ _____

The angle the ladder makes with the barn is about _____.

2.5 **7.** Find the length of each indicated side to the nearest tenth of a centimetre.

a) RS

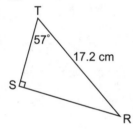

The measure of ∠T is known.
Use the _____ ratio.

b) NQ

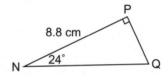

The measure of ∠N is known.
Use the _____ ratio.

RS is about _____ long.

NQ is about _____ long.

8. An escalator is 14.5 m long. The escalator makes an angle of 27° with the ground. What is the height of the escalator? Give your answer to the nearest tenth of a metre.

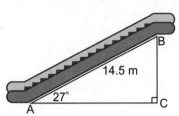

To find the length of BC, use the _____ ratio.

BC = _____

The escalator is about _____ high.

2.6 **9.** Solve this triangle. Give side lengths to the nearest tenth of a centimetre.

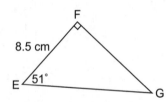

Find the length of FG.

Use the _____ ratio.

Find the length of EG.

Use the _____ ratio.

FG is about _____ long.

The acute angles have a sum of _____.

So, $\angle G = 90° -$ _____

$\angle G = 90° -$ _____

$\angle G =$ _____

EG is about _____ long.

10. Two buildings are 25 m apart. From the top of the shorter building, the angles of elevation and depression of the top and bottom of the taller building are 31° and 48° respectively. What is the height of the taller building? Give your answer to the nearest metre.

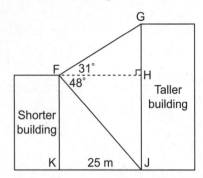

We want to find the length of GJ.

GJ = _____ + _____

The angle of depression of point J is _____.

Use △FHJ to find the length of HJ.

Use the _____ ratio.

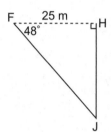

HJ = _____

The angle of elevation of point G is _____.

Use △FGH to find the length of GH.

Use the _____ ratio.

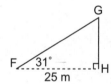

GH = _____

To find the height of the taller building, add:

_____ + _____ = _____

The taller building is about _____ tall.

Factors and Products

What You'll Learn

- use different strategies to find factors and multiples of whole numbers

- identify prime factors and write the prime factorization of a number

- find square roots of perfect squares and cube roots of perfect cubes

- use different strategies to multiply and factor polynomials

Why It's Important

Factors and products are used by:

- cryptologists, to design codes to protect electronic data from being accessed illegally.

- actuaries, to design plans to help insurance companies make a profit

Key Words

prime number	perfect square, square root
prime factorization	perfect cube, cube root
greatest common factor	factoring
common multiple	perfect square trinomial
least common multiple	difference of squares

3.1 Skill Builder

Divisibility Rules

We can use rules to find out if a number is a factor of another number.

To find out if 2, 4, 5, 8, or 10 is a factor, look at the last digits in the number:
- 2 is a factor of 35**4** because the last digit, 4, is even.
- 4 is a factor of 5**24** because 4 is a factor of the last two digits, 24.
- 5 is a factor of 58**5** because the last digit is 5.
- 8 is a factor of 3**400** because 8 is a factor of the last three digits, 400.
- 10 is a factor of 21**0** because the last digit is 0.

A number that ends in 5 or 0 is divisible by 5.

To find out if 3 or 9 is a factor, add the digits in the number:
- 3 is a factor of 411 because 3 is a factor of the sum of the digits:
  $4 + 1 + 1 = 6$
- 9 is a factor of 747 because 9 is a factor of the sum of the digits:
  $7 + 4 + 7 = 18$

To find out if 6 is a factor, use the rules for 2 and 3:
- 6 is a factor of 216 because the last digit, 6, is even, and 3 is a factor of the sum of the digits: $2 + 1 + 6 = 9$

Check

1. Write yes or no to answer each question.

a) Is 2 a factor of 457?

Is the last digit even? _____
So, is 2 a factor of 457? _____

b) Is 3 a factor of 732?

The sum of the digits is _____.
So, is 3 a factor of 732? _____

c) Is 5 a factor of 734?

Is the last digit 5 or 0? _____
So, is 5 a factor of 734? _____

d) Is 4 a factor of 712?

The last 2 digits are _____.
Is 4 a factor of 12? _____
Is 4 a factor of 712? _____

e) Is 6 a factor of 558?

Is the last digit even? _____
The sum of the digits is _____.
Is 3 a factor of 558? _____
So, is 6 a factor of 558? _____

f) Is 8 a factor of 1064?

The last 3 digits are _____.
Is 8 a factor of 64? _____
So, is 8 a factor of 1064? _____

▶ 3.1 Factors and Multiples of Whole Numbers

FOCUS Find prime factors, greatest common factors, and least common multiples of whole numbers.

We can factor 24 in different ways:

24 = 1 × 24   Write 24 as: 2 × 12

   = 1 × 2 × 12   Write 12 as: 2 × 6

   = 1 × 2 × 2 × 6   Write 6 as: 2 × 3

   = 1 × 2 × 2 × 2 × 3   All these numbers, except 1, are prime numbers.

> *A **prime number** has only two factors: itself and 1*

The **prime factorization** of 24 is:

$24 = 2 \times 2 \times 2 \times 3$ We can use powers: $2 \times 2 \times 2 = 2^3$

So, $24 = 2^3 \times 3$

> *The prime factorization of a number is the product of its prime factors.*

| Example 1 | Writing the Prime Factorization of a Whole Number |

Write the prime factorization of 324.

Solution

Draw a factor tree.
The last digit is even, so 2 is a factor.
$324 \div \mathbf{2} = 162$
The last digit is even, so 2 is a factor.
$162 \div \mathbf{2} = 81$
The sum of the digits is 9, so 3 is a factor.
$81 \div \mathbf{3} = 27$
Continue to divide by 3.
$27 \div \mathbf{3} = 9$
$9 \div \mathbf{3} = 3$
$3 \div \mathbf{3} = 1$
Write the product of the prime factors.
The prime factorization of 324 is:
$2 \times 2 \times 3 \times 3 \times 3 \times 3$, or $2^2 \times 3^4$

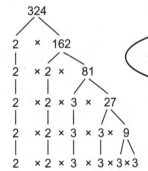

> *Use divisibility rules to find factors. Keep dividing until all the factors are prime.*

> *If you started dividing by a different prime factor, the factor tree would be different, but the prime factorization would be the same.*

> *Write the prime factors in order from least to greatest.*

1. Complete the factor tree for 120. Continue dividing until all factors are prime.

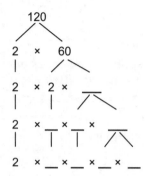

The prime factorization of 120 is: ___ × ___ × ___ × ___ × ___, or ___ × ___ × ___

2. Draw a factor tree for 280.

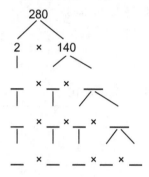

The prime factorization of 280 is: ___ × ___ × ___ × ___ × ___, or ___ × ___ × ___

The **greatest common factor (GCF)** of two numbers is the greatest factor the numbers have in common.

For example,

12 ÷ 1 = 12   and   12 ÷ 2 = **6**   and   12 ÷ 3 = 4

18 ÷ 1 = 18   and   18 ÷ 2 = 9   and   18 ÷ 3 = **6**

The factors of 12 are: 1, 2, 3, 4, **6**, 12

The factors of 18 are: 1, 2, 3, **6**, 9, 18

6 is the GCF of 12 and 18 because 6 is the greatest factor common to both 12 and 18.

Example 2 | **Finding the Greatest Common Factor**

Find the GCF of 24 and 60.

Solution

List the factors of 24   and   the factors of 60.

$24 \div 1 = 24$

$24 \div 2 = 12$

$24 \div 3 = 8$

$24 \div 4 = 6$

Stop dividing when the next division will give you a factor you already have.

$60 \div 1 = 60$

$60 \div 2 = 30$

$60 \div 3 = 20$

$60 \div 4 = 15$

$60 \div 5 = 12$

$60 \div 6 = 10$

As you divide, you identify two factors.

Factors of 24: 1, 2, 3, 4, 6, 8, **12**, 24

Factors of 60: 1, 2, 3, 4, 5, 6, 10, **12**, 15, 20, 30, 60

Identify the greatest factor that is in both lists.

The GCF of 24 and 60 is 12.

Check

1. a) Find the GCF of 40 and 56.

List the factors of 40   and   the factors of 56.

$40 \div 1 =$ _____

$40 \div 2 =$ _____

$40 \div$ _____ $=$ _____

$40 \div$ _____ $=$ _____

$56 \div 1 =$ _____

$56 \div 2 =$ _____

$56 \div$ _____ $=$ _____

$56 \div$ _____ $=$ _____

Factors of 40: _____

Factors of 56: _____

The GCF of 40 and 56 is _____.

Find the greatest factor that is in both lists.

b) Find the GCF of 45 and 99.

List the factors of 45   and   the factors of 99.

$45 \div 1 =$ ____

$45 \div$ ____ $=$ ____

$45 \div$ ____ $=$ ____

$99 \div 1 =$ ____

$99 \div$ ____ $=$ ____

$99 \div$ ____ $=$ ____

Factors of 45: _____

Factors of 99: _____

The GCF of 45 and 99 is ____.

The first five multiples of 6 are:

$6 \times 1 = 6$ $6 \times 2 = 12$ $6 \times 3 = 18$ $6 \times 4 = 24$ $6 \times 5 = 30$

The first five multiples of 4 are:

$4 \times 1 = 4$ $4 \times 2 = 8$ $4 \times 3 = 12$ $4 \times 4 = 16$ $4 \times 5 = 20$

The first ten multiples of 6 are: 6, **12**, 18, **24**, 30, **36**, 42, 48, 54, 60

The first ten multiples of 4 are: 4, 8, **12**, 16, 20, **24**, 28, 32, **36**, 40

> To get a multiple of a whole number, multiply it by a counting number.

12, 24, and 36 are **common multiples** of 6 and 4, because they are in both lists of multiples.

12 is the **least common multiple (LCM)** of 6 and 4, because 12 is the *least* number that is in both lists of multiples.

Example 3 | Finding the Least Common Multiple

Find the LCM of 12 and 15.

Solution

List multiples of 12.

12, 24, 36, 48, **60**, 72, ...

List multiples of 15 until you see a multiple of 12.

15, 30, 45, **60**, ...

The LCM of 12 and 15 is 60.

Check

1. Find the LCM of 20 and 25.

Multiples of 20: 20, 40, _____

Multiples of 25: 25, 50, _____

The LCM of 20 and 25 is _____.

> Stop when you see the same number in both lists.

2. Find the LCM of 10 and 45.

Multiples of 10: 10, _____

Multiples of 45: 45, _____

The LCM of 10 and 45 is _____.

Example 4 | **Using Greatest Common Factor to Solve a Problem**

Two ribbons are 24 cm and 42 cm long. Each ribbon is to be cut into equal pieces and all pieces must have the same length that is a whole number of centimetres. What is the greatest possible length of each piece?

Solution

Each ribbon is to be cut into equal lengths, so the lengths must be factors of 24 and factors of 42.
Factors of 24: 1, 2, 3, 4, **6**, 8, 12, 24
Factors of 42: 1, 2, 3, **6**, 7, 14, 21, 42

The possible lengths, in centimetres, are the common factors of 24 and 42:
1, 2, 3, and 6
The greatest length is the GCF: 6
The greatest possible length of each piece is 6 cm.

Check

1. Two ropes are 48 m and 32 m long. Each rope is to be cut into equal pieces and all pieces must have the same length that is a whole number of metres. What is the greatest possible length of each piece?

The lengths of the ropes must be factors of 48 and factors of 32.
Factors of 48: _____
Factors of 32: _____

The possible lengths, in metres, are the common factors of 48 and 32:

_____

The greatest length is the GCF: _____
The greatest possible length of each piece is _____.

1. Complete each factor tree.

a)   144
     2 × 72
     | /\
   __ × __ × /\
   | |
   __ × __ × __ × /\
   | | |
   __ × __ × __ × __ × /\
   | | | |
   __ × __ × __ × __ × __

b)   600
     2 × 300
     | /\
   __ × __ × /\
   | |
   __ × __ × __ × /\
   | | |
   __ × __ × __ × __ × /\
   | | | |
   __ × __ × __ × __ × __

2. Use each factor tree in question 1 to write the prime factorization of:

   a) 144 = ____ × ____ × ____ × ____ × ____ × ____, or ____ × ____
   b) 600 = ____ × ____ × ____ × ____ × ____ × ____, or ____ × ____ × ____

3. For each number, draw a factor tree, then write the prime factorization.

   a)   252
        /\

   b)   900
        /\

   The prime factorization of 252 is:

   _____, or _____

   The prime factorization of 900 is:

   _____, or _____

4. Find the GCF of each pair of numbers.

a) 44 and 70

List the factors of 44   and   the factors of 70.

44 ÷ 1 = _____   70 ÷ 1 = _____

44 ÷ _____ = _____   70 ÷ _____ = _____

44 ÷ _____ = _____   70 ÷ _____ = _____

                                                          70 ÷ _____ = _____

Factors of 44: _____

Factors of 70: _____

The GCF of 44 and 70 is _____.

b) 36 and 48

Factors of 36: _____

Factors of 48: _____

The GCF of 36 and 48 is _____.

5. a) List the first 10 multiples of each number.

Multiples of 7: 7, _____

Multiples of 10: 10, _____

b) The LCM of 7 and 10 is _____.

6. Find the LCM of each pair of numbers.

a) 12 and 30

Multiples of 12: 12, 24, _____

Multiples of 30: 30, _____

The LCM of 12 and 30 is _____.

b) 16 and 18

Multiples of 16: _____

Multiples of 18: _____

The LCM of 16 and 18 is _____.

7. Hamburger patties come in packages of 8. Buns come in packages of 6.
What is the least number of hamburgers that can be made with
no patties or buns left over?

The total number of patties are multiples of 8: _____, _____, _____, _____, _____, ⋯

The total number of buns are multiples of 6: _____, _____, _____, _____, _____, ⋯

For there to be no patties or buns left over, the numbers of patties
and buns must be the same.

Find the _____ of 6 and 8: _____

The least number of hamburgers is _____.

3.2 Perfect Squares, Perfect Cubes, and Their Roots

FOCUS Find square roots of perfect squares and cube roots of perfect cubes.

A **perfect square** is the square of a whole number.

For example, 16 is a perfect square because $16 = 4^2$

We say: 4 is the **square root** of 16.

We write: $\sqrt{16} = 4$

16 square units — 4 units

100 is a perfect square.

The prime factorization of 100 is:

$100 = 2 \times 2 \times 5 \times 5$, or $2^2 \times 5^2$

The prime factors occur in pairs.

This is true for any perfect square.

So, we can use prime factorization to find the square root of a perfect square.

Example 1 | Finding the Square Root of a Perfect Square

Find $\sqrt{324}$.

Solution

Draw a factor tree.

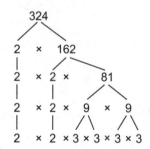

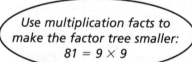
Use multiplication facts to make the factor tree smaller:
$81 = 9 \times 9$

The prime factorization of 324 is:

$324 = 2 \times 2 \times 3 \times 3 \times 3 \times 3$

$\quad\ \ = (2 \times 3 \times 3) \times (2 \times 3 \times 3)$

$\quad\ \ = 18 \times 18$

Since $324 = 18 \times 18$, or 18^2

Then, $\sqrt{324} = 18$

Group the factors as 2 equal products.
Multiply the factors.

Check

1. Find $\sqrt{576}$.

Complete this factor tree.

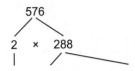

The prime factorization of 576 is:

$576 = \underline{\ }\times\underline{\ }\times\underline{\ }\times\underline{\ }\times\underline{\ }\times\underline{\ }\times\underline{\ }\times\underline{\ }$ Group the factors as 2 equal products.

$\quad\ = (2\times\underline{\ }\times\underline{\ }\times\underline{\ })\times(2\times\underline{\ }\times\underline{\ }\times\underline{\ })$ Multiply the factors.

$\quad\ = \underline{\qquad}\times\underline{\qquad}$

So, $\sqrt{576} = \underline{\qquad}$

A **perfect cube** is the cube of a whole number.

For example, 125 is a perfect cube because $125 = 5^3$

We say: 5 is the **cube root** of 125.

We write: $\sqrt[3]{125} = 5$

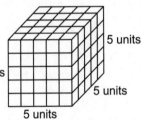

Volume = 125 cubic units

5 units
5 units
5 units

Example 2 | Finding the Cube Root of a Perfect Cube

Find $\sqrt[3]{2744}$.

Solution

Draw a factor tree.

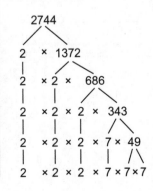

Write the prime factorization of 2744.

2744 = 2 × 2 × 2 × 7 × 7 × 7   Group the factors as 3 equal products.
  = (2 × 7) × (2 × 7) × (2 × 7)   Multiply the factors.
  = 14 × 14 × 14
Since 2744 = 14 × 14 × 14, or 14^3
Then, $\sqrt[3]{2744}$ = 14

Check

1. Find $\sqrt[3]{216}$.

Complete this factor tree.

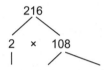

Use multiplication facts to make the factor tree smaller.

The prime factorization of 216 is:

216 = ___ × ___ × ___ × ___ × ___ × ___   Group the factors as ___ equal products.
 = (2 × ___) × (2 × ___) × (2 × ___)   _____ the factors.
 = ___ × ___ × ___
So, $\sqrt[3]{216}$ = ___

Example 3 | Using Roots to Solve a Problem

A rectangular prism has dimensions 16 cm by 8 cm by 4 cm. What is the edge length of a cube with the same volume?

Solution

First find the volume of the prism.
Volume of the rectangular prism is:
$V = lwh$ Substitute: l = 16, w = 8, and h = 4
$V = 16 × 8 × 4$
$V = 512$

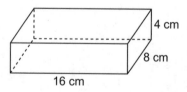

Now consider a cube with the same volume as the prism.
A cube has equal edge lengths.
Let the edge length be e centimetres.
Volume of the cube is:

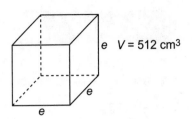

$V = e^3$ Substitute: $V = 512$

$512 = e^3$

$e = \sqrt[3]{512}$

Use a calculator to find the prime factors of 512.

$512 = 2 \times 2 \times 2 \times 2 \times 2 \times 2 \times 2 \times 2 \times 2$ Group the factors as 3 equal products.

$= (2 \times 2 \times 2) \times (2 \times 2 \times 2) \times (2 \times 2 \times 2)$

$= 8 \times 8 \times 8$

So, $\sqrt[3]{512} = 8$

The edge length of the cube is 8 cm.

Check

1. A rectangular prism has dimensions 8 in. by 4 in. by 2 in. What is the edge length of a cube with the same volume?

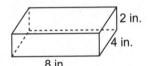

2 in.

4 in.

8 in.

First find the volume of the prism.

Volume of the rectangular prism is:

$V = \underline{\hspace{1cm}}$ Substitute: \underline{\hspace{5cm}}

$V = \underline{\hspace{0.6cm}} \times \underline{\hspace{0.6cm}} \times \underline{\hspace{0.6cm}}$

$V = \underline{\hspace{1cm}}$

Now think of a cube with the same volume.

Let the edge length of the cube be e centimetres.
Volume of the cube is:

e

e

e

$V = e^3$ Substitute: $V = \underline{\hspace{1cm}}$

$\underline{\hspace{1cm}} = e^3$

$e = \sqrt[3]{\underline{\hspace{1cm}}}$

Use a calculator or a factor tree to find the prime factors of \underline{\hspace{1cm}}.

$\underline{\hspace{1cm}} = 2 \times \underline{\hspace{0.6cm}} \times \underline{\hspace{0.6cm}} \times \underline{\hspace{0.6cm}} \times \underline{\hspace{0.6cm}} \times \underline{\hspace{0.6cm}}$ Group the factors as \underline{\hspace{1cm}} equal

$= (\underline{\hspace{1cm}}) \times (\underline{\hspace{1cm}}) \times (\underline{\hspace{1cm}})$ products.

$= \underline{\hspace{0.6cm}} \times \underline{\hspace{0.6cm}} \times \underline{\hspace{0.6cm}}$

So, $\sqrt[3]{\underline{\hspace{1cm}}} = \underline{\hspace{1cm}}$

The edge length of the cube is \underline{\hspace{1.5cm}}.

1. Use prime factorization to find each square root.

a) $\sqrt{225}$

225

225 = ____ × ____ × ____ × ____

    = (____ × ____) × (____ × ____)

    = ____ × ____

So, $\sqrt{225}$ = ____

3 ×

b) $\sqrt{196}$

196

196 = ____ × ____ × ____ × ____

    = (____ × ____) × (____ × ____)

    = ____ × ____

So, $\sqrt{196}$ = ____

2 ×

c) $\sqrt{1225}$

1225

1225 = ____ × ____ × ____ × ____

    = (_____) × (_____)

    = ____ × ____

So, $\sqrt{1225}$ = ____

2. Use prime factorization to find each cube root.

729

a) $\sqrt[3]{729}$

729 = ____ × ____ × ____ × ____ × ____ × ____

    = (____ × ____) × (____ × ____) × (____ × ____)

    = ____ × ____ × ____

So, $\sqrt[3]{729}$ = ____

3 ×

b) $\sqrt[3]{3375}$

3375

3375 = ____ × ____ × ____ × ____ × ____ × ____

    = (____ × ____) × (____ × ____) × (____ × ____)

    = ____ × ____ × ____

So, $\sqrt[3]{3375}$ = ____

3 ×

c) $\sqrt[3]{9261}$

$9261 = \underline{} \times \underline{} \times \underline{} \times \underline{} \times \underline{} \times \underline{}$

$ = (\underline{}) \times (\underline{}) \times (\underline{})$

$ = \underline{} \times \underline{} \times \underline{}$

So, $\sqrt[3]{9261} = \underline{}$

9261

3. Find the edge length of this cube.

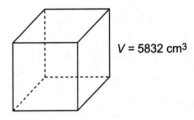

$V = 5832 \text{ cm}^3$

So, $\sqrt[3]{\underline{}} = \underline{}$

The edge length of the cube is _____.

CHECKPOINT 1

Can you...

- write the prime factorization of a number?
- find the greatest common factor and least common multiple of two numbers?
- find the square root of a perfect square?
- find the cube root of a perfect cube?

3.1 **1.** Complete each factor tree. Then write each prime factorization.

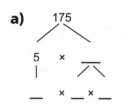

a) 175

5 × ___

___ × ___ × ___

175 = ___ × ___ × ___,
or _____

b) 450

10 × ___

___ × ___ × ___

___ × ___ × ___ × ___ × ___

450 = ___ × ___ × ___ × ___ × ___,
or _____

2. Find the GCF of 42 and 50.

List the factors of 42   and   the factors of 50.

42 ÷ 1 = _____   50 ÷ 1 = _____

42 ÷ _____ = _____   50 ÷ _____ = _____

42 ÷ _____ = _____   50 ÷ _____ = _____

42 ÷ _____ = _____

> Look for the same factor in both lines.

Factors of 42: _____

Factors of 50: _____

The GCF of 42 and 50 is _____.

3. Find the LCM of each pair of numbers.

a) 9 and 21

Multiples of 9 are: 9, _____

Multiples of 21: 21,_____ ◄─── Stop when you see a multiple of 9.

The LCM of 9 and 21 is _____.

b) 14 and 22

Multiples of 14: 14, _____

Multiples of 22: _____

The LCM of 14 and 22 is _____.

4. Find each square root.

a) $\sqrt{484}$

484

Draw a factor tree.

484 = _____

= (_____) × (_____)

= _____ × _____

So, $\sqrt{484}$ = _____

b) $\sqrt{1764}$

1764

Draw a factor tree.

1764 = _____

= (_____) × (_____)

= _____ × _____

So, $\sqrt{1764}$ = _____

5. Find each cube root.

a) $\sqrt[3]{343}$

343 = _____

So, $\sqrt[3]{343}$ = _____

b) $\sqrt[3]{8000}$

8000 = _____

= (_____) × (_____) × (_____)

= _____ × _____ × _____

So, $\sqrt[3]{8000}$ = _____

3.3 Skill Builder

Multiplying and Dividing a Binomial by a Constant

A **polynomial** is 1 term or the sum of terms. Here are 3 types of polynomials:

A **monomial** has 1 term; for example, $5a$, 6, $2x^2$

A **binomial** has 2 terms; for example, $2c + 5$, $3y^2 - 2y$

A **trinomial** has 3 terms; for example, $4b^2 - 5b + 2$

We can use algebra tiles to model polynomials.

This is a 1-tile. ▪ This is an x-tile. ▭ This is an x^2-tile.

A grey tile represents a positive term.

- To multiply $2(3x + 1)$:

  Using algebra tiles

  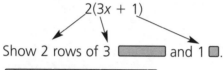
  $$2(3x + 1)$$

  Show 2 rows of 3 ▭ and 1 ▪.

  There are 6 ▭ and 2 ▪.

  So, $2(3x + 1) = 6x + 2$

  Using the distributive property
  Multiply each term in the binomial by the constant.

  $2(3x + 1) = 2(3x) + 2(1)$
  $ = 6x + 2$

- To divide $\dfrac{4x^2 + 8x}{2}$:

  Using algebra tiles

  $$\dfrac{4x^2 + 8x}{2}$$

  Arrange 4 ▭ and 8 ▭ in 2 equal rows.

  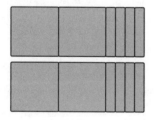

  Using division
  Divide each term of the binomial by 2.

  $\dfrac{4x^2 + 8x}{2} = \dfrac{4x^2}{2} + \dfrac{8x}{2}$
  $\phantom{\dfrac{4x^2 + 8x}{2}} = 2x^2 + 4x$

  The x-tile can be used to represent any variable, such as a y-tile or a c-tile. The x^2-tile may represent a y^2-tile or a c^2-tile.

  In each row, there are 2 and 4 ▭.

  So, $\dfrac{4x^2 + 8x}{2} = 2x^2 + 4x$

Check

1. Multiply: $3(4b + 2)$

Using algebra tiles

Sketch ____ rows of ____ ▭ and ____ ▪.

There are _____ ▭ and ____ ▪.

So, $3(4b + 2) =$ _____

Using the distributive property

Multiply each term of the binomial by the constant.

$3(4b + 2) = 3(\underline{}) + 3(\underline{})$

$= \underline{} + \underline{}$

2. Divide: $\dfrac{9r^2 + 6r}{3}$

Using algebra tiles

Sketch ____ ⬛ and ____ ▭ in ____ equal rows.

Using division

Divide each term of the binomial by ____.

$\dfrac{9r^2 + 6r}{\underline{}} = \dfrac{9r^2}{\underline{}} + \dfrac{6r}{\underline{}}$

$= \underline{}r^2 + \underline{}r$

In each row, there are ____ ⬛ and ____ ▭.

So, $\dfrac{9r^2 + 6r}{3} =$ _____

Multiplying and Dividing a Binomial by a Monomial

- To multiply $2x(3x + 1)$:

Using algebra tiles

Outline a rectangle with length 3 ▭ and 1 ▫, and width 2 ▭.

Fill in the rectangle with and ▭.

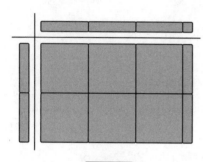

There are 6 ▭ and 2 ▭.
So, $2x(3x + 1) = 6x^2 + 2x$

Using the distributive property

Multiply each term of the binomial by $2x$.

$$2x(3x + 1) = 2x(3x) + 2x(1)$$
$$= 6x^2 + 2x$$

- To divide $\dfrac{4x^2 + 8x}{2x}$:

Using algebra tiles

Arrange 4 ▭ and 8 ▭ in a rectangle with width 2 ▭.

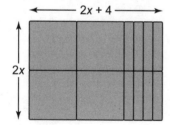

The length of the rectangle is
2 ▭ and 4 ▫.

So, $\dfrac{4x^2 + 8x}{2x} = 2x + 4$

Using division

Divide each term of the binomial by $2x$.

$$\frac{4x^2 + 8x}{2x} = \frac{4x^2}{2x} + \frac{8x}{2x}$$
$$= 2x + 4$$

Remember that
$\dfrac{x^2}{x} = x$ *and* $\dfrac{x}{x} = 1.$

Check

1. Multiply: $3b(4b + 2)$

Using algebra tiles
Outline a rectangle with length ____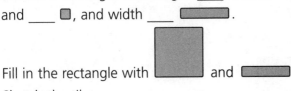
and ____ ■, and width ____ ⬛.

Fill in the rectangle with ⬛ and ▬.
Sketch the tiles.

Using the distributive property
Multiply each term of the binomial by $3b$.

$3b(4b + 2) = 3b(\underline{\quad}) + 3b(\underline{\quad})$

$\quad\quad\quad\quad = \underline{\quad} + \underline{\quad}$

There are ____ ⬛ and ____ ▬.
So, $3b(4b + 2) = \underline{\quad\quad\quad}$

2. Divide: $\dfrac{6a^2 + 8a}{2a}$

Using algebra tiles

Arrange ____ ⬛ and ____ ▬
in a rectangle with width ____ ▬.
Sketch the tiles. Label the rectangle.

Using division
Divide each term of the binomial by ____.

$\dfrac{6a^2 + 8a}{\underline{\quad}} = \dfrac{6a^2}{\underline{\quad}} + \dfrac{8a}{\underline{\quad}}$

$\quad\quad\quad\quad = \underline{\quad} + \underline{\quad}$

The length of the rectangle is
____ ▬ and ____ ■.

So, $\dfrac{6a^2 + 8a}{2a} = \underline{\quad\quad\quad}$

3.3 Common Factors of a Polynomial

To factor a polynomial, we write it as a product of polynomials.

This rectangle models the polynomial $6x^2 + 2x$.

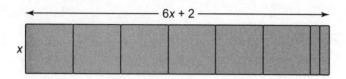

The length and width of the rectangle are *factors* of the polynomial.

The length is $6x + 2$ and the width is x.

So, $6x + 2$ and x are factors of $6x^2 + 2x$.

We write: $6x^2 + 2x = x(6x + 2)$

This binomial can be factored further because both terms have a common factor, 2.

This rectangle also models the polynomial $6x^2 + 2x$.

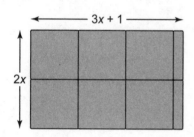

$2x$ and $3x + 1$ are **factors** of $6x^2 + 2x$.
$2x$ is the **greatest common factor** of $6x^2 + 2x$.

The length is $3x + 1$ and the width is $2x$.

We write: $6x^2 + 2x = 2x(3x + 1)$

To factor a polynomial means to factor fully.

This binomial cannot be factored further, so the polynomial is *factored fully*.

Example 1 **Using Algebra Tiles to Factor a Binomial**

Factor each binomial.

a) $4x + 6$

b) $3b^2 + 6b$

Solution

a) Use algebra tiles to model $4x + 6$ as a rectangle.

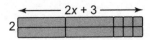

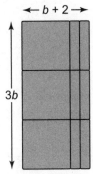

The length of the rectangle is $2x + 3$.

The width of the rectangle is 2.

So, $4x + 6 = 2(2x + 3)$

Since 2 is the greatest common factor (GCF) of 4 and 6, make 2 equal rows of tiles.

The factoring is complete because $2x + 3$ cannot be factored further.

We can check the factors by multiplying.
$2(2x + 3) = 2(2x) + 2(3)$
$= 4x + 6$

b) Use algebra tiles to model $3b^2 + 6b$ as a rectangle.

Since 3 is the GCF of 3 and 6, make 3 equal rows of tiles.

The length of the rectangle is $b + 2$.

The width of the rectangle is $3b$.

So, $3b^2 + 6b = 3b(b + 2)$

Check

1. Factor each binomial.

a) $5c + 10$

Use algebra tiles to model $5c + 10$ as a rectangle.
Since _____ is the GCF of 5 and 10,
make _____ equal rows of tiles.
Sketch the tiles.
The length of the rectangle is _____.
The width of the rectangle is _____.
So, $5c + 10 = $ _____

b) $4n^2 + 14n$

Use algebra tiles to model $4n^2 + 14n$ as a rectangle.
Since _____ is the GCF of 4 and 14,
make _____ equal rows of tiles.
Sketch the tiles.
The length of the rectangle is _____.
The width of the rectangle is _____.
So, $4n^2 + 14n = $ _____

If the numbers in the polynomial are large or if the numbers are negative,
we factor by dividing.

Example 2 | Factoring Binomials by Dividing

Factor each binomial.

a) $10a - 8$ **b)** $-6m^2 + 4m$

Solution

a) $10a - 8$

Find the GCF of the terms of the binomial.
Factor each term of the binomial.
$10a = \mathbf{2} \times 5 \times a$
$8 = \mathbf{2} \times 2 \times 2$
The GCF is 2. ◄—— This is one factor of the binomial.
Divide each term of the binomial by 2 to get another factor.

$$\frac{10a - 8}{2} = \frac{10a}{2} - \frac{8}{2}$$

$$= 5a - 4 \quad \text{◄—— This is the other factor of the binomial.}$$

So, $10a - 8 = 2(5a - 4)$

b) $-6m^2 + 4m$

Find the GCF of the terms of the binomial.

Factor each term of the binomial.

$6m^2 = \mathbf{2} \times 3 \times \mathbf{m} \times m$

$4m = \mathbf{2} \times 2 \times \mathbf{m}$

Multiply the factors that are in both lists.

When we list the factors of a negative term, we don't need to write the negative sign.

The GCF is $2 \times m = 2m$. ◄— This is one factor of the binomial.

Divide each term of the binomial by $2m$ to get the other factor.

$\dfrac{-6m^2 + 4m}{2m} = -\dfrac{6m^2}{2m} + \dfrac{4m}{2m}$

$= -3m + 2$ ◄— This is the other factor of the binomial.

So, $-6m^2 + 4m = 2m(-3m + 2)$

Check

1. Factor each binomial.

a) $4n - 32$

Factor each term of the binomial.

$4n = \underline{} \times \underline{} \times \underline{}$

$32 = \underline{} \times \underline{} \times \underline{} \times \underline{} \times \underline{}$

Circle the factors that are in both lists.

The GCF is $\underline{} \times \underline{} = \underline{}$.

Divide each term of the binomial by $\underline{}$.

$\dfrac{4n - 32}{\underline{}} = \dfrac{4n}{\underline{}} - \dfrac{32}{\underline{}}$

$= \underline{} - \underline{}$

So, $4n - 32 = \underline{}$

b) $-18r^2 + 12r$

Factor each term of the binomial.

$18r^2 = \underline{} \times \underline{} \times \underline{} \times \underline{} \times \underline{}$

$12r = \underline{} \times \underline{} \times \underline{} \times \underline{}$

The GCF is $\underline{} \times \underline{} \times \underline{} = \underline{}$.

Divide each term of the binomial by $\underline{}$.

$\dfrac{-18r^2 + 12r}{\underline{}} = -\dfrac{18r^2}{\underline{}} + \dfrac{12r}{\underline{}}$

$= \underline{} + \underline{}$

So, $-18r^2 + 12r = \underline{}$

When we use algebra tiles to factor a trinomial with positive terms, we may not be able to make a rectangle so we make equal groups of tiles instead.

Example 3 | Factoring Trinomials with a Common Factor

Factor each trinomial.

a) $2n^2 + 4n + 6$ **b)** $3n^2 - 12n - 9$

Solution

a) $2n^2 + 4n + 6$

Since all the terms are positive, use algebra tiles.

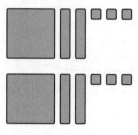

Use 2 ▢, 4 ▭, and 6 ◻.

Since 2 is the GCF of 2, 4, and 6, arrange the tiles in 2 equal groups.

There are 2 equal groups, so 2 is one factor.

Each group models $n^2 + 2n + 3$, so this polynomial is the other factor.

Write the factors as a product.

So, $2n^2 + 4n + 6 = 2(n^2 + 2n + 3)$

b) $3n^2 - 12n - 9$

Since some terms are negative, divide by the GCF to find the factors.

Factor each term of the trinomial.

$3n^2 = \mathbf{3} \times n \times n$

$12n = 2 \times 2 \times \mathbf{3} \times n$

$9 = \mathbf{3} \times 3$

The GCF is 3.

Divide each term of the trinomial by 3.

$$\frac{3n^2 - 12n - 9}{3} = \frac{3n^2}{3} - \frac{12n}{3} - \frac{9}{3}$$

$$= n^2 - 4n - 3$$

So, $3n^2 - 12n - 9 = 3(n^2 - 4n - 3)$

Check

1. Factor each trinomial.

a) $6n^2 + 3n + 9$

Since all the terms are positive, use algebra tiles.

Use _____ ▢ , _____ ▬ , and _____ ▪ .
Since _____ is the GCF of 6, 3, and 9, arrange the tiles in _____ equal groups.
Sketch the tiles.

There are _____ equal groups, so _____ is one factor.
Each group models _____ $n^2 +$ _____ $n +$ _____ , so this polynomial is the other factor.
So, $6n^2 + 3n + 9 =$ _____

b) $-12v^2 + 8v - 16$

Since some terms are negative, divide by the GCF to find the factors.

$12v^2 =$ _____ × _____ × _____ × _____ × _____
$8v =$ _____ × _____ × _____ × _____
$16 =$ _____ × _____ × _____ × _____
The GCF is _____ × _____ = _____ .
Divide each term of the trinomial by _____ .

> Circle the factors that are in both lists, then multiply.

$$\frac{-12v^2 + 8v - 16}{\rule{2em}{0.4pt}} = -\frac{12v^2}{\rule{2em}{0.4pt}} + \frac{8v}{\rule{2em}{0.4pt}} - \frac{16}{\rule{2em}{0.4pt}}$$

$$= \_\_\_ v^2 + \_\_\_ v - \_\_\_ .$$

So, $-12v^2 + 8v - 16 =$ _____ (_____ $v^2 +$ _____ $v -$ _____)

As we remove -1 as a common factor,
multiply each term in the brackets by -1.

> When the 1st term in the trinomial is negative, we remove -1 as a common factor.

_____ (_____ $v^2 +$ _____ $v -$ _____) = _____ (_____ $v^2 -$ _____ $v +$ _____)

So, $-12v^2 + 8v - 16 =$ _____

1. a) Write the binomial modelled by
   these algebra tiles: _____

   b) The length of the rectangle is _____.
   The width of the rectangle is _____.
   Factor the binomial: _____

2. Use algebra tiles to factor each binomial.

   a) $8w + 12$

   Since _____ is the GCF of 8 and 12, make _____ equal rows of tiles.
   Sketch the tiles.
   The length of the rectangle is _____.
   The width of the rectangle is _____.
   So, $8w + 12 =$ _____

   b) $6x^2 + 15x$

   Since _____ is the GCF of 6 and 15, make _____ equal rows of tiles.
   Sketch the tiles.
   The length of the rectangle is _____.
   The width of the rectangle is _____.
   So, $6x^2 + 15x =$ _____

3. Factor each binomial by dividing.

   a) $-9z + 36$

   Factor each term of the binomial.
   $9z =$ _____ $\times$ _____ $\times$ _____
   $36 =$ _____ $\times$ _____ $\times$ _____ $\times$ _____
   The GCF is _____ $\times$ _____ $=$ _____.
   Divide each term of the binomial by _____.

   $$\frac{-9z + 36}{\rule{1cm}{0.4pt}} = -\frac{9z}{\rule{1cm}{0.4pt}} + \frac{36}{\rule{1cm}{0.4pt}}$$

   $$= \rule{1cm}{0.4pt} + \rule{1cm}{0.4pt}$$

   So, $-9z + 36 =$ _____

   b) $25t^2 - 10t$

   Factor each term of the binomial.
   $25t^2 =$ _____ $\times$ _____ $\times$ _____ $\times$ _____
   $10t =$ _____ $\times$ _____ $\times$ _____
   The GCF is _____ $\times$ _____ $=$ _____.

   Divide each term of the binomial by _____.

   $$\frac{25t^2 - 10t}{\rule{1cm}{0.4pt}} = \frac{\rule{0.8cm}{0.4pt}}{\rule{0.8cm}{0.4pt}} - \frac{\rule{0.8cm}{0.4pt}}{\rule{0.8cm}{0.4pt}}$$

   $$= \rule{1cm}{0.4pt} - \rule{1cm}{0.4pt}$$

   So, $25t^2 - 10t =$ _____

4. Factor each trinomial.

a) $4x^2 + 8x + 2$

Since all the terms are positive, use algebra tiles.

Use ____ ⬛, ____ ▭, and ____ ◼.

Since ____ is the GCF of 4, 8, and 2, arrange the tiles in ____ equal groups.

Sketch the tiles.

There are ____ equal groups, so ____ is one factor.

Each group models ____ + ____ + ____,

so this polynomial is the other factor.

So, $4x^2 + 8x + 2 = $ _____

b) $-15a^2 + 10a - 30$

Factor each term of the trinomial.

The GCF is ____.

Divide each term of the trinomial by ____.

Remove -1 as a common factor.

So, $-15a^2 + 10a - 30 = $ _____

c) $24n^2 - 16n - 8$

So, $24n^2 - 16n - 8 = $ _____

3.4 Math Lab: Modelling Trinomials as Binomial Products

Explore trinomials with algebra tiles.

We can use the distributive property and an area model to show the product of two 2-digit numbers.

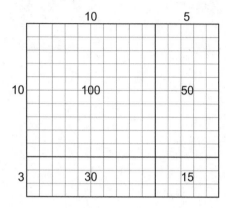

$13 \times 15 = (10 + 3)(10 + 5)$
$= 10(10 + 5) + 3(10 + 5)$
$= 10(10) + 10(5) + 3(10) + 3(5)$
$= 100 + 50 + 30 + 15$
$= 195$

We can use the same process to show the product of two binomials.

Try This

Use only positive algebra tiles.

Part A

• This rectangle represents the trinomial $x^2 + 2x + 1$.
Write each side length on the rectangle.
Use the side lengths to write the polynomial as a product:
$x^2 + 2x + 1 = (x + \underline{\hspace{1cm}})(x + \underline{\hspace{1cm}})$

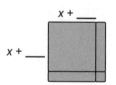

• Sketch as many ▭ and ▢ as you need
to complete this rectangle to show the
trinomial $x^2 + 3x + 2$. Write as a product:
$x^2 + 3x + 2 = (x + \underline{\hspace{1cm}})(x + \underline{\hspace{1cm}})$

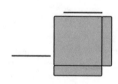
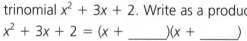

- Sketch as many 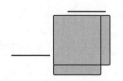 and ☐ as you need to complete this rectangle to show the trinomial $x^2 + 4x + 4$. Write as a product:

$x^2 + 4x + 4 = ($ _____ $+$ _____ $)($ _____ $+$ _____ $)$

- Sketch as many 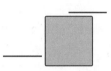 and ☐ as you need to complete this rectangle to show a different trinomial. Write as a product:

_____

- Use 1 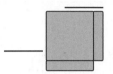 and as many ▭ and ☐ as you need to make, then sketch a rectangle to show a different trinomial. Write as a product:

_____

Part B

- This rectangle represents the trinomial $2x^2 + 3x + 1$. Write each side length on the rectangle. Write as a product:

$2x^2 + 3x + 1 = (2x +$ _____ $)(x +$ _____ $)$

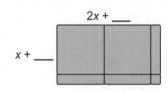

- Sketch as many ▭ and ☐ as you need to complete this rectangle to show the trinomial $2x^2 + 7x + 3$. Write as a product:

$2x^2 + 7x + 3 = (2x +$ _____ $)(x +$ _____ $)$

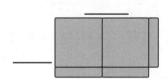

- Sketch as many ▭ and ☐ as you need to complete this rectangle to show the trinomial $2x^2 + 4x + 2$. Write as a product:

$2x^2 + 4x + 2 = ($ _____ $+$ _____ $)($ _____ $+$ _____ $)$

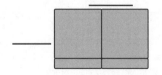

- Sketch as many ▭ and ☐ as you need to complete this rectangle to show a different trinomial. Write as a product:

_____

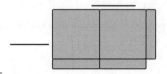

- Use 2 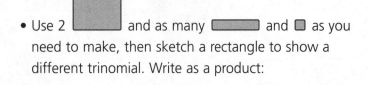 and as many ▭ and ▪ as you need to make, then sketch a rectangle to show a different trinomial. Write as a product:

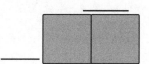

_____

Part C

From Part A, copy 3 trinomials and their products below.

How are the numbers in each trinomial related to the numbers in its product?

_____

_____

Here is a trinomial and its product from Part B:

$$2x^2 + 7x + 3 = (2x + 1)(x + 3)$$

- How is this term in the   …these terms in
  trinomial related to…   the product?

_____

$$2x^2 + 7x + 3 = (2x + 1)(x + 3)$$

- How is this term in the trinomial related to the indicated terms in the product?

_____

_____

$$2x^2 + 7x + 3 = (2x + 1)(x + 3)$$

- How is this term in the   …these terms in
  trinomial related to…   the product?

_____

1. For each set of algebra tiles below:
   - Write the trinomial.
   - Write the trinomial as a product.

   a)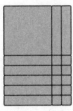

   The trinomial is: $x^2 +$ _____ $x +$ _____
   The product is: $(x +$ _____$)(x +$ _____$)$

   b)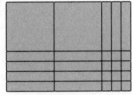

   The trinomial is: _____ $x^2 +$ _____ $x +$ _____
   The product is: (_____ $x +$ _____$)(x +$ _____$)$

   c)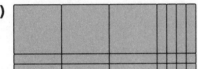

   The trinomial is: _____
   The product is: _____

2. a) Use 1 ⬜ , 6 ▭ , and 8 ◻ to make a rectangle.
   Sketch the rectangle.

   b) Write the trinomial: _____

   c) Write the trinomial as a product: _____ = _____

3.5 Skill Builder

Adding and Subtracting Binomials

To add or subtract binomials, group like terms, then combine the terms by adding their coefficients.

- To add:

  $(4x + 2) + (-3x - 6)$ Remove brackets.

  $= 4x + 2 - 3x - 6$ Group like terms.

  $= 4x - 3x + 2 - 6$ Combine like terms.

  $= x - 4$

- To subtract:

  $(2x - 3) - (4x - 1)$ Remove brackets.

                                Change the signs of the subtracted terms.

  $= 2x - 3 - 4x + 1$ Group like terms.

  $= 2x - 4x - 3 + 1$ Combine like terms.

  $= -2x - 2$

Check

1. Add.

a) $(4x + 2) + (5x + 1)$

    $= 4x + 2 + 5x + 1$

    $= 4x + \underline{} + 2 + \underline{}$

    $= \underline{}x + \underline{}$

b) $(5n - 3) + (-n + 6)$

    $= 5n - 3 - \underline{} + \underline{}$

    $= 5n - \underline{} - 3 + \underline{}$

    $= \underline{} + \underline{}$

c) $(-6x + 3) + (3x - 4)$

    $= \underline{}x + \underline{} + \underline{}x - \underline{}$

    $= \underline{} + \underline{} + \underline{} - \underline{}$

    $= \underline{}$

d) $(-4s - 5) + (3s - 1)$

    $= \underline{}$

    $= \underline{}$

    $= \underline{}$

2. Subtract.

a) $(2m + 5) - (m + 3)$

    $= 2m + 5 - m - 3$

    $= \underline{} - \underline{} + \underline{} - \underline{}$

    $= \underline{} + \underline{}$

b) $(5 - 3h) - (2 - 4h)$

    $= \underline{} - \underline{} - \underline{} + \underline{}$

    $= \underline{} - \underline{} - \underline{} + \underline{}$

    $= \underline{}$

c) $(t + 2) - (-2t + 4)$

    $= \underline{} + \underline{} + \underline{} - \underline{}$

    $= \underline{} + \underline{} + \underline{} - \underline{}$

    $= \underline{}$

d) $(2r - 1) - (-3r - 2)$

    $= \underline{}$

    $= \underline{}$

    $= \underline{}$

3.5 Polynomials of the Form $x^2 + bx + c$

FOCUS Use different strategies to multiply binomials and to factor trinomials.

These algebra tiles and the rectangle diagram model the trinomial $x^2 + 7x + 10$.

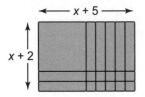

	x	5
x	$(x)(x) = x^2$	$(x)(5) = 5x$
2	$(2)(x) = 2x$	$(2)(5) = 10$

$(x + 5)(x + 2) = x^2 + 7x + 10$

$(x + 5)(x + 2) = x^2 + 5x + 2x + 10$
$\qquad\qquad\qquad = x^2 + 7x + 10$

We can use these models to multiply, or expand, two binomials.

Example 1 | Using Models and Diagrams to Multiply Two Binomials

Expand, then simplify.

a) $(x + 6)(x + 3)$
b) $(n - 5)(n - 2)$

Solution

a) $(x + 6)(x + 3)$

Since all the terms are positive, use algebra tiles.
Use 1 ▭ and 6 ☐ as the length of a rectangle.
Use 1 ▭ and 3 ☐ as the width of the rectangle.
Use algebra tiles to make the rectangle.

The tiles used are: 1 ▢, 9 ▭, and 18 ☐
So, $(x + 6)(x + 3) = x^2 + 9x + 18$

b) $(n - 5)(n - 2)$

Since some terms are negative, use a rectangle diagram.
Sketch a rectangle with length $n - 5$ and width $n - 2$.
Divide the rectangle into smaller rectangles.

Multiply the terms that label the sides of each small rectangle.

Add the products from the smaller rectangles.
$(n - 5)(n - 2) = n^2 - 5n - 2n + 10$
$\qquad\qquad\qquad = n^2 - 7n + 10$

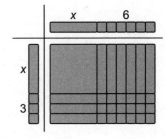

	n	-5
n	$n \times n = n^2$	$n \times (-5) = -5n$
-2	$(-2) \times n = -2n$	$(-2) \times (-5) = 10$

Check

1. Expand, then simplify.

a) $(x + 7)(x + 2)$

Use algebra tiles.

Use _____ 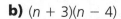 and _____ ▫ as the length
of a rectangle.
Use _____ ▭ and _____ ▫ as the width
of a rectangle.
To make the rectangle, use these tiles:

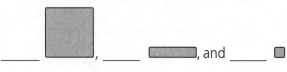

_____ ⬛, _____ ▭, and _____ ▫

So, $(x + 7)(x + 2) = x^2 +$ _____ $x +$ _____

Sketch the tiles.

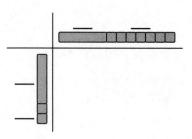

b) $(n + 3)(n - 4)$

Use a rectangle diagram.
Sketch a rectangle with length _____ and width _____.
Divide the rectangle into smaller rectangles.

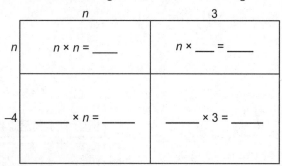

	n	3
n	$n \times n =$ _____	$n \times$ ___ $=$ _____
-4	_____ $\times n =$ _____	_____ $\times 3 =$ _____

Add the products from the smaller rectangles.

$(n + 3)(n - 4) =$ _____ $+$ _____ $-$ _____ $-$ _____

$=$ _____

We can use the distributive property to multiply two binomials.

$(z + 5)(z + 3) = z(z + 3) + 5(z + 3)$

$\qquad = z(z) + z(3) + 5(z) + 5(3)$

$\qquad = z^2 + 3z + 5z + 15$

$\qquad = z^2 + 8z + 15$

Example 2 | **Multiplying Two Binomials**

Expand, then simplify.

a) $(x + 6)(x - 3)$ **b)** $(n - 6)(n - 4)$

Solution

Use the distributive property.

a) $(x + 6)(x - 3) = x(x - 3) + 6(x - 3)$

$\qquad\qquad\qquad = x(x) + x(-3) + 6(x) + 6(-3)$ Multiply.

$\qquad\qquad\qquad = x^2 - 3x + 6x - 18$ Combine like terms.

$\qquad\qquad\qquad = x^2 + 3x - 18$

b) $(n - 6)(n - 4) = n(n - 4) - 6(n - 4)$

$\qquad\qquad\qquad = n(n) + n(-4) - 6(n) - 6(-4)$

$\qquad\qquad\qquad = n^2 - 4n - 6n + 24$

$\qquad\qquad\qquad = n^2 - 10n + 24$

Check

1. Expand, then simplify.

a) $(x - 5)(x - 3)$

$= x(\underline{\qquad}) - 5(\underline{\qquad})$ Use the distributive property.

$= x(\underline{\quad}) + x(\underline{\quad}) - 5(\underline{\quad}) - 5(\underline{\quad})$ Multiply.

$= \underline{\quad} - \underline{\quad} - \underline{\quad} + \underline{\quad}$ Combine like terms.

$= \underline{\qquad\qquad\qquad}$

b) $(v - 7)(v + 3)$

$= v(\underline{\qquad}) - 7(\underline{\qquad})$

$= v(\underline{\quad}) + v(\underline{\quad}) - 7(\underline{\quad}) - 7(\underline{\quad})$

$= \underline{\quad} + \underline{\quad} - \underline{\quad} - \underline{\quad}$

$= \underline{\qquad\qquad\qquad}$

In *Examples 1* and *2*, we multiplied two binomials, then simplified the product to get a trinomial.

When we reverse the process and write a trinomial as a product of two binomials, we *factor* the trinomial.

Example 3 | Using Algebra Tiles to Factor a Trinomial

Use algebra tiles to factor $x^2 + 6x + 5$.

Solution

To model $x^2 + 6x + 5$, use 1 ⬜, 6 ▭, and 5 ▫.

To form a rectangle:

Place ⬜ at the top left.

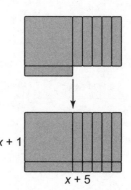

Arrange 6 ▭ beneath and to the right of ⬜.
Use 5 ▫ to complete the rectangle.
The length and width of the rectangle are the factors.
So, $x^2 + 6x + 5 = (x + 5)(x + 1)$

$x + 1$

$x + 5$

Check

1. Use algebra tiles to factor $x^2 + 7x + 12$.

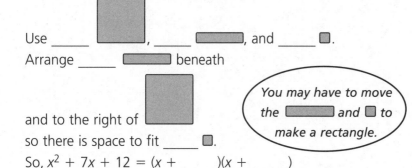

Use _____ ⬜, _____ ▭, and _____ ▫.
Arrange _____ ▭ beneath

and to the right of ⬜
so there is space to fit _____ ▫.
So, $x^2 + 7x + 12 = (x + $ _____ $)(x + $ _____ $)$

You may have to move the ▭ and ▫ to make a rectangle.

Sketch the tiles.
Label the length and width.

We can use the patterns in the numbers in a trinomial and its factors to help factor a trinomial.

When we factor a trinomial, we find two numbers whose sum is the coefficient of the x-term in the trinomial and whose product is the constant term.

$7 = 3 + 4$

$x^2 + 7x + 12 = (x + 3)(x + 4)$

$12 = 3 \times 4$

Remember the patterns you discovered in Lesson 3.4.

Example 4 | Using Algebra to Factor Trinomials

Factor each trinomial.

a) $x^2 + 5x + 6$

b) $x^2 - x - 12$

Solution

a) $x^2 + 5x + 6$

The coefficient of x is 5.

The constant term is 6.

Write pairs of factors of 6: 1×6 and 2×3

There are 2 pairs of factors, so there are 2 possible binomials:

$(x + 1)(x + 6)$ $(x + 2)(x + 3)$

Multiply to find which trinomial has the term $5x$.

$\quad (x + 1)(x + 6) \qquad\qquad (x + 2)(x + 3)$

$= x^2 + 6x + 1x + 6 \qquad = x^2 + 3x + 2x + 6$

$= x^2 + 7x + 6 \qquad\qquad = x^2 + 5x + 6 \; \longleftarrow$ This is the correct trinomial.

So, $x^2 + 5x + 6 = (x + 2)(x + 3)$

> *The coefficient of x is positive, so we don't need to list negative factors.*

b) $x^2 - x - 12$

Think of $x^2 - x - 12$ as $x^2 - 1x - 12$.

The coefficient of x is -1, so the sum of the factors is -1.

The constant term is -12, so the product of the factors is -12.

Factors of -12	Sum of the factors	
$1 \times (-12)$	$1 - 12 = -11$	X
$(-1) \times 12$	$-1 + 12 = 11$	X
$2 \times (-6)$	$2 - 6 = -4$	X
$(-2) \times 6$	$-2 + 6 = 4$	X
$3 \times (-4)$	$\mathbf{3 - 4 = -1}$	✓
$(-3) \times 4$	$-3 + 4 = 1$	X

> *Use a table to list pairs of factors of -12, and their sum. It helps to list the factors in order, starting with 1.*

> *You may be able to use mental math to identify factors, then find their sum.*

So, the factors of -12 are 3 and -4.

Then, $x^2 - x - 12 = (x + 3)(x - 4)$

> *You can expand to check the binomial factors are correct.*

Not all trinomials can be factored as a product of two binomials.
For example, $x^2 + 5x + 12$ cannot be factored because
we cannot form a rectangle with the algebra tiles, and
no pair of factors of 12 has a sum of 5.

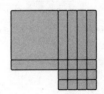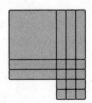

Check

1. Factor each trinomial.

a) $x^2 - 6x + 8$

The coefficient of x is _____, so the sum of the factors is _____.

The constant term is _____, so the product of the factors is _____.

Factors of _____	Sum of the factors
$1 \times$ _____	$1 +$ _____ $=$ _____ _____
$(-1) \times$ _____	$-1 -$ _____ $=$ _____ _____
$2 \times$ _____	$2 +$ _____ $=$ _____ _____
$(-2) \times$ _____	$-2 -$ _____ $=$ _____ _____

8 is positive, so both its factors have the same sign. The x-term is negative, so both factors must be negative.

So, the factors of _____ are _____ and _____.

Then, $x^2 - 6x + 8 = (x -$ _____$)(x -$ _____$)$

b) $c^2 + 2c - 15$

The coefficient of c is _____, so the sum of the factors is _____.

The constant term is _____, so the product of the factors is _____.

Factors of _____	Sum of the factors
$1 \times ($ _____ $)$	$1 -$ _____ $=$ _____ _____
$(-1) \times$ _____	$-1 +$ _____ $=$ _____ _____
$3 \times ($ _____ $)$	$3 -$ _____ $=$ _____ _____
$(-3) \times$ _____	$-3 +$ _____ $=$ _____ _____

The factors of _____ are _____ and _____.

So, $c^2 + 2c - 15 = (c -$ _____$)(c +$ _____$)$

Practice

1. Expand, then simplify.

a) $(x + 3)(x + 5)$

Use algebra tiles to make a rectangle.

Use _____ [tile] and _____ [tile] as the length.

Use _____ [tile] and _____ [tile] as the width.

To make the rectangle, use these tiles:

Sketch the tiles.
Label the length and width.

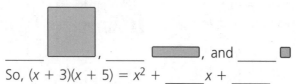

_____ [tile], _____ [tile], and _____ [tile]

So, $(x + 3)(x + 5) = x^2 +$ _____ $x +$ _____

b) $(n - 5)(n + 7)$

Use a rectangle diagram.
Sketch a rectangle with length _____ and width _____.
Divide the rectangle into smaller rectangles.

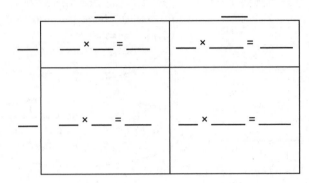

Add the products from the smaller rectangles.

$(n - 5)(n + 7) =$ _____ − _____ + _____ − _____

= _____

2. Use the distributive property to multiply, then simplify.

a) $(x - 10)(x + 4) = x($_____$) - 10($_____$)$

$= x($_____$) + x($_____$) - 10($_____$) - 10($_____$)$

= _____ + _____ − _____ − _____

= _____

b) $(n + 9)(n - 6) = n($_____$) + 9($_____$)$

$= n($_____$) + n($_____$) + 9($_____$) + 9($_____$)$

= _____ − _____ + _____ − _____

= _____

c) $(h - 7)(h - 4) =$ _____

= _____

3. Factor each trinomial.

a) $x^2 + 10x + 9$

Use algebra tiles.   Sketch the tiles.
                                                 Label the length and width.

Use _____ ⬛ , _____ ▭ , and _____ ◻ .
Arrange _____ ▭ so
there is space to fit _____ ◻ .
So, $x^2 + 10x + 9 = (x +$ _____$)(x +$ _____$)$

b) $x^2 - 13x + 12$

The coefficient of x is _____, so the sum of the factors is _____.
The constant term is _____, so the product of the factors is _____.

Factors of ____	Sum of the factors
$1 \times$ ____	$1 +$ ____ $=$ ____ ____
$(-1) \times$ (____)	$-1 -$ ____ $=$ ____ ____
$2 \times$ ____	$2 +$ ____ $=$ ____ ____
$(-2) \times$ (____)	$-2 -$ ____ $=$ ____ ____
$3 \times$ ____	$3 +$ ____ $=$ ____ ____
$(-3) \times$ (____)	$-3 -$ ____ $=$ ____ ____

____ is positive, so both its factors have the same sign. The x-term is _____, so both factors must be _____.

Once you have found the sum you need, you don't have to add any more factors.

The factors of _____ are _____ and _____.
So, $x^2 - 13x + 12 = (x -$ _____$)(x -$ _____$)$

c) $n^2 - 8n - 20$

The sum of the factors is _____.
The product of the factors is _____.

Factors of ____	Sum of the factors
_____	_____ _____
_____	_____ _____
_____	_____ _____
_____	_____ _____
_____	_____ _____
_____	_____ _____

So, $n^2 - 8n - 20 =$ _____

d) $c^2 + 7c - 18$

So, $c^2 + 7c - 18 =$ _____

▶ 3.6 Polynomials of the Form $ax^2 + bx + c$

FOCUS Multiply binomials and factor trinomials.

In Lesson 3.5, all the trinomials had x^2-terms with coefficient 1.
In this lesson, we will work with trinomials whose x^2-terms have coefficients
that are not 1.

These algebra tiles model the trinomial $2x^2 + 11x + 12$.

The lengths of the sides of the rectangle can be used to write
the trinomial as a product.
$2x^2 + 11x + 12 = (2x + 3)(x + 4)$

We can use this model to help us multiply two binomials.

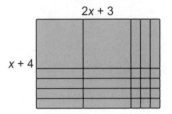

| **Example 1** | **Using Models and Diagrams to Multiply Two Binomials** |

Expand, then simplify.

a) $(2x + 4)(3x + 1)$ **b)** $(3n − 5)(4n − 7)$

Solution

a) $(2x + 4)(3x + 1)$

Since all the terms are positive, use algebra tiles
to make a rectangle.
Use 2 ▭ and 4 ▫ as the length.
Use 3 ▭ and 1 ▫ as the width.
These tiles were used to make the rectangle:

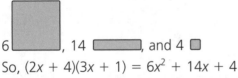

6 ▭, 14 ▭, and 4 ▫
So, $(2x + 4)(3x + 1) = 6x^2 + 14x + 4$

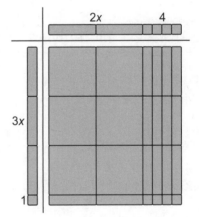

b) $(3n − 5)(4n − 7)$

Since some terms are negative, use a
rectangle diagram.
Sketch a rectangle with length $3n − 5$
and width $4n − 7$.

Divide the rectangle into smaller rectangles.
Add the products from the smaller rectangles.

$(3n − 5)(4n − 7) = 12n^2 − 20n − 21n + 35$
$= 12n^2 − 41n + 35$

	$3n$	$−5$
$4n$	$4n × 3n = 12n^2$	$4n × (−5) = −20n$
$−7$	$(−7) × 3n = −21n$	$(−7) × (−5) = 35$

Check

1. Expand, then simplify.

a) $(4x + 2)(2x + 3)$

Use algebra tiles to make a rectangle.
Use ____ 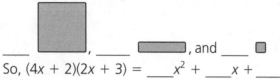 and ____ ▢ for the length.
Use ____ ▭ and ____ ▢ for the width.
To make the rectangle, use these tiles:

____ ▢ , ____ ▭ , and ____ ▢
So, $(4x + 2)(2x + 3) =$ ____ $x^2 +$ ____ $x +$ ____

b) $(5n - 2)(3n + 7)$

Use a rectangle diagram.
Sketch a rectangle with length _____
and width _____.
Divide the rectangle into smaller rectangles.
Add the products from the smaller rectangles.
$(5n - 2)(3n + 7) =$ ____ − ____ + ____ − ____
$=$ _____

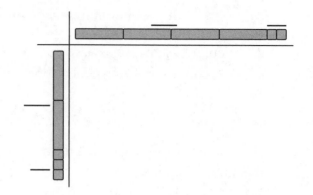

We can use the distributive property to multiply two binomials.

Example 2 | Multiplying Two Binomials

Expand, then simplify.
a) $(4n + 3)(2n + 2)$ **b)** $(-3f + 4)(2f - 5)$

Solution

Use the distributive property.

a) $(4n + 3)(2n + 2) = 4n(2n + 2) + 3(2n + 2)$
$= 4n(2n) + 4n(2) + 3(2n) + 3(2)$ Multiply.
$= 8n^2 + 8n + 6n + 6$ Combine like terms.
$= 8n^2 + 14n + 6$

b) $(-3f + 4)(2f - 5) = -3f(2f - 5) + 4(2f - 5)$
$= (-3f)(2f) + (-3f)(-5) + 4(2f) + 4(-5)$
$= -6f^2 + 15f + 8f - 20$
$= -6f^2 + 23f - 20$

Check

1. Expand, then simplify.

a) $(3f - 4)(2f + 6)$

Use the distributive property.

$(3f - 4)(2f + 6) = 3f(_____) - 4(_____)$

$= 3f(\_\_\_\_) + 3f(\_\_\_\_) - 4(\_\_\_\_) - 4(\_\_\_\_)$ Multiply.

$= \_\_\_\_ + \_\_\_\_ - \_\_\_\_ - \_\_\_\_$ Combine like terms.

$= \_\_\_\_ + \_\_\_\_ - \_\_\_\_$

b) $(4m + 9)(-5m - 2)$

Use the distributive property.

$(4m + 9)(-5m - 2) = 4m(_____) + 9(_____)$

$= 4m(_____) + 4m(\_\_\_\_) + 9(_____) + 9(\_\_\_\_)$

$= _____m^2 - _____m - _____m - _____$

$= _____$

In *Examples 1* and *2*, we multiplied two binomials. We now reverse the process and factor a trinomial.

Example 3 | Factoring a Trinomial with Positive Terms

Factor each trinomial.

a) $2x^2 + 7x + 6$ **b)** $3n^2 + 8n + 4$

Solution

a) $2x^2 + 7x + 6$

Use algebra tiles to factor.

Use 2 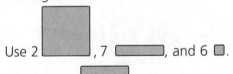 , 7 ▭ , and 6 ▫ .

Start with 2 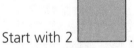 .

Arrange 7 ▭ beneath and to the

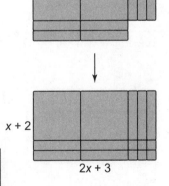

right of the rectangle formed by 2 ⬜ .

Use 6 ▫ to complete the rectangle.

The length and width of the rectangle are the factors.

So, $2x^2 + 7x + 6 = (2x + 3)(x + 2)$

b) $3n^2 + 8n + 4$

$$3n^2 + 8n + 4$$

The 1st term is $3n^2$.
Write this term as
a product of factors:
$3n^2 = 3n \times n$

These factors are the
1st terms in the binomials.

The 3rd term is 4.
Write this term as
a product of factors.
$4 = 4 \times 1 \qquad 4 = 2 \times 2$

The factors in one of these
pairs are the 2nd terms in the binomials.

Write all possible binomials.

$(3n + 4)(n + 1)$ $\qquad$ $(3n + 1)(n + 4)$ $\qquad$ $(3n + 2)(n + 2)$

Multiply, then add to find which product has the term $8n$.

$(3n + 4)(n + 1)$	$(3n + 1)(n + 4)$	$(3n + 2)(n + 2)$
$= 3n^2 + 3n + 4n + 4$	$= 3n^2 + 12n + n + 4$	$= 3n^2 + 6n + 2n + 4$
$= 3n^2 + 7n + 4$	$= 3n^2 + 13n + 4$	$= 3n^2 + 8n + 4$

This product has the term $8n$.

So, $3n^2 + 8n + 4 = (3n + 2)(n + 2)$

Expand factors to check the binomial.

Check

1. Factor each trinomial.

a) $2x^2 + 9x + 4$

Use algebra tiles to factor.

Sketch the tiles. Label the length and width.

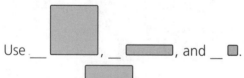

Use __ , __ [   ], and __ ▪.

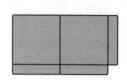

Start with __ [   ].
Arrange __ [   ] beneath and
to the right of the rectangle

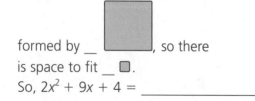

formed by __ [   ], so there
is space to fit __ ▪.
So, $2x^2 + 9x + 4 =$ _____

b) $7n^2 + 16n + 4$

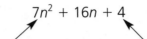

$$7n^2 + 16n + 4$$

The 1st term is $7n^2$.
Write this term as
a product of factors:
$7n^2 = 7n \times$ _____

The 3rd term is _____.
Write this term as
a product of factors:
_____ = _____ × _____   _____ = _____ × _____

Write all possible binomials.
$(7n +$ _____$)($_____$+$ ___$)$ $(7n +$ ___$)($___$+$ ___$)$ $(7n +$ ___$)($___$+$ ___$)$

Multiply to find which product has the term $16n$.

$(7n +$ _____$)($_____$+$ _____$)$ $(7n +$ ___$)($___$+$ ___$)$
$= 7n^2 +$ _____ $+$ _____ $+$ _____ $=$ _____ $+$ _____ $+$ _____ $+$ _____
$= 7n^2 +$ _____ $+$ _____ $=$ _____ $+$ _____ $+$ _____

$(7n +$ _____$)($_____$+$ _____$)$
$=$ _____ $+$ _____ $+$ _____ $+$ _____
$=$ _____ $+$ _____ $+$ _____

So, $7n^2 + 16n + 4 =$ _____

Look at the trinomial $7n^2 + 16n + 4$ and its factored form $(7n + 2)(1n + 2)$.
In the trinomial:
The 1st term is $7n^2$, and the factors of 7 are 1 and 7.
The 3rd term is 4, and the factors of 4 are 2 and 2.
We write one pair of factors next to the other.
When we multiply the numbers as shown then add, we get:
$(1 \times 2) + (7 \times 2) = 2 + 14$

$\qquad = 16$ ◄— This is the coefficient of n in the trinomial.

We can use this strategy to find the terms for the binomial factors of any trinomial.
For example, to factor $5x^2 + 17x + 6$:
The 1st term is $5x^2$, and the factors of 5 are 1 and 5.
The 3rd term is 6, and its factors are 1 and 6; 2 and 3.
Write each pair of factors of 6 next to a pair of factors of 5.

Multiply, then add:
$(1 \times 6) + (5 \times 1)$ $(1 \times 1) + (5 \times 6)$ $(1 \times 3) + (5 \times 2)$ $(1 \times 2) + (5 \times 3)$
$= 6 + 5$ $= 1 + 30$ $= 3 + 10$ $= 2 + 15$
$= 11$ $= 31$ $= 13$ $= 17$ ◄— This is the
                                                                                                                        coefficient
                                                                                                                        of x.

So, the factors of 5 are 1 and 5; and the factors of 6 are 3 and 2.

The coefficient of x and $\longrightarrow$ 1   3
the constant term in   5   2 $\longleftarrow$ The coefficient of x
one binomial   and the constant term
                                      in the other binomial

The binomial factors are $(1x + 3)(5x + 2)$.
Then, $5x^2 + 17x + 6 = (x + 3)(5x + 2)$

Example 4 | Factoring a Trinomial with Negative Terms

Factor each trinomial.

a) $7x^2 + 18x - 9$ **b)** $6n^2 - 7n + 2$

Solution

a) $7x^2 + 18x - 9$

$$7x^2 + 18x - 9$$

The 1st term is $7x^2$.   The 3rd term is -9.
The factors of 7 are: The factors of -9 are:
1 and 7   1 and -9; -1 and 9; 3 and -3

Write each pair of factors of -9 next to a pair of factors of 7. Find the products.

1   1 $[1 \times (-9)] + (7 \times 1) = -9 + 7$
7   -9 $= -2$

1   -9 $(1 \times 1) + [7 \times (-9)] = 1 - 63$
7   1 $= -62$

We stop when we get 18 as the sum of the products.

1   -1 $(1 \times 9) + [7 \times (-1)] = 9 - 7$
7   9 $= 2$

1   9 $[1 \times (-1)] + (7 \times 9) = -1 + 63$
7   -1 $= 62$

1   3 $[1 \times (-3)] + (7 \times 3) = -3 + 21$
7   -3 $= 18$ $\longleftarrow$ This is the coefficient of x.

So, the factors of 7 are 1 and 7; and the factors of -9 are 3 and -3.
The binomial factors are $(1x + 3)(7x - 3)$.
Then, $7x^2 + 18x - 9 = (x + 3)(7x - 3)$

b) $6n^2 - 7n + 2$

$$6n^2 - 7n + 2$$

The 1st term is $6n^2$.
The factors of 6 are:
1 and 6; 2 and 3

The 3rd term is 2.
The factors of 2 are:
-1 and -2

> *The 2nd term of the trinomial is negative, and the 3rd term is positive, so write only the negative factors of 2.*

Write the pair of factors of 2 next to each pair of factors of 6. Find the products.

1   -1
6   -2

$[1 \times (-2)] + [6 \times (-1)] = -2 - 6$
$= -8$

> *We stop when we get -7 as the sum of the products.*

1   -2
6   -1

$[1 \times (-1)] + [6 \times (-2)] = -1 - 12$
$= -13$

2   -1
3   -2

$[2 \times (-2)] + [3 \times (-1)] = -4 - 3$
$= -7$ ← This is the coefficient of n.

So, the factors of 6 are 2 and 3;
and the factors of 2 are -1 and -2.
The binomial factors are $(2n - 1)(3n - 2)$.
Then, $6n^2 - 7n + 2 = (2n - 1)(3n - 2)$

> *You can check the binomial factors by expanding to see if you get the original trinomial.*

Check

1. Factor this trinomial: $8m^2 - 2m - 3$

The 1st term is $8m^2$.
The factors of ____ are:
1 and ____; 2 and ____

The 3rd term is -3.
The factors of ____ are:
1 and ____; -1 and ____

Write each pair of factors of ____ next to a pair of factors of ____. Find the products.

$[\_\_ \times (\_\_)] + (\_\_ \times \_\_) = \_\_ + \_\_$
$= \_\_$

$(\_\_ \times \_\_) + [\_\_ \times (\_\_)] = \_\_ - \_\_$
$= \_\_$

$(\_\_ \times \_\_) + [\_\_ \times (\_\_)] = \_\_ - \_\_$
$= \_\_$

> *Stop when you get ____ as the sum of the products.*

$[\_\_ \times (\_\_)] + [\_\_ \times \_\_] = \_\_ + \_\_$
$= \_\_$

So, the factors of ____ are ____ and ____; and the factors of ____ are ____ and ____.
The binomial factors are $(\_\_ + \_\_)(\_\_ - \_\_)$.
So, $8m^2 - 2m - 3 =$ _____

1. Expand, then simplify.

a) $(3x + 5)(x + 1)$

Use algebra tiles to make a rectangle.

Use ____ 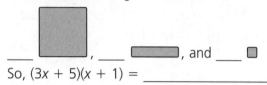 and ____ ▢ for the length.

Use ____ ⬛ and ____ ▢ for the width.

To make the rectangle, use these tiles:

____ ⬛ , ____ ▭ , and ____ ▢

So, $(3x + 5)(x + 1) =$ _____

Sketch the tiles. Label the length and width.

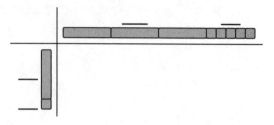

b) $(4w - 3)(5w - 9)$

Use a rectangle diagram.

Sketch a rectangle with length _____ and width _____.

Divide the rectangle into smaller rectangles.

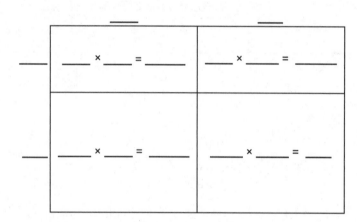

Add the products in the smaller rectangles.

$(4w - 3)(5w - 9) =$ _____ − _____ − _____ + _____

$=$ _____

2. Expand, then simplify.

a) $(-2v + 6)(5v - 3) = (-2v)(_____) + 6(_____)$

$= (-2v)(\_\_\_\_) + (-2v)(\_\_\_\_) + 6(\_\_\_\_) + 6(\_\_\_\_)$

$=$ _____ + _____ + _____ − _____

$=$ _____

b) $(7c - 8)(-4c + 1) =$ _____

$=$ _____

3. Factor each trinomial.

a) $2x^2 + 15x + 7$

Use algebra tiles to factor.   Sketch the tiles.

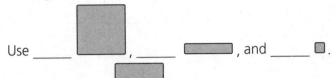

Use _____ ⬛ , _____ ▭ , and _____ ▫ .

Start with _____ ⬛ .

Arrange _____ ▭ so there is space to fit _____ ▫ .

So, $2x^2 + 15x + 7 =$ _____

b) $5m^2 + 16m + 3$

$$5m^2 + 16m + 3$$

The 1st term is _____.   The 3rd term is _____.
Its factors are: _____ × _____   Its factors are: _____ × _____

Write all possible binomials.
Multiply to find which product has the term $16m$.

(_____ + _____)(_____ + _____)   (_____ + _____)(_____ + _____)

= _____ + _____ + _____ + _____   = _____ + _____ + _____ + _____

= _____ + _____ + _____   = _____ + _____ + _____

So, $5m^2 + 16m + 3 =$ _____

4. Factor each trinomial.

a) $3x^2 - 5x - 2$

$$3x^2 - 5x - 2$$

The 1st term is _____.   The 3rd term is _____.
The factors of _____ are: The factors of _____ are:
_____ and _____   _____ and _____ ; _____ and _____

Write each pair of factors of _____ next to the pair of factors of _____.
Find the products.

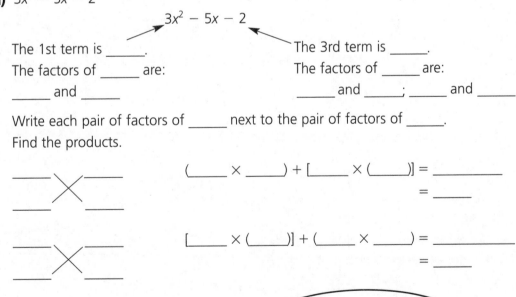

(_____ × _____) + [_____ × (_____)] = _____

= _____

[_____ × (_____)] + (_____ × _____) = _____

= _____

Stop when you get _____ as the sum of the products.

_____ ⟍⟋ _____   [_____ × (_____)] + (_____ × _____) = _____
_____ ⟋⟍ _____   = _____

_____ ⟍⟋ _____   (_____ × _____) + [_____ × (_____)] = _____
_____ ⟋⟍ _____   = _____

So, the factors of _____ are _____ and _____; and the factors of _____ are _____ and _____.

The binomial factors are: _____

So, $3x^2 - 5x - 2 =$ _____

b) $2x^2 - 13x + 15$

$$2x^2 - 13x + 15$$

The 1st term is _____.   The 3rd term is _____.
The factors of _____ are: The factors of _____ are:
_____ and _____   _____ and _____; _____ and _____

Write each pair of factors of _____ next to the pair of
factors of _____.

Find the products.

The 2nd term of the trinomial is
_____, and the 3rd term is
_____, so write only the
_____ factors of _____.

Stop when you get
_____ as the sum of
the products.

So, the factors of _____ are _____ and _____;
and the factors of _____ are _____ and _____.
The binomial factors are: _____

So, $2x^2 - 13x + 15 =$ _____

CHECKPOINT 2

Can you...

- find the common factor of a binomial or a trinomial?
- multiply two binomials?
- factor trinomials?

3.3 **1.** Factor each polynomial by dividing.

   a) $15q + 25$

   Factor each term of the binomial.
   $15q =$ ____ × ____ × ____
   $25 =$ ____ × ____
   The GCF is ____.
   Divide each term of the binomial by ____.

   $$\frac{15q + 25}{\rule{2em}{0.4pt}} = \frac{}{\rule{3em}{0.4pt}} + \frac{}{\rule{3em}{0.4pt}}$$

   $$= \rule{2em}{0.4pt} + \rule{2em}{0.4pt}$$

   So, $15q + 25 =$ _____

   b) $18s^2 - 24s - 6$

   Factor each term of the trinomial.
   $18s^2 =$ ____ × ____ × ____ × ____ × ____
   $24s =$ ____ × ____ × ____ × ____ × ____
   $6 =$ ____ × ____
   The GCF is ____ × ____ = ____.
   Divide each term of the trinomial by ____.

   $$\frac{18s^2 - 24s - 6}{\rule{2em}{0.4pt}} = \frac{}{\rule{3em}{0.4pt}} - \frac{}{\rule{3em}{0.4pt}} - \frac{}{\rule{3em}{0.4pt}}$$

   $$= \rule{2em}{0.4pt} - \rule{2em}{0.4pt} - \rule{2em}{0.4pt}$$

   So, $18s^2 - 24s - 6 =$ _____

3.5 **2.** Expand, then simplify: $(t - 9)(t + 5)$

   Use the distributive property.
   $(t - 9)(t + 5) = t(\rule{4em}{0.4pt}) - 9(\rule{4em}{0.4pt})$
   $ = t(\rule{2em}{0.4pt}) + t(\rule{2em}{0.4pt}) - 9(\rule{2em}{0.4pt}) - 9(\rule{2em}{0.4pt})$
   $ = \rule{2em}{0.4pt} + \rule{2em}{0.4pt} - \rule{2em}{0.4pt} - \rule{2em}{0.4pt}$
   $ = \rule{5em}{0.4pt}$

3. Factor $x^2 - 5x - 6$.

The sum of the factors is _____.
The product of the factors is _____.

Factors of _____	Sum of the factors		
_____ × (_____)	_____ − _____ = _____	_____
(_____) × _____	_____ + _____ = _____	_____
_____ × (_____)	_____ − _____ = _____	_____
(_____) × _____	_____ + _____ = _____	_____

So, $x^2 - 5x - 6 =$ _____

3.6 **4.** Expand, then simplify.

$(3a - 5)(-2a + 6) = 3a(\underline{\hspace{2cm}}) - 5(\underline{\hspace{2cm}})$
$= 3a(\underline{\hspace{1cm}}) + 3a(\underline{\hspace{1cm}}) - 5(\underline{\hspace{1cm}}) - 5(\underline{\hspace{1cm}})$
$= \underline{\hspace{1cm}} + \underline{\hspace{1cm}} + \underline{\hspace{1cm}} - \underline{\hspace{1cm}}$
$= \underline{\hspace{4cm}}$

5. Factor $3u^2 - 11u + 6$.

$$3u^2 - 11u + 6$$

The 1st term is _____.   The 3rd term is _____.
The factors of _____ are: The factors of _____ are:
_____ and _____   _____ and _____;
                                  _____ and _____

Write only the _____ factors of __.

Write each pair of factors of _____ next to the pair of factors of _____.
Find the products.

_____ ╳ _____   [_____ × (_____)] + [_____ × (_____)] = _____ − _____
                                                              = _____

_____ ╳ _____   [_____ × (_____)] + [_____ × (_____)] = _____ − _____
                                                              = _____

_____ ╳ _____   [_____ × (_____)] + [_____ × (_____)] = _____ − _____
                                                              = _____

_____ ╳ _____   [_____ × (_____)] + [_____ × (_____)] = _____ − _____
                                                              = _____

The binomial factors are (_____ − _____)(_____ − _____).
So, $3u^2 - 11u + 6 =$ _____

Stop when you get _____ as the sum of the products.

▶ 3.7 Multiplying Polynomials

FOCUS Multiply polynomials.

We used the distributive property to multiply two binomials.
We can use the same property to multiply two polynomials.

Example 1 | Multiplying Polynomials with Positive Terms

Expand, then simplify and verify.

a) $(3n)(2n^2 + 4n + 5)$

b) $(5p + 2)(3p^2 + 2p + 4)$

Solution

a) $(3n)(2n^2 + 4n + 5)$ Multiply each term in the trinomial by $3n$.

$= 3n(2n^2) + 3n(4n) + 3n(5)$

$= (3 \times 2 \times n \times n^2) + (3 \times 4 \times n \times n) + (3 \times 5 \times n)$

> *Multiply the numbers, then multiply the variables.*

$= 6n^3 + 12n^2 + 15n$

Verify. Substitute $n = 2$.

Left side

$(3n)(2n^2 + 4n + 5)$

$= (3 \times 2)(2 \times 2^2 + 4 \times 2 + 5)$

$= (6)(8 + 8 + 5)$

$= (6)(21)$

$= 126$

Right side

$6n^3 + 12n^2 + 15n$

$= 6 \times 2^3 + 12 \times 2^2 + 15 \times 2$

$= 48 + 48 + 30$

$= 126$

> *We could choose any value for n. We chose 2 because it is easy to work with.*

The numbers match, so the product is likely correct.

b) $(5p + 2)(3p^2 + 2p + 4)$

$= 5p(3p^2 + 2p + 4) + 2(3p^2 + 2p + 4)$

$= 5p(3p^2) + 5p(2p) + 5p(4) + 2(3p^2) + 2(2p) + 2(4)$

$= 15p^3 + 10p^2 + 20p + 6p^2 + 4p + 8$

$= 15p^3 + 10p^2 + 6p^2 + 20p + 4p + 8$

$= 15p^3 + 16p^2 + 24p + 8$

> *Multiply each term in the trinomial by each term in the binomial.*

> *Group like terms, then combine them.*

Verify. Substitute $p = 2$.

Left side

$(5p + 2)(3p^2 + 2p + 4)$

$= (5 \times 2 + 2)(3 \times 2^2 + 2 \times 2 + 4)$

$= (10 + 2)(12 + 4 + 4)$

$= (12)(20)$

$= 240$

Right side

$15p^3 + 16p^2 + 24p + 8$

$= 15 \times 2^3 + 16 \times 2^2 + 24 \times 2 + 8$

$= 120 + 64 + 48 + 8$

$= 240$

The numbers match, so the product is likely correct.

Check

1. Expand, then simplify and verify.

$(3z + 4)(2z^2 + 4z + 7) = 3z(2z^2 + 4z + 7) + 4(2z^2 + 4z + 7)$

$= 3z(\underline{\hspace{1cm}}) + 3z(\underline{\hspace{1cm}}) + 3z(\underline{\hspace{1cm}}) + 4(\underline{\hspace{1cm}}) + 4(\underline{\hspace{1cm}}) + 4(\underline{\hspace{1cm}})$

$= \underline{\hspace{0.5cm}}z^3 + \underline{\hspace{0.5cm}}z^2 + \underline{\hspace{0.5cm}}z + \underline{\hspace{0.5cm}}z^2 + \underline{\hspace{0.5cm}}z + \underline{\hspace{0.5cm}}$

$= \underline{\hspace{0.5cm}}z^3 + \underline{\hspace{0.5cm}}z^2 + \underline{\hspace{0.5cm}}z^2 + \underline{\hspace{0.5cm}}z + \underline{\hspace{0.5cm}}z + \underline{\hspace{0.5cm}}$

$= \underline{\hspace{0.5cm}}z^3 + \underline{\hspace{0.5cm}}z^2 + \underline{\hspace{0.5cm}}z + \underline{\hspace{0.5cm}}$

Verify. Substitute $z = 2$.

Left side

$(3z + 4)(2z^2 + 4z + 7)$

$= (\underline{\hspace{0.5cm}} \times 2 + \underline{\hspace{0.5cm}})(\underline{\hspace{0.5cm}} \times 2^2 +$
$\underline{\hspace{0.5cm}} \times 2 + \underline{\hspace{0.5cm}})$

$= (\underline{\hspace{0.5cm}} + \underline{\hspace{0.5cm}})(\underline{\hspace{0.5cm}} + \underline{\hspace{0.5cm}} + \underline{\hspace{0.5cm}})$

$= (\underline{\hspace{0.5cm}})(\underline{\hspace{0.5cm}})$

$= \underline{\hspace{1cm}}$

Right side

$\underline{\hspace{0.5cm}}z^3 + \underline{\hspace{0.5cm}}z^2 + \underline{\hspace{0.5cm}}z + \underline{\hspace{0.5cm}}$

$= \underline{\hspace{0.5cm}} \times 2^3 + \underline{\hspace{0.5cm}} \times 2^2 +$
$\underline{\hspace{0.5cm}} \times 2 + \underline{\hspace{0.5cm}}$

$= \underline{\hspace{0.5cm}} + \underline{\hspace{0.5cm}} + \underline{\hspace{0.5cm}} + \underline{\hspace{0.5cm}}$

$= \underline{\hspace{0.5cm}}$

The numbers match, so the product is likely correct.

Example 2	Multiplying Polynomials with Negative Terms

Expand, then simplify and verify.

a) $(-5p)(3p^2 + 2p - 4)$

b) $(4n - 2)(-2n^2 - 4n - 5)$

Solution

a) $(-5p)(3p^2 + 2p - 4)$

$= (-5p)(3p^2) + (-5p)(2p) + (-5p)(-4)$

$= [(-5) \times 3 \times p \times p^2] + [(-5) \times 2 \times p \times p] + [(-5) \times (-4) \times p]$

$= -15p^3 + (-10p^2) + (20p)$

$= -15p^3 - 10p^2 + 20p$

> Multiply each term in the trinomial by $-5p$.

> As you multiply, check the signs.

Verify. Substitute $p = 2$.

Left side

$(-5p)(3p^2 + 2p - 4)$

$= ((-5) \times 2)(3 \times 2^2 + 2 \times 2 - 4)$

$= (-10)(12 + 4 - 4)$

$= (-10)(12)$

$= -120$

Right side

$-15p^3 - 10p^2 + 20p$

$= (-15) \times 2^3 - 10 \times 2^2 + 20 \times 2$

$= -120 - 40 + 40$

$= -120$

The numbers match, so the product is likely correct.

 978-0-321-61066-9

b) $(4n - 2)(-2n^2 - 4n - 5)$

$= 4n(-2n^2 - 4n - 5) - 2(-2n^2 - 4n - 5)$

$= 4n(-2n^2) + 4n(-4n) + 4n(-5) - 2(-2n^2) - 2(-4n) - 2(-5)$

$= -8n^3 + (-16n^2) + (-20n) - (-4n^2) - (-8n) - (-10)$

$= -8n^3 - 16n^2 - 20n + 4n^2 + 8n + 10$

$= -8n^3 - 16n^2 + 4n^2 - 20n + 8n + 10$

$= -8n^3 - 12n^2 - 12n + 10$

Multiply each term in the trinomial by each term in the binomial.

Verify. Substitute $n = 2$.

Left side

$(4n - 2)(-2n^2 - 4n - 5)$

$= (4 \times 2 - 2)((-2) \times 2^2 - 4 \times 2 - 5)$

$= (8 - 2)(-8 - 8 - 5)$

$= (6)(-21)$

$= -126$

Right side

$-8n^3 - 12n^2 - 12n + 10$

$= (-8) \times 2^3 - 12 \times 2^2 - 12 \times 2 + 10$

$= -64 - 48 - 24 + 10$

$= -126$

The numbers match, so the product is likely correct.

Check

1. Expand, then simplify and verify.

$(3n - 1)(4n^2 - 6n - 2) = 3n(\underline{\hspace{3cm}}) - 1(\underline{\hspace{2cm}})$

$= 3n(\underline{\hspace{0.6cm}}) + 3n(\underline{\hspace{0.6cm}}) + 3n(\underline{\hspace{0.6cm}}) - 1(\underline{\hspace{0.6cm}}) - 1(\underline{\hspace{0.6cm}}) - 1(\underline{\hspace{0.6cm}})$

$= \underline{\hspace{0.6cm}}n^3 + (\underline{\hspace{0.6cm}}n^2) + (\underline{\hspace{0.6cm}}n) - (\underline{\hspace{0.6cm}}n^2) - (\underline{\hspace{0.6cm}}n) - (\underline{\hspace{0.6cm}})$

$= \underline{\hspace{0.6cm}}n^3 - \underline{\hspace{0.6cm}}n^2 - \underline{\hspace{0.6cm}}n - \underline{\hspace{0.6cm}}n^2 + \underline{\hspace{0.6cm}}n + \underline{\hspace{0.6cm}}$

$= \underline{\hspace{0.6cm}}n^3 - \underline{\hspace{0.6cm}}n^2 - \underline{\hspace{0.6cm}}n^2 - \underline{\hspace{0.6cm}}n + \underline{\hspace{0.6cm}}n + \underline{\hspace{0.6cm}}$

$= \underline{\hspace{1.2cm}} - \underline{\hspace{1.2cm}} + \underline{\hspace{1.2cm}}$

Verify. Substitute $n = 2$.

Left side

$(3n - 1)(4n^2 - 6n - 2)$

$= (\underline{\hspace{0.6cm}} \times 2 - \underline{\hspace{0.6cm}})(\underline{\hspace{0.6cm}} \times 2^2 -$

$\underline{\hspace{0.6cm}} \times 2 - \underline{\hspace{0.6cm}})$

$= (\underline{\hspace{0.6cm}} - \underline{\hspace{0.6cm}})(\underline{\hspace{0.6cm}} - \underline{\hspace{0.6cm}} - \underline{\hspace{0.6cm}})$

$= (\underline{\hspace{0.6cm}})(\underline{\hspace{0.6cm}})$

$= \underline{\hspace{1.2cm}}$

Right side

$\underline{\hspace{1cm}} - \underline{\hspace{1cm}} + \underline{\hspace{1cm}}$

$= \underline{\hspace{0.6cm}} \times 2^3 - \underline{\hspace{0.6cm}} \times 2^2 + \underline{\hspace{0.6cm}}$

$= \underline{\hspace{0.6cm}} - \underline{\hspace{0.6cm}} + \underline{\hspace{0.6cm}}$

$= \underline{\hspace{0.6cm}}$

The numbers match, so the product is likely correct.

Practice

1. Expand, then simplify.

a) $(5n)(3n^2 + 2n + 1)$

$= 5n(\underline{\hspace{0.8cm}}) + 5n(\underline{\hspace{0.8cm}}) + 5n(\underline{\hspace{0.8cm}})$

$= \underline{\hspace{3cm}}$

Multiply each term in the $\underline{\hspace{2cm}}$ by $\underline{\hspace{0.8cm}}$.

b) $(4b + 3)(2b^2 + 4b + 3)$

$= 4b(\underline{\hspace{3cm}}) + 3(\underline{\hspace{3cm}})$

$= 4b(\underline{\hspace{1cm}}) + 4b(\underline{\hspace{1cm}}) + 4b(\underline{\hspace{1cm}}) + 3(\underline{\hspace{1cm}}) + 3(\underline{\hspace{1cm}}) + 3(\underline{\hspace{1cm}})$

$= \underline{\hspace{0.7cm}}b^3 + \underline{\hspace{0.7cm}}b^2 + \underline{\hspace{0.7cm}}b + \underline{\hspace{0.7cm}}b^2 + \underline{\hspace{0.7cm}}b + \underline{\hspace{0.7cm}}$

$= \underline{\hspace{0.7cm}}b^3 + \underline{\hspace{0.7cm}}b^2 + \underline{\hspace{0.7cm}}b^2 + \underline{\hspace{0.7cm}}b + \underline{\hspace{0.7cm}}b + \underline{\hspace{0.7cm}}$

$= \underline{\hspace{5cm}}$

2. Expand, then simplify. Verify for parts a and b.

a) $(2n)(-2n^2 + 4n - 5) = 2n(\underline{\hspace{1cm}}) + 2n(\underline{\hspace{1cm}}) + 2n(\underline{\hspace{1cm}})$

$\qquad\qquad\qquad\qquad\qquad = \underline{\hspace{4cm}}$

Verify. Substitute $n = 2$.

Left side

$\qquad(2n)(-2n^2 + 4n - 5)$

$= \underline{\hspace{5cm}}$

$= \underline{\hspace{4cm}}$

$= \underline{\hspace{2.5cm}}$

$= \underline{\hspace{1.5cm}}$

Right side

$\underline{\hspace{6cm}}$

$= \underline{\hspace{6cm}}$

$= \underline{\hspace{5cm}}$

$= \underline{\hspace{1.5cm}}$

The numbers match, so the product is likely correct.

b) $(4b - 5)(b^2 - 7b + 8)$

$= 4b(\underline{\hspace{3cm}}) - 5(\underline{\hspace{3cm}})$

$= 4b(\underline{\hspace{1cm}}) + 4b(\underline{\hspace{1.5cm}}) + 4b(\underline{\hspace{1cm}}) - 5(\underline{\hspace{1cm}}) - 5(\underline{\hspace{1cm}}) - 5(\underline{\hspace{1cm}})$

$= \underline{\hspace{0.7cm}}b^3 - \underline{\hspace{0.7cm}}b^2 + \underline{\hspace{0.7cm}}b - \underline{\hspace{0.7cm}}b^2 + \underline{\hspace{0.7cm}}b - \underline{\hspace{0.7cm}}$

$= \underline{\hspace{1cm}} - \underline{\hspace{1cm}} - \underline{\hspace{1cm}} + \underline{\hspace{1cm}} + \underline{\hspace{1cm}} - \underline{\hspace{1cm}}$

$= \underline{\hspace{5cm}}$

Verify. Substitute $b = 2$.

Left side

$\qquad(4b - 5)(b^2 - 7b + 8)$

$= \underline{\hspace{5cm}}$

$= \underline{\hspace{4cm}}$

$= \underline{\hspace{2.5cm}}$

$= \underline{\hspace{1.5cm}}$

Right side

$\underline{\hspace{6cm}}$

$= \underline{\hspace{6cm}}$

$= \underline{\hspace{5cm}}$

$= \underline{\hspace{1.5cm}}$

The numbers match, so the product is likely correct.

c) $(-4y + 3)(4y^2 + 3y - 7)$

$= \underline{\hspace{5cm}}$

▶ 3.8 Factoring Special Polynomials

FOCUS Factor special polynomials.

When we multiply a binomial by itself, we *square* the binomial.

There are patterns in the terms.

$(a + 4)^2 = (a + 4)(a + 4)$
$= a^2 + 4a + 4a + 16$
$= a^2 + 8a + 16$

$(\boldsymbol{a} + \boldsymbol{4})^2 = a^2 \quad + 8a \quad + 16$
$\quad\quad\quad\quad \uparrow \quad\quad \uparrow \quad\quad \uparrow$
$\quad\quad\quad\quad (\boldsymbol{a})^2 \quad 2(\boldsymbol{4})(\boldsymbol{a}) \quad (\boldsymbol{4})^2$

$(t - 3)^2 = (t - 3)(t - 3)$
$= t^2 - 3t - 3t + 9$
$= t^2 - 6t + 9$

$(\boldsymbol{t} - \boldsymbol{3})^2 = t^2 \quad - 6t \quad + 9$
$\quad\quad\quad\quad \uparrow \quad\quad \uparrow \quad\quad \uparrow$
$\quad\quad\quad\quad (\boldsymbol{t})^2 \quad 2(\boldsymbol{-3})(\boldsymbol{t}) \quad (\boldsymbol{-3})^2$

$(5n + 3)^2 = (5n + 3)(5n + 3)$
$= 25n^2 + 15n + 15n + 9$
$= 25n^2 + 30n + 9$

$(\boldsymbol{5n} + \boldsymbol{3})^2 = 25n^2 \quad + 30n \quad + 9$
$\quad\quad\quad\quad\quad \uparrow \quad\quad \uparrow \quad\quad \uparrow$
$\quad\quad\quad\quad\quad (\boldsymbol{5n})^2 \quad 2(\boldsymbol{3})(\boldsymbol{5n}) \quad (\boldsymbol{3})^2$

$(3a - 4)^2 = (3a - 4)(3a - 4)$
$= 9a^2 - 12a - 12a + 16$
$= 9a^2 - 24a + 16$
$\quad\quad\quad \uparrow$

$(\boldsymbol{3a} - \boldsymbol{4})^2 = 9a^2 \quad -24a \quad + 16$
$\quad\quad\quad\quad\quad \uparrow \quad\quad \uparrow \quad\quad \uparrow$
$\quad\quad\quad\quad\quad (\boldsymbol{3a})^2 \quad 2(\boldsymbol{-4})(\boldsymbol{3a}) \quad (\boldsymbol{-4})^2$

Each trinomial above is a **perfect square trinomial**.

We can use these patterns to factor perfect square trinomials.

Example 1 | Factoring Perfect Square Trinomials

Factor each perfect square trinomial.

a) $w^2 - 14w + 49$

b) $25n^2 + 20n + 4$

Solution

a) $w^2 - 14w + 49$
The 2nd term is negative,
so the factors of 49 are negative.
$w^2 - 14w + 49$
$\uparrow \quad\quad\quad \uparrow$
$(w)^2 \quad\quad (-7)^2$
So, $w^2 - 14w + 49 = (w - 7)(w - 7)$
$\quad\quad\quad\quad\quad\quad = (w - 7)^2$

b) $25n^2 + 20n + 4$
The 2nd term is positive,
so the factors of 4 are positive.
$25n^2 + 20n + 4$
$\uparrow \quad\quad\quad \uparrow$
$(5n)^2 \quad\quad (2)^2$
So, $25n^2 + 20n + 4 = (5n + 2)(5n + 2)$
$\quad\quad\quad\quad\quad\quad = (5n + 2)^2$

You can expand to check the factors.

Check

1. Factor each perfect square trinomial.

   a) $r^2 + 6r + 9$

   The 2nd term is _____,

   so the factors of 9 are _____.

   $$r^2 + 6r + 9$$

   ↑   ↑

   (___)²   (___)²

   So, $r^2 + 6r + 9$

   = (___ + ___)(___ + ___)

   = (___ + ___)²

   b) $9m^2 - 12m + 4$

   The 2nd term is _____,

   so the factors of ___ are _____.

   $$9m^2 - 12m + 4$$

   ↑   ↑

   (___)²   (___)²

   So, $9m^2 - 12m + 4 = $ _____

   = (_____)²

All the binomial products you have seen so far produce trinomials.

There are special binomial products that produce binomials.

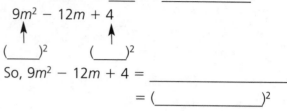

There are patterns in the terms.

$(a + 4)(a - 4) = a^2 - 4a + 4a - 16$
$\qquad\qquad = a^2 - 16$

$\boldsymbol{(a + 4)(a - 4) = a^2 - 16}$

$\qquad\qquad\quad ↑ \qquad ↑$

$\qquad\qquad (\boldsymbol{a})^2 \ (\boldsymbol{4})^2$

$(t + 3)(t - 3) = t^2 - 3t + 3t - 9$
$\qquad\qquad = t^2 - 9$

$\boldsymbol{(t + 3)(t - 3) = t^2 - 9}$

$\qquad\qquad\quad ↑ \qquad ↑$

$\qquad\qquad (\boldsymbol{t})^2 \ (\boldsymbol{3})^2$

$(5n + 3)(5n - 3) = 25n^2 - 15n + 15n - 9$
$\qquad\qquad\qquad = 25n^2 - 9$

$\boldsymbol{(5n + 3)(5n - 3) = 25n^2 - 9}$

$\qquad\qquad\qquad ↑ \qquad ↑$

$\qquad\qquad (\boldsymbol{5n})^2 \ (\boldsymbol{3})^2$

$(3a + 4)(3a - 4) = 9a^2 - 12a + 12a - 16$
$\qquad\qquad\qquad = 9a^2 - 16$

$\boldsymbol{(3a + 4)(3a - 4) = 9a^2 - 16}$

$\qquad\qquad\qquad ↑ \qquad ↑$

$\qquad\qquad (\boldsymbol{3a})^2 \ (\boldsymbol{4})^2$

Each binomial above is a **difference of squares**.

We can use these patterns to factor a difference of squares.

Example 2 | Factoring a Difference of Squares

Factor each difference of squares.

a) $x^2 - 64$

b) $4v^2 - 49$

Solution

a) $x^2 - 64$

Write 64 as a perfect square:

$64 = 8^2$

$x^2 - 64 = x^2 - 8^2$

$\qquad\qquad = (x + 8)(x - 8)$

b) $4v^2 - 49$

Write $4v^2$ as a perfect square:

$4v^2 = 2v \times 2v$, or $(2v)^2$

Write 49 as a perfect square: $49 = 7^2$

$4v^2 - 49 = (2v)^2 - 7^2$

$\qquad\qquad = (2v + 7)(2v - 7)$

Check

1. Factor each difference of squares.

   a) $x^2 - 100$

   Write 100 as a perfect square:

   $100 = $ _____

   $x^2 - 100$

   $= $ _____ $- $ _____

   $= ($ _____ $+ $ _____ $)($ _____ $- $ _____ $)$

   b) $25h^2 - 81$

   Write $25h^2$ and 81 as perfect squares:

   $25h^2 = $ _____ $\times$ _____, or $($ _____ $)^2$

   $81 = $ _____

   $25h^2 - 81 = $ _____ $- $ _____

   $= $ _____

Practice

1. Factor each perfect square trinomial.

   a) $r^2 - 18r + 81$

   The 2nd term is _____,

   so the factors of 81 are _____.

   $r^2 - 18r + 81$

   $($ _____ $)^2$ $($ _____ $)^2$

   So, $r^2 - 18r + 81$

   $= ($ _____ $- $ _____ $)($ _____ $- $ _____ $)$

   $= ($ _____ $- $ _____ $)^2$

   b) $25b^2 + 40b + 16$

   The 2nd term is _____,

   so the factors of _____ are _____.

   $25b^2 + 40b + 16$

   $($ _____ $)^2$ $($ _____ $)^2$

   So, $25b^2 + 40b + 16$

   $= $ _____

   $= ($ _____ $)^2$

2. Factor each difference of squares.

   a) $x^2 - 36$

   Write _____ as a perfect square:

   _____ $= $ _____

   $x^2 - 36 = $ _____ $- $ _____

   $= $ _____

   b) $9w^2 - 1$

   Write _____ and _____ as perfect squares:

   _____ $= $ _____ $\times$ _____, or $($ _____ $)^2$

   _____ $= $ _____

   $9w^2 - 1 = $ _____ $- $ _____

   $= $ _____

3. Factor.

   a) $100c^2 - 49$

   This is a _____.

   $100c^2 - 49 = $ _____

   b) $64m^2 - 16m + 1$

   This is a _____.

   $64m^2 - 16m + 1$

   $($ _____ $)^2$ $($ _____ $)^2$

   So, $64m^2 - 16m + 1$

   $= $ _____

   $= ($ _____ $)^2$

Chapter 3 Puzzle

Match and Decipher

Cut out each puzzle piece. Arrange the pieces to make a 4-by-4 square.
The expressions on adjacent sides must be equal.
Follow the instructions that are revealed when you complete the puzzle.

$(4x - 7)(4x + 7)$ **A** $(-2x)(2x + 1)$ — left: $(3x + 2)(x + 2)$	$x^2 - 10x + 25$ left: $4x^2 + 12x + 5$ **A** $4x^2 + 12x + 5$ — right: $(-4x)(x - 2)$	$-4x^2 - 2x$ **B** $6x + 12$ — right: $-4(2x - 1)$	$3(x - 2)$ left: $(1 + x)(1 - x)$ **D** right: $(2x + 1)(2x + 5)$
left: $(2x + 3)(2x - 3)$ **H** $(x + 3)(x + 4)$	**H** $16x^2 - 49$ — right: $(x + 4)(x - 2)$	$6(x + 2)$ **H** right: $x^2 - 1$	
$3x^2 + 8x + 4$ left: $-8x + 4$ **I** $3x - 6$ — right: $(2x - 1)(3x - 4)$	left: $(9 - x^2 + x)$ **M** $(3x - 4)^2$ — right: $4x^2 - 9$	$-15x^2 - 20x$ left: $3x^2 + 8x + 4$ **P** $(3x + 2)(x + 2)$ — right: $(x + 2)(x + 2)$	
$9x^2 - 24x + 16$ left: $x^2 + 4x + 4$ **P** $(x - 4)(x + 1)$ — right: $x^2 - 25$	$x^2 - 3x - 4$ left: $6x^2 - 11x + 4$ **R** $(x - 5)(x - 5)$ — right: $(2x + 3)(2x + 3)$	$3x^2 + 3x$ left: $4x^2 + 12x + 9$ **T** $(x + 3)(x + 1)$	
left: $x^2 + 2x - 8$ **U** $(-5x)(3x + 4)$ — right: $(x + 3)(x - 2)$	$x^2 + 4x + 3$ left: $-4x^2 + 8x$ **Y** 	$x^2 + 7x + 12$ left: $(x + 5)(x - 5)$ **Y** $3x(x + 1)$	

194 978-0-321-61066-9 Copyright © 2011 Pearson Canada Inc.

Skill	Description	Example
Write the prime factorization of a number.	Write the prime factors of a number as a product.	The prime factorization of 18 is: $2 \times 3 \times 3$, or 2×3^2
Find the greatest common factor (GCF) of two numbers.	List the factors of each number. Identify the greatest factor that is in both lists.	Find the GCF of 12 and 16: Factors of 12: 1, 2, 3, **4**, 6, 12 Factors of 16: 1, 2, **4**, 8, 16 The GCF of 12 and 16 is 4.
Find the least common multiple (LCM) of two numbers.	List multiples of each number. Identify the least multiple that is in both lists.	Find the LCM of 12 and 16: Multiples of 12: 12, 24, 36, **48**, 60, … Multiples of 16: 16, 32, **48**, 64, 80, … The LCM of 12 and 16 is 48.
Find the square root of a perfect square and the cube root of a perfect cube.	Group the prime factors.	Find $\sqrt{64}$: $64 = (2 \times 2 \times 2) \times (2 \times 2 \times 2)$ $\sqrt{64} = 2 \times 2 \times 2$, or 8 Find $\sqrt[3]{64}$: $64 = (2 \times 2) \times (2 \times 2) \times (2 \times 2)$ $\sqrt[3]{64} = 2 \times 2$, or 4
Factor polynomials with a common factor.	Find the GCF of the terms. Divide to find the other factor.	Factor $6n^2 - 18n$: The GCF of $6n^2$ and $18n$ is $6n$. $6n^2 - 18n = 6n(n - 3)$
Multiply polynomials.	Multiply each term in one polynomial by each term in the other polynomial.	Multiply $(b - 4)(2b + 3)$: $(b - 4)(2b + 3)$ $= b(2b + 3) - 4(2b + 3)$ $= 2b^2 + 3b - 8b - 12$ $= 2b^2 - 5b - 12$
Factor trinomials.	Factor the 1st and 3rd terms. Write the possible binomials.	Factor $x^2 + 4x + 3$: List factors of 3: (1, 3) $x^2 + 4x + 3 = (x + 1)(x + 3)$
Factor special polynomials.	Factor a difference of squares and a perfect square trinomial.	Factor $4a^2 - 9$: $4a^2 - 9 = (2a)^2 - 3^2$ $4a^2 - 9 = (2a + 3)(2a - 3)$ Factor $9m^2 + 24m + 16$: Write the 1st and 3rd terms as perfect squares. $9m^2 = (3m)^2$ and $16 = 4^2$ $9m^2 + 24m + 16 = (3m + 4)(3m + 4)$ $\qquad\qquad\qquad = (3m + 4)^2$

Chapter 3 Review

3.1 **1. a)** Draw a factor tree for 250. 250

   b) The prime factorization of 250 is:

   _____

2. Find the GCF of 20 and 45.

   Factors of 20   Factors of 45
   20 ÷ _____ = _____   45 ÷ _____ = _____
   20 ÷ _____ = _____   45 ÷ _____ = _____
   20 ÷ _____ = _____   45 ÷ _____ = _____

   Factors of 20: _____
   Factors of 45: _____
   The GCF of 20 and 45 is _____.

3. Find the LCM of 16 and 20.

   Multiples of 16: 16, _____
   Multiples of 20: 20, _____
   The LCM of 16 and 20 is _____.

3.2 **4.** Find $\sqrt{2025}$.   2025

   Use prime factorization.
   $2025 =$ _____ $\times$ _____ $\times$ _____ $\times$ _____ $\times$ _____ $\times$ _____
   $=$ (_____ $\times$ _____ $\times$ _____) $\times$ (_____ $\times$ _____ $\times$ _____)
   $=$ _____ $\times$ _____

   So, $\sqrt{2025} =$ _____

5. Find $\sqrt[3]{2744}$.   2744

   Use prime factorization.
   $2744 =$ _____ $\times$ _____ $\times$ _____ $\times$ _____ $\times$ _____ $\times$ _____
   $=$ (_____) $\times$ (_____) $\times$ (_____)
   $=$ _____ $\times$ _____ $\times$ _____

   So, $\sqrt[3]{2744} =$ _____

6. Use algebra tiles to factor $12p + 18$.

Model $12p + 18$ as a rectangle.
Since _____ is the GCF of 12 and 18, make _____ equal rows.
Sketch the tiles. Label the length and width.

The length of the rectangle is _____.
The width of the rectangle is _____.
So, $12p + 18 =$ _____

7. Use division to factor each polynomial.

a) $9x^2 - 12x$

Factor each term of the binomial.
$9x^2 =$ _____ $\times$ _____ $\times$ _____ $\times$ _____
$12x =$ _____ $\times$ _____ $\times$ _____ $\times$ _____
The GCF is _____ $\times$ _____ $=$ _____.
Divide each term of the binomial by _____.

$$\frac{9x^2 - 12x}{\rule{2cm}{0.4pt}} = \frac{\rule{2cm}{0.4pt}}{\rule{2cm}{0.4pt}} - \frac{\rule{2cm}{0.4pt}}{\rule{2cm}{0.4pt}}$$

$$= \rule{2cm}{0.4pt} - \rule{2cm}{0.4pt}$$

So, $9x^2 - 12x =$ _____

b) $-10m^2 - 15m + 5$

Factor each term of the trinomial.
$10m^2 =$ _____ $\times$ _____ $\times$ _____ $\times$ _____
$15m =$ _____ $\times$ _____ $\times$ _____
$5 =$ _____
The GCF is _____.
Divide each term of the trinomial by _____.

$$\frac{-10m^2 - 15m + 5}{\rule{2cm}{0.4pt}} = \frac{\rule{2cm}{0.4pt}}{\rule{2cm}{0.4pt}} - \frac{\rule{2cm}{0.4pt}}{\rule{2cm}{0.4pt}} + \frac{\rule{2cm}{0.4pt}}{\rule{2cm}{0.4pt}}$$

$$= \rule{4cm}{0.4pt}$$

So, $-10m^2 - 15m + 5 =$ _____

Remove -1 as a common factor.

_____ $=$ _____ (_____ $+$ _____ $-$ _____)

So, $-10m^2 - 15m + 5 =$ _____

3.5 **8. a)** Use a rectangle diagram to expand, then simplify $(c - 6)(c - 5)$.

Sketch a rectangle with length _____ and width _____.

Divide the rectangle into smaller rectangles.

Add the products from the smaller rectangles.

$(c - 6)(c - 5)$

$=$ _____ $-$ _____ $-$ _____ $+$ _____

$=$ _____

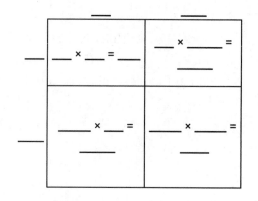

b) Use the distributive property to expand, then simplify $(h - 4)(h + 7)$.

$(h - 4)(h + 7) = h($ _____ $) - 4($ _____ $)$

$=$ _____

9. a) Use algebra tiles to factor $x^2 + 9x + 8$.

Use _____ ⬛ , _____ ▬ , and _____ ◾.

Arrange _____ ▬ beneath and

to the right of ⬛ , so there

is space to fit _____ ◾.

So, $x^2 + 9x + 8 =$ _____

Sketch the tiles.
Label the length and width.

b) Factor $x^2 - 8x + 15$.

The coefficient of x is _____, so the sum of the factors is _____.

The constant term is _____, so the product of the factors is _____.

Factors of _____	Sum of the factors
$(-1) \times$ _____	$-1 -$ _____ $=$ _____ _____
$(-3) \times$ _____	$-3 -$ _____ $=$ _____ _____

_____ is positive, so both its factors have the same sign. The x-term is _____, so both factors must be _____.

The factors of _____ for the binomials are _____ and _____.

So, $x^2 - 8x + 15 =$ _____

3.6 **10.** Expand, then simplify $(2x - 5)(3x + 6)$.

Use the distributive property.

$(2x - 5)(3x + 6) = 2x($ _____ $+$ _____ $) - 5($ _____ $+$ _____ $)$

$= 2x($ _____ $) +$ _____ $($ _____ $) - 5($ _____ $) -$ _____ $($ _____ $)$

$=$ _____ $+$ _____ $-$ _____ $-$ _____

$=$ _____

11. Use algebra tiles to factor $2x^2 + 11x + 5$.   Sketch the tiles.

Use _____ 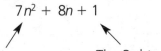 , _____ ▭ , and _____ ▪.
Arrange _____ ▭ beneath and to
the right of the rectangle formed

by _____ ▭ , so there is space to fit _____ ▪.
So, $2x^2 + 11x + 5 =$ _____

12. Factor each trinomial.

a) $7n^2 + 8n + 1$

$$7n^2 + 8n + 1$$

The 1st term is _____.   The 3rd term is _____.
The factors of _____ are: The factors of _____ are:
_____ and _____   _____ and _____

There is only 1 possible binomial product.

$7n^2 + 8n + 1 = ($_____ $+$ _____$)($_____ $+$ _____$)$

b) $3v^2 - 8v + 4$

$$3v^2 - 8v + 4$$

The 1st term is _____.   The 3rd term is _____.
The factors of _____ are: The factors of _____ are:
_____ and _____   _____ and _____ ;
                                    _____ and _____

> The 2nd term of the trinomial is _____, and the 3rd term is _____, so write only the _____ factors of _____.

Write each pair of factors of _____ next to the pair of factors of _____.
Find the products. Stop when you get _____ as the sum of the products.

_____ ✕ _____   [_____ ✕ (_____)] + [_____ ✕ (_____)] = _____ − _____
_____ ✕ _____   = _____

_____ ✕ _____   [_____ ✕ (_____)] + [_____ ✕ (_____)] = _____ − _____
_____ ✕ _____   = _____

_____ ✕ _____   [_____ ✕ (_____)] + [_____ ✕ (_____)] = _____ − _____
_____ ✕ _____   = _____

The binomial factors are $($_____ $-$ _____$)($_____ $-$ _____$)$.
So, $3v^2 - 8v + 4 =$ _____

13. Expand, then simplify and verify.

a) $(3m + 2)(2m^2 + m + 5)$

$= 3m(\underline{\hspace{1cm}} + \underline{\hspace{1cm}} + \underline{\hspace{1cm}}) + 2(\underline{\hspace{1cm}} + \underline{\hspace{1cm}} + \underline{\hspace{1cm}})$

$= \underline{\hspace{2cm}} + \underline{\hspace{1.5cm}} + \underline{\hspace{1.5cm}} + \underline{\hspace{1.5cm}} + \underline{\hspace{1.5cm}} + \underline{\hspace{1.5cm}}$

$= \underline{\hspace{1cm}} + \underline{\hspace{1cm}} + \underline{\hspace{1cm}} + \underline{\hspace{1cm}} + \underline{\hspace{1cm}} + \underline{\hspace{1cm}}$

$= \underline{\hspace{1cm}} + \underline{\hspace{1cm}} + \underline{\hspace{1cm}} + \underline{\hspace{1cm}} + \underline{\hspace{1cm}} + \underline{\hspace{1cm}}$

$= \underline{\hspace{1cm}} + \underline{\hspace{1cm}} + \underline{\hspace{1cm}} + \underline{\hspace{1cm}}$

Verify. Substitute $m = 2$.

Left side

$(3m + 2)(2m^2 + m + 5)$

$= (\underline{\hspace{1cm}} \times 2 + \underline{\hspace{1cm}})(\underline{\hspace{1cm}} \times 2^2 + \underline{\hspace{1cm}} \times 2 + \underline{\hspace{1cm}})$

$= (\underline{\hspace{1cm}} + \underline{\hspace{1cm}})(\underline{\hspace{1cm}} + \underline{\hspace{1cm}} + \underline{\hspace{1cm}})$

$= (\underline{\hspace{1cm}})(\underline{\hspace{1cm}})$

$= \underline{\hspace{2cm}}$

Right side

$\underline{\hspace{5cm}}$

$= \underline{\hspace{1cm}} \times 2^3 + \underline{\hspace{1cm}} \times 2^2 + \underline{\hspace{1cm}} \times 2 + \underline{\hspace{1cm}}$

$= \underline{\hspace{1cm}} + \underline{\hspace{1cm}} + \underline{\hspace{1cm}} + \underline{\hspace{1cm}}$

$= \underline{\hspace{2cm}}$

The numbers match, so the product is likely correct.

b) $(3z - 2)(z^2 - 3z - 4) = \underline{\hspace{1cm}}(\underline{\hspace{1cm}} - \underline{\hspace{1cm}} - \underline{\hspace{1cm}}) - \underline{\hspace{1cm}}(\underline{\hspace{1cm}} - \underline{\hspace{1cm}} - \underline{\hspace{1cm}})$

$= \underline{\hspace{4cm}}$

Verify. Substitute $z = 2$.

Left side   Right side

The numbers match, so the product is likely correct.

14. Factor.

a) $4c^2 + 20c + 25$

This is a $\underline{\hspace{4cm}}$.
The 2nd term is $\underline{\hspace{2cm}}$,
so the factors of $\underline{\hspace{1cm}}$ are $\underline{\hspace{2cm}}$.

$\quad 4c^2 + 20c + 25$

$\qquad \uparrow \qquad\qquad \uparrow$

$(\underline{\hspace{1cm}})^2 \qquad (\underline{\hspace{1cm}})^2$

So, $4c^2 + 20c + 25 = \underline{\hspace{3cm}}$

$= \underline{\hspace{3cm}}$

b) $16m^2 - 81$

This is a $\underline{\hspace{4cm}}$.
$16m^2 = \underline{\hspace{2cm}}$
$81 = \underline{\hspace{2cm}}$
So, $16m^2 - 81$

$= \underline{\hspace{3cm}}$

Roots and Powers

What You'll Learn

- Estimate and calculate roots of numbers.

- Identify and order irrational numbers.

- Use exponent laws to simplify expressions involving roots and powers.

Why It's Important

Roots and powers are used by:

- biologists, to estimate body measurements of mammals

- health researchers, to predict the percent of medication remaining in a person

- financial planners, to estimate the growth of investments

Key Words

square root	cube root
radical	index
radicand	rational number
irrational number	power
exponent	entire radical
mixed radical	

▶ 4.1 Skill Builder

Estimating Square Roots

We can use perfect squares and their square roots to estimate other square roots.

Number	0	1	4	9	16	25	36	49	64	81	100
Square root	0	1	2	3	4	5	6	7	8	9	10

To estimate $\sqrt{30}$:

From the 1st row in the table, 30 is between 25 and 36.

From the 2nd row in the table, $\sqrt{30}$ is between 5 and 6.

Estimate to 1 decimal place: $\sqrt{30} \doteq 5.5$

Square the estimate: $5.5^2 = 30.25$ This is high.

Revise the estimate: $\sqrt{30} \doteq 5.4$

Square the estimate: $5.4^2 = 29.16$ This is low.

30.25 is closer to 30, so $\sqrt{30}$ is about 5.5.

Use a calculator to square the estimates.

Check

1. Estimate each square root to 1 decimal place.

a) $\sqrt{8}$

Use the table above to help.

8 is between _____ and _____, but much closer to _____.

So, $\sqrt{8}$ is between _____ and _____, but much closer to _____.

Estimate to 1 decimal place: $\sqrt{8} \doteq$ _____

Square the estimate: _____ = _____   This is: _____

Revise the estimate: $\sqrt{8} \doteq$ _____

Square the estimate: _____ = _____   This is: _____

_____ is closer to 8, so $\sqrt{8}$ is about _____.

b) $\sqrt{52}$

52 is between _____ and _____, but much closer to _____.

So, $\sqrt{52}$ is between _____ and _____, but much closer to _____.

Estimate to 1 decimal place: $\sqrt{52} \doteq$ _____

Square the estimate: _____ = _____   This is: _____

Revise the estimate: $\sqrt{52} \doteq$ _____

Square the estimate: _____ = _____   This is: _____

_____ is closer to 52, so $\sqrt{52}$ is about _____.

Estimating Cube Roots

We can use perfect cubes and their cube roots to estimate other cube roots.

Number	0	1	8	27	64	125	216	343	512	729	1000
Cube root	0	1	2	3	4	5	6	7	8	9	10

To estimate $\sqrt[3]{30}$:

From the 1st row in the table, 30 is between 27 and 64, but much closer to 27.

From the 2nd row in the table, $\sqrt[3]{30}$ is between 3 and 4, but much closer to 3.

Estimate to 1 decimal place: $\sqrt[3]{30} \doteq 3.1$

Cube the estimate: $3.1^3 = 29.791$　　　　　　This is low.

Revise the estimate: $\sqrt[3]{30} \doteq 3.2$

Cube the estimate: $3.2^3 = 32.768$　　　　　　This is high.

29.791 is closer to 30, so $\sqrt[3]{30}$ is about 3.1.

> Use a calculator to cube the estimates.

Check

1. Estimate each cube root to 1 decimal place.

> Use the table above to help.

a) $\sqrt[3]{20}$

20 is between _____ and _____, and closer to _____.

So, $\sqrt[3]{20}$ is between _____ and _____, and closer to _____.

Estimate to 1 decimal place: $\sqrt[3]{20} \doteq$ _____

Cube the estimate: _____ = _____　　　This is: _____

Revise the estimate: $\sqrt[3]{20} \doteq$ _____

Cube the estimate: _____ = _____　　　This is: _____

_____ is closer to 20, so $\sqrt[3]{20}$ is about: _____

b) $\sqrt[3]{600}$

600 is between _____ and _____, and closer to _____.

So, $\sqrt[3]{600}$ is between _____ and _____, and closer to _____.

Estimate to 1 decimal place: $\sqrt[3]{600} \doteq$ _____

Cube the estimate: _____ = _____　　　This is: _____

Revise the estimate: $\sqrt[3]{600} \doteq$ _____

Cube the estimate: _____ = _____　　　This is: _____

_____ is closer to 600, so $\sqrt[3]{600}$ is about: _____

4.1 Math Lab: Estimating Roots

FOCUS Write the root of a number as a decimal.

You have worked with square roots and cube roots.

$\sqrt{25} = 5$ because $5 \times 5 = 25$

$\sqrt[3]{216} = 6$ because $6 \times 6 \times 6 = 216$

We can also find other roots.

$\sqrt[4]{81} = 3$ because $3 \times 3 \times 3 \times 3 = 81$

In the table below:

• Find the exact value or estimate the approximate value of each radical.

• State whether the value is exact or approximate.

Radical	Value	Is the Value Exact or Approximate?
$\sqrt{16}$	4	Exact
$\sqrt{27}$	5.2	Approximate
$\sqrt{\dfrac{16}{81}}$	$\dfrac{4}{9}$, or $0.\overline{4}$	Exact
$\sqrt{0.64}$		
$\sqrt[3]{16}$		
$\sqrt[3]{27}$		
$\sqrt[3]{\dfrac{16}{81}}$		
$\sqrt[3]{0.64}$		
$\sqrt[3]{-0.64}$		
$\sqrt[4]{16}$		
$\sqrt[4]{27}$		
$\sqrt[4]{\dfrac{16}{81}}$		
$\sqrt[4]{0.64}$		

Fill in the last 3 rows with radicals you choose.

1. Find the value of each radical.

a) $\sqrt[3]{125}$

125 = 5 × 5 × 5

So, $\sqrt[3]{125}$ = _____

b) $\sqrt[3]{343}$

343 = 7 × _____ × _____

So, $\sqrt[3]{343}$ = _____

c) $\sqrt[3]{512}$

512 = _____ × _____ × _____

So, $\sqrt[3]{512}$ = _____

d) $\sqrt[4]{10\ 000}$

10 000 = _____

So, $\sqrt[4]{10\ 000}$ = _____

2. Evaluate each radical.

a) $\sqrt{144} = \sqrt{\underline{\quad} \times \underline{\quad}}$

= _____

b) $\sqrt{10\ 000} = \sqrt{\underline{\quad} \times \underline{\quad}}$

= _____

c) $\sqrt[3]{-27} = \sqrt[3]{\underline{\quad} \times \underline{\quad} \times \underline{\quad}}$

= _____

d) $\sqrt[3]{64}$ = _____

= _____

3. Use a checkmark to indicate if the value of each radical is exact or approximate.

Radical	Exact	Approximate	Radical	Exact	Approximate
$\sqrt{100}$			$\sqrt{15}$		
$\sqrt{3}$			$\sqrt[3]{-1}$		
$\sqrt{10}$			$\sqrt[3]{1000}$		
$\sqrt{49}$			$\sqrt[3]{100}$		

4. Complete each statement to find two whole numbers between which the value of the radical lies.

a) Since 11 is between 9 and 16, then $\sqrt{11}$ is between $\sqrt{\underline{\quad}}$ and $\sqrt{\underline{\quad}}$

So, $\sqrt{11}$ is between _____ and _____.

b) Since 45 is between 27 and 64, then $\sqrt[3]{45}$ is between $\sqrt[3]{\underline{\quad}}$ and $\sqrt[3]{\underline{\quad}}$

So, $\sqrt[3]{45}$ is between _____ and _____.

c) Since 5 is between 1 and 8, then $\sqrt[3]{5}$ is between $\sqrt[3]{\underline{\quad}}$ and $\sqrt[3]{\underline{\quad}}$

So, $\sqrt[3]{5}$ is between _____ and _____.

▶ 4.2 Irrational Numbers

FOCUS Identify and order radicals that are irrational numbers.

A **rational number** is a number that can be written as a fraction, with denominator not 0.
Rational numbers have decimal values that either terminate or repeat.
For example,

$$\sqrt{\frac{4}{9}} = \frac{2}{3}$$

$$\qquad = 0.6666\ldots$$

$$\qquad = 0.\overline{6}$$

$$\sqrt[3]{1.331} = 1.1$$

This decimal terminates.

This decimal repeats.

> *All integers are rational.*

So, $\sqrt{\frac{4}{9}}$ and $\sqrt[3]{1.331}$ are rational numbers.

Numbers whose decimals don't repeat or don't terminate are **irrational numbers**.
For example, $\sqrt[3]{12} = 2.289\ 428\ 485\ldots$

Example 1 | Classifying Numbers

Tell whether each number is rational or irrational.

a) $\sqrt{625}$ **b)** $\sqrt[3]{26}$ **c)** $\sqrt{\frac{9}{100}}$

Solution

Use a calculator.

a) $\sqrt{625} = 25$

25 can be written as $\frac{25}{1}$, or 25.0; so $\sqrt{625}$ is rational.

b) $\sqrt[3]{26} = 2.962\ 496\ 068\ldots$

This decimal doesn't terminate or repeat, so $\sqrt[3]{26}$ is irrational.

c) $\sqrt{\frac{9}{100}} = 0.3$

This decimal terminates, so $\sqrt{\frac{9}{100}}$ is rational.

Check

1. Tell whether each number is rational or irrational.

Use a calculator.

a) $\sqrt{5} =$ _____, which _____ terminate or repeat

So, $\sqrt{5}$ is _____.

b) $\sqrt[3]{7} =$ _____, which _____ terminate or repeat

So, $\sqrt[3]{7}$ is _____.

c) $\sqrt[3]{\dfrac{1}{27}} =$ _____, which _____

So, $\sqrt[3]{\dfrac{1}{27}}$ is _____.

> When you use your calculator to find the cube root of a fraction, you may need to input the fraction in brackets.

Example 2 | Ordering Irrational Numbers on a Number Line

Use the number line below to order these numbers from least to greatest:
$\sqrt{17}, \sqrt[3]{-8}, \sqrt[3]{6}$

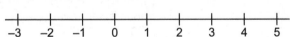

Solution

Estimate $\sqrt{17}$:

17 is between the perfect squares 16 and 25, and is closer to 16.

So, $\sqrt{17}$ is between 4 and 5, and closer to 4.

> Use the table of perfect squares on page 202.

$\sqrt[3]{-8}$ is the least number because it is negative and all the other radicals are positive.

$\sqrt[3]{-8} = -2$

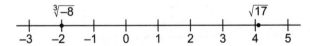

> Use the table of perfect cubes on page 203. The cube root of a negative number is negative.

Estimate $\sqrt[3]{6}$:

6 is between 1 and 8, and is closer to 8.

So, $\sqrt[3]{6}$ is between 1 and 2, and closer to 2.

Use the table of perfect cubes on page 203.

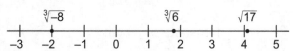

From the number line above, the order from least to greatest is: $\sqrt[3]{-8}, \sqrt[3]{6}, \sqrt{17}$

Check

1. Use the number line below to order these numbers from least to greatest:

$\sqrt{18}, \sqrt[3]{-30}, \sqrt[3]{27}$

18 is between the perfect squares _____ and _____, and is closer to 16.
So, $\sqrt{18}$ is between _____ and _____, and closer to _____.

−30 is between the perfect cubes _____, and is closer to _____.
So, $\sqrt[3]{-30}$ is between _____ and _____, and closer to _____.

$\sqrt[3]{27} =$ _____

Remember that the cube root of a negative number is negative.

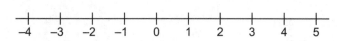

The order from least to greatest is: _____

Practice

1. Tell whether each number is rational or irrational.

a) $\sqrt{36} =$ _____, which _____. So, $\sqrt{36}$ is _____.

b) $\sqrt[3]{12} =$ _____, which _____ terminate or repeat.
So, $\sqrt[3]{12}$ is _____.

c) $\sqrt[3]{-8} =$ _____, which _____. So, $\sqrt[3]{-8}$ is _____.

d) $\sqrt{\dfrac{81}{4}} =$ _____, which _____. So, $\sqrt{\dfrac{81}{4}}$ is _____.

2. Place each number in the correct column:

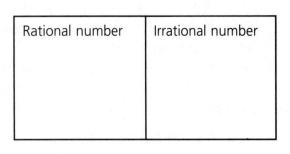

Rational number	Irrational number

$4 = \dfrac{}{1}$

$\sqrt{1.1} = $ _____

$1.\overline{6} = $ _____

$\sqrt[3]{-1} = $ _____

$1\dfrac{3}{4} = \dfrac{}{4}$

$\sqrt[3]{10} = $ _____

$-16 = $ _____

3. Look at each calculator screen. Is the radical rational or irrational?

a)

√(0.25)

0.5

_____

b)

√(25/36)

0.833333333

_____

4. a) Find each square root. Identify any that are irrational.

$\sqrt{4}, \sqrt{5}, \sqrt{9}, \sqrt{100}$

$\sqrt{4} = $ _____

$\sqrt{5} = $ _____

$\sqrt{9} = $ _____

$\sqrt{100} = $ _____

The decimal form of _____ does not terminate or repeat.

So, _____ is irrational.

b) Find each cube root. Identify any that are irrational.

$\sqrt[3]{-216}, \sqrt[3]{64}, \sqrt[3]{1}, \sqrt[3]{100}$

$\sqrt[3]{-216} = $ _____

$\sqrt[3]{64} = $ _____

$\sqrt[3]{1} = $ _____

$\sqrt[3]{100} = $ _____

The decimal form of _____ does not terminate or repeat.

So, _____ is irrational.

5. Compare each pair of numbers. Replace each ? with < or >.

a) $5 \ ? \ \sqrt{9}$

$\sqrt{9} =$ _____

Compare: 5 _____ _____

So, 5 _____ $\sqrt{9}$

b) $\sqrt{9} \ ? \ \sqrt{10}$

Compare: 9 _____ _____

So, $\sqrt{9}$ _____ $\sqrt{10}$

c) $-3 \ ? \ \sqrt[3]{-8}$

$\sqrt[3]{-8} =$ _____

Compare: -3 _____ _____

So, -3 _____ $\sqrt[3]{-8}$

d) $\sqrt[3]{42} \ ? \ \sqrt{12}$

$\sqrt[3]{42} =$ _____

$\sqrt{12} =$ _____

Compare: _____ _____ _____

So, $\sqrt[3]{42}$ _____ $\sqrt{12}$

6. Each point on the number line below represents one of these numbers. Write a letter to identify each number.

$\sqrt[3]{60}:$ _____ $\sqrt{9}:$ _____ $\sqrt[3]{-9}:$ _____ $\sqrt{3}:$ _____

```
        B               C    D   A
  +--+--•--+--+--+--•--+--+--•--+
 -3   -2  -1   0   1   2   3   4
```

7. Is this statement true or false? Explain.

$\sqrt[3]{8} > \sqrt{8}$

_____

_____

_____

 978-0-321-61066-9 Copyright © 2011 Pearson Canada Inc.

4.3 Skill Builder

Power of a Product of Integers

We can see patterns in powers of products. For example:

$(4 \times 3)^2 = (4 \times 3) \times (4 \times 3)$

$\qquad = 4 \times 3 \times 4 \times 3$ Rearrange the factors.

$\qquad = 4 \times 4 \times 3 \times 3$

$\qquad = 4^2 \times 3^2$

And, $(6 \times 4)^3 = (6 \times 4) \times (6 \times 4) \times (6 \times 4)$

$\qquad = 6 \times 4 \times 6 \times 4 \times 6 \times 4$ Rearrange the factors.

$\qquad = 6 \times 6 \times 6 \times 4 \times 4 \times 4$

$\qquad = 6^3 \times 4^3$

In general:

> **Multiplication Property of Powers**
>
> $(ab)^n = a^n \times b^n$
>
> where n is a natural number, and a and b are real numbers.

Check

1. Write each product of factors as a product of powers.

a) $7 \times 11 \times 7 \times 11 \times 7 \times 11$

$= (7 \times \underline{\hspace{1cm}} \times \underline{\hspace{1cm}}) \times (11 \times \underline{\hspace{1cm}} \times \underline{\hspace{1cm}})$

$= 7^{\underline{\hspace{0.3cm}}} \times 11^{\underline{\hspace{0.3cm}}}$

b) $8 \times 13 \times 8 \times 13 \times 8 \times 13 \times 8 \times 13$

$= (\underline{\hspace{3cm}}) \times (\underline{\hspace{3cm}})$

$= \underline{\hspace{2cm}}$

Remember that order doesn't matter when you multiply.

2. In each pair of expressions, replace ? with = or ≠.

a) $(7 \times 2)^2 \ ? \ 7^2 \times 2^2$

$(7 \times 2)^2 = 7^{\underline{\hspace{0.3cm}}} \times 2^{\underline{\hspace{0.3cm}}}$

So, $(7 \times 2)^2 \underline{\hspace{1.5cm}} 7^2 \times 2^2$

b) $(5 \times 9)^3 \ ? \ 9^3 \times 5^3$

$(5 \times 9)^3 = \underline{\hspace{1cm}} \times \underline{\hspace{1cm}}$

So, $(5 \times 9)^3 \underline{\hspace{1.5cm}} 9^3 \times 5^3$

c) $(6 \times 10)^4 \ ? \ 6 \times 10^4$

$(6 \times 10)^4 = \underline{\hspace{1cm}} \times \underline{\hspace{1cm}}$

So, $(6 \times 10)^4 \underline{\hspace{1.5cm}} 6 \times 10^4$

d) $(8 \times 5)^3 \ ? \ (8 \times 5)(8 \times 5)(8 \times 5)$

$(8 \times 5)^3 = (\underline{\hspace{0.5cm}} \times \underline{\hspace{0.5cm}}) \times (\underline{\hspace{0.5cm}} \times \underline{\hspace{0.5cm}}) \times (\underline{\hspace{0.5cm}} \times \underline{\hspace{0.5cm}})$

So, $(8 \times 5)^3 \underline{\hspace{1.5cm}} (8 \times 5)(8 \times 5)(8 \times 5)$

4.3 Mixed and Entire Radicals

Writing mixed radicals and entire radicals.

We can see patterns in products involving radicals. For example,

$\sqrt{4 \cdot 9} = \sqrt{36}$ and $\sqrt{4} \cdot \sqrt{9} = 2 \cdot 3$

$\qquad = 6$ $\qquad = 6$

So, $\sqrt{4 \cdot 9} = \sqrt{4} \cdot \sqrt{9}$

> *We sometimes use a dot, ·, instead of a multiplication sign.*

Also, $\sqrt[3]{8 \cdot 125} = \sqrt[3]{1000}$ and $\sqrt[3]{8} \cdot \sqrt[3]{125} = 2 \cdot 5$

$\qquad = 10$ $\qquad = 10$

So, $\sqrt[3]{8 \cdot 125} = \sqrt[3]{8} \cdot \sqrt[3]{125}$

> *When numerical expressions are equivalent, they have the same value.*

In general:

Multiplication Property of Radicals

$\sqrt[n]{ab} = \sqrt[n]{a} \cdot \sqrt[n]{b}$

where n is a natural number, and a and b are real numbers.

Example 1 | Simplifying Radicals Using Perfect Powers

Write each radical in simplest form. Check by evaluating each radical.

a) $\sqrt{99}$ **b)** $\sqrt{72}$ **c)** $\sqrt[3]{72}$

Solution

a) $\sqrt{99}$

Write 99 as a product of factors, one of which is a perfect square.

$99 = 9 \times 11$

$\sqrt{99} = \sqrt{9 \times 11}$ Use the multiplication property.

$\qquad = \sqrt{9} \times \sqrt{11}$

$\qquad = 3 \times \sqrt{11}$

$\qquad = 3\sqrt{11}$

> *$3\sqrt{11}$ is the simplest form because the radicand 11 has no factors, other than 1, that are perfect squares.*

Check: Use a calculator to evaluate each radical.

$\sqrt{99} = 9.9498\ldots$ and $3\sqrt{11} = 9.9498\ldots$

The decimal values appear to be equal.

> *$3\sqrt{11}$ is a **mixed radical**.*

b) $\sqrt{72}$

Write 72 as a product with one perfect-square factor.

$72 = 4 \times 18$, or $72 = 9 \times 8$, or $72 = 36 \times 2$

> *$\sqrt{72}$ is an **entire radical**.*

Use the product with the greatest perfect-square factor:

$72 = 36 \times 2$

$\sqrt{72} = \sqrt{36 \times 2}$ Use the multiplication property.

$\qquad = \sqrt{36} \times \sqrt{2}$

$\qquad = 6 \times \sqrt{2}$

$\qquad = 6\sqrt{2}$

Check: Use a calculator to evaluate each radical.

$\sqrt{72} = 8.4852...$ and $6\sqrt{2} = 8.4852...$

The decimal values appear to be equal.

c) $\sqrt[3]{72}$

Write 72 as a product with one perfect-cube factor.

$72 = 8 \times 9$

$\sqrt[3]{72} = \sqrt[3]{8 \times 9}$ Use the multiplication property.

$= \sqrt[3]{8} \times \sqrt[3]{9}$

$= 2 \times \sqrt[3]{9}$

$= 2\sqrt[3]{9}$

Use the table of perfect cubes on page 203.

Check: Use a calculator to evaluate each radical.

$\sqrt[3]{72} = 4.1601...$ and $2\sqrt[3]{9} = 4.1601...$

The decimal values appear to be equal.

Check

1. Write each radical in simplest form. Check by evaluating each radical.

a) $\sqrt{32}$

Write 32 as a product with one perfect-square factor.

$32 = 4 \times$ _____, or $32 = 16 \times$ _____

Use the product with the greatest perfect-square factor: $32 = 16 \times$ _____

$\sqrt{32} = \sqrt{16 \times \_\_\_\_}$ Use the multiplication property.

$= \_\_\_\_\_ \times \_\_\_\_\_$

$= \_\_\_\_\_ \times \_\_\_\_\_$

$= \_\_\_\_\_$

Check: Use a calculator to evaluate each radical.

$\sqrt{32} = \_\_\_\_\_$ and $\_\_\_\_\_ = \_\_\_\_\_$

b) $\sqrt[3]{56}$

Write 56 as a product with one perfect-cube factor.

$56 = 8 \times$ _____

$\sqrt[3]{56} = \sqrt[3]{8 \times \_\_\_\_}$ Use the multiplication property.

$= \_\_\_\_\_ \times \_\_\_\_\_$

$= \_\_\_\_\_$

$= \_\_\_\_\_$

Check: Use a calculator to evaluate each radical.

$\sqrt[3]{56} = \_\_\_\_\_$ and $\_\_\_\_\_ = \_\_\_\_\_$

To work with larger numbers, start by writing each number as a product of prime factors.

Example 2 | Simplifying Radicals Using Prime Factors

Simplify: $\sqrt[3]{432}$

Solution

$\sqrt[3]{432}$

Write 432 as a product of prime factors.

$432 = 2 \cdot 2 \cdot 2 \cdot 2 \cdot 3 \cdot 3 \cdot 3$

So, $\sqrt[3]{432} = \sqrt[3]{2 \cdot 2 \cdot 2 \cdot 2 \cdot 3 \cdot 3 \cdot 3}$

Use a calculator to keep dividing by prime numbers, then list the factors. Or, you could use a factor tree.

For the cube root, identify groups of 3 equal factors.

$\sqrt[3]{432} = \sqrt[3]{(2 \cdot 2 \cdot 2) \cdot 2 \cdot (3 \cdot 3 \cdot 3)}$ Use the multiplication property.

$\qquad = \sqrt[3]{2 \cdot 2 \cdot 2} \cdot \sqrt[3]{2} \cdot \sqrt[3]{3 \cdot 3 \cdot 3}$

$\qquad = 2 \cdot \sqrt[3]{2} \cdot 3$

$\qquad = 2 \cdot 3 \cdot \sqrt[3]{2}$

$\qquad = 6\sqrt[3]{2}$

Check

1. Simplify: $\sqrt{1260}$

Write 1260 as a product of prime factors.

$1260 = $ _____

So, $\sqrt{1260} = $ _____

For the square root, identify groups of _____ equal factors.

$\sqrt{1260} = $ _____

$\qquad = $ _____

$\qquad = $ _____

$\qquad = $ _____

Example 3 | **Writing a Mixed Radical as an Entire Radical**

Write each mixed radical as an entire radical.

a) $2\sqrt{7}$ **b)** $5\sqrt[3]{3}$

> Example 3 reverses the process of Examples 1 and 2.

Solution

a) $2\sqrt{7}$

Write 2 as a radical with index 2.

$2 = \sqrt{2 \cdot 2}$, or $\sqrt{4}$

Replace the factor 2 with $\sqrt{4}$.

> $\sqrt{7}$ is a square root, so write 2 as a square root.

$2\sqrt{7} = \sqrt{4} \cdot \sqrt{7}$ Use the multiplication property.

$= \sqrt{4 \cdot 7}$

$= \sqrt{28}$

> You can check by evaluating $2\sqrt{7}$ and $\sqrt{28}$, then comparing results.

b) $5\sqrt[3]{3}$

Write 5 as a radical with index 3.

$5 = \sqrt[3]{5 \cdot 5 \cdot 5}$, or $\sqrt[3]{125}$

Replace the factor 5 with $\sqrt[3]{125}$.

> $\sqrt[3]{3}$ is a cube root, so write 5 as a cube root.

$5\sqrt[3]{3} = \sqrt[3]{125} \cdot \sqrt[3]{3}$ Use the multiplication property.

$= \sqrt[3]{125 \cdot 3}$

$= \sqrt[3]{375}$

Check

1. Write each mixed radical as an entire radical.

a) $7\sqrt{2} = \sqrt{7 \cdot 7} \cdot \sqrt{2}$ **b)** $10\sqrt[3]{3} = \sqrt[3]{10 \cdot 10 \cdot 10 \cdot \underline{\hspace{1cm}}}$

$= \sqrt{49} \cdot \sqrt{2}$ $= \sqrt[3]{1000 \cdot \underline{\hspace{1cm}}}$

$= \underline{\hspace{2cm}}$ $= \underline{\hspace{2cm}}$

$= \underline{\hspace{2cm}}$ $= \underline{\hspace{2cm}}$

Practice

1. List all the perfect squares that are factors of each number. Do not include 1.

a) 18: $\underline{\hspace{2cm}}$ **b)** 24: $\underline{\hspace{2cm}}$ **c)** 48: $\underline{\hspace{2cm}}$ **d)** 98: $\underline{\hspace{2cm}}$

2. List all the perfect cubes that are factors of each number. Do not include 1.

   a) 32: _____   **b)** 48: _____   **c)** 54: _____   **d)** 108: _____

3. Circle the expression you would use to simplify each radical at the left.

   a) $\sqrt{24}$ $\sqrt{2 \cdot 12}$ $\sqrt{3 \cdot 8}$ $\sqrt{4 \cdot 6}$

   b) $\sqrt{108}$ $\sqrt{2 \cdot 54}$ $\sqrt{3 \cdot 36}$ $\sqrt{4 \cdot 27}$

   c) $\sqrt[3]{40}$ $\sqrt[3]{2 \cdot 20}$ $\sqrt[3]{4 \cdot 10}$ $\sqrt[3]{5 \cdot 8}$

   d) $\sqrt[3]{162}$ $\sqrt[3]{2 \cdot 81}$ $\sqrt[3]{3 \cdot 54}$ $\sqrt[3]{6 \cdot 27}$

4. Simplify each radical.

   a) $\sqrt{320} = \sqrt{64 \cdot 5}$ **b)** $\sqrt{735} = \sqrt{\underline{\hspace{1cm}} \cdot \underline{\hspace{1cm}}}$

            $= \underline{\hspace{2cm}}$ $= \underline{\hspace{2cm}}$

            $= \underline{\hspace{2cm}}$ $= \underline{\hspace{2cm}}$

   c) $\sqrt[3]{189} = \sqrt[3]{27 \cdot 7}$ **d)** $\sqrt[3]{576} = \sqrt[3]{\underline{\hspace{1cm}} \cdot \underline{\hspace{1cm}}}$

            $= \underline{\hspace{2cm}}$ $= \underline{\hspace{2cm}}$

            $= \underline{\hspace{2cm}}$ $= \underline{\hspace{2cm}}$

5. a) Write each number as the product of its prime factors.

    i) $96 = \underline{\hspace{4cm}}$ **ii)** $200 = \underline{\hspace{4cm}}$

   b) Use each product in part a to simplify each radical.

    i) $\sqrt{96} = \underline{\hspace{4cm}}$ **ii)** $\sqrt[3]{200} = \underline{\hspace{4cm}}$

               $= \underline{\hspace{3cm}}$ $= \underline{\hspace{3cm}}$

               $= \underline{\hspace{3cm}}$ $= \underline{\hspace{3cm}}$

               $= \underline{\hspace{3cm}}$ $= \underline{\hspace{3cm}}$

               $= \underline{\hspace{3cm}}$ $= \underline{\hspace{3cm}}$

6. Write each mixed radical as an entire radical.

   a) $3\sqrt{11} = \sqrt{3 \cdot 3} \cdot \sqrt{11}$ **b)** $2\sqrt{13} = \underline{\hspace{1.5cm}} \cdot \underline{\hspace{1.5cm}}$

            $= \sqrt{9} \cdot \underline{\hspace{1.5cm}}$ $= \underline{\hspace{1.5cm}} \cdot \underline{\hspace{1.5cm}}$

            $= \underline{\hspace{2cm}}$ $= \underline{\hspace{2cm}}$

            $= \underline{\hspace{2cm}}$ $= \underline{\hspace{2cm}}$

   c) $3\sqrt[3]{4} = \sqrt[3]{3 \cdot 3 \cdot 3} \cdot \sqrt[3]{4}$ **d)** $2\sqrt[3]{15} = \underline{\hspace{2cm}} \cdot \underline{\hspace{1cm}}$

            $= \sqrt[3]{27} \cdot \underline{\hspace{1.5cm}}$ $= \underline{\hspace{1.5cm}} \cdot \underline{\hspace{1cm}}$

            $= \underline{\hspace{2cm}}$ $= \underline{\hspace{2cm}}$

            $= \underline{\hspace{2cm}}$ $= \underline{\hspace{2cm}}$

CHECKPOINT 1

Can you...

- estimate the value of a radical?
- identify a radical as a rational or an irrational number?
- order radicals?
- simplify a radical?
- write a mixed radical as an entire radical?

4.1 **1.** Estimate the value of each radical to 1 decimal place.

a) $\sqrt{11}$

11 is between the perfect squares: _____

So, $\sqrt{11}$ is between: _____

Estimate to 1 decimal place: $\sqrt{11} \doteq$ _____

Square the estimate: _____ = _____

Revise the estimate: $\sqrt{11} \doteq$ _____

Square the estimate: _____ = _____

_____ is closer to 11, so $\sqrt{11}$ is about: _____

b) $\sqrt[3]{60}$

60 is between the perfect cubes: _____

So, $\sqrt[3]{60}$ is between: _____

Estimate to 1 decimal place: $\sqrt[3]{60} \doteq$ _____

Cube the estimate: _____ = _____

Revise the estimate: $\sqrt[3]{60} \doteq$ _____

Cube the estimate: _____ = _____

_____ is closer to 60, so $\sqrt[3]{60}$ is about: _____

4.2 **2.** Is each number rational or irrational?

a) $\sqrt{8} =$ _____, which _____ terminate or repeat

So, $\sqrt{8}$ is _____.

b) $\sqrt[3]{-27} =$ _____, which _____

So, $\sqrt[3]{-27}$ is _____.

c) $\sqrt[3]{\dfrac{125}{64}} =$ _____, which _____

So, $\sqrt[3]{\dfrac{125}{64}}$ is _____.

3. a) Estimate the location of each number on the number line below.

$\sqrt{30}$, $\sqrt{5}$, $\sqrt[3]{-7}$

30 is between the perfect squares: _____

So, $\sqrt{30}$ is between: _____

5 is between: _____

So, $\sqrt{5}$ is between: _____

−7 is between: _____

$\sqrt[3]{-7}$ is between: _____

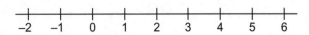

$$\begin{array}{ccccccccc} \,| & | & | & | & | & | & | & | & | \\ -2 & -1 & 0 & 1 & 2 & 3 & 4 & 5 & 6 \end{array}$$

b) The order from least to greatest is: _____

4.3 **4.** Simplify each radical.

a) $\sqrt{124} = \sqrt{4 \cdot 31}$

= _____

= _____

b) $\sqrt[3]{400} =$ _____

= _____

= _____

5. Write each mixed radical as an entire radical.

a) $3\sqrt{10} = \sqrt{3 \cdot 3} \cdot \sqrt{10}$

= _____

= _____

= _____

b) $5\sqrt{5} = \sqrt{5 \cdot 5} \cdot$ _____

= _____

= _____

= _____

c) $2\sqrt[3]{40} = \sqrt[3]{2 \cdot 2 \cdot 2} \cdot$ _____

= _____

= _____

= _____

d) $5\sqrt[3]{7} =$ _____

= _____

= _____

= _____

4.4 Fractional Exponents and Radicals

FOCUS Use a fractional exponent to represent a radical.

Investigation with a calculator suggests that:

- Raising a number to the exponent $\frac{1}{2}$ is the same as finding its square root.

- Raising a number to the exponent $\frac{1}{3}$ is the same as finding its cube root.
  For example,

$$\sqrt{3} = 3^{\frac{1}{2}} \quad \text{and} \quad 10^{\frac{1}{2}} = \sqrt{10}$$
$$\sqrt[3]{4} = 4^{\frac{1}{3}} \quad \text{and} \quad 21^{\frac{1}{3}} = \sqrt[3]{21}$$

> **Powers with Fractional Exponents with Numerator 1**
>
> $x^{\frac{1}{n}} = \sqrt[n]{x}$, where n is a natural number, and x is a rational number

---

Example 1 | Evaluating Powers and Radicals

a) Evaluate each power.

  i) $16^{\frac{1}{2}}$ **ii)** $(-64)^{\frac{1}{3}}$ **iii)** $16^{\frac{1}{4}}$

> *Raising a number to the exponent $\frac{1}{4}$ is the same as finding the fourth root of the number.*

b) Find the value of each power and radical to 2 decimal places.

  i) $7^{\frac{1}{2}}$ **ii)** $24^{\frac{1}{3}}$ **iii)** $\sqrt[3]{120}$ **iv)** $\sqrt[4]{68}$

Solution

a) i) $16^{\frac{1}{2}} = \sqrt{16}$ **ii)** $(-64)^{\frac{1}{3}} = \sqrt[3]{-64}$ **iii)** $16^{\frac{1}{4}} = \sqrt[4]{16}$
     $= 4$ $= -4$ $= 2$

> *Use the tables of roots on pages 202 and 203.*

b) i) $7^{\frac{1}{2}}$ **ii)** $24^{\frac{1}{3}}$

  Use the ^ key: Use the ^ key:

```
7^(1/2)
          2.645751311
```

```
24^(1/3)
          2.884499141
```

  So, $7^{\frac{1}{2}} \doteq 2.65$ So, $24^{\frac{1}{3}} \doteq 2.89$

iii) $\sqrt[3]{120}$

Use the $\sqrt[x]{}$ key:

```
3ˣ√(120)
            4.932424149
```

So, $\sqrt[3]{120} \doteq 4.9$

iv) $\sqrt[4]{68}$

Use the $\sqrt[x]{}$ key:

```
4ˣ√(68)
            2.871621711
```

So, $\sqrt[4]{68} \doteq 2.9$

Check

1. Evaluate each power.

a) $81^{\frac{1}{2}} = \sqrt{\underline{}}$

$= \underline{}$

b) $(-125)^{\frac{1}{3}} = \sqrt[3]{\underline{}}$

$= \underline{}$

c) $10\,000^{\frac{1}{4}} = \sqrt[4]{\underline{}}$

$= \underline{}$

2. Find the value of each power and radical to 2 decimal places.

a) $10^{\frac{1}{2}} \doteq \underline{}$

b) $75^{\frac{1}{3}} \doteq \underline{}$

c) $\sqrt[3]{11} \doteq \underline{}$

d) $\sqrt[4]{25} \doteq \underline{}$

Some fractional exponents have numerators greater than 1.

For example, $16^{\frac{3}{4}}$ $\frac{3}{4}$ can be written as $3 \times \frac{1}{4}$ or $\frac{1}{4} \times 3$

So, $16^{\frac{3}{4}}$ can be written as:

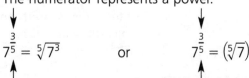

$16^{\frac{3}{4}} = 16^{3 \times \frac{1}{4}}$

$= (16^3)^{\frac{1}{4}}$

$= \sqrt[4]{16^3}$

$\uparrow$

The 4th root of 16^3

or

$16^{\frac{3}{4}} = 16^{\frac{1}{4} \times 3}$

$= \left(16^{\frac{1}{4}}\right)^3$

$= \left(\sqrt[4]{16}\right)^3$

$\uparrow$

The cube of the 4th root of 16

The numerator represents a power.

$\downarrow$

$7^{\frac{3}{5}} = \sqrt[5]{7^3}$

$\uparrow$

or

$\downarrow$

$7^{\frac{3}{5}} = \left(\sqrt[5]{7}\right)^3$

$\uparrow$

The denominator represents a root.

In general:

Powers with Fractional Exponents

$x^{\frac{m}{n}} = \sqrt[n]{x^m}$ or $x^{\frac{m}{n}} = \left(\sqrt[n]{x}\right)^m$

where m and n are natural numbers, and x is a rational number

| Example 2 | Writing a Power as a Radical |

Write $15^{\frac{2}{3}}$ as a radical in two ways.

Solution

$15^{\frac{2}{3}}$ ←——— the exponent of the power
      ←——— the index of the root

As the root of a power: $15^{\frac{2}{3}} = \sqrt[3]{15^2}$

As the power of a root: $15^{\frac{2}{3}} = \left(\sqrt[3]{15}\right)^2$

Check

1. Write each power as a radical in two ways.

a) $82^{\frac{5}{2}} = \sqrt{\underline{\quad\quad}}$ or $82^{\frac{5}{2}} = \left(\sqrt{\underline{\quad\quad}}\right)^{\underline{\quad}}$

b) $9^{\frac{2}{3}} = \sqrt[3]{\underline{\quad\quad}}$ or $9^{\frac{2}{3}} = \left(\sqrt[3]{\underline{\quad\quad}}\right)^{\underline{\quad}}$

| Example 3 | Writing a Radical as a Power |

Write as a power with a fractional exponent.

a) $\sqrt[3]{5^2}$ **b)** $\left(\sqrt[4]{7}\right)^3$

Solution

       ——— denominator in the exponent

a) $\sqrt[3]{5^2}$ ←——— numerator in the exponent

$\sqrt[3]{5^2} = 5^{\frac{2}{3}}$

       ——— denominator in the exponent

b) $\left(\sqrt[4]{7}\right)^3$ ←——— numerator in the exponent

$\left(\sqrt[4]{7}\right)^3 = 7^{\frac{3}{4}}$

For a square root, the exponent of the power is a fraction with denominator 2.

For example, $\sqrt{6^3} = 6^{\frac{3}{2}}$ and $\left(\sqrt{6}\right)^3 = 6^{\frac{3}{2}}$

Check

1. Write as a power with a fractional exponent.

a) $\sqrt{57^5} = 57^{\underline{}}$

b) $\left(\sqrt[3]{3}\right)^4 = 3^{\underline{}}$

c) $\sqrt[4]{6^5} = $ _____

d) $\left(\sqrt{10}\right)^7 = $ _____

| **Example 4** | **Evaluating Powers and Radicals** |

a) Evaluate each power.

i) $16^{\frac{3}{2}}$

ii) $27^{\frac{2}{3}}$

b) Evaluate: $\sqrt[3]{2^6}$

Solution

a) i) $16^{\frac{3}{2}} = \left(\sqrt{16}\right)^3$

$\phantom{16^{\frac{3}{2}}} = (4)^3$

$\phantom{16^{\frac{3}{2}}} = 64$

ii) $27^{\frac{2}{3}} = \left(\sqrt[3]{27}\right)^2$

$\phantom{27^{\frac{2}{3}}} = (3)^2$

$\phantom{27^{\frac{2}{3}}} = 9$

b) $\sqrt[3]{2^6}$

$2^6 = 64$

So, $\sqrt[3]{2^6} = \sqrt[3]{64}$

$\phantom{So, \sqrt[3]{2^6}} = 4$

The root and the power can be calculated in either order. It is usually easier to find the root first.

Check

1. Evaluate each power and radical.

a) $4^{\frac{5}{2}} = \left(\sqrt{\underline{}}\right)^5$

$= $ _____

$= $ _____

b) $27^{\frac{4}{3}} = \left(\sqrt[3]{\underline{}}\right)^4$

$= $ _____

$= $ _____

c) $\sqrt[3]{10^6}$

$10^6 = $ _____

So, $\sqrt[3]{10^6} = \sqrt[3]{\underline{}}$

$= $ _____

 978-0-321-61066-9

1. Write each power as a radical.

    a) $8^{\frac{1}{2}} = \sqrt{\underline{\hphantom{000}}}$ **b)** $32^{\frac{1}{3}} = \sqrt[3]{\underline{\hphantom{000}}}$ **c)** $12^{\frac{1}{4}} = \underline{\hphantom{00000}}$

2. Write each radical as a power.

    a) $\sqrt{35} = \underline{\hphantom{0000}}^{\frac{1}{2}}$ **b)** $\sqrt[3]{11} = \underline{\hphantom{0000}}^{\frac{1}{3}}$ **c)** $\sqrt[4]{6} = \underline{\hphantom{00000}}$

3. Evaluate each power.

    a) $100^{\frac{1}{2}} = \sqrt{\underline{\hphantom{000}}}$ **b)** $125^{\frac{1}{3}} = \sqrt[3]{\underline{\hphantom{000}}}$ **c)** $81^{\frac{1}{4}} = \underline{\hphantom{00000}}$

            $= \underline{\hphantom{0000}}$ $= \underline{\hphantom{0000}}$ $= \underline{\hphantom{0000}}$

4. Find the value of each power and radical to 2 decimal places.

    a) $22^{\frac{1}{2}} \doteq \underline{\hphantom{0000}}$ **b)** $30^{\frac{1}{3}} \doteq \underline{\hphantom{0000}}$ **c)** $\sqrt[4]{250} \doteq \underline{\hphantom{0000}}$

5. Use $2^{10} = 1024$ to evaluate $1024^{\frac{1}{10}}$.

    $1024^{\frac{1}{10}} = \sqrt[10]{\underline{\hphantom{0000}}}$

              $= \underline{\hphantom{00000}}$

              $= \underline{\hphantom{00000}}$

6. Use a radical to show another way to write $52^{\frac{3}{4}}$.

    $52^{\frac{3}{4}} = \sqrt[4]{52^3}$ or $52^{\frac{3}{4}} = \underline{\hphantom{00000}}$

7. Write each power as a radical in two ways.

    a) $114^{\frac{3}{2}} = \underline{\hphantom{0000}}$, or $\underline{\hphantom{0000}}$ **b)** $92^{\frac{2}{3}} = \underline{\hphantom{0000}}$, or $\underline{\hphantom{0000}}$

8. Write each radical as a power with a fractional exponent.

    a) $\sqrt{537^3} = \underline{\hphantom{000}}$ **b)** $\left(\sqrt[3]{15}\right)^4 = \underline{\hphantom{000}}$ **c)** $\left(\sqrt[4]{63}\right)^5 = \underline{\hphantom{000}}$

9. Evaluate each power.

    a) $25^{\frac{3}{2}} = \left(\sqrt{\underline{\hphantom{00}}}\right)^{\underline{\hphantom{0}}}$ **b)** $64^{\frac{2}{3}} = \left(\sqrt[3]{\underline{\hphantom{00}}}\right)^{\underline{\hphantom{0}}}$ **c)** $16^{\frac{3}{4}} = \underline{\hphantom{000}}$

             $= \underline{\hphantom{0000}}$ $= \underline{\hphantom{0000}}$ $= \underline{\hphantom{0000}}$

             $= \underline{\hphantom{0000}}$ $= \underline{\hphantom{0000}}$ $= \underline{\hphantom{0000}}$

▶ 4.5 Negative Exponents and Reciprocals

FOCUS Relate negative exponents and reciprocals.

A power such as 2^{-4} is equivalent to $\frac{1}{2^4}$.

And, $\frac{1}{3^{-5}}$ is equivalent to 3^5.

> 2^4 is the reciprocal of 2^{-4}.

In general:

> **Powers with Negative Exponents**
>
> $x^{-n} = \frac{1}{x^n}$ and $x^n = \frac{1}{x^{-n}}$
>
> where x is any number, except 0, and n is a rational number

---

| **Example 1** | **Evaluating Powers with Negative Integer Exponents** |

Evaluate each power.

a) 5^{-3} 　　　　**b)** 1000^{-2} 　　　　**c)** $\frac{1}{3^{-4}}$

Solution

a) $5^{-3} = \frac{1}{5^3}$ 　　　　**b)** $1000^{-2} = \frac{1}{1000^2}$ 　　　　**c)** $\frac{1}{3^{-4}} = 3^4$

$\quad = \frac{1}{125}$ 　　　　　　　$= \frac{1}{1\ 000\ 000}$ 　　　　　$= 81$

Check

1. Evaluate each power.

a) $7^{-2} = \dfrac{1}{\rule{1cm}{0.4pt}}$

$\quad = \dfrac{\ }{\rule{1cm}{0.4pt}}$

b) $10^{-4} = \dfrac{1}{\rule{1cm}{0.4pt}}$

$\quad = \dfrac{\ }{\rule{1cm}{0.4pt}}$

c) $\dfrac{1}{4^{-3}} = 4\rule{1cm}{0.4pt}$

$\quad = \rule{1.5cm}{0.4pt}$

> Leave the answers in parts a and b as fractions.

Example 2 | **Evaluating Powers with Negative Unit-Fraction Exponents**

Evaluate each power.

a) $4^{-\frac{1}{2}}$

b) $(-27)^{-\frac{1}{3}}$

Solution

a) $4^{-\frac{1}{2}} = \dfrac{1}{4^{\frac{1}{2}}}$

$= \dfrac{1}{\sqrt{4}}$

$= \dfrac{1}{2}$

To check part a, we could use a calculator to evaluate $4^{-\frac{1}{2}}$ and $\frac{1}{2}$.

b) $(-27)^{-\frac{1}{3}} = \dfrac{1}{(-27)^{\frac{1}{3}}}$

$= \dfrac{1}{\sqrt[3]{-27}}$

$= \dfrac{1}{-3}$, or $-\dfrac{1}{3}$

Check

1. Evaluate each power.

a) $16^{-\frac{1}{2}} = \dfrac{1}{\rule{2cm}{0.4pt}}$

$= \dfrac{1}{\rule{2cm}{0.4pt}}$

$= \dfrac{\rule{2cm}{0.4pt}}{\rule{2cm}{0.4pt}}$

b) $(-8)^{-\frac{1}{3}} = \dfrac{1}{\rule{2cm}{0.4pt}}$

$= \dfrac{1}{\rule{2cm}{0.4pt}}$

$= \dfrac{\rule{2cm}{0.4pt}}{\rule{2cm}{0.4pt}}$

Leave the answers as fractions.

Example 3 | **Evaluating Powers with Negative Rational Exponents**

Evaluate each power.

a) $16^{-\frac{3}{4}}$

b) $27^{-\frac{2}{3}}$

Solution

a) $16^{-\frac{3}{4}} = \dfrac{1}{16^{\frac{3}{4}}}$

$= \dfrac{1}{\left(\sqrt[4]{16}\right)^3}$

$= \dfrac{1}{(2)^3}$

$= \dfrac{1}{8}$

b) $27^{-\frac{2}{3}} = \dfrac{1}{27^{\frac{2}{3}}}$

$= \dfrac{1}{\left(\sqrt[3]{27}\right)^2}$

$= \dfrac{1}{(3)^2}$

$= \dfrac{1}{9}$

Check

1. Write as a power with a positive exponent.

a) $10^{-\frac{3}{2}} = \dfrac{1}{10^{\underline{\quad}}}$

b) $120^{-\frac{2}{3}} = \dfrac{1}{\underline{\quad\quad}}$

2. Evaluate each power.

a) $49^{-\frac{3}{2}} = \dfrac{1}{49^{\underline{\quad}}}$

$= \dfrac{1}{\left(\sqrt{\underline{\quad}}\right)^3}$

$= \underline{\quad\quad}$

$= \underline{\quad\quad}$

b) $10\,000^{-\frac{3}{4}} = \dfrac{1}{10\,000^{\underline{\quad}}}$

$= \dfrac{1}{\left(\sqrt[4]{\underline{\quad}}\right)^3}$

$= \underline{\quad\quad}$

$= \underline{\quad\quad}$

To write the reciprocal of a fraction, transpose the numerator and denominator.

For example, $\dfrac{2}{5}$ is the reciprocal of $\dfrac{5}{2}$

When a power has a rational base and an integer exponent, we can write this:

$\left(\dfrac{2}{5}\right)^{-3} = \left(\dfrac{5}{2}\right)^3$ and $\left(\dfrac{5}{2}\right)^{-3} = \left(\dfrac{2}{5}\right)^3$

In general:

> **Negative Exponents and Reciprocals**
>
> $\left(\dfrac{a}{b}\right)^{-n} = \left(\dfrac{b}{a}\right)^{n}$
>
> where a and b are not equal to 0, and n is a rational number.

$\left(\dfrac{2}{5}\right)^3$ is a power of a quotient.

$\left(\dfrac{2}{5}\right)^3$ means $\left(\dfrac{2}{5}\right) \cdot \left(\dfrac{2}{5}\right) \cdot \left(\dfrac{2}{5}\right) = \dfrac{2 \cdot 2 \cdot 2}{5 \cdot 5 \cdot 5}$

$= \dfrac{2^3}{5^3}$

 978-0-321-61066-9

| Example 4 | Evaluating Powers with Rational Bases |

Evaluate each power.

a) $\left(\dfrac{2}{5}\right)^{-3}$

b) 1.7^{-2}

Solution

a) $\left(\dfrac{2}{5}\right)^{-3}$ Write the reciprocal with a positive exponent.

$= \left(\dfrac{5}{2}\right)^{3}$

$= \dfrac{5^3}{2^3}$

$= \dfrac{125}{8}$

b) 1.7^{-2}

Use a calculator.

```
1.7^(-2)
         0.346020761
```

$1.7^{-2} = 0.3460\ldots$

> *When you input a negative number, use the change sign key (−) and not the subtraction key.*

Check

1. Write with a positive exponent.

a) $\left(\dfrac{3}{5}\right)^{-2} = \left(\dfrac{5}{3}\right)^{\underline{\quad}}$ **b)** $\left(\dfrac{6}{7}\right)^{-4} = \left(\underline{\quad}\right)$ **c)** $\left(\dfrac{9}{4}\right)^{-3} = \underline{\qquad}$

2. Evaluate each power.

a) $\left(\dfrac{4}{3}\right)^{-3} = \left(\dfrac{3}{4}\right)^{\underline{\quad}}$ **b)** $\left(\dfrac{7}{5}\right)^{-2} = \left(\dfrac{5}{7}\right)^{\underline{\quad}}$

$= \underline{\qquad}$ $= \underline{\qquad}$

$= \underline{\qquad}$ $= \underline{\qquad}$

c) 0.8^{-3}

Use a calculator.

Input: 0.8^(_____)

The calculator displays: _____

$0.8^{-3} = $ _____

1. Evaluate each power.

a) $6^{-2} = \dfrac{1}{6^{\underline{\hspace{1cm}}}}$

$= \underline{\hspace{1.5cm}}$

b) $5^{-1} = \underline{\hspace{2cm}}$

c) $2^{-5} = \underline{\hspace{2cm}}$

$= \underline{\hspace{2cm}}$

d) $\dfrac{1}{2^{-4}} = 2^{\underline{\hspace{1cm}}}$

$= \underline{\hspace{2cm}}$

e) $\dfrac{1}{3^{-3}} = \underline{\hspace{1.5cm}}$

$= \underline{\hspace{1.5cm}}$

f) $\dfrac{1}{10^{-1}} = \underline{\hspace{1.5cm}}$

2. Use the fact that $4^3 = 64$. Write 4^{-3} as a fraction.

$4^{-3} = \dfrac{1}{\underline{\hspace{1cm}}}$

$= \underline{\hspace{2cm}}$

3. Write each power as a fraction with a radical in the denominator.

a) $3^{-\frac{1}{2}} = \dfrac{1}{3^{\underline{\hspace{1cm}}}}$

$= \underline{\hspace{2cm}}$

b) $2^{-\frac{1}{3}} = \dfrac{1}{2^{\underline{\hspace{1cm}}}}$

$= \underline{\hspace{2cm}}$

c) $8^{-\frac{1}{4}} = $

$\underline{\hspace{2.5cm}}$

$= \underline{\hspace{2.5cm}}$

4. Write each power with a positive exponent.

a) $3^{-\frac{2}{3}} = $

$\underline{\hspace{2.5cm}}$

b) $2^{-\frac{3}{2}} = $

$\underline{\hspace{2.5cm}}$

c) $\left(\dfrac{5}{6}\right)^{-4} = \underline{\hspace{2cm}}$

5. Evaluate each power.

a) $100^{-\frac{1}{2}} = \dfrac{1}{100^{\underline{}}}$

$= \dfrac{1}{\sqrt{\underline{}}}$

$= \underline{}$

b) $(-125)^{-\frac{1}{3}} = \dfrac{1}{(-125)^{\underline{}}}$

$= \dfrac{1}{\sqrt[3]{\underline{}}}$

$= \underline{}$

c) $16^{-\frac{1}{4}} =$

$\underline{}$

$= \underline{}$

$= \underline{}$

6. Evaluate each power.

a) $100^{-\frac{3}{2}} = \dfrac{1}{100^{\underline{}}}$

$= \dfrac{1}{\left(\sqrt{\underline{}}\right)^3}$

$= \underline{}$

$= \underline{}$

b) $(-125)^{-\frac{4}{3}} = \dfrac{1}{(-125)^{\underline{}}}$

$= \dfrac{1}{\left(\sqrt[3]{\underline{}}\right)^4}$

$= \underline{}$

$= \underline{}$

c) $16^{-\frac{5}{4}} =$

$\underline{}$

$= \underline{}$

$= \underline{}$

7. Evaluate each power.

a) $\left(\dfrac{5}{6}\right)^{-2} = \left(\dfrac{6}{5}\right)^{\underline{}}$

$= \underline{}$

$= \underline{}$

b) $\left(\dfrac{2}{7}\right)^{-3} = \underline{}$

$= \underline{}$

$= \underline{}$

c) 2.9^{-4}

Use a calculator.

$\underline{}$

Can you...

• relate radicals to powers?

• evaluate powers with rational and negative exponents?

4.4 **1.** Write each power as a radical.

a) $13^{\frac{1}{2}}$ = _____

b) $(-2)^{\frac{1}{3}}$ = _____

c) $15^{\frac{1}{4}}$ = _____

2. Evaluate each power.

a) $25^{\frac{1}{2}}$ = _____

= _____

b) $(-1000)^{\frac{1}{3}}$ = _____

= _____

c) $1^{\frac{1}{4}}$ = _____

= _____

3. This formula is used to estimate the thickness of ice, t millimetres, needed to support a mass, m kilograms, safely: $t = 3.8\,m^{\frac{1}{2}}$

To the nearest millimetre, estimate the thickness of ice needed to support each mass.

a) a person with a mass of 75 kg

Use: $t = 3.8m^{\frac{1}{2}}$ Substitute: $m = 75$

$t =$ _____

$t =$ _____

The thickness is about: _____

b) a car with a mass of 800 kg

Use: $t = 3.8m^{\frac{1}{2}}$ Substitute: _____

$t =$ _____

$t =$ _____

The thickness is about: _____

4. Write each radical as a power with a fractional exponent.

a) $\sqrt{5^3}$ = _____$^{\frac{3}{2}}$

b) $\left(\sqrt{27}\right)^5 = 27$___

c) $\sqrt[3]{25^4}$ = _____

d) $\left(\sqrt[4]{11}\right)^3$ = _____

5. Evaluate each expression.

a) $\left(\sqrt[3]{-8}\right)^2 = (\underline{\hspace{1cm}})^2$

$= \underline{\hspace{1.5cm}}$

b) $\sqrt{4^3} = \sqrt{\underline{\hspace{1cm}}}$

$= \underline{\hspace{1.5cm}}$

c) $(-64)^{\frac{2}{3}} = \left(\sqrt[3]{\underline{\hspace{1cm}}}\right)^2$

$= \underline{\hspace{1.5cm}}$

$= \underline{\hspace{1.5cm}}$

d) $81^{\frac{5}{4}} = \underline{\hspace{2cm}}$

$= \underline{\hspace{1.5cm}}$

$= \underline{\hspace{1.5cm}}$

4.5 **6.** Write each power with a positive exponent.

a) $7^{-3} = \underline{\hspace{1.5cm}}$

b) $\dfrac{1}{2^{-3}} = \underline{\hspace{1.5cm}}$

c) $5^{-\frac{3}{2}} = \underline{\hspace{1.5cm}}$

d) $\left(\dfrac{4}{9}\right)^{-5} = \underline{\hspace{1.5cm}}$

7. Evaluate each power.

a) $36^{-\frac{1}{2}} = \dfrac{1}{36\underline{\hspace{1cm}}}$

$= \underline{\hspace{2cm}}$

$= \underline{\hspace{2cm}}$

b) $8^{-\frac{1}{3}} = \dfrac{1}{\underline{\hspace{1cm}}^{\frac{1}{3}}}$

$= \underline{\hspace{2cm}}$

$= \underline{\hspace{2cm}}$

c) $27^{-\frac{2}{3}} = \dfrac{1}{\underline{\hspace{1cm}}^{\frac{2}{3}}}$

$= \dfrac{1}{\left(\sqrt[3]{\underline{\hspace{1cm}}}\right)^2}$

$= \underline{\hspace{2cm}}$

$= \underline{\hspace{2cm}}$

▶ 4.6 Skill Builder

Multiplying and Dividing Powers with the Same Base

Multiply:

$2^5 \cdot 2^3 = (2 \cdot 2 \cdot 2 \cdot 2 \cdot 2) \cdot (2 \cdot 2 \cdot 2)$

$\qquad = 2 \cdot 2 \cdot 2 \cdot 2 \cdot 2 \cdot 2 \cdot 2 \cdot 2$

$\qquad = 2^8$

To multiply two powers with the same base, add the exponents:

$2^5 \cdot 2^3 = 2^{5+3}$

$\qquad = 2^8$

Divide:

$\dfrac{3^6}{3^4} = \dfrac{3 \cdot 3 \cdot 3 \cdot 3 \cdot 3 \cdot 3}{3 \cdot 3 \cdot 3 \cdot 3}$

$\qquad = \dfrac{\cancel{3} \cdot \cancel{3} \cdot \cancel{3} \cdot \cancel{3} \cdot 3 \cdot 3}{\cancel{3} \cdot \cancel{3} \cdot \cancel{3} \cdot \cancel{3}}$

$\qquad = 3^2$

To divide two powers with the same base, subtract the exponents:

$\dfrac{3^6}{3^4} = 3^{6-4}$

$\qquad = 3^2$

Check

1. Multiply or divide.

a) $2^7 \cdot 2^3 = 2^{\underline{\quad}+\underline{\quad}}$

$\qquad = \underline{\hspace{2cm}}$

c) $2^9 \div 2^3 = 2^{\underline{\quad}-\underline{\quad}}$

$\qquad = \underline{\hspace{2cm}}$

b) $3^2 \cdot 3^2 = 3^{\underline{\quad}+\underline{\quad}}$

$\qquad = \underline{\hspace{2cm}}$

d) $3^7 \div 3^6 = 3^{\underline{\quad}}$

$\qquad = \underline{\hspace{2cm}}$

When a number does not show an exponent, its exponent is 1; for example, $3 = 3^1$

Raising a Power to a Power

Simplify: $(6^2)^4 = (6^2) \cdot (6^2) \cdot (6^2) \cdot (6^2)$ Add the exponents.

$\qquad\qquad = 6^{2+2+2+2}$

$\qquad\qquad = 6^8$

To raise a power to a power, multiply the exponents: $(6^2)^4 = 6^{2 \times 4}$

$\qquad\qquad\qquad\qquad\qquad\qquad\qquad\qquad\quad = 6^8$

Check

1. Simplify.

a) $(2^9)^3 = 2^{\underline{\quad}\times\underline{\quad}}$

$\qquad = \underline{\hspace{2cm}}$

b) $(3^3)^4 = 3^{\underline{\quad}\times\underline{\quad}}$

$\qquad = \underline{\hspace{2cm}}$

▶ 4.6 Applying the Exponent Laws

FOCUS Apply the exponent laws to simplify expressions.

The exponent laws apply for rational bases and rational exponents.

Exponent Laws

Product of powers: $a^m \cdot a^n = a^{m+n}$
Quotient of powers: $a^m \div a^n = a^{m-n}, a \neq 0$
Power of a power: $(a^m)^n = a^{mn}$
Power of a product: $(ab)^m = a^m b^m$

Power of a quotient: $\left(\dfrac{a}{b}\right)^m = \dfrac{a^m}{b^m}, b \neq 0$

Example 1 | **Simplifying Numerical Expressions with Integer Exponents**

Simplify each expression by writing it as a power with a positive exponent.

a) $3^{-7} \cdot 3^3$ **b)** $(5^{-7})^2 \cdot (5^{-2})^3$ **c)** $\dfrac{(6^{-8})(6^4)}{6^{-3}}$

Solution

Use the exponent laws.

a) $3^{-7} \cdot 3^3$ Multiply powers by adding exponents.
$= 3^{-7+3}$
$= 3^{-4}$ Write as a power with a positive exponent.
$= \dfrac{1}{3^4}$

b) $(5^{-7})^2 \cdot (5^{-2})^3$ Find the power of a power by multiplying exponents.
$= (5^{-7 \times 2}) \cdot (5^{-2 \times 3})$
$= 5^{-14} \cdot 5^{-6}$ Multiply powers by adding exponents.
$= 5^{-14 + (-6)}$
$= 5^{-20}$ Write as a power with a positive exponent.
$= \dfrac{1}{5^{20}}$

c) $\dfrac{(6^{-8})(6^4)}{6^{-3}}$ 　　　In the numerator, multiply powers by adding exponents.

$= \dfrac{6^{-8\,+\,4}}{6^{-3}}$

$= \dfrac{6^{-4}}{6^{-3}}$ 　　　Divide powers by subtracting exponents.

$= 6^{-4\,-\,(-3)}$

$= 6^{-4\,+\,3}$

$= 6^{-1}$ 　　　Write as a power with a positive exponent.

$= \dfrac{1}{6}$

Check

1. Simplify each expression by writing it as a power with a positive exponent.

a) $2^{-4} \cdot 2^{-3}$ 　　　Multiply powers by adding exponents.

$= 2^{\underline{\qquad}}$

$= \underline{\qquad}$ 　　　Write as a power with a positive exponent.

$= \underline{\qquad}$

b) $(3^{-2} \cdot 3^4)^{-2}$ 　　　Multiply powers by _____.

$= (\underline{\qquad})^{-2}$

$= \underline{\qquad}$ 　　　Find the power of a power by _____.

$= \underline{\qquad}$ 　　　Write as a power with a positive exponent.

$= \underline{\qquad}$

c) $\dfrac{11^{-2}}{(11^{-4})(11^{-5})}$ 　　　In the denominator, multiply powers by _____.

$= \dfrac{11^{\overline{\qquad}}}{11^{\underline{\qquad}}}$

$= \underline{\qquad}$ 　　　Divide powers by _____.

$= 11^{\underline{\qquad}}$

$= \underline{\qquad}$

$= \underline{\qquad}$

 978-0-321-61066-9 Copyright © 2011 Pearson Canada Inc.

| Example 2 | Simplifying Numerical Expressions with Rational Exponents |

Simplify each expression by writing it as a power with a positive exponent.

a) $3^{\frac{1}{2}} \cdot 3^{\frac{1}{4}}$

b) $2^{-\frac{1}{3}} \cdot (2^{-2})^{\frac{1}{2}}$

c) $\dfrac{(5^{-0.5})(5^{1.5})}{5^{0.5}}$

Solution

a) $\quad 3^{\frac{1}{2}} \cdot 3^{\frac{1}{4}}$ Multiply powers by adding exponents.

$= 3^{\frac{1}{2}+\frac{1}{4}}$ Write the exponents with a common denominator.

$= 3^{\frac{2}{4}+\frac{1}{4}}$

$= 3^{\frac{3}{4}}$

b) $\quad 2^{-\frac{1}{3}} \cdot (2^{-2})^{\frac{1}{2}}$ In the 2nd factor, find the power of a power by multiplying exponents.

$= 2^{-\frac{1}{3}} \cdot 2^{(-2)\left(\frac{1}{2}\right)}$

$= 2^{-\frac{1}{3}} \cdot 2^{-1}$ Multiply powers by adding exponents.

$= 2^{-\frac{1}{3}-1}$ Write the exponents with a common denominator.

$= 2^{-\frac{1}{3}-\frac{3}{3}}$

$= 2^{-\frac{4}{3}}$ Write as a power with a positive exponent.

$= \dfrac{1}{2^{\frac{4}{3}}}$

c) $\quad \dfrac{(5^{-0.5})(5^{1.5})}{5^{0.5}}$ In the numerator, multiply powers by adding exponents.

$= \dfrac{5^{-0.5+1.5}}{5^{0.5}}$

$= \dfrac{5^{1}}{5^{0.5}}$ Divide powers by subtracting exponents.

$= 5^{1-0.5}$

$= 5^{0.5}$

Check

1. Simplify each expression by writing as a power with a positive exponent.

a) $\left(4^{\frac{1}{2}} \cdot 4^{-\frac{1}{4}}\right)^3$ Multiply powers by _____ .

$= \left(4^{\underline{\quad\quad}}\right)^3$ Write the exponents with a common denominator.

$= \left(4^{\underline{\quad\quad}}\right)^3$

$= \left(4^{\underline{\quad\quad}}\right)^3$ Find the power of a power by _____ .

$= 4^{\underline{\quad\quad}}$

$= \underline{\quad\quad\quad}$

b) $\left(2^{-\frac{1}{3}}\right)^3 \cdot (2^{-2})^{-\frac{1}{3}}$ Find the power of a power by _____

$= 2^{\underline{\quad\quad}} \cdot 2^{\underline{\quad\quad}}$

$= 2^{\underline{\quad\quad}} \cdot 2^{\underline{\quad\quad}}$ Multiply powers by _____ .

$= 2^{\underline{\quad\quad}}$

$= \underline{\quad\quad\quad}$ Write as a power with _____

$=$

$\underline{\quad\quad\quad}$

c) $\left[\dfrac{5^{-1.5}}{(5^{1.5})(5^{-0.25})}\right]^4$ In the denominator, multiply powers by _____ .

$= \left[\dfrac{5^{\underline{\quad\quad}}}{5^{\underline{\quad\quad}}}\right]^4$

$= \left[\dfrac{5^{\underline{\quad\quad}}}{5^{\underline{\quad\quad}}}\right]^4$ Divide powers by _____ .

$= \left[5^{\underline{\quad\quad}}\right]^{\underline{\quad\quad}}$

$= \left[5^{\underline{\quad\quad}}\right]^{\underline{\quad\quad}}$ Find the power of a power by _____

$= \underline{\quad\quad\quad}$ Write as a power with _____

$=$

$\underline{\quad\quad\quad}$

We can use letters to represent numbers, so all the exponent laws apply when we use algebraic expressions.

Example 3 | Simplifying Algebraic Expressions with Integer Exponents

Simplify.

a) $3a^2 \cdot a^{-5} \cdot a^4$ **b)** $(2x^2 \cdot 3x^{-5})^3$ **c)** $\dfrac{12a^2}{3a^{-3}}$

Solution

a) $3a^2 \cdot a^{-5} \cdot a^4$ Multiply powers by adding exponents.

$= 3 \cdot a^{2-5+4}$

$= 3 \cdot a^1$

$= 3a$

b) $(2x^2 \cdot 3x^{-5})^3$ Group like factors; put coefficients together and variables together.

$= (2 \cdot 3 \cdot x^2 \cdot x^{-5})^3$ Multiply coefficients. Multiply powers by adding exponents.

$= (6 \cdot x^{2-5})^3$

$= (6 \cdot x^{-3})^3$ Find the power of a power by multiplying exponents.

$= 6^3 \cdot x^{(-3) \times (3)}$

$= 216 \cdot x^{-9}$ Write x^{-9} with a positive exponent.

$= 216 \cdot \dfrac{1}{x^9}$

$= \dfrac{216}{x^9}$

c) $\dfrac{12a^2}{3a^{-3}}$ Group like factors.

$= \dfrac{12}{3} \cdot \dfrac{a^2}{a^{-3}}$ Divide coefficients. Divide powers by subtracting exponents.

$= 4 \cdot a^{2-(-3)}$

$= 4 \cdot a^{2+3}$

$= 4 \cdot a^5$

$= 4a^5$

Check

1. Simplify. Write an expression with positive exponents where necessary.

a) $2x^3 \cdot x^4 \cdot x^{-9}$

$= 2 \cdot x\rule{2cm}{0.4pt}$

Multiply powers by _____.

$= 2 \cdot x\rule{1.5cm}{0.4pt}$

Write _____ with a _____.

$= 2 \cdot \dfrac{1}{\rule{1cm}{0.4pt}}$

$= \rule{1.5cm}{0.4pt}$

b) $(2a^5 \cdot 3a^{-1})^2$

Group _____.

$= (2 \cdot 3 \cdot a\rule{1cm}{0.4pt} \cdot a\rule{1cm}{0.4pt})^2$

Multiply _____. Multiply powers by _____ _____.

$= (6 \cdot a\rule{1cm}{0.4pt})^2$

$= (6 \cdot a\rule{1cm}{0.4pt})^2$

Find the power of a power by _____.

$= 6\rule{1cm}{0.4pt} \cdot a\rule{1.5cm}{0.4pt}$

$= \rule{2.5cm}{0.4pt}$

$= \rule{2.5cm}{0.4pt}$

c) $\dfrac{3y^2}{6y^{-4}}$

Group _____.

$= \dfrac{3}{\rule{1cm}{0.4pt}} \cdot \dfrac{y^2}{\rule{1cm}{0.4pt}}$

Divide _____. Divide powers by _____ _____.

$= \rule{3cm}{0.4pt}$

$= \rule{3cm}{0.4pt}$

Example 4 | **Simplifying Algebraic Expressions with Rational Exponents**

Simplify.

a) $x^{\frac{3}{2}} \cdot x^{-1}$

b) $\dfrac{10a^{\frac{9}{4}}}{8a^3}$

Solution

a) $\quad x^{\frac{3}{2}} \cdot x^{-1}$ 　　　　Multiply powers by adding exponents.

$\quad = x^{\frac{3}{2}-1}$ 　　　　Write exponents with a common denominator.

$\quad = x^{\frac{3}{2}-\frac{2}{2}}$

$\quad = x^{\frac{1}{2}}$

b) $\quad \dfrac{10a^{\frac{9}{4}}}{8a^3}$ 　　　　Group like factors.

$\quad = \dfrac{10}{8} \cdot \dfrac{a^{\frac{9}{4}}}{a^3}$ 　　　　Divide coefficients. Divide powers by subtracting exponents.

$\quad = \dfrac{5}{4} \cdot a^{\frac{9}{4}-3}$ 　　　　Write exponents with a common denominator.

$\quad = \dfrac{5}{4} \cdot a^{\frac{9}{4}-\frac{12}{4}}$

$\quad = \dfrac{5}{4} \cdot a^{-\frac{3}{4}}$ 　　　　Write $a^{-\frac{3}{4}}$ with a positive exponent.

$\quad = \dfrac{5}{4} \cdot \dfrac{1}{a^{\frac{3}{4}}}$

$\quad = \dfrac{5}{4a^{\frac{3}{4}}}$

Check

1. Simplify.

a) $x^{\frac{5}{2}} \cdot x^{-\frac{3}{2}}$ 　　　　　　　Multiply powers by _____.

$= x^{\underline{\quad\quad}}$

$= x^{\underline{\quad\quad}}$

$= \underline{\quad\quad\quad}$

b) $\dfrac{8a^{\frac{1}{3}}}{6a^{-\frac{4}{3}}}$ 　　　　　　　Group _____.

$= \dfrac{\underline{\quad\quad}}{\underline{\quad\quad}} \cdot \dfrac{a^{\underline{\quad}}}{a^{\underline{\quad}}}$ 　　　　Divide _____. Divide powers by _____.

$= \underline{\quad\quad} \cdot a^{\underline{\quad}}$

$= \underline{\quad\quad} \cdot a^{\underline{\quad}}$

$= \underline{\quad\quad}$

Practice

1. Write as a power with a positive exponent.

a) $5^7 \cdot 5^4 \cdot 5^{-7} = 5^{\underline{\quad\quad}}$

　　　$= \underline{\quad\quad}$

b) $\dfrac{11^2}{11^{-3}} = 11^{\underline{\quad\quad}}$

　　　$= \underline{\quad\quad}$

c) $(3^2 \cdot 3^2)^{-2} = (3^{\underline{\quad\quad}})^{-2}$

　　　$= (3^{\underline{\quad}})^{-2}$

　　　$= 3^{\underline{\quad} \times \underline{\quad}}$

　　　$= \underline{\quad\quad}$

　　　$= \underline{\quad\quad}$

d) $\left(\dfrac{8^2}{8^3}\right)^{-4} = (8^{\underline{\quad\quad}})^{-4}$

　　　$= \underline{\quad\quad}$

　　　$= \underline{\quad\quad}$

　　　$= \underline{\quad\quad}$

2. Evaluate.

a) $(7^{-2})^{-1} = 7 \underline{\qquad} \times \underline{\qquad}$

$= \underline{\qquad}$

$= \underline{\qquad}$

b) $5^3 \cdot (5^{-2})^2 = 5^3 \cdot 5 \underline{\qquad} \times 2$

$= 5^3 \cdot \underline{\qquad}$

$= \underline{\qquad}$

$= \underline{\qquad}$

c) $\left(\dfrac{4^{-3} \cdot 4^{-1}}{4^{-2}} \right)^2 = \left(\dfrac{4 \underline{\qquad}}{4 \underline{\qquad}} \right)^2$

$= \left(\underline{\qquad} \right)$

$= \underline{\qquad}$

$= \underline{\qquad}$

$= \underline{\qquad}$

$= \underline{\qquad}$

Each answer should be an integer or a fraction.

3. Write as a power with a positive exponent.

a) $5^{\frac{3}{4}} \cdot 5^{-\frac{1}{4}} = 5 \underline{\qquad}$

$= \underline{\qquad}$

$= \underline{\qquad}$

b) $(7^{-0.5} \cdot 7^{2.5})^{-2} = \left(7 \underline{\qquad} \right)^{-2}$

$= \left(7 \underline{\qquad} \right)^{-2}$

$= \underline{\qquad}$

$= \underline{\qquad}$

$= \underline{\qquad}$

c) $\dfrac{3^{-\frac{2}{3}}}{3^{\frac{4}{3}}} = 3 \underline{\qquad}$

$= \underline{\qquad}$

$= \underline{\qquad}$

d) $\left(\dfrac{2^{-1.75}}{2^{-0.25}} \right)^3 = \left(2 \underline{\qquad} \right)^3$

$= \left(2 \underline{\qquad} \right)^3$

$= \underline{\qquad}$

$= \underline{\qquad}$

4. Circle the expressions that equal 1.

a) $x \cdot x^{-1}$

b) $(a \cdot a^{-1})^3$

c) $\dfrac{y}{y^{-1}}$

d) $\dfrac{\left(x^{\frac{1}{2}}\right)^{-2}}{x^{-1}}$

Remember, $x^0 = 1$

5. Write this expression with positive exponents: $\dfrac{a}{b^{-1}} = $ _____

6. Simplify. Write an expression with positive exponents where necessary.

a) $3y \cdot y^{-2} \cdot y^4 = 3 \cdot y$————

$= $ ____ $\cdot$ ____

$= $ _____

b) $(4x^3 \cdot 3x^{-4})^2 = ($ ____ $\cdot$ ____ $\cdot x$—— $\cdot x$——$)^2$

$= ($ ____ $\cdot x$—— $\cdot x$——$)^2$

$= ($ ____ $\cdot x$————$)^2$

$= ($ ____ $\cdot x$——$)^2$

$= $ ____ $\cdot$ ____

$= $ _____

$= $ _____

c) $\dfrac{25b^3}{10b^{-2}} = $ _____ $\cdot \dfrac{b——}{b——}$

$= $ _____ $\cdot b$——

$= $ _____

d) $\dfrac{(7a^{-3})^2}{a^{-4}} = \dfrac{\text{____} \cdot a——}{\text{_____}}$

$= $ ____ $\cdot a$——

$= $ _____

$= $ _____

7. Simplify. Write an expression with positive exponents where necessary.

a) $x^{-\frac{1}{2}} \cdot x^{-3} = x$————

$= x$————

$= $ _____

$= $ _____

b) $\dfrac{16a^{\frac{1}{3}}}{24a^{-1}} = $ _____

$= $ _____

$= $ _____

$= $ _____

Chapter 4 Puzzle

How Irrational Is It?

The radical $\sqrt{26}$ and the power $2^{\frac{3}{2}}$ went to a bank to apply for credit cards.
"I'm sorry," said the bank manager, "You may not have credit cards."
"Why not?," asked the radical and power, "Is it because we are irrational?"

Why did the bank manager not give them credit cards?

To find out, evaluate or simplify each expression below.
Then, write the matching letter above the matching answer on the underline below.

$\sqrt[3]{-8} = \underline{\hspace{1cm}} = U$

$4^{\frac{3}{2}} = \underline{\hspace{1cm}} = E$

$2^{\frac{1}{2}} = \underline{\hspace{1cm}} = H$

$5^{-3} = \underline{\hspace{1cm}} = Y$

$3^{\frac{2}{3}} = \underline{\hspace{1cm}} = A$

$\left(\frac{3}{4}\right)^{-2} = \underline{\hspace{1cm}} = N$

$2^{-5} \cdot 2^4 = \underline{\hspace{1cm}} = R$

$\dfrac{5^{-3} \cdot 5^4}{5^{-2}} = \underline{\hspace{1cm}} = I$

$\left(4^{\frac{2}{3}}\right)^3 = \underline{\hspace{1cm}} = G$

$7^{\frac{1}{2}} \cdot 7^{\frac{1}{4}} = \underline{\hspace{1cm}} = T$

$\left(2^{\frac{1}{3}} \cdot 2^{\frac{1}{2}}\right)^6 = \underline{\hspace{1cm}} = D$

$\overline{\sqrt[4]{7^3}} \quad \overline{\sqrt{2}} \quad \overline{8} \quad \overline{\dfrac{1}{125}} \qquad \overline{\sqrt[3]{9}} \quad \overline{\dfrac{1}{2}} \quad \overline{8} \qquad \overline{-2} \quad \overline{\dfrac{16}{9}} \quad \overline{32} \quad \overline{8} \quad \overline{\dfrac{1}{2}}$

$\overline{8} \quad \overline{125} \quad \overline{16} \quad \overline{\sqrt{2}} \quad \overline{\sqrt[4]{7^3}} \quad \overline{8} \quad \overline{8} \quad \overline{\dfrac{16}{9}}$

Skill	Description	Example
Classify radicals as rational or irrational numbers.	A radical is rational if it can be written as: a fraction, a terminating decimal, or a repeating decimal.	Classify each radical as rational or irrational. $\sqrt{2.25} = 1.5$, so $\sqrt{2.25}$ is rational $\sqrt{2} = 1.4142...$, so $\sqrt{2}$ is irrational
Simplify a radical.	Write the radicand as a product with a perfect power as one factor. Then write the radical as the product of a whole number and a radical.	Simplify. $\sqrt{24}$ $\begin{aligned} \sqrt{24} &= \sqrt{4 \cdot 6} \\ &= \sqrt{4} \cdot \sqrt{6} \\ &= 2\sqrt{6} \end{aligned}$
Write a mixed radical as an entire radical.	Write the whole number as the root of a perfect power. Then multiply the perfect power and the radicand to get the new radicand.	Express $2\sqrt[3]{5}$ as an entire radical. $2 = \sqrt[3]{2 \cdot 2 \cdot 2}$, or $\sqrt[3]{8}$ So, $\begin{aligned} 2\sqrt[3]{5} &= \sqrt[3]{8} \cdot \sqrt[3]{5} \\ &= \sqrt[3]{8 \cdot 5} \\ &= \sqrt[3]{40} \end{aligned}$
Write a power with a rational number exponent as a radical.	The numerator of the exponent is the power to which the base is raised. The denominator of the exponent is the index of the radical.	Express $7^{\frac{2}{3}}$ as a radical. $7^{\frac{2}{3}} = \sqrt[3]{7^2}$ or $7^{\frac{2}{3}} = \left(\sqrt[3]{7}\right)^2$
Write a power with a negative exponent as a power with a positive exponent.	Write the reciprocal of the base, and change the exponent from negative to positive.	Write each power with a positive exponent. $\left(\frac{3}{5}\right)^{-4} = \left(\frac{5}{3}\right)^4$ $2^{-3} = \frac{1}{2^3}$
Apply exponent laws to simplify expressions.	The exponent laws apply for rational and integer exponents and bases, and for variable bases. The expression is usually written with positive exponents.	Simplify. $\begin{aligned} x^{-\frac{1}{2}} \cdot x^{-2} &= x^{-\frac{1}{2} - 2} \\ &= x^{-\frac{1}{2} - \frac{4}{2}} \\ &= x^{-\frac{5}{2}}, \text{ or } \frac{1}{x^{\frac{5}{2}}} \end{aligned}$

Chapter 4 Review

4.1 **1.** Evaluate each radical.

a) $\sqrt{121}$

121 = _____ × _____

So, $\sqrt{121}$ = _____

b) $\sqrt{400}$

400 = _____ × _____

So, $\sqrt{400}$ = _____

c) $\sqrt[3]{64}$

64 = _____ × _____ × _____

So, $\sqrt[3]{64}$ = _____

d) $\sqrt[3]{-125}$

−125 = (____) × (____) × (____)

So, $\sqrt[3]{-125}$ = _____

2. Estimate $\sqrt{13}$ to 1 decimal place.

13 is between the perfect squares _____ and _____, and is closer to _____.
So, $\sqrt{13}$ is between _____ and _____, and is closer to _____.
Estimate to 1 decimal place: $\sqrt{13} \doteq$ _____
Square the estimate: _____ = _____
Revise the estimate: $\sqrt{13} \doteq$ _____
Square the estimate: _____ = _____
_____ is closer to 13, so $\sqrt{13}$ is about _____.

4.2 **3.** Identify each number as rational or irrational.

a) $\sqrt{8}$

$\sqrt{8}$ = _____, which _____ terminate or repeat

So, $\sqrt{8}$ is _____.

b) $\sqrt[3]{343}$

$\sqrt[3]{343}$ = _____, which _____

So, $\sqrt[3]{343}$ is _____.

4. Each point on the number line below represents one of these numbers. Write a letter to identify each number.

$\sqrt[3]{64}$: _____ $\sqrt[3]{-3}$: _____ $\sqrt{14}$: _____ $\sqrt{8}$: _____

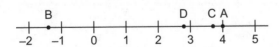

5. a) Estimate the location of each number on the number line below.
$\sqrt{5}$, $\sqrt[3]{-9}$, $\sqrt[3]{35}$

5 is between the perfect squares: _____

So, $\sqrt{5}$ is between: _____

−9 is between: _____

So, $\sqrt[3]{-9}$ is between: _____

35 is between: _____

So, $\sqrt[3]{35}$ is between: _____

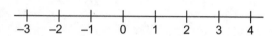

b) From the number line above, least to greatest is: _____

4.3 **6. a)** List all the perfect squares that are factors of each number. Do not include 1.
Circle the greatest perfect square.

i) 32: _____   **ii)** 63: _____   **iii)** 90: _____

b) Use your answers to part a to simplify each radical.

i) $\sqrt{32} = \sqrt{\underline{\quad} \times \underline{\quad}}$ **ii)** $\sqrt{63} = \sqrt{\underline{\quad} \times \underline{\quad}}$ **iii)** $\sqrt{90} = \underline{\qquad}$

$ = \sqrt{\underline{\quad}} \times \sqrt{\underline{\quad}}$ $ = \underline{\quad} \times \underline{\quad}$ $ = \underline{\qquad}$

$ = \underline{\qquad}$ $ = \underline{\qquad}$ $ = \underline{\qquad}$

c) Write the greatest perfect cube that is a factor of each number.

i) 54: _____   **ii)** 60: _____   **iii)** 72: _____

d) Use your answers to part c to simplify each radical, if possible.

i) $\sqrt[3]{54} = \sqrt[3]{\underline{\quad} \times \underline{\quad}}$ **ii)** $\sqrt[3]{60} = \underline{\quad}$ **iii)** $\sqrt[3]{72} = \underline{\qquad}$

$ = \sqrt[3]{\underline{\quad}} \times \sqrt[3]{\underline{\quad}}$ $ = \underline{\qquad}$

$ = \underline{\qquad}$ $ = \underline{\qquad}$

7. Simplify each radical.

a) $\sqrt{52} = \underline{\hspace{2cm}}$

$= \underline{\hspace{2cm}}$

b) $\sqrt[3]{405} = \underline{\hspace{2cm}}$

$= \underline{\hspace{2cm}}$

8. a) Write 1080 as a product of prime factors: $\underline{\hspace{3cm}}$

b) Use the factors in part a to simplify each radical.

i) $\sqrt{1080} = \underline{\hspace{4cm}}$

$= \underline{\hspace{4cm}}$

$= \underline{\hspace{4cm}}$

$= \underline{\hspace{4cm}}$

$= \underline{\hspace{4cm}}$

ii) $\sqrt[3]{1080} = \underline{\hspace{4cm}}$

$= \underline{\hspace{4cm}}$

$= \underline{\hspace{4cm}}$

$= \underline{\hspace{4cm}}$

9. Write each mixed radical as an entire radical.

a) $3\sqrt{14} = \sqrt{3 \cdot 3} \cdot \sqrt{\underline{\hspace{1cm}}}$

$= \sqrt{9} \cdot \sqrt{\underline{\hspace{1cm}}}$

$= \underline{\hspace{2cm}}$

b) $5\sqrt[3]{2} = \sqrt[3]{5 \cdot 5 \cdot 5} \cdot \sqrt[3]{\underline{\hspace{1cm}}}$

$= \sqrt[3]{\underline{\hspace{1cm}}} \cdot \underline{\hspace{1cm}}$

$= \underline{\hspace{2cm}}$

4.4 **10.** Evaluate each power.

a) $36^{\frac{1}{2}} = \sqrt{\underline{\hspace{1cm}}}$

$= \underline{\hspace{2cm}}$

b) $125^{\frac{1}{3}} = \underline{\hspace{2cm}}$

$= \underline{\hspace{2cm}}$

c) $81^{\frac{3}{4}} = \left(\sqrt[4]{\underline{\hspace{1cm}}}\right)^3$

$= \underline{\hspace{2cm}}$

$= \underline{\hspace{2cm}}$

11. a) Write each radical as a power, then use a calculator to find the value to 2 decimal places.

i) $\sqrt[5]{18^2}$: $\underline{\hspace{3cm}}$

ii) $\left(\sqrt[4]{21}\right)^3$: $\underline{\hspace{3cm}}$

b) Write each power as a radical, then use a calculator to find the value to 2 decimal places.

i) $25^{\frac{4}{3}}$: $\underline{\hspace{4cm}}$

ii) $75^{\frac{2}{5}}$: $\underline{\hspace{4cm}}$

12. Write each power with a positive exponent.

a) $8^{-5} =$ _____

b) $6^{-\frac{2}{3}} =$ _____

c) $\dfrac{1}{3^{-10}} =$ _____

d) $\left(\dfrac{9}{2}\right)^{-3} =$ _____

13. Evaluate each power.

a) $3^{-3} =$ _____

$=$ _____

b) $\left(\dfrac{3}{10}\right)^{-3} =$ _____

$=$ _____

$=$ _____

c) $4^{-\frac{3}{2}} = \dfrac{1}{\rule{2cm}{0.4pt}}$

$= \dfrac{1}{\rule{2cm}{0.4pt}}$

$= \dfrac{\rule{2cm}{0.4pt}}{\rule{2cm}{0.4pt}}$

$= \dfrac{\rule{2cm}{0.4pt}}{\rule{2cm}{0.4pt}}$

14. Evaluate.

a) $(3^{-2})^{-2} = 3^{\rule{1.5cm}{0.4pt}}$

$=$ _____

$=$ _____

b) $\left(4^{\frac{1}{2}} \cdot 4^{\frac{3}{2}}\right)^{-1} = \left(4^{\rule{1cm}{0.4pt}}\right)^{-1}$

$=$ _____

$=$ _____

$=$ _____

15. Simplify. Write an expression with a positive exponent where necessary.

a) $x^{\frac{2}{3}} \cdot x^{-2} = x^{\rule{1.5cm}{0.4pt}}$

$=$ _____

$=$ _____

$=$ _____

b) $\dfrac{18x^{\frac{1}{2}}}{24x^{-\frac{3}{2}}} = \dfrac{\rule{1cm}{0.4pt}}{\rule{1cm}{0.4pt}} \cdot \dfrac{x^{\rule{1cm}{0.4pt}}}{x^{\rule{1cm}{0.4pt}}}$

$= \dfrac{\rule{2cm}{0.4pt}}{\rule{2cm}{0.4pt}} \cdot x^{\rule{1cm}{0.4pt}}$

$= \dfrac{\rule{2cm}{0.4pt}}{\rule{2cm}{0.4pt}}$

$= \dfrac{\rule{2cm}{0.4pt}}{\rule{2cm}{0.4pt}}$

Relations and Functions

What You'll Learn

- Describe a relation in words and represent it using a set of ordered pairs, an arrow diagram, a table of values, and a graph.

- Find the domain and range of a relation and decide if the relation is a function.

- Interpret graphs that represent situations.

- Find the rate of change and the intercepts of the graph of a linear function.

Why It's Important

Relations and functions are used by:

- advertising specialists, to analyze trends in sales

- bank tellers, to convert Canadian dollars to foreign currency

- nurses, to relate a patient's mass to the drug dosage required

Key Words

relation	independent variable
arrow diagram	function notation
domain	rate of change
range	linear function
function	horizontal intercept
dependent variable	vertical intercept

▶ 5.1 Representing Relations

FOCUS Represent relations in different ways.

A *set* is a collection of objects.

An *element* of a set is one object in the set.

A **relation** associates the elements of one set with the elements of another set.

We can represent a relation in different ways.

Example 1 | Representing a Relation Given as a Table

Athletes can be associated with their sports.

Athlete	Sport
Jennifer Botterill	Ice hockey
Jennifer Jones	Curling
Jeremy Wotherspoon	Speed skating
Jonathan Cheechoo	Ice hockey

> *The columns represent the sets in the relation. The heading of each column describes each set.*

a) Describe this relation in words.

b) Represent this relation as a set of ordered pairs.

c) Represent this relation as an **arrow diagram**.

Solution

a) The relation shows the association "takes part in" from a set of athletes to a set of sports. For example, Jennifer Botterill takes part in ice hockey.

b) The ordered pairs are:

{(Jennifer Botterill, ice hockey), (Jennifer Jones, curling), (Jeremy Wotherspoon, speed skating), (Jonathan Cheechoo, ice hockey)}

> *The athletes are the 1st elements in the ordered pairs and the sports are the 2nd elements.*

c) The athletes are written in the 1st set of the arrow diagram. The sports are written in the 2nd set; each sport is written only once.

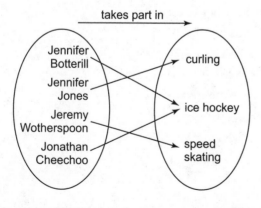

> *Each arrow associates an element in the 1st set with an element in the 2nd set. The order is important; a relation has direction from the 1st set to the 2nd set.*

Check

1. Tourist attractions can be associated with the provinces or territories they are in.

Tourist Attraction	Province
Butchart Gardens	British Columbia
Icefields Parkway	Alberta
Royal Canadian Mint	Manitoba
Stanley Park	British Columbia

a) Describe this relation in words.

The relation shows the association _____ from a set of

_____ to a set of _____.

For example, _____

b) Represent this relation as a set of ordered pairs.

The ordered pairs are: _____

_____

c) Represent this relation as an arrow diagram.

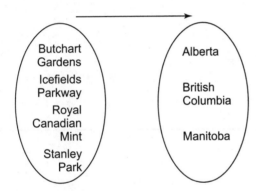

We usually list the elements of each set in alphabetical or numerical order.

When the elements of one or both sets are numbers, the relation can be represented as a bar graph.

Example 2 | Representing a Relation Given as a Bar Graph

Consider the relation represented by this graph.
Represent the relation:

a) as a table

b) as an arrow diagram

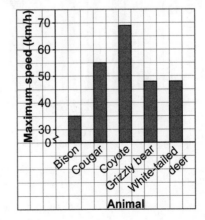

Maximum Speeds of Different Animals

Solution

a) In the table, write the types of animals in the 1st column and estimates of the maximum speeds in kilometres per hour in the 2nd column.

Animal	Maximum Speed (km/h)
Bison	35
Cougar	55
Coyote	69
Grizzly bear	48
White-tailed deer	48

b) The association is: "has a maximum speed (km/h) of"
In the arrow diagram, write the types of animals in the 1st set and the maximum speeds in kilometres per hour in the 2nd set.

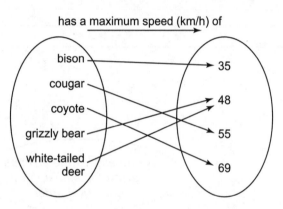

Check

1. Consider the relation represented by this graph.

Canada's Medal Count at the Summer Olympics

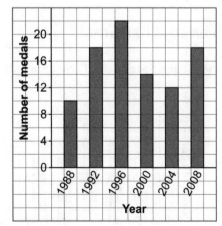

Represent the relation:

a) as a table

Year	Number of Medals

b) as an arrow diagram

The association is:

_____

_____

Practice

1. Consider the relation represented by this table.

Capital City	Province or Territory
Yellowknife	Northwest Territories
Iqaluit	Nunavut
Whitehorse	Yukon
Victoria	British Columbia
Edmonton	Alberta
Regina	Saskatchewan
Winnipeg	Manitoba

a) Complete this sentence.

The relation associates a set of _____ with a set of

_____

b) Circle the best choice of association for the relation above.

i) is the province of

ii) is the capital city of

iii) is a village in

iv) is a territory in

c) Circle the ordered pair that belongs to the relation above.

i) (Edmonton, Saskatchewan)

ii) (Nunavut, Iqaluit)

iii) (Calgary, Alberta)

iv) (Winnipeg, Manitoba)

d) Draw an arrow diagram to represent the relation.

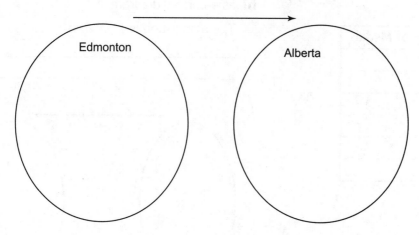

2. Properties in the board game *Monopoly®* can be associated with their colours.

Property	Colour
Atlantic Avenue	Yellow
Baltic Avenue	Purple
Boardwalk	Dark Blue
Marvin Gardens	Yellow
Pacific Avenue	Green

a) Describe this relation in words.

The relation shows the association _____ from a set
of _____ to a set of _____
For example, _____

b) Represent this relation as a set of ordered pairs.

The ordered pairs are: _____

_____

c) Represent this relation as an arrow diagram.

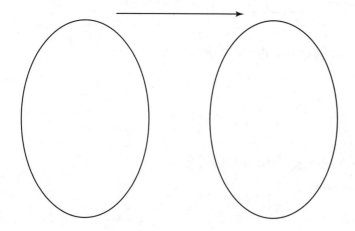

3. Consider the relation represented by this graph.

Number of Vowels in a Word

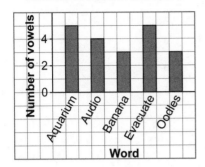

a) Represent the relation as a table.

Word	Number of Vowels

b) Describe the relation in words.

The relation shows the association _____

_____

c) List 2 ordered pairs that belong to the relation.

Two ordered pairs are: _____

4. Here are some Canadian prime ministers and the year they died.
(Pierre Trudeau, 2000); (John Diefenbaker, 1979); (Lester B. Pearson, 1972);
(Robert Borden, 1937); (John A. Macdonald, 1891)
Use these data to represent each association below in the stated way.

a) "died in" as a table

b) "is the year of death of" as an arrow diagram

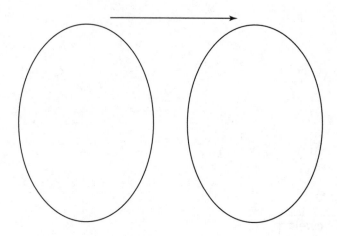

c) Does it matter if you reverse the ovals in the arrow diagram? Explain.

_____

_____

5. a) Create a table of values to represent the association "is the number of legs on" for different types of animals.

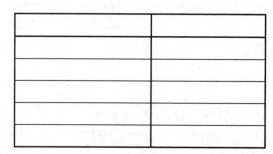

b) Represent the relation in two different ways.

_____

_____

_____

_____

_____

5.2 Skill Builder

Evaluating Expressions

We can evaluate algebraic expressions when given the values of the variables.

To evaluate $7k + 2$ for $k = 4$:

$7k + 2 = 7(4) + 2$
$\qquad = 28 + 2$
$\qquad = 30$

> $7k$ means $7 \times k$.

Check

1. Evaluate each expression when $x = 3$.

a) $3x + 4$

$3(\underline{\hspace{1cm}}) + 4 = \underline{\hspace{1cm}} + 4$

$\qquad = \underline{\hspace{1cm}}$

b) $5x - 7$

$\underline{\hspace{2cm}} = \underline{\hspace{1.5cm}}$

$\qquad = \underline{\hspace{1.5cm}}$

Solving Equations

To solve an equation, find the value of the variable that makes the equation true.

To solve $3x + 4 = 28$:

$\qquad 3x + 4 = 28$ Isolate $3x$: subtract 4 from each side.

$3x + 4 - 4 = 28 - 4$

$\qquad\qquad 3x = 24$ Divide each side by 3.

$\qquad\qquad x = 8$

Check

1. Solve each equation.

a) $\qquad 3x - 4 = 23$

$3x - 4 + \underline{\hspace{1cm}} = 23 + \underline{\hspace{1cm}}$

$\underline{\hspace{1cm}} = \underline{\hspace{1cm}}$

$x = \underline{\hspace{1cm}}$

b) $\qquad 5x + 7 = 42$

$x = \underline{\hspace{1cm}}$

5.2 Properties of Functions

Develop an understanding of functions.

The set of 1st elements of a relation is its **domain**.
The set of related 2nd elements of a relation is its **range**.

> A **function** is a special type of relation where each element in
> the domain is associated with exactly one element in the range.

Example 1 | Identifying Functions

For each relation below:
- Identify its domain and range.
- Decide whether the relation is a function.

a) A relation that associates 5 foods to the food groups to which they belong:
{(orange, fruit), (cheese, dairy), (broccoli, vegetable), (milk, dairy), (kiwi, fruit)}

b)

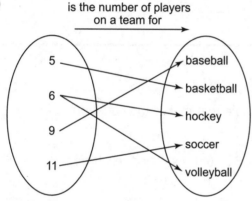

is the number of players
on a team for

Solution

a) {(orange, fruit), (cheese, dairy), (broccoli, vegetable), (milk, dairy), (kiwi, fruit)}
The domain is the set of 1st elements of the ordered pairs:
{orange, cheese, broccoli, milk, kiwi}
The range is the set of 2nd elements of the ordered pairs:
{fruit, dairy, vegetable}

> *When we list the elements
> of the domain and range, we do
> not repeat an element that
> occurs more than once.*

Check to see if any ordered pairs have the same 1st element:
{(*orange*, fruit), (*cheese*, dairy), (*broccoli*, vegetable), (*milk*, dairy), (*kiwi*, fruit)}
Each ordered pair has a different 1st element.
So, the relation is a function.

b) The domain is the set of elements in the 1st set: {5, 6, 9, 11}
The range is the set of elements in the 2nd set:
{baseball, basketball, hockey, soccer, volleyball}
Check to see if there is more than one arrow from any element in the 1st set.
Since there are two arrows from 6 in the 1st set, the relation is not a function.

Check

1. For each relation below:
- Identify its domain and range.
- Decide whether the relation is a function.

a) A relation that associates the numbers of tickets required for different rides at Galaxyland in the West Edmonton Mall:

{(4, Cosmo's Space Derby), (6, Galaxy Twister), (7, Mindbender),
(4, Galaxyland Raceway), (3, Balloon Race)}

The domain is the set of 1st elements: _____

The range is the set of 2nd elements: _____

_____

_____ ordered pairs have the same 1st element: _____

So, the relation _____ a function.

b)

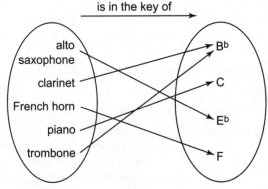

is in the key of

The domain is: _____

The range is: _____

There is _____ arrow from each element in the 1st set.

So, the relation _____ a function.

This table shows the masses of different numbers of Canadian quarters.

independent variable ⟶

dependent variable ⟵

domain {

range }

Number of Quarters, n	Mass, m (g)
1	4.4
2	8.8
3	13.2
4	17.6
5	22.0

The mass of the quarters, m, depends on the number of quarters, n.
So, we say m is the **dependent variable** and n is the **independent variable**.

Example 2 Describing Functions

This table shows sample costs for a pay-as-you-go cell phone plan.

Number of Minutes, *n*	Cost, *C* ($)
10	2
20	4
30	6
40	8
50	10

A table of values usually represents a sample of the ordered pairs in a relation.

a) Why is this relation also a function?

b) Identify the dependent variable and the independent variable.

c) Write the domain and range.

Solution

a) No two numbers in the 1st column are the same. So, the relation is a function.

b) The cost, *C*, depends on the number of minutes, *n*.
So, *C* is the dependent variable and *n* is the independent variable.

c) The 1st column of the table represents the domain.
The domain is: {10, 20, 30, 40, 50, ...}
The 2nd column of the table represents the range.
The range is: {2, 4, 6, 8, 10, ...}

The symbol "..." shows that the domain and range may continue.

Check

1. This table shows the Calories burned for various running times, at an average speed of 8 km/h.

Number of Minutes, *n*	Calories Burned per Kilogram, *C*
5	0.67
10	1.34
15	2.01
20	2.68
25	3.35

a) Why is this relation also a function?

b) Identify the dependent variable and the independent variable.

The _____ depends on _____

_____ So, _____ is the dependent variable and _____ is the independent variable.

c) Write the domain and range.

The domain is: _____

The range is: _____

We can write an equation that represents a function using **function notation**.

For example, to show that $C = 15 + 2n$ represents a function, we write: $C(n) = 15 + 2n$

> We say: "C of n is equal to 15 + 2n."

This notation shows that C is the dependent variable and that C depends on n.

| Example 3 | Using Function Notation to Find Values |

Carmen works for a research company in a shopping mall. The equation $P = 5n + 30$ represents her daily pay, P dollars, when she conducts n surveys.

a) Describe the function. Write the equation using function notation.

b) Find the value of $P(8)$.

What does this number represent?

c) Find the value of n when $P(n) = 90$.

What does this number represent?

Solution

a) Carmen's pay is a function of the number of surveys she conducts.

In function notation: $P(n) = 5n + 30$

b) To find $P(8)$, use:

$P(n) = 5n + 30$ Substitute: $n = 8$

$P(8) = 5(8) + 30$

$P(8) = 40 + 30$

> $P(8)$ is the value of P when $n = 8$.

$P(8) = 70$

This means that when Carmen conducts 8 surveys, she earns $70.

c) To find the value of n when $P(n) = 90$, use:

$P(n) = 5n + 30$ Substitute: $P(n) = 90$

$90 = 5n + 30$ Solve for n. Subtract 30 from each side.

$90 - 30 = 5n + 30 - 30$

$60 = 5n$ Divide each side by 5.

$\dfrac{60}{5} = \dfrac{5n}{5}$

$n = 12$

$P(n) = 90$ when $n = 12$

This means that when Carmen conducts 12 surveys, she earns $90.

Check

1. Frank sells memberships to a local gym. The equation $E = 50n + 150$ represents his weekly earnings, E dollars, when he sells n memberships.

a) Describe the function. Write the equation using function notation.

_____ are a function of _____.

In function notation: E_____ = _____ + 150

b) Find the value of $E(9)$.
What does this number represent?

$E(n) = 50n + 150$ Substitute: $n = 9$

$E(9) = 50(\_\_\_\_) + 150$

$E(9) = $ _____

$E(9) = $ _____

This means that when Frank sells _____ memberships, he earns _____.

c) Find the value of n when $E(n) = 850$.
What does this number represent?

$E(n) = 50n + 150$ Substitute: $E(n) = 850$

_____ $= 50n + 150$

$n = $ _____

$E(n) = 850$ when $n = $ _____

This means that when Frank sells _____ memberships, he earns _____.

Practice

1. For each relation below, decide whether the relation is a function. How do you know?

a)

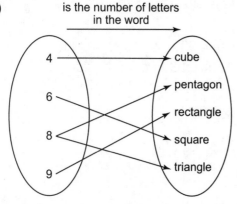

is the number of letters in the word

_____

So, the relation _____ a function.

b) A relation that associates cities to famous people who were born there:
{(Winnipeg, Chantal Kreviazuk), (Vancouver, Michael J. Fox), (Calgary, Stephen Harper), (Regina, Steve Nash), (Vancouver, Pamela Anderson)}

_____

So, the relation _____ a function.

c) A relation that associates a number with its double:
{(1, 2), (2, 4), (3, 6), (4, 8), (5, 10)}

_____

So, the relation _____ a function.

2. Identify the domain and range of each relation in question 1.

a) The domain is: _____
The range is: _____

b) The domain is: _____
The range is: _____

_____

c) The domain is: _____
The range is: _____

3. This table shows Alberta's speeding fines for different speeds in a 60 km/h zone.

Speed, s (km/h)	Fine, f ($)
75	89
80	124
85	150
90	177
100	264
110	351

a) Why is this relation also a function?

_____

b) Identify the dependent variable and the independent variable.
The _____ depends on _____.
So, _____ is the dependent variable and _____ is the independent variable.

c) Write the domain and range.
The domain is: _____
The range is: _____

4. Write in function notation.

a) $P = 2s + 15$

_____

b) $y = -3x + 5$

_____

> When an equation has the form "y =," we use symbols such as f(x), g(x), or h(x), to name the function.

5. Write as an equation in two variables.

a) $d(t) = 4t - 7$

$d =$ _____

b) $g(x) = -2x - 3$

_____

6. For the function $P(n) = 7n - 18$, find:

a) $P(3)$

$P(n) = 7n - 18$

$P(3) = 7(\underline{}) - 18$

$P(3) = \underline{} - 18$

$P(3) = \underline{}$

b) $P(8)$

$P(8) = \underline{}$

7. Patty lifts weights at the local gym. The equation $M = 5n + 2.5$ represents the mass lifted, M kilograms, when the number of 5-kg masses on the bar is n.

a) Describe the function. Write the equation using function notation.

_____ is a function of _____.

In function notation: _____

b) Find the value of $M(6)$.
What does this number represent?

$M(n) = 5n + 2.5$

Substitute: $n =$ _____

$M(6)$ is the value of _____ when _____.

This means that when there are _____ 5-kg masses on the bar, Patty lifts _____ kg.

c) Find the value of n when $M(n) = 42.5$.
What does this number represent?

$M(n) = 5n + 2.5$

Substitute: _____

$n =$ _____

$M(n) = 42.5$ when $n =$ _____

This means that when there are _____ 5-kg masses on the bar, Patty lifts _____ kg.

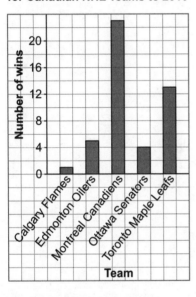

CHECKPOINT 1

Can you...

- describe a relation in words and represent it using a set of ordered pairs, an arrow diagram, and a table of values?
- decide whether a relation is a function?
- list the elements of the domain and range?
- identify the dependent and independent variables?
- write an equation using function notation?

5.1 **1.** Consider the relation represented by this graph.

Number of Stanley Cup Wins for Canadian NHL Teams to 2010

a) Represent the relation as a table.

Team	Number of Wins

b) Describe the relation in words.

The relation shows the association _____

from a set of _____ to a set of _____.

c) Represent the relation as an arrow diagram.

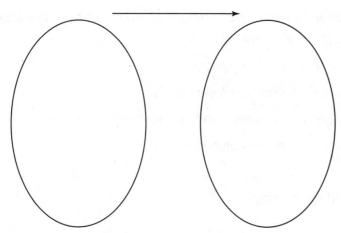

d) List 2 ordered pairs that belong to the relation.
Two ordered pairs are:

_____

5.2 **2.** For each relation below:
- Identify its domain and range.
- Decide whether the relation is a function.

a) A relation that associates a game to what is needed to play it:

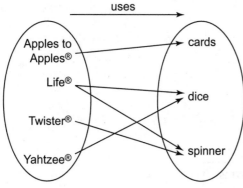

The domain is: _____

The range is: _____

There are _____ arrows from _____ in the 1st set.
So, the relation _____ a function.

b) A relation that associates a book to its author:
{(*Lord of the Flies*, Golding), (*Romeo and Juliet*, Shakespeare), (*Harry Potter*, Rawlings),
(*Catcher in the Rye*, Salinger), (*Of Mice and Men*, Steinbeck)}
The domain is: _____

_____

The range is: _____

_____

So, the relation _____ a function.

3. This table shows the daily rates for emergency medical coverage while travelling outside Canada for 14 days.

Age, a (years)	Daily Rate, r ($)
49	2.88
54	2.95
59	2.98
64	3.04
69	3.91
74	4.88
79	7.73
84	13.34
85	19.32

a) Why is this relation also a function?

_____

b) Identify the dependent variable and the independent variable.

The _____ depends on _____.

So, _____ is the dependent variable and _____ is the independent variable.

c) Write the domain and range.

The domain is: _____

The range is: _____

4. Write each equation in function notation.

a) $A = 5n + 32$

_____

b) $y = -7x + 12$

_____

5. Write each equation as an equation in two variables.

a) $P(n) = 8n - 5$

_____

b) $g(x) = 4x - 1$

_____

6. For the function $g(x) = 3x - 5$, find:

a) $g(8)$

$g(x) = 3x - 5$

$g(8) = 3(\text{_____}) - 5$

$g(8) = $ _____

$g(8) = $ _____

b) the value of x when $g(x) = 31$

$g(x) = 3x - 5$

_____ $= 3x - 5$

$x = $ _____

5.3 Skill Builder

Interpreting Graphs

We can tell a lot from a graph.

The title tells us this graph shows the temperatures in Port Hardy, BC, at different times on January 4, 2010.

From the graph, we see that from 00:00 to 12:00, the line segments go up to the right.
This shows that the temperature increases from midnight to noon.

From 12:00 to 20:00, the line segments go down to the right.
This shows that the temperature decreases from noon to 8 P.M.

The highest point on the graph is (12:00, 8).
This means the highest temperature on January 4th was about 8°C at noon.

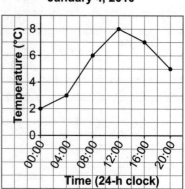

Temperatures in Port Hardy, BC, January 4, 2010

Check

1. Look at the graph below.

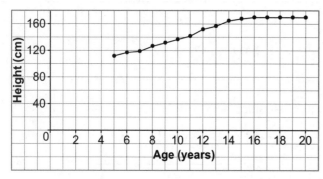

Jodie's Height

a) What does this graph show?

The graph shows Jodie's _____ from _____ to _____ years of age.

b) What happened between 5 and 16 years of age? Jodie _____.
How do you know? _____

c) What happened between 16 and 20 years of age? Jodie _____
How do you know? _____

d) About how tall is Jodie? Jodie is about _____ cm tall.

5.3 Interpreting and Sketching Graphs

FOCUS Describe a possible situation for a graph.

Example 1 | Interpreting a Graph

Each point on this graph represents a person.

a) Which person has the greatest hourly wage? What is this wage?

b) Which person has worked for the least number of years?
What is this number?

c) Which two people have the same hourly wage? What is this wage?

d) Which two people have worked for the same number of years?
What is this number?

Wages and Years Worked

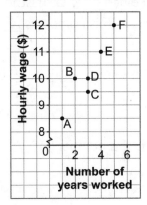

Solution

a) The vertical axis represents hourly wage.
Point F is the highest point, so person F has the greatest hourly wage.
This wage is $12/h.

b) The horizontal axis represents number of years worked. Point A is farthest to the left,
so person A has worked for the least number of years.
This number is 1 year.

c) Hourly wage is on the vertical axis.
Points B and D lie on the same horizontal line.
The line passes through 10 on the *Hourly wage* axis.
So, both persons B and D have an hourly wage of $10.

> Look across from the vertical axis for points on the same horizontal line.

d) Number of years worked is on the horizontal axis.
Points C and D lie on the same vertical line.
The line passes through 3 on the *Number of years worked* axis.
So, both persons C and D have worked for 3 years.

> Look up from the horizontal axis for points on the same vertical line.

Check

1. Each point on this graph represents a package of AA batteries.

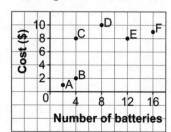

Packages of AA Batteries

a) Which package is the most expensive? What does it cost?

The _____ axis represents the cost. Point ____ is the highest point.

So, Package ____ is the most expensive. It costs _____.

b) Which package has the greatest number of batteries? What is this number?

The _____ axis represents the number of batteries. Point ____ is farthest to the

_____. So, Package ____ has the greatest number of batteries. This number is ____.

c) Which packages cost the same? What is this cost?

Cost is on the _____ axis. Points ____ and ____ lie on the same _____ line.

The line passes through ____ on the _____ axis.

So, Packages ____ and ____ cost the same. The cost is ____.

d) Which packages have the same number of batteries? What is this number?

Number of batteries is on the _____ axis.

Points ____ and ____ lie on the same _____ line.

The line passes through ____ on the _____ axis.

So, Packages ____ and ____ have the same number of batteries. The number is ____.

Example 2 | Describing a Possible Situation for a Graph

Describe a possible situation for this graph.

Volume of Water in Emiko's Water Bottle

> *Read the graph labels to help you interpret the graph.*

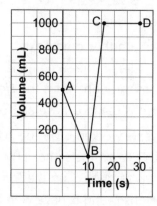

Solution

The graph shows how the volume of water in Emiko's water bottle changes over time.
Each segment on the graph represents a different type of change.

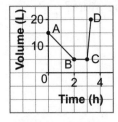

A table can organize your work.

Segment	Description	Possible Situation
AB	The graph goes down to the right. So, the volume of water in the bottle is decreasing.	Emiko has 500 mL of water in her bottle. She drinks all the water in 10 s.
BC	The graph goes up to the right. So, the volume of water in the bottle is increasing.	Emiko fills her water bottle. It takes about 6 s to put 1000 mL of water in the bottle.
CD	The graph is horizontal. So, the volume of water in the bottle stays the same.	Emiko does not drink any water from her water bottle.

Check

1. Describe a possible situation for this graph.

Volume of Gas in Winston's Motorcycle

This graph shows _____

_____

Complete the table below by describing each segment of the graph, and describing a possible situation for each segment.

Segment	Description	Possible Situation
AB	The graph goes _____ to the right. So, the volume of gas in the tank is _____.	Winston starts with _____ of gas in his tank. He drives for _____, then has _____ of gas remaining.
BC	The graph is _____. So, the volume of gas in the tank _____.	Winston stops for _____.
CD	The graph goes _____. So, the volume of gas in the tank is _____.	

1. Each point on this graph represents a possible winter vacation destination.

Graph of Temperature against Humidity

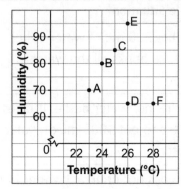

a) Which destination has the highest temperature? What is this temperature?

The _____ axis represents temperature. Point _____ is farthest

to the _____ on the graph. So, Destination _____ has the highest temperature.

The temperature is _____.

b) Which destination has the greatest humidity? What is this humidity?

The _____ axis represents humidity. Point _____ is the _____ point.

So, Destination _____ has the greatest humidity. This humidity is _____.

c) Which destinations have the same temperature? What is this temperature?

Temperature is on the _____ axis.

Points _____ and _____ lie on the same _____ line.

The line passes through _____ on the _____ axis.

So, Destinations _____ and _____ have the same temperature.

The temperature is _____.

d) Which destinations have the same humidity? What is this humidity?

Humidity is on the _____ axis. Points _____ and _____ lie

on the same _____ line.

The line passes through _____ on the _____ axis.

So, Destinations _____ and _____ have the same humidity. The humidity is _____.

2. Each point on this graph represents a container of orange juice.

Costs of Containers of Orange Juice

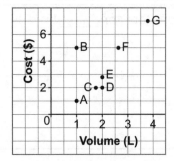

Is each statement true or false?

a) Containers D and E cost the same.

Points D and E lie on the same _____ line. So, they have the same _____.
The statement is _____.

b) Containers B and F cost the same.

Points B and F lie on the same _____ line. So, they have the same _____.
The statement is _____.

c) Container G is the most expensive.

The vertical axis represents _____. Point G is the _____ point.
So, Container G is the _____. The statement is _____.

d) Container F has a greater volume than Container B.

The horizontal axis represents _____. Point F is farther _____ than
point B. So, Container F has the _____ volume. The statement is _____.

3. Describe a possible situation for this graph.

Troy's Hike

This graph shows _____

_____

Complete the table below by describing each segment of the graph, and describing a
possible situation for each segment.

Segment	Description	Possible Situation
OA	The graph goes _____. So, the distance from home is _____.	
AB	The graph goes _____. So, the distance from home is _____.	
BC	The graph is _____. So, the distance from home _____.	
CD	The graph goes _____. So, the distance from home is _____.	

4. This graph shows how Gabrielle's distance from the ski lodge changes on her cross-country ski tour.

Gabrielle's Cross-Country Ski Tour

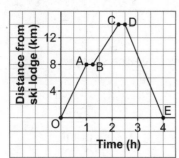

Complete the description of the graph representing Gabrielle's tour.

From O to A, Gabrielle skis _____ the lodge; she skis _____ km in _____ h.

From A to B, Gabrielle's distance from the lodge _____; she rests for _____ min.

From B to C, Gabrielle skis _____ the lodge; she skis _____ km in _____ h.

From C to D, Gabrielle's distance from the lodge _____; she rests for _____ min.

From D to E, Gabrielle skis _____ the lodge; she skis _____ km in _____ h.

5. Describe a possible situation for this graph.

Ryan's Heart Rate

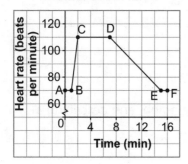

▶ 5.4 Skill Builder

Graphing on a Coordinate Grid

An ordered pair tells you the position of a point on a coordinate grid.

$(2, -3)$

— The 1st number tells you the distance left or right of the origin.

— The 2nd number tells you the distance up or down from the origin.

*The numbers in an ordered pair are the **coordinates** of a point.*

To plot:

Point A(10, 15): Start at 10 on the horizontal axis, then move up 15 units.

Point B(0, −5): Start at 0 on the horizontal axis, then move down 5 units.

Point C(−10, 0): Start at −10 on the horizontal axis, then move up 0 units.

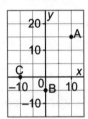

On this grid, 1 square represents 5 units. We chose this scale because all the numbers are divisible by 5.

Check

1. Write the coordinates of each point on the grid.

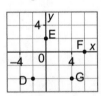

Point D: (_____, _____)

Point E: (_____, _____)

Point F: (_____, _____)

Point G: (_____, _____)

2. Plot and label these points on the coordinate grid below.

P(12, −8), Q(0, 4), R(−8, 8), S(8, 0), T(−4, −12)

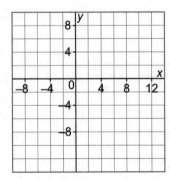

5.4 Math Lab: Graphing Data

FOCUS Graph data and investigate the domain and range when the data represent a function.

Try This

Work with a partner.

The materials you need are listed on page 285 of the Student Text.

Part A

Record all measurements in the table below.

Measure the length of rope without any knots.

Tie one knot in the rope. Measure the length of the rope with 1 knot.

Tie a second knot. Measure the length of the rope with 2 knots.

Continue this process until you have 5 knots.

Number of Knots	Length of Rope (cm)
0	
1	
2	
3	
4	
5	

Try to make all knots the same size and tightness.

Part B

Graph the data.

Choose a scale for the vertical axis.

Scale: 1 square = _____ cm

Graph of Length of a Rope with Knots

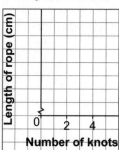

Does it make sense to join the points? Explain.

_____

Part C

Is the relation between the number of knots and the length of rope a function? _____

How do you know? _____

What is the domain? _____

What is the range? _____

Could the graph be extended to the right? Explain.

_____

Could the graph be extended to the left? Explain.

_____

Practice

1. Would you join the points on a graph that represents each relation below? Circle your choice.

   Can you have a fraction of each item in the relation?

   a) the relation between the mass and age of a baby   Yes   No

   b) the relation between the number of ice cream cones
      sold and the outside temperature   Yes   No

   c) the relation between the volume of gas in a car and
      the distance travelled   Yes   No

   d) the relation between the outside temperature and
      the time of day   Yes   No

   e) the relation between the number of T-shirts sold and
      the profit   Yes   No

2. This table shows the number of cars in a school parking lot during a day.

   a) Graph the data.

Time	Number of cars
7 A.M.	0
8 A.M.	20
9 A.M.	35
10 A.M.	35
11 A.M.	35
12 noon	10
1 P.M.	25
2 P.M.	30
3 P.M.	30
4 P.M.	5

Choose a scale for the vertical axis.
The greatest number of cars is _____.
So, let 1 square = _____ cars
Plot the points: (7, 0), (8, 20), and so on

Number of Cars in School Parking Lot

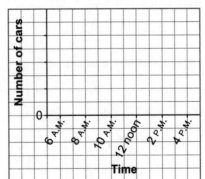

b) Does it make sense to join the points? Explain.

_____

c) Is the relation a function? Explain.

_____

d) What is the domain? _____

_____

What is the range? _____

3. This table shows the height of water in a rain barrel over time.

a) Graph the data.

Time (months)	Height of water (mm)
0	0
1	15
2	75
3	120
4	150
5	165
6	180

Height of Water in a Rain Barrel

Choose a scale for the vertical axis.

The greatest height of water is _____.

So, let 1 square = _____ mm

Plot the points: (0, 0), (1, 15), and so on

b) Does it make sense to join the points? Explain.

_____

_____

c) Is the relation a function? Explain.

_____

▶ 5.5 Skill Builder

Inequalities

We can use *inequality signs* to compare two quantities.

The inequality signs are:

Symbol	Meaning
<	less than
>	greater than
≤	less than or equal to
≥	greater than or equal to

Remember that the symbol always points toward the lesser number.

For example, to write each statement as an inequality:
* *a* is *greater than* 3 $a > 3$
* *b* is *less than or equal to* 7 $b \leq 7$

A *double inequality* has 2 inequality signs in one statement.
To write this statement as a double inequality:

g is greater than or equal to 5 and less than 11.

Break the statement into 2 parts:
* *g* is *greater than or equal to* 5 $g \geq 5$
  Another way to write this is: $5 \leq g$
* *g* is less than 11 $g < 11$
Then combine: $5 \leq g < 11$

We combine the statements so the variable is in the middle and the signs point in the same direction.

Check

1. Use a symbol to write an inequality for each statement.

   a) *c* is less than 6.

   c _____ 6

   b) *d* is greater than or equal to 0.

   d _____ 0

   c) *e* is greater than −2.

   _____

   d) *f* is less than or equal to 4.

   _____

2. Use symbols to write a double inequality for each statement.

   a) *g* is greater than 2 and less than 10.

   Break the statement into 2 parts.
   * *g* is greater than 2.   *g* _____
     Another way to write this is: _____ *g*
   * *g* is less than 10.   *g* _____
   Combine: _____

   b) *h* is greater than −5 and less than or equal to 6.

   Break the statement into 2 parts.
   * *h* is greater than −5.   *h* _____
     Another way to write this is: _____ *h*
   * *h* is less than or equal to 6.   _____
   Combine: _____

5.5 Graphs of Relations and Functions

FOCUS Use the properties of the graphs of relations and functions.

On the graph of a function, any vertical line will always pass through no more than one point.

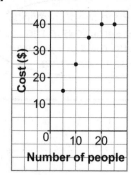

On the graph of a relation that is not a function, a vertical line may pass through more than one point.

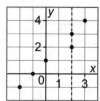

Vertical Line Test for a Function

Place a ruler vertically on a graph. Slide the ruler across the graph. If one edge of the ruler always intersects the graph at *no more than* one point, the graph represents a function.

Example 1 | Identifying the Graph of a Function

Decide whether each graph represents a function.

a) Cost of Admission

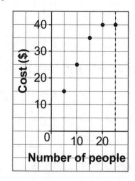

b) Number of Siblings My Friends Have

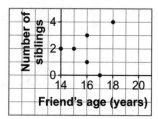

Solution

Use the vertical line test for each graph.

a) Cost of Admission

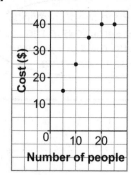

Any vertical line passes through 0 points or 1 point. So, the graph represents a function.

b) Number of Siblings My Friends Have

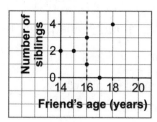

Two points lie on the same vertical line. So, the graph does not represent a function.

Check

1. Which of these graphs represent functions? Circle the correct answers.

a) **Points Scored by Players in a Basketball Game**

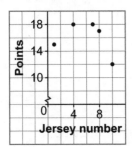

Is there a vertical line that passes through more than 1 point? Yes/No
So, the graph does/does not represent a function.

b) **Goals Scored by Players in a Hockey Tournament**

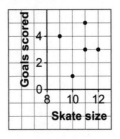

Draw vertical lines or use a straightedge to help you decide.

Is there a vertical line that passes through more than 1 point? Yes/No
So, the graph does/does not represent a function.

When the points on a graph are joined, we use inequality symbols to write the domain and range.

Example 2 | Finding the Domain and Range of a Function

Find the domain and range of each graph.

a)

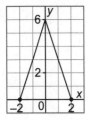

b)

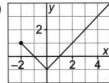

A dot at the end of a graph tells us the graph stops at that point. No dot means the graph continues.

Solution

a)

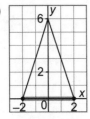

Visualize the shadow on the *x*-axis.
This is the domain.
The shadow on the *x*-axis starts at −2 and ends at 2.
So, the domain is:
$-2 \leq x \leq 2$

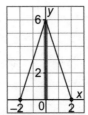

Visualize the shadow on the *y*-axis.
This is the range.
The shadow on the *y*-axis starts at 0 and ends at 6.
So, the range is:
$0 \leq y \leq 6$

Imagine a flashlight shone on the graph from above, then from the right.

b) The dot at the left tells us that the graph stops at that point.
There is no dot at the right, so the graph continues.

Visualize the shadow on the *x*-axis.
This is the domain.

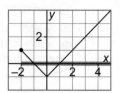

Visualize the shadow on the *y*-axis.
This is the range.

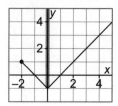

The shadow on the *x*-axis
starts at −2 and continues right.
So, the domain is: $x \geq -2$

The shadow on the *y*-axis
starts at −1 and continues up.
So, the range is: $y \geq -1$

Check

1. Each graph is drawn twice.
Use the 1st graph to find the domain.
Use the 2nd graph to find the range.

a)

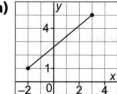

The shadow on the *x*-axis
starts at _____ and ends at _____.
So, the _____ is:
_____ $\leq x \leq$ _____

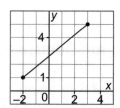

The shadow on the *y*-axis
starts at _____ and ends at _____.
So, the _____ is:
_____ $\leq$ _____ $\leq$ _____

b)

The shadow on the *x*-axis
starts at _____ and continues _____.
So, the _____ is: $x \leq$ _____

The shadow on the *y*-axis
starts at _____ and continues _____.
So, the _____ is: _____

Example 3 | **Finding Values from the Graph of a Function**

Here is the graph of a function $y = f(x)$.

a) Find the range value when the domain value is 2.

b) Find the domain value when the range value is -3.

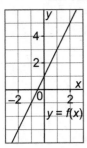

A domain value is a value of x.
A range value is a value of y.

Solution

a) To find the value of y when $x = 2$, start at
$x = 2$ on the x-axis.
Draw a vertical line to the graph, then a horizontal
line to the y-axis.

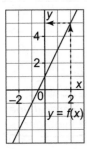

The line intersects the y-axis at 5.
So, the range value is 5.

b) To find the value of x when $y = -3$, start at
$y = -3$ on the y-axis.
Draw a horizontal line to the graph,
then a vertical line to the x-axis.

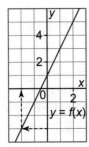

The line intersects the x-axis at -2.
So, the domain value is -2.

Check

1. Use each graph of the function $y = g(x)$.

a) Find the range value when the domain value is –2.

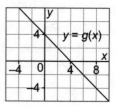

Start at _____ = –2 on the _____-axis.

Draw a _____ line to the graph,

then a _____ line to the _____-axis.

The line intersects the _____-axis at _____.

So, the range value is _____.

b) Find the domain value when the range value is –4.

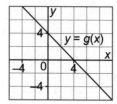

Start at _____ = –4 on the _____-axis.

Draw a _____ line to the graph,

then a _____ line to the _____-axis.

The line intersects the _____-axis at _____.

So, the domain value is _____.

Practice

1. Decide whether each graph represents a function. Circle the correct answers.

a)

Is there a vertical line that passes through more than 1 point? Yes/No
So, the graph does/does not represent a function.

b)

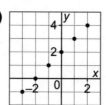

Draw vertical lines to help you decide.

Is there a vertical line that passes through more than 1 point? Yes/No
So, the graph does/does not represent a function.

2. Write the domain and range of each graph in question 1.

a) The domain is the set of *x*-values.

The domain is: _____

The range is the set of *y*-values.

The range is: _____

We do not repeat a number that occurs more than once.

b) The domain is: _____

The range is: _____

3. Does each graph represent a function?

Graph A **Graph B** 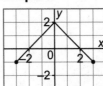 **Graph C**

Graph A _____ represent a function because a vertical line passes through _____

Graph B _____ represent a function because a vertical line passes through _____

Graph C _____ represent a function because a vertical line passes through _____

4. Find the domain and range of each graph.

a)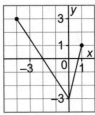

The shadow on the x-axis starts at _____ and ends at _____. So, the domain is:

_____ ≤ x ≤ _____

The shadow on the _____-axis starts at _____ and ends at _____. So, the range is:

_____ ≤ _____ ≤ _____

b)

The shadow on the _____ starts at _____ and continues _____. So, the domain is:

_____

The shadow on the _____ starts at _____ and continues _____. So, the range is:

_____

5. Match each graph to its domain and range.

Graph A **Graph B**

a) Domain: x ≥ −3   Range: y ≤ 2   Graph _____

b) Domain: −3 ≤ x ≤ 3   Range: −1 ≤ y ≤ 2   Graph _____

6. Here is the graph of a function $y = g(x)$.

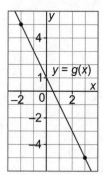

a) Find the range value when the domain value is 3.

Start at _____ = 3 on the _____-axis.
Draw a _____ line to the graph,
then a _____ line to the _____-axis.
The line intersects the _____-axis at _____.
So, the range value is _____.

b) Find the domain value when the range value is 5.

Start at _____ = 5 on the _____ -axis.
Draw a _____ line to the graph,
then a _____ line to the _____-axis.
The line intersects the _____-axis at _____.
So, the domain value is _____.

7. Here is the graph of a function $y = f(x)$.

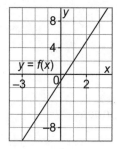

a) Find the range value when the domain value is 2.

The range value is: _____

b) Find the domain value when the range value is −7.

The domain value is: _____

Can you...

- interpret a graph?
- describe a possible situation for a graph?
- graph a table of values that represents a relation and analyze the data?
- identify the graph of a function and its domain and range?
- find values from the graph of a function?

5.3 **1.** Describe a possible situation for this graph.

Volume of Water in Marty's Kitchen Sink

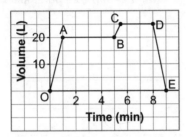

This graph shows _____

_____

Complete the table below by describing each segment of the graph, and describing a possible situation for each segment.

Segment	Description	Possible Situation
OA	The graph goes _____ to the right. So, the volume of water is _____.	
AB	The graph is _____. So, the volume of water _____.	
BC	The graph goes _____. So, the volume of water is _____.	
CD	The graph is _____. So, the volume of water _____.	
DE	The graph goes _____. So, the volume of water is _____.	

5.4 **2.** This table shows the cost of prizes for the school carnival.

  a) Graph the data.

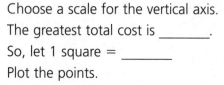

Number of prizes	Total Cost ($)
1	6
2	12
6	24
12	42
20	60

Cost of Prizes for the School Carnival

Choose a scale for the vertical axis.

The greatest total cost is _____.

So, let 1 square = _____

Plot the points.

  b) Does it make sense to join the points?

  _____

  c) Is the relation a function? _____

  _____

  d) What is the domain? _____

  What is the range? _____

5.5 **3.** Does each graph represent a function?

Graph A

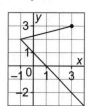

Graph B

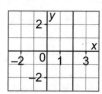

Graph C

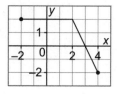

Graph A _____ represent a function because a vertical line passes
through _____

Graph B _____ represent a function because a vertical line passes
through _____

Graph C _____ represent a function because a vertical line passes
through _____

4. Find the domain and range of this graph.

The shadow on the _____-axis
starts at _____ and continues _____.
So, the domain is:

_____

The shadow on the _____-axis
starts at _____ and continues _____.
So, the range is:

_____

5. Here is the graph of a function $y = f(x)$.

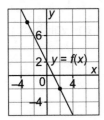

a) Find the range value when the domain value is 2.

Start at _____ = 2 on the _____-axis.
Draw a _____ line to the graph,
then a _____ line to the _____-axis.
The line intersects the _____-axis at _____.
So, the range value is _____.

b) Find the domain value when the range value is 8.

So, the domain value is _____.

▶ 5.6 Skill Builder

Creating Tables of Values

To create a table of values for an equation, substitute values
of x into the equation, then solve for y.
For example,

$y = 4x - 3$

x	Substitution	y
−2	$4(−2) − 3 = −11$	−11
−1	$4(−1) − 3 = −7$	−7
0	$4(0) − 3 = −3$	−3
1	$4(1) − 3 = 1$	1
2	$4(2) − 3 = 5$	5

Or, do the work
in your head.

$y = 4x - 3$

x	y
−2	−11
−1	−7
0	−3
1	1
2	5

For the equation $y = 3$, for any value of x,
y is always 3.

$y = 3$

x	y
−2	3
−1	3
0	3
1	3
2	3

For the equation $x = −5$, for any value of y,
x is always −5.

$x = −5$

x	y
−5	−2
−5	−1
−5	0
−5	1
−5	2

Check

1. Complete the table of values for each equation below.

a) $y = 3x + 4$

x	Substitution	y
−2	$3(−2) + 4 =$	
−1	$3(−1) + 4 =$	
0	$3(\_\_\_) + 4 =$	
1	$3(\_\_\_) + 4 =$	
2	$3(\_\_\_) + 4 =$	

b) $y = −2x + 5$

x	Substitution	y
−2	$−2(\_\_\_) + 5 =$	
−1	$−2(\_\_\_) + 5 =$	

5.6 Properties of Linear Relations

FOCUS Identify and represent linear relations in different ways.

The graph of a linear relation is a straight line.
For example, this graph represents a linear relation.

We can find patterns in a table of values
that we build from the graph.

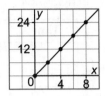

x	y
0	0
2	6
4	12
6	18
8	24

For a linear relation,
when the changes in the
1st column are the same
from one row to the next...

+2
+2
+2
+2

+6
+6
+6
+6

...the changes in
the 2nd column
are the same.

Example 1 | Deciding whether a Table of Values Represents a Linear Relation

Does this table of values represent a linear relation?

Time, t	Distance, d
0	1
2	5
4	25
6	125
8	625

*To find the change in 2 values,
subtract the first value from
the second value; for example,
5 − 1 = 4*

Solution

Find the change in each variable.

Time, t	Distance, d
0	1
2	5
4	25
6	125
8	625

+2
+2
+2
+2

+4
+20
+100
+500

The changes in the 1st column are the
same, but the changes in the 2nd column
are different. So, the table of values does not represent a linear relation.

Plot the points to check. Since the points do
not lie on a straight line, the relation is not
linear.

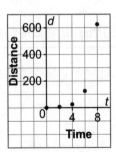

Check

1. Does each table of values represent a linear relation? Circle the correct answers.

a) Find the change in each variable.

5 − 0 = ____
10 − 5 = ____

_____
_____

Time, *t*	Volume, *V*
0	18
5	21
10	24
15	27
20	30

21 − 18 = ____
24 − 21 = ____

_____
_____

The changes in the 1st column are: the same   different

The changes in the 2nd column are: the same   different

The relation is: linear   not linear

b) Find the change in each variable.

5 − 0 = ____

_____
_____
_____

Time, *t*	Volume, *V*
0	19
5	22
10	26
15	31
20	37

22 − 19 = ____

_____
_____
_____

The changes in the 1st column are: the same   different

The changes in the 2nd column are: the same   different

The relation is: linear   not linear

When the graph of an equation lies on a straight line, the equation represents a linear relation.

Example 2 | Deciding whether an Equation Represents a Linear Relation

Does each equation represent a linear relation?

a) $y = -x - 2$

b) $y = x^2 + 1$

Solution

Make a table of values for each equation, then graph the data.

a) $y = -x - 2$

x	Substitution	y
−2	−(−2) − 2 = 0	0
−1	−(−1) − 2 = −1	−1
0	−(0) − 2 = −2	−2
1	−(1) − 2 = −3	−3
2	−(2) − 2 = −4	−4

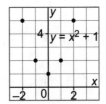

Use a ruler to check, or join the points.

Since the points lie on a straight line,
$y = -x - 2$ represents a linear relation.

b) $y = x^2 + 1$

x	Substitution	y
−2	(−2)² + 1 = 5	5
−1	(−1)² + 1 = 2	2
0	(0)² + 1 = 1	1
1	(1)² + 1 = 2	2
2	(2)² + 1 = 5	5

Since the points do not lie on a straight line,
$y = x^2 + 1$ does not represent a linear relation.

Check

1. Does each equation represent a linear relation?

a) $y = x^2 - 1$

Make a table of values.

x	Substitution	y
−2	(−2)² − 1 =	
−1	(___)² − 1 =	
0		
1		
2		

Plot the points on the grid.

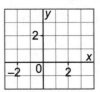

Do the points lie on a straight line? _____
Does $y = x^2 - 1$ represent a linear relation? _____

b) $y = x + 2$

Make a table of values.

x	Substitution	y
−2	−2 + 2 =	
−1	___ + 2 =	
0		
1		
2		

Plot the points on the grid.

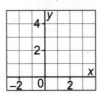

Do the points lie on a straight line? _____
Does $y = x + 2$ represent a linear relation? _____

We've seen that linear relations involve variables changing at a constant rate. We can find the **rate of change** of a linear relation.

> The rate of change of a linear relation is the fraction: $\dfrac{\text{change in dependent variable}}{\text{change in independent variable}}$
>
> The dependent variable is plotted on the vertical axis.
> The independent variable is plotted on the horizontal axis.

Example 3 | Finding the Rate of Change from a Graph

This graph shows the altitude of a helicopter as it lifts off.

Helicopter Lifting Off

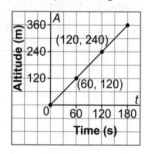

Altitude is the height above the ground.

a) Identify the dependent and independent variables.

b) Find the rate of change. What does it represent?

Solution

a) The dependent variable is plotted on the vertical axis.
It is *A*, the altitude.
The independent variable is plotted on the horizontal axis.
It is *t*, the time.

b) Rate of change

$= \dfrac{\text{change in dependent variable}}{\text{change in independent variable}}$

$= \dfrac{\text{change in altitude}}{\text{change in time}}$

Use the given points.

Find the change in each variable.

Change in altitude:
240 m − 120 m = 120 m

Change in time:
120 s − 60 s = 60 s

Helicopter Lifting Off

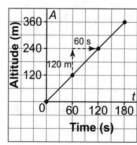

Rate of change

$$= \frac{120 \text{ m}}{60 \text{ s}}$$

$= 2$ m/s

The rate of change is 2 m/s. This is positive.

So, every second, the helicopter climbs 2 m.

> *When a graph goes up to the right, the rate of change is positive.*

Check

1. This graph shows the altitude of a helicopter as it descends to land.

Helicopter Descending to Land

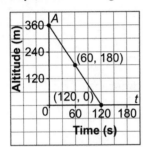

a) Identify the dependent and independent variables.

The dependent variable is plotted on the _____ axis.

It is _____, the _____.

The independent variable is plotted on the _____ axis.

It is _____, the _____.

b) Find the rate of change. What does it represent?

> *Start with the point farthest right on the graph.*

Change in altitude:

0 m − _____ = _____

Change in time:

120 s − _____ = _____

Rate of change

$$= \frac{\text{change in } \rule{1.5cm}{0.15mm} \text{ variable}}{\text{change in } \rule{1.5cm}{0.15mm} \text{ variable}}$$

$$= \frac{\text{change in } \rule{1.2cm}{0.15mm}}{\text{change in } \rule{1.2cm}{0.15mm}}$$

Helicopter Descending to Land

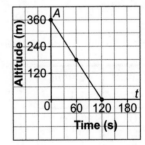

$$= \frac{\rule{1.5cm}{0.15mm}}{}$$

$= \underline{\quad}$ m/s

> *When a graph goes down to the right, the rate of change is _____.*

The rate of change is _____ m/s. This is _____.

So, every _____, the helicopter _____.

1. Does each table of values represent a linear relation? Circle the correct answers.

a) Find the change in each variable.

Time, t	Distance, d
0	8
3	13
6	23
9	38
12	58

The changes in the 1st column are: the same   different

The changes in the 2nd column are: the same   different

The relation is: linear   not linear

b) Find the change in each variable.

Number, n	Cost, C
0	0
4	15
8	30
12	45
16	60

The changes in the 1st column are: the same   different

The changes in the 2nd column are: the same   different

The relation is: linear   not linear

2. Does each table of values represent a linear relation? Circle the correct answers.

a)

Time, t	Volume, V
0	2
2	4
4	6
6	8
8	10

linear   not linear

b)

Time, t	Height, h
0	0
10	6
20	11
30	15
40	16

linear   not linear

c)

x	y
−2	3
−1	3
0	3
1	3
2	3

linear   not linear

3. Circle each graph that represents a linear relation.

a)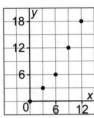

b)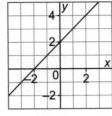

c)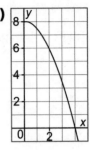

4. Does each equation represent a linear relation?

a) $y = 2x^2 - 3$

Make a table of values.

Plot the points on the grid.

x	Substitution	y
−2	2(____)² − 3 =	

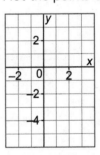

Do the points lie on a straight line? _____

Does $y = 2x^2 - 3$ represent a linear relation? _____

b) $y = 2x - 1$

Make a table of values.

Plot the points on the grid.

x	y
−2	
−1	

Do the points lie on a straight line? _____

Does $y = 2x - 1$ represent a linear relation? _____

5. This graph shows a car's distance from Edmonton during a journey.

Distance from Edmonton

a) Identify the dependent and independent variables.

The dependent variable is plotted on the _____

axis. It is _____, the _____.

The independent variable is plotted on the _____

axis. It is _____, the _____.

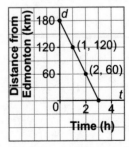

978-0-321-61066-9 Copyright © 2011 Pearson Canada Inc.

b) Find the rate of change.
What does it mean?

Change in distance from Edmonton:

_____

Change in time:

_____

Rate of change:

$\dfrac{\text{change in } \underline{\hspace{2cm}} \text{ variable}}{\text{change in } \underline{\hspace{2cm}} \text{ variable}}$

$= \dfrac{\text{change in } \underline{\hspace{3cm}}}{\text{change in } \underline{\hspace{1.5cm}}}$

$= \underline{\hspace{2cm}}$

$= \underline{\hspace{2cm}}$

The rate of change is _____. This is _____.
So, every _____, the car is _____ to Edmonton.

Check: The graph goes down to the right, so the rate of change is _____.

6. This graph shows the money raised at a fundraiser.

a) Identify the dependent and independent variables.

b) Find the rate of change.
What does it mean?

Money Raised at a Fundraiser

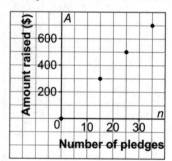

▶ 5.7 Interpreting Graphs of Linear Functions

FOCUS Use intercepts, rate of change, domain, and range to describe the graph of a linear function.

Any graph of a line that is not vertical represents a function.
We call these functions **linear functions**.

We can use the intercepts to describe the graph of a linear function.
This graph intersects the horizontal axis at 2.
So, the **horizontal intercept** is 2.
The coordinates of this point are (2, 0).

The graph intersects the vertical axis at 5.
So, the **vertical intercept** is 5.
The coordinates of this point are (0, 5).

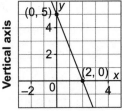

Horizontal axis

Example 1 — Finding Intercepts, Domain, and Range of a Graph

This graph shows the temperature
in a location over a 12-h period.

a) Find the vertical and horizontal intercepts.
What do they represent?

b) Find the domain and range.

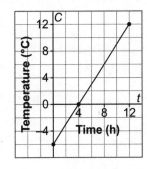

Solution

a) The graph intersects the vertical axis at −6.
So, the vertical intercept is −6.
This represents the starting temperature,
or the temperature at 0 h: −6°C

*The intercepts can also be named by their axes.
The C-intercept is −6.
The t-intercept is 4.*

The graph intersects the horizontal axis at 4.
So, the horizontal intercept is 4.
This represents the time when the temperature is 0°C: after 4 h

b) The dot at each end of the graph tells us that
the graph stops at that point.
Visualize the shadows on the axes.

On the horizontal axis, the shadow starts at 0 and ends at 12.
So, the domain is: $0 \leq t \leq 12$

On the vertical axis, the shadow starts at −6 and ends at 12.
So, the range is: $-6 \leq C \leq 12$

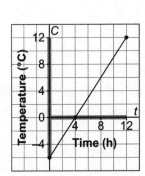

Check

1. This graph shows a person's distance from the finish line for a bicycle race.

a) Find the vertical and horizontal intercepts. What do they represent?

The graph intersects the vertical axis at _____.
So, the vertical intercept is: _____
This represents the distance from the finish line
at the _____ of the race, at _____ h: _____ km

The graph intersects the horizontal axis at _____.
So, the horizontal intercept is: _____
This represents the time when the distance
from the finish line is _____ km: after _____ h

b) Find the domain and range.

Draw the shadows on the axes.

On the _____ axis, the shadow
starts at _____ and ends at _____.
So, the domain is: _____ ≤ t ≤ _____

On the _____ axis, the shadow
starts at _____ and ends at _____.
So, the range is: _____ ≤ d ≤ _____

Bicycle Race

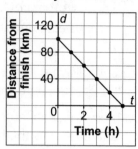

Bicycle Race

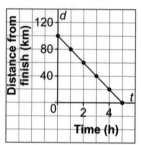

We can find intercepts algebraically.
This is the graph of the linear function $y = 2x - 3$.

When the graph intersects the x-axis, $y = 0$.
So, to find the x-intercept, substitute $y = 0$.
$y = 2x - 3$
$0 = 2x - 3$ Solve for x.
$3 = 2x$
$\dfrac{3}{2} = \dfrac{2x}{2}$
$x = 1.5$

When the graph intersects the y-axis, $x = 0$.
So, to find the y-intercept, substitute $x = 0$.
$y = 2x - 3$
$y = 2(0) - 3$
$y = -3$

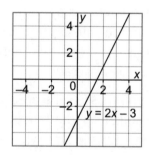

When the intercepts are integers, it is more efficient to use intercepts to graph rather than a table of values.

We can use the intercepts to graph a linear function.

To find the y-intercept, substitute $x = 0$.

To find the x-intercept, substitute $y = 0$.

Example 2 | Sketching a Graph Using Intercepts

Use intercepts to sketch the linear function $y = 2x - 4$.

Solution

$y = 2x - 4$

To find the y-intercept, substitute $x = 0$.   To find the x-intercept, substitute $y = 0$.

$y = 2(0) - 4$ $0 = 2x - 4$ Add 4 to both sides.

$y = -4$ $0 + 4 = 2x - 4 + 4$

                                                  $4 = 2x$ Divide both sides by 2.

                                                  $\dfrac{4}{2} = \dfrac{2x}{2}$

                                                  $x = 2$

> We only need 2 points to sketch a graph. We find a third point in case we made an error when finding the intercepts.

Find the coordinates of another point on the graph.

Substitute $x = 1$ in $y = 2x - 4$.

$y = 2(1) - 4$

$y = -2$

This point has coordinates $(1, -2)$.

Mark points at -4 on the y-axis; at 2 on the x-axis; and at $(1, -2)$. Draw a line through the points.

Check

1. Use intercepts to sketch the linear function $y = -2x + 6$.

To find the y-intercept,   To find the x-intercept,

substitute $x = $ _____.   substitute _____.

$y = -2(\_\_\_\_) + 6$ _____ $= -2x + 6$ Subtract ____ from both sides.

$y = $ _____ $0 - $ _____ $= -2x + 6 - $ _____   Simplify.

                          _____ $= $ _____   Divide both sides by _____.

                          $\dfrac{\_\_\_\_}{\_\_\_\_} = \dfrac{\_\_\_\_}{\_\_\_\_}$

                          $x = $ _____

Find the coordinates of another point on the graph.

Substitute $x = 1$ in $y = -2x + 6$.

$y = -2(\underline{\hspace{1cm}}) + 6$

$y = \underline{\hspace{1cm}}$

This point has coordinates ($\underline{\hspace{1cm}}$, $\underline{\hspace{1cm}}$).

Mark points at $\underline{\hspace{1cm}}$ on the y-axis;

at $\underline{\hspace{1cm}}$ on the x-axis; and at ($\underline{\hspace{1cm}}$, $\underline{\hspace{1cm}}$).

Draw a line through the points.

Example 3 — Matching a Graph to a Given Rate of Change and Vertical Intercept

Which graph has a rate of change of 1 and a vertical intercept of 8?

Graph A

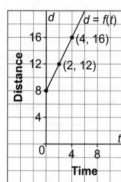

Graph B

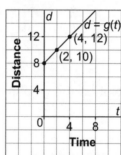

Solution

Both graphs have a vertical intercept of 8.
Find each rate of change.

For each graph, the rate of change is:

$$\frac{\text{change in dependent variable}}{\text{change in independent variable}} = \frac{\text{change in distance}}{\text{change in time}}$$

For Graph A:

Rate of change

$= \dfrac{16 - 12}{4 - 2}$

$= \dfrac{4}{2}$

$= 2$

For Graph B:

Rate of change

$= \dfrac{12 - 10}{4 - 2}$

$= \dfrac{2}{2}$

$= 1$

The rate of change is 2.   The rate of change is 1.

This is not the correct graph.   This is the correct graph.

So, Graph B has a rate of change of 1 and a vertical intercept of 8.

Check

1. Which graph has a rate of change of 1 and a vertical intercept of 9?

Graph A

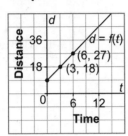

Graph B

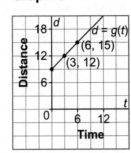

Both graphs have a vertical intercept of _____.

For each graph, the rate of change is:

$$\frac{\text{change in dependent variable}}{\text{change in independent variable}} = \frac{\text{change in _____}}{\text{change in _____}}$$

For Graph A: For Graph B:

Rate of change   Rate of change

= _____   = _____

= _____   = _____

= _____   = _____

The rate of change is _____.   The rate of change is _____.

This _____ the correct graph.   This _____ the correct graph.

So, Graph _____ has a rate of change of 1 and a vertical intercept of 9.

Practice

1. This graph shows how the height of oil in a camping lantern changes over time.
Find the vertical and horizontal intercepts.
What do they represent?

Height of Oil in Lantern

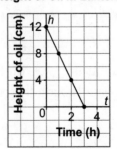

The vertical intercept is: _____

This represents the height of oil in the lantern

at the _____, at _____ h of burning: _____ cm

The horizontal intercept is: _____

This represents the time when the height of oil

in the lantern is _____ cm: after _____ h

2. This graph shows the temperature in a location over a 12-h period. Find the domain and range.

Temperature in a Location

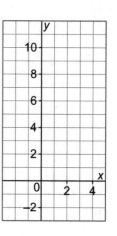

Draw the shadows on the axes.

The shadow on the horizontal axis starts at _____ and ends at _____.

So, the _____ is: _____ ≤ _____ ≤ _____

The shadow on the vertical axis starts at _____ and ends at _____.

So, the _____ is: _____ ≤ _____ ≤ _____

3. Use intercepts to sketch the linear function $y = 3x + 6$.

To find the *y*-intercept, substitute $x =$ _____.

$y = 3(\underline{}) + 6$

$y =$ _____

To find the *x*-intercept, substitute $y =$ _____.

_____ $= 3x + 6$

$0 -$ _____ $= 3x + 6 -$ _____

_____ $=$ _____

$\dfrac{}{} = \dfrac{}{}$

$x =$ _____

Find the coordinates of another point on the graph.

Substitute $x = 1$ in $y = 3x + 6$.

$y = 3(\underline{}) + 6$

$y =$ _____

Mark points at _____ on the *y*-axis;

at _____ on the *x*-axis; and at _____.

Draw a line through the points.

4. Use intercepts to sketch the linear function $y = -x + 5$.

Find the intercepts and the coordinates of a 3rd point on the line.

	When...	Then...
y-intercept	$x = 0$	$y = -(\underline{}) + 5$ $y =$ _____
x-intercept		
3rd point		

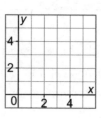

Mark points at _____ on the *y*-axis; at _____ on the *x*-axis; and at _____.

Draw a line through the points.

5. The graphs below show how the temperature changes over time at different locations. Match each graph to its rate of change and vertical intercept.

Graph A

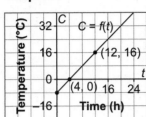

Graph B

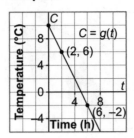

Graph C

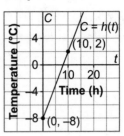

a) rate of change: 1   vertical intercept: −8
b) rate of change: 2   vertical intercept: −8
c) rate of change: −2   vertical intercept: 10

Both Graphs _____ and _____ have a vertical intercept of _____.
Graph _____ has a vertical intercept of 10.
So, Graph _____ matches part c.

Find the rate of change for Graphs _____ and _____.
For each graph, the rate of change is:

$$\frac{\text{change in dependent variable}}{\text{change in independent variable}} = \frac{\text{change in} \underline{\hspace{3cm}}}{\text{change in} \underline{\hspace{2cm}}}$$

For Graph _____:
Rate of change

= _____

= _____

= _____

Rate of change is: _____
This matches part _____.

For Graph _____:
Rate of change

= _____

= _____

= _____

Rate of change is: _____
This matches part _____.

So, the matches are:
Graph _____ and part _____, Graph _____ and part _____,
and Graph _____ and part _____.

Mystery Picture

What is the title of this picture?

Use these functions:

Function A: $y = 2x + 5$

Function B: $y = -3x - 12$

Function C:

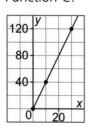

Function D:

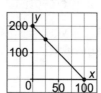

Find each value below.

		Code Value	Code Letter
1. The x-intercept of Function D:		_____	P
2. The rate of change of Function C:		_____	N
3. The range of Function D: $0 \leq y \leq$ _____		_____	E
4. The value of Function C when $x = 30$:		_____	S
5. The y-intercept of Function B:		_____	G
6. The rate of change of Function D:		_____	I
7. The x-intercept of Function B:		_____	O
8. The value of Function D when $x = 75$:		_____	D
9. The value of Function A when $x = -1$:		_____	A
10. The x-intercept of Function C:		_____	R
11. The y-intercept of Function A:		_____	W
12. In Function C, the value of x when y is 80:		_____	F

To find the title of the picture, write the code letter that corresponds to each code value.

Picture Title:

−12	−2	0	3	20	20	200

100	3	120	120	−2	4	−12

3

5	−2	4	50	−4	5

Skill	Description	Example
Find the domain and range of a function.	The domain is the set of 1st elements of the ordered pairs in a function. The range is the set of related 2nd elements. For a graph, the domain is represented by the shadow of the graph on the horizontal axis. The range is represented by the shadow of the graph on the vertical axis.	For the set of ordered pairs: {(−1, 4), (0, 6), (1, 8)} The domain is: {−1, 0, 1} The range is: {4, 6, 8} For the graph: The domain is: $0 \le t \le 6$ The range is: $2 \le d \le 8$
Find the rate of change from the graph of a linear function.	The rate of change of a linear function is: $$\frac{\text{change in dependent variable}}{\text{change in independent variable}}$$ The rate of change is positive when the graph goes up to the right, and negative when the graph goes down to the right.	**Distance against Time** Rate of change $$= \frac{100 \text{ km} - 50 \text{ km}}{4 \text{ h} - 2 \text{ h}}$$ $$= \frac{50 \text{ km}}{2 \text{ h}}$$ $$= 25 \text{ km/h}$$
Find the intercepts of the graph of a linear function.	To find the x-intercept, substitute $y = 0$. To find the y-intercept, substitute $x = 0$.	For the linear function $y = -2x + 8$: When $y = 0$, $0 = -2x + 8$ $2x = 8$ $x = 4$ The x-intercept is 4. When $x = 0$, $y = -2(0) + 8$ $y = 8$ The y-intercept is 8.

5.1 **1.** Consider the relation represented by this graph.

Memory of iPods in 2010

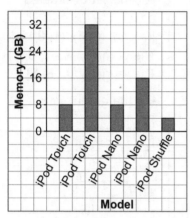

a) Represent the relation as a table.

Model	Memory (GB)

b) Describe the relation in words.
The relation shows the association _____ from a set of _____ to a set of _____.

c) List 2 ordered pairs that belong to the relation.

_____

5.2 **2.** Which sets of ordered pairs represent functions? Circle the correct answers.

a) {(1, 1), (–1, 1), (2, 4), (–2, 4)}
Each ordered pair has/does not have a different 1st element.
So, the relation is/is not a function.

b) {(2, 3), (2, 4), (2, 5), (2, 6)}
Each ordered pair has/does not have a different 1st element.
So, the relation is/is not a function.

3. Write each equation in function notation.

a) $y = 7x - 2$ **b)** $C = 15n + 50$

_____   _____

4. For the function $g(x) = -x + 9$, find:

a) $g(5)$

$g(x) = -x + 9$

$g(5) = -(\underline{\hspace{1cm}}) + 9$

$g(5) = \underline{\hspace{2cm}}$

$g(5) = \underline{\hspace{2cm}}$

b) the value of x when $g(x) = 12$

$g(x) = -x + 9$

$\underline{\hspace{1cm}} = -x + 9$

$x = \underline{\hspace{1cm}}$

5.3 **5.** Describe a possible situation for this graph.

Volume of Toby's Television

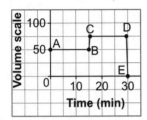

This graph shows _____

_____

Complete the table below by describing each segment of the graph, and describing a possible situation for each segment.

Segment	Description	Possible Situation
AB	The graph is _____. So, the volume of the television _____.	
BC	The graph goes _____. So, the volume is _____.	
CD	The graph is _____. So, the volume of the television _____.	
DE	The graph goes _____. So, the volume is _____.	

5.4 **6.** This table shows the attendance for a weekly after-school yoga class.

a) Graph the data.

Week	Number of students
1	20
2	25
3	25
4	20
5	15
6	10

Choose a scale for the vertical axis.
The greatest number of students is _____.
So, let 1 square = _____ students
Plot the points.

**Attendance at the
After-School Yoga Class**

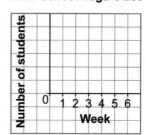

b) Does it make sense to join the points? Explain.

_____

c) Is the relation a function? Explain.

_____

d) What is the domain? _____
What is the range? _____

5.5 **7.** Decide whether each graph represents a function.

a) **The Minimum Wage in Manitoba**

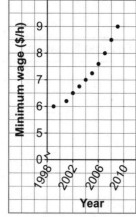

b) **Number of Pets
My Friends Have**

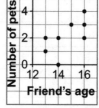

*Draw vertical lines
to help you decide.*

Is there a vertical line that passes
through more than 1 point? _____
So, the graph _____
represent a function.

Is there a vertical line that passes
through more than 1 point? _____
So, the graph _____
represent a function.

8. Here is the graph of a function $y = g(x)$.
a) Find the range value when
the domain value is –4.

The range value is: _____

b) Find the domain value when
the range value is 2.

The domain value is: _____

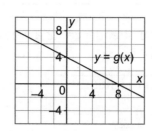

*Draw arrows on the
graph to help.*

9. Does each table of values represent a linear relation?

Circle the correct answers.

a)

Number, n	Profit, P
20	10
40	20
60	30
80	40
100	50

linear   not linear

b)

Time, t	Distance, d
0	5
4	9
8	13
12	17
16	21

linear   not linear

c)

x	y
1	4
2	7
3	12
4	19
5	28

linear   not linear

10. Does each equation represent a linear relation?

a) $y = 5x$

Make a table of values.   Plot the points on the grid.

x	Substitution	y
−2	$5(-2) =$	
−1		

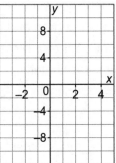

Do the points lie on a straight line? _____

Does $y = 5x$ represent a linear relation? _____

b) $y = 2x^2 + 2$

Make a table of values.   Plot the points on the grid.

x	Substitution	y
−2		
−1		

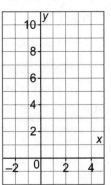

Do the points lie on a straight line? _____

Does $y = 2x^2 + 2$ represent a linear relation? _____

5.7 **11.** Use intercepts to sketch the linear function $y = -2x - 6$.
Find the intercepts and the coordinates of a 3rd point on the line.

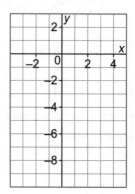

	When...	Then...
y-intercept	$x = 0$	$y = -2(\underline{\quad}) - 6$ $y = \underline{\quad}$
x-intercept		
3rd point		

Mark points at _____ on the *y*-axis;
at _____ on the *x*-axis; and at _____.
Draw a line through the points.

12. This graph shows the temperature at a location over time.

a) Find the vertical and horizontal intercepts.
What do they represent?
The vertical intercept is: _____.
This represents _____
_____

The horizontal intercept is: _____
This represents _____
_____

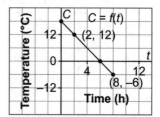

b) Find the domain and range.
Draw the shadows on the axes.
The domain is: ____ ≤ ____ ≤ ____
The range is: ____ ≤ ____ ≤ ____

c) Find the rate of change. What does it represent?
The rate of change is:
$$\frac{\text{change in dependent variable}}{\text{change in independent variable}} = \frac{\text{change in} \underline{\qquad}}{\text{change in} \underline{\quad}}$$

$$= \frac{\underline{\quad}}{\underline{\quad}}$$

$$= \underline{\quad}$$

Rate of change is ____°C/h.

_____

Linear Functions

What You'll Learn

- Find the slope of a line segment and a line.

- Graph a line, given different forms of its equation.

- Find the equation of a line, given different information about the line.

Why It's Important

Linear functions are used by:

- graphic designers, to produce images and designs

- financial planners, to study business trends

Key Words

slope	slope-intercept form
rise	slope-point form
run	general form
negative reciprocals	

▶ 6.1 Slope of a Line

FOCUS **Find the slope of a line segment and a line.**

The steepness or **slope** of a line segment is given by:

$$\text{Slope} = \frac{\text{rise}}{\text{run}}$$

The **rise** is the change in the vertical distance.
Moving up is positive; moving down is negative.

The **run** is the change in the horizontal distance.
Moving right is positive; moving left is negative.

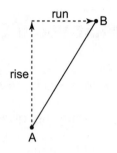

A line segment that
goes up to the right
has a positive
slope.

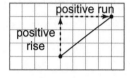

A line segment that
goes up to the left
has a negative
slope.

We can also say that
this line segment goes down
to the right.

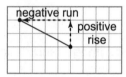

A horizontal line
has slope 0.

When the line or line segment is on a grid, we can count
squares to find the rise and the run.

Example 1 | **Finding the Slope of a Line Segment**

Find the slope of each line segment.

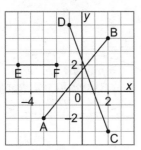

Solution

Line segment AB goes up to the right,
so its slope is positive.

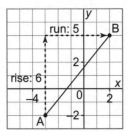

From A to B, the rise is 6 and the run is 5.

$$\text{Slope} = \frac{\text{rise}}{\text{run}}$$

$$= \frac{6}{5}$$

Line segment CD goes up to the left, so its slope is negative.

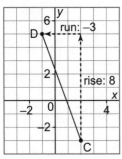

From C to D, the rise is 8 and the run is −3.

$$\text{Slope} = \frac{\text{rise}}{\text{run}}$$

$$= \frac{8}{-3}, \text{ or } -\frac{8}{3}$$

The negative fraction
can be expressed as:
$$\frac{8}{-3}, \frac{-8}{3}, \text{ or } -\frac{8}{3}$$

Line segment EF is horizontal, so its slope is 0.

Check

1. The rise and run of a line segment are given. Find the slope of each segment.

   a) Rise: 3; run: 4

       Slope = $\dfrac{\text{rise}}{\text{run}}$

            = _____

   b) Rise: 1; run: −2

       Slope = _____

Remember to write fractions in simplest form.

   c) Rise: 4; run: −2

       Slope = _____

   d) Rise: 2; run: 10

       Slope = _____

2. Find the slope of each line segment.

   a)

Line segment BA goes up to the _____, so its slope is _____.

Rise = _____

Run = _____

Slope = _____

   b)

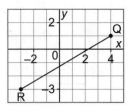

Line segment RQ goes up to the _____, so its slope is _____.

Rise = _____

Run = _____

Slope = _____

Example 2 | Drawing a Line Segment Given Its Slope

Draw a line segment with each slope.

a) 3

b) $-\dfrac{4}{5}$

Solution

a) A slope of 3 can be written as $\dfrac{3}{1}$, with rise 3 and run 1.

Choose any point on the grid.

Label it A.

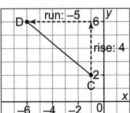

A line segment with a positive slope goes up to the right.

From A, move 3 units up and 1 unit right. Label the point B. Join AB.

Line segment AB has slope 3.

b) A slope of $-\dfrac{4}{5}$ can be written as $\dfrac{4}{-5}$, with rise 4 and run −5.

Choose any point on the grid.

Label it C.

A line segment with a negative slope goes up to the left.

From C, move 4 units up and 5 units left.

Label the point D. Join CD.

Line segment CD has slope $-\dfrac{4}{5}$.

Check

1. Draw a line segment EF with each slope.

a) 2

A slope of 2 can be written as _____.
So, rise is _____ and run is _____.
Choose any point on the grid.
Label it E.
From E, move _____ units _____ and
_____ unit _____. Label the point F. Join EF.

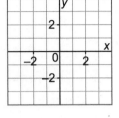

b) $-\dfrac{5}{3}$

A slope of $-\dfrac{5}{3}$ can be written as _____.

So, rise is _____ and run is _____.
Choose any point E on the grid.
From E, move _____ units _____ and
_____ units _____. Label the point F. Join EF.

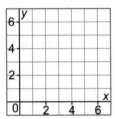

Different line segments on this line have these slopes:

$$\dfrac{3}{1} = 3 \qquad\qquad \dfrac{6}{2} = 3$$

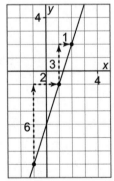

A slope of 3 can be written as any of these fractions: $\dfrac{3}{1}$, $\dfrac{6}{2}$, and so on.
So, this line has slope 3.
We can find the slope of a line by choosing any 2 points on the line.
The choice of points does not affect the value of the slope.

> The slope of a line is equal to the slope of any segment of the line.

| Example 3 | Finding Slope Using Two Points on a Line |

Find the slope of this line.

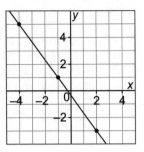

Solution

The line goes up to the left, so its slope is negative.

Choose any 2 points on the line,

such as C(2, −3) and D(−1, 1).

From C to D:

Rise = 4

Run = −3

Slope = $\frac{\text{rise}}{\text{run}}$

$\quad = \frac{4}{-3}$, or $-\frac{4}{3}$

The slope of the line is $-\frac{4}{3}$.

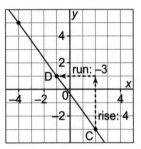

Check

1. Find the slope of this line.

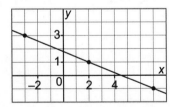

Choose P(−3, 3) and Q(2, 1).

From Q to P:

Rise = _____

Run = _____

Slope = $\frac{\text{rise}}{\text{run}}$

$\quad =$

_____

The slope of the line is: _____

In *Examples 1* to *3*, we counted squares to find the rise and the run.
When the line is not drawn, we can use a formula to find the slope.

Slope of a Line

A line passes through two points $A(x_1, y_1)$ and $B(x_2, y_2)$.

Slope of AB $= \dfrac{y_2 - y_1}{x_2 - x_1}$

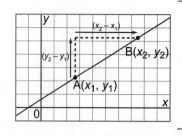

It doesn't matter which points are chosen, as long as the x- and y-coordinates are subtracted in the same order.

Example 4 | Using a Formula to Find the Slope of a Line

Find the slope of the line that passes through D(−3, −2) and E(10, 5).
Check by sketching the line.

Solution

Use the formula: Slope $= \dfrac{y_2 - y_1}{x_2 - x_1}$

Let D be (x_1, y_1) and E be (x_2, y_2).

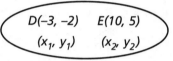

D(−3, −2)   E(10, 5)
 (x_1, y_1) (x_2, y_2)

Slope of DE $= \dfrac{y_2 - y_1}{x_2 - x_1}$ Substitute: $x_1 = -3$, $y_1 = -2$, $x_2 = 10$, and $y_2 = 5$

Slope of DE $= \dfrac{5 - (-2)}{10 - (-3)}$

Slope of DE $= \dfrac{7}{13}$

The slope of the line is $\dfrac{7}{13}$.

Check:
The line goes up to the right.
This agrees with the positive value of the slope above.

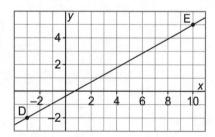

Check

1. Find the slope of the line that passes through G(−4, −7) and H(3, 8).
   Check by sketching the line.

   Use the formula: Slope $= \dfrac{y_2 - y_1}{x_2 - x_1}$

   Let G be (x_1, y_1) and H be (x_2, y_2).

   Slope of GH $= \dfrac{y_2 - y_1}{x_2 - x_1}$ Substitute: $x_1 =$ _____, $y_1 =$ _____, $x_2 =$ _____, and $y_2 =$ _____

   Slope of GH $=$ _____

   Slope of GH $=$ _____

   The slope of the line is: _____

   Check:
   Plot G and H on this grid.
   Draw a line through the points.
   The line goes up to the _____.
   This agrees with the _____
   value of the slope above.

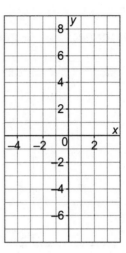

Practice

1. Draw lines to match each statement with a line segment and the description of its slope.

The line segment goes up to the right.		positive slope
The line segment goes up to the left.		0 slope
The line segment is horizontal.		negative slope

2. Find the slope of segment ST.

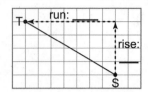

Rise = _____

Run = _____

Slope =
_____

3. Complete this table for each line segment at the right.

Line segment	Rise	Run	Slope
AB			
CD			
EF			
GH			

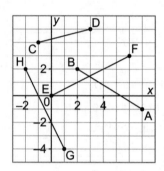

4. Draw a line segment with each slope.

a) $\frac{4}{3}$

The rise is _____ and the run is _____.
Choose any point on the grid below.
Label it E.
From E, move _____ units _____ and _____ units _____.
Label the point F. Join EF.

Check: A line segment with a positive slope
goes up to the _____.

b) $-\dfrac{3}{4}$

A slope of $-\dfrac{3}{4}$ can be written as _____.

So, the rise is _____ and the run is _____.

Choose any point G on the grid below.

From G, move _____ units _____ and _____ units _____.

Label the point H. Join GH.

Check: A line segment with a negative slope goes _____.

5. Find the slope of the line that passes through N(7, 11) and Q(−1, −5).

Use the formula: Slope $= \dfrac{y_2 - y_1}{x_2 - x_1}$

Let N be _____ and Q be _____

Slope of NQ $= \dfrac{y_2 - y_1}{x_2 - x_1}$ Substitute: _____

Slope of NQ $=$
_____

Slope of NQ $=$
_____

The slope of the line is _____.

6. Draw a line GH through G(−2, −1) with slope $\dfrac{5}{2}$.

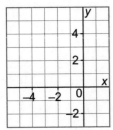

Plot point G(−2, −1).

The slope of GH is $\dfrac{5}{2}$; so, the rise is _____ and the run is _____.

From G, move _____.

Mark a point H.

Draw a line through GH.

▶ 6.2 Slopes of Parallel and Perpendicular Lines

FOCUS Use slope to find out if two lines are parallel or perpendicular.

These two lines are parallel.

Slope of line AB = $\dfrac{6}{-3}$

             = -2

Slope of line CD = $\dfrac{4}{-2}$

             = -2

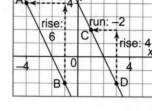

These two lines have the same slope.

In general:

> **Slopes of Parallel Lines**
> Parallel lines have the same slope.

Example 1	Identifying Parallel Lines

Line EF passes through E(-4, -3) and F(0, 3).
Line PQ passes through P(-3, -5) and Q(2, 3).
Line RS passes through R(0, -3) and S(4, 3).
Are the lines parallel?

Solution

Graph the lines.

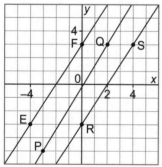

All of them appear to be parallel.
Find the slopes to check.
Use the formula for slope.

Slope $= \dfrac{y_2 - y_1}{x_2 - x_1}$

E(−4, −3) and F(0, 3)
To find the slope of EF, substitute:
$x_1 = -4$, $y_1 = -3$,
$x_2 = 0$, and $y_2 = 3$
Slope of EF $= \dfrac{3 - (-3)}{0 - (-4)}$
$= \dfrac{6}{4}$, or $\dfrac{3}{2}$

P(−3, −5) and Q(2, 3)
To find the slope of PQ, substitute:
$x_1 = -3$, $y_1 = -5$,
$x_2 = 2$, and $y_2 = 3$
Slope of PQ $= \dfrac{3 - (-5)}{2 - (-3)}$
$= \dfrac{8}{5}$

R(0, −3) and S(4, 3)
To find the slope of RS, substitute:
$x_1 = 0$, $y_1 = -3$,
$x_2 = 4$, and $y_2 = 3$
Slope of RS $= \dfrac{3 - (-3)}{4 - 0}$
$= \dfrac{6}{4}$, or $\dfrac{3}{2}$

The slopes of EF and RS are equal, so these two lines are parallel.
Although PQ appears to be parallel, it is not.

Check

1. The slope of each line is given. Circle the lines that are parallel.

a) Slope AB: −4   **b)** Slope CD: 3   **c)** Slope EF: 4   **d)** Slope GH: −4

2. Line AB passes through A(3, 6) and B(−1, −2).
Line CD passes through C(4, 5) and D(−1, −5).
Line EF passes through E(3, 1) and F(6, 6).
Are the lines parallel?

Graph the lines.

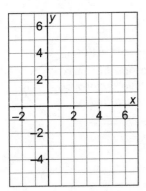

Lines _____ and _____ appear to be parallel.
Find the slopes to check.

Use the formula: Slope $= \dfrac{y_2 - y_1}{x_2 - x_1}$

A(3, 6) and B(−1, −2)
For the slope of AB,
substitute:

$x_1 =$ _____ , $y_1 =$ _____ ,
$x_2 =$ _____ , $y_2 =$ _____

Slope =

_____

=

_____

Slope of AB is _____.

C(4, 5) and D(−1, −5)
For the slope of CD,
substitute:

$x_1 =$ _____ , $y_1 =$ _____ ,
$x_2 =$ _____ , $y_2 =$ _____

Slope =

_____

=

_____

Slope of CD is _____.

E(3, 1) and F(6, 6)
For the slope of EF,
substitute:

$x_1 =$ _____ , $y_1 =$ _____ ,
$x_2 =$ _____ , $y_2 =$ _____

Slope =

_____

=

_____

Slope of EF is _____.

Lines _____ and _____ have _____ slope, so they are _____ .

Lines PQ and RS are perpendicular.

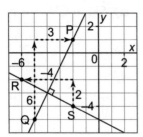

> *Perpendicular lines intersect at right angles.*

Slope of PQ $= \dfrac{6}{3}$

$= 2$

Slope of RS $= \dfrac{2}{-4}$

$= -\dfrac{1}{2}$

> *Two numbers are negative reciprocals if their product is −1.*

Since $2 \times \left(-\dfrac{1}{2}\right) = -1$,

then $-\dfrac{1}{2}$ is the *negative reciprocal* of 2.

In general:

Slopes of Oblique Perpendicular Lines
The slopes of two oblique perpendicular lines are
negative reciprocals; that is, a line with slope m is
perpendicular to a line with slope $-\dfrac{1}{m}$; $m \neq 0$.

> *Recall that any line that is not horizontal or vertical is an **oblique** line.*

Example 2 | **Examining Slopes to Compare Lines**

Line PQ passes through P(−1, −1) and Q(2, 8).
Line RS passes through R(6, −3) and S(0, −1).
Line TU passes through T(4, 6) and U(2, 1).
Are the lines perpendicular?

Solution

Graph the lines.

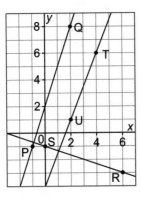

Both PQ and TU appear to be perpendicular to SR.
Find the slopes to check.
Use the formula.

$$\text{Slope} = \frac{y_2 - y_1}{x_2 - x_1}$$

P(−1, −1) and Q(2, 8)
To find the slope of PQ, substitute:
$x_1 = -1$, $y_1 = -1$,
$x_2 = 2$, and $y_2 = 8$

$$\text{Slope of PQ} = \frac{8 - (-1)}{2 - (-1)}$$
$$= \frac{9}{3}$$
$$= 3$$

R(6, −3) and S(0, −1)
To find the slope of RS, substitute:
$x_1 = 6$, $y_1 = -3$,
$x_2 = 0$, and $y_2 = -1$

$$\text{Slope of RS} = \frac{-1 - (-3)}{0 - 6}$$
$$= \frac{2}{-6}$$
$$= -\frac{1}{3}$$

T(4, 6) and U(2, 1)
To find the slope of TU, substitute:
$x_1 = 4$, $y_1 = 6$,
$x_2 = 2$, and $y_2 = 1$

$$\text{Slope of TU} = \frac{1 - 6}{2 - 4}$$
$$= \frac{-5}{-2}$$
$$= \frac{5}{2}$$

Multiply slopes to check:

$$3 \times \left(-\frac{1}{3}\right) = -1$$

The slopes of PQ and RS are negative reciprocals,
so these lines are perpendicular.

Check

1. The slope of each line is given. Circle the lines that are perpendicular.

a) Slope AB: -2 **b)** Slope CD: $\dfrac{1}{2}$ **c)** Slope EF: $-\dfrac{1}{2}$ **d)** Slope GH: -1

2. Line PQ passes through P(1, 4) and Q(2, 8).
Line RS passes through R(−1, 4) and S(−2, 8).
Line TU passes through T(4, 4) and U(8, 5).
Are the lines perpendicular?

Graph the lines.

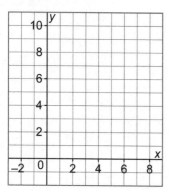

Lines _____ and _____ appear to be perpendicular.

Find the slopes to check.

Use the formula: Slope $= \dfrac{y_2 - y_1}{x_2 - x_1}$

P(1, 4) and Q(2, 8)	R(−1, 4) and S(−2, 8)	T(4, 4) and U(8, 5)
For the slope of PQ, substitute:	For the slope of RS, substitute:	For the slope of TU, substitute:

$x_1 =$ _____, $y_1 =$ _____, $x_2 =$ _____, $y_2 =$ _____

$x_1 =$ _____, $y_1 =$ _____, $x_2 =$ _____, $y_2 =$ _____

$x_1 =$ _____, $y_1 =$ _____, $x_2 =$ _____, $y_2 =$ _____

Slope = _____

$=$ _____

Slope of PQ is _____.

Slope = _____

$=$ _____

Slope of RS is _____.

Slope = _____

$=$ _____

Slope of TU is _____.

Multiply slopes to check:

PQ and TU:

RS and TU:

PQ and RS:

_____ × _____ = _____

_____ × _____ = _____

_____ × _____ = _____

The slopes of _____ and _____ are _____, so these lines are

_____.

Example 3 | Using Slope to Identify a Polygon

Is quadrilateral BCDE a trapezoid?

> *A trapezoid has one pair of parallel sides.*

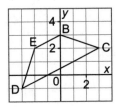

Solution

From the diagram, sides ED and BC are not parallel because the slope of ED is positive and the slope of BC is negative. To check if EB is parallel to DC, compare their slopes.

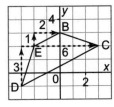

Slope of EB = $\dfrac{1}{2}$

Slope of DC = $\dfrac{3}{6}$, or $\dfrac{1}{2}$

The slopes of EB and DC are equal, so EB and DC are parallel and BCDE is a trapezoid.

Check

1. Is △ABC a right triangle?

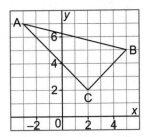

> *Count squares to find each rise and run.*

From the diagram, ∠_____ looks like a right angle.
Find the slopes of sides _____ and _____ to check.

Slope of _____ = _____

Slope of _____ = _____

The slopes _____ negative reciprocals, so sides _____ and _____ _____ perpendicular, and △ABC _____ a right triangle.

1. The slopes of lines are given. Circle the slopes of parallel lines.

  a) Slope: $\frac{5}{3}$ **b)** Slope: $-\frac{5}{3}$ **c)** Slope: $\frac{10}{6}$ **d)** Slope: $-\frac{3}{5}$

2. The slopes of lines are given. Circle the slopes of perpendicular lines.

  a) Slope: $-\frac{5}{8}$ **b)** Slope: $\frac{5}{8}$ **c)** Slope: $\frac{8}{5}$ **d)** Slope: $\frac{10}{16}$

3. a) Line AB has slope -3. A line perpendicular to AB has slope: _____

  b) Line CD has slope $\frac{3}{4}$. A line perpendicular to CD has slope: _____

  c) Line EF has slope $-\frac{7}{8}$. A line perpendicular to EF has slope: _____

  d) Line GH has slope 1. A line perpendicular to GH has slope: _____

4. Write *parallel, perpendicular,* or *neither* to indicate how the lines in each pair are related.

  a) Slope EF: $\frac{1}{4}$ **b)** Slope MN: $\frac{1}{3}$ **c)** Slope JK: $\frac{8}{3}$

   Slope GH: 4   Slope PQ: -3 Slope MN: $\frac{16}{6}$

   _____   _____   _____

5. Line AB passes through A(-3, 2) and B(3, 0).
   Line CD passes through C(1, -1) and D(4, -2).
   Are the lines parallel?

   Graph the lines.
   They _____ parallel.
   Find the slopes to check.
   Use the formula for slope.

   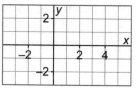

   Slope $= \dfrac{y_2 - y_1}{x_2 - x_1}$

   A(-3, 2) and B(3, 0)   C(1, -1) and D(4, -2)
   To find the slope of AB, substitute: To find the slope of CD, substitute:
   $x_1 =$ _____, $y_1 =$ _____, $x_1 =$ _____, $y_1 =$ _____,
   $x_2 =$ _____, and $y_2 =$ _____ $x_2 =$ _____, and $y_2 =$ _____

   Slope of AB =   Slope of CD =
      _____   _____

      =   =
      _____   _____

   The slopes of AB and CD are _____, so these lines are _____.

330 978-0-321-61066-9 Copyright © 2011 Pearson Canada Inc.

6. Line QR passes through Q(−6, 0) and R(2, 2).
Line ST passes through S(−3, 5) and T(−1, −3).
Are the lines perpendicular?
Graph the lines.

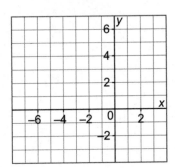

Lines _____ and _____ appear to be _____.

Find the slopes to check.

Use the formula:

$$\text{Slope} = \frac{y_2 - y_1}{x_2 - x_1}$$

Q(−6, 0) and R(2, 2)
For the slope of QR, substitute:

$x_1 = \underline{\quad}, y_1 = \underline{\quad},$
$x_2 = \underline{\quad}, y_2 = \underline{\quad}$

Slope = _____

= _____

S(−3, 5) and T(−1, −3)
For the slope of ST, substitute:

$x_1 = \underline{\quad}, y_1 = \underline{\quad},$
$x_2 = \underline{\quad}, y_2 = \underline{\quad}$

Slope = _____

= _____

Multiply slopes to check:

_____ × _____ = _____

The slopes of _____ and _____ are _____,

so these lines are _____.

7. Draw quadrilateral ABCD with vertices: A(0, 4), B(6, 6), C(8, 3) and D(2, 1)
Is quadrilateral ABCD a parallelogram?

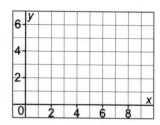

From the diagram:

Sides _____ and _____ appear to be _____.

Sides _____ and _____ appear to be _____.

To check if _____ is parallel to _____, compare their slopes.

Slope of _____ = _____

Slope of _____ = _____

The slopes of _____ and _____ are _____,

so _____ and _____ are _____.

To check if _____ is parallel to _____, compare their slopes.

Slope of _____ = _____

Slope of _____ = _____

The slopes of _____ and _____ are _____,

so _____ and _____ are _____.

Sides _____ and _____ are _____.

Sides _____ and _____ are _____.

The opposite sides of the quadrilateral _____ parallel,

so ABCD _____ a parallelogram.

Can you...

- find the slope of a line segment by using its rise and run?
- find the slope of a line given two points on the line?
- draw a line given its slope and one point on the line?
- use slope to find out if lines are parallel, perpendicular, or neither?

6.1 **1.** Write the rise, the run, and the slope of each line segment.

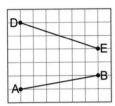

For line segment AB:

Rise = _____

Run = _____

Slope =

_____

For line segment DE:

Rise = _____

Run = _____

Slope =

_____

2. Find the slope of the line that passes through Q(4, 7) and R(10, 10).

Use the formula: Slope $= \dfrac{y_2 - y_1}{x_2 - x_1}$

Let Q be (x_1, y_1) and R be (x_2, y_2).

Slope of QR $= \dfrac{y_2 - y_1}{x_2 - x_1}$

Substitute: $x_1 =$ _____, $y_1 =$ _____, $x_2 =$ _____, and $y_2 =$ _____

Slope of QR =

_____

$=$

_____

Slope of QR is:

_____

3. Draw line EF that passes through E(5, −2) and has slope $-\frac{3}{4}$.

The slope $-\frac{3}{4}$ can be written as _____.

So, the rise is _____ and the run is _____.
Plot point E(5, −2).
From E, move: _____
Mark a point F.
Draw a line through EF.

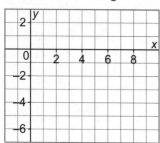

4. a) Two lines are parallel. What do you know about their slopes?

_____

b) Two lines are perpendicular. What do you know about their slopes?

_____

5. Triangle ABC has vertices: A(−3, 7), B(−1, 5), and C(−5, 2)
Is △ABC a right triangle?

Draw △ABC.

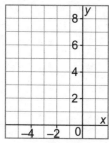

From the diagram, ∠_____ looks like a right angle.
Find the slopes of sides _____ and _____ to check.

Slope of _____ = _____

Slope of _____ = _____

The slopes _____ negative reciprocals, so sides _____

_____ perpendicular, and △ABC _____

a right triangle.

6.3 Math Lab: Investigating Graphs of Linear Functions

FOCUS Compare the graph and the equation of a line.

Use a graphing calculator or a computer with graphing software.

Graph $y = mx + 6$ for the different values of m given.
Record your results as shown in the 2nd row.

It may be easier to identify patterns if you enter all the equations before graphing, rather than graphing the equations one by one.

Part A

Equation	Value of m	Sketch of the graphs	Slope of the graph	x-intercept	y-intercept
$y = -2x + 6$	-2		-2	3	6
$y = -x + 6$	-1				
$y = 0x + 6$	0				
$y = x + 6$	1				
$y = 2x + 6$	2				

Part B

Predict the result for each column of the table in Part A when you graph each equation.
Graph to check each prediction.

- $y = -3x + 6$

  $m =$ _____   slope = _____ x-intercept = _____ y-intercept = _____

  Graph of $y = -3x + 6$

  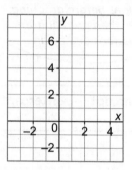

- $y = 3x + 6$

  $m =$ _____   slope = _____ x-intercept = _____ y-intercept = _____

  Graph of $y = 3x + 6$

  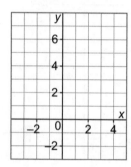

How does changing the value of m change the line?

When m is positive, the line goes _____.
When m is negative, the line goes _____.

What does m represent? _____

Part C

Graph $y = 2x + b$ for the different values of b given.

Record your results in the table.

Equation	Value of b	Sketch of the graphs	Slope of the graph	x-intercept	y-intercept
$y = 2x - 4$	-4		2	2	-4
$y = 2x - 2$	-2				
$y = 2x - 0$	0				
$y = 2x + 2$	2				
$y = 2x + 4$	4				

Part D

Predict the result for each column of the table in part c when you graph each equation.

Graph to check each prediction.

- $y = 2x - 6$

  $b =$ _____   slope = _____ x-intercept = _____ y-intercept = _____

  Graph of $y = 2x - 6$

  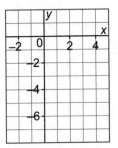

- $y = 2x + 6$

    $b =$ _____   slope = _____ x-intercept = _____ y-intercept = _____

    Graph of $y = 2x + 6$

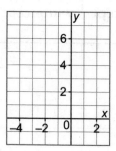

How does changing the value of b change the line?

When b increases, the line moves _____.
When b decreases, the line moves _____.

What does b represent? _____

Practice

1. In the screen below, each mark on the x-axis and y-axis represents 1 unit.

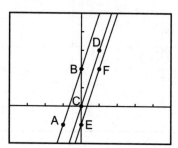

   a) Write the y-intercept of each line.

   AB: _____   CD: _____   EF: _____

   b) Write the slope of each line.

   AB: _____   CD: _____   EF: _____

2. a) Describe the graph of $y = -4x + 2$.

The graph is a line that goes _____.
Its slope is _____ and its y-intercept is _____.

b) How are the graphs of $y = -4x + 4$ and $y = -4x + 2$ alike?
How are the graphs different?

Both graphs have the same _____, which is _____. The graph of $y = -4x + 4$
has y-intercept _____, and the graph of $y = -4x + 2$ has y-intercept _____.

3. a) Graph $y = 2x + 5$ without using a table of values.

The y-intercept is _____; so, mark a point at _____ on the y-axis.
The slope is _____; so, from the plotted point, move _____ units _____ and
_____ unit _____.
Draw a line through the two points.

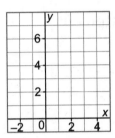

b) How could you use the graph in part a to help you draw the graph of $y = 2x + 6$?

The graph of $y = 2x + 6$ and $y = 2x + 5$ have the same _____; so, the
graphs are _____.
The graph of $y = 2x + 6$ has y-intercept _____.
So, I would draw a line that passes through _____ on the _____-axis and is
_____ the graph of $y = 2x + 5$.

4. a) How do you know that the graphs of $y = 2x$ and $y = -\frac{1}{2}x$ are perpendicular?

b) Give another example of the equations of two lines that are perpendicular.

6.4 Slope-Intercept Form of the Equation for a Linear Function

FOCUS Relate the graph of a line to its equation in slope-intercept form.

The equation of any line that is not vertical can be written in **slope-intercept form**.

> **Slope-Intercept Form of the Equation of a Line**
> The equation of a line, when written as $y = mx + b$, gives information about the line: m is the slope of the line and b is its y-intercept

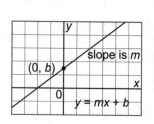

Example 1 | Writing an Equation Given Slope and y-Intercept

A line has slope $-\dfrac{7}{4}$ and y-intercept 5. Write an equation for this line.

Solution

The slope is $-\dfrac{7}{4}$, so $m = -\dfrac{7}{4}$.

The y-intercept is 5, so $b = 5$.

Use:

$y = mx + b$ Substitute: $m = -\dfrac{7}{4}$ and $b = 5$

$y = -\dfrac{7}{4}x + 5$

An equation is: $y = -\dfrac{7}{4}x + 5$

Check

1. A line has slope $\dfrac{1}{2}$ and y-intercept -3. Circle the correct equation.

a) $y = -3x + \dfrac{1}{2}$ **b)** $y = -\dfrac{1}{2}x + 3$ **c)** $y = \dfrac{1}{2}x - 3$

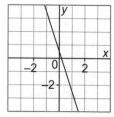 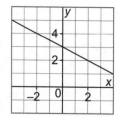 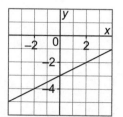

2. A line has slope $\frac{1}{4}$ and y-intercept -6. Write an equation for this line.

In $y = mx + b$, substitute: $m =$ _____ and $b =$ _____

An equation is: _____

Example 2 | Graphing a Line Given Its Equation in Slope-Intercept Form

Use slope and y-intercept to graph the line $y = -\frac{5}{4}x - 2$.

Solution

Compare: $y = -\frac{5}{4}x - 2$

with: $\quad y = mx + b$

The slope of the line is: $m = -\frac{5}{4}$

The y-intercept is: $b = -2$

On a grid, mark a point at the y-intercept -2.

The slope of the line is:

$\dfrac{\text{rise}}{\text{run}} = -\dfrac{5}{4}$, or $\dfrac{5}{-4}$

So, the rise is 5 and the run is -4.

From the y-intercept, move 5 units up and 4 units left, then mark a point.

Draw a line through the points.

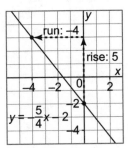

Check

1. Use slope and y-intercept to graph the line $y = 5x + 2$.

Compare: $y = 5x + 2$

with : $y = mx + b$

The slope of the line is: $m = $ _____

Write the slope as _____.
So, the rise is _____ and the run is _____.

The y-intercept is: $b = $ _____
Mark a point at the y-intercept, then move: _____ units _____
and _____ unit _____
Mark a point.

Draw a line through the points.

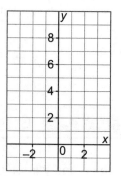

Example 3	Writing an Equation Given a Graph

Write an equation to describe this line.

We need to know the slope, m, of the line and its y-intercept, b.

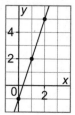

Solution

Use the equation: $y = mx + b$
From the graph, the rise is 3 when the run is 1.

So, $m = \dfrac{3}{1}$, or 3
The line intersects the y-axis at -1.
So, $b = -1$
Substitute for m and b in $y = mx + b$.
$y = 3x - 1$
An equation for the line is: $y = 3x - 1$

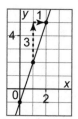

You could check this equation by making a table of values, to see that the points lie on the line.

Check

1. Write an equation to describe this line.

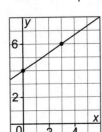

From the graph,

Rise = _____

Run = _____

So, slope, $m =$ _____

The y-intercept is _____; so, $b =$ _____

In $y = mx + b$, substitute:

$m =$ _____ and $b =$ _____

An equation is: _____

---

1. A line has slope -2 and y-intercept $\frac{3}{4}$.

Circle the correct equation for this line.

a) $y = \frac{3}{4}x - 2$ **b)** $y = -2x + \frac{3}{4}$ **c)** $y = 2x - \frac{3}{4}$

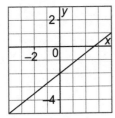 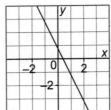 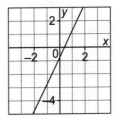

2. For each equation, write the slope and y-intercept of its graph.

a) $y = 2x + 6$

Slope = _____

y-intercept = _____

c) $y = \frac{1}{4}x$

Slope = _____

y-intercept = _____

b) $y = -\frac{1}{2}x + \frac{3}{2}$

Slope = _____

y-intercept = _____

d) $y = -x + 1$

Slope = _____

y-intercept = _____

3. Write an equation for the line that:

a) has slope −2 and *y*-intercept 3

Use: *y* = *mx* + *b*
Substitute: *m* = _____ and *b* = _____
An equation is: _____

b) has slope $\frac{1}{4}$ and *y*-intercept −2

m = _____ and *b* = _____

An equation is: _____

c) passes through S(0, −3) and has slope 4

The point S has *x*-coordinate _____
and *y*-coordinate _____.
So, the *y*-intercept is: _____
m = _____ and *b* = _____
An equation is: _____

d) passes through the origin and has slope $-\frac{3}{4}$

The *y*-intercept is: _____

m = _____ and *b* = _____

An equation is: _____

4. Write an equation to describe this line.

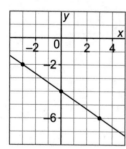

Rise = _____
Run = _____

Slope, *m* = _____

y-intercept, *b* = _____
In *y* = *mx* + *b*,

substitute: *m* = _____ and *b* = _____

An equation is: _____

 978-0-321-61066-9

5. Graph the line with each given *y*-intercept and slope.
Write an equation of the line.

a) *y*-intercept is 1, slope is $-\dfrac{3}{2}$

The rise is _____.
The run is _____.
From a point at _____ on the *y*-axis, move _____ units _____
and _____ units _____.
Mark a point, then draw a line through the two points.

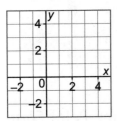

In *y* = *mx* + *b*,

substitute: *m* = _____ and *b* = _____

An equation is: _____

b) *y*-intercept is −3, slope is $\dfrac{7}{4}$

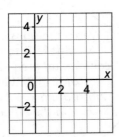

An equation is: _____

6.5 Slope-Point Form of the Equation for a Linear Function

Relate the graph of a line to its equation in slope-point form.

We can write the equation of a line when we know its slope and *y*-intercept. We can also write the equation of a line when we know its slope and the coordinates of a point on the line.

In general:

> **Slope-Point Form of the Equation of a Line**
> The equation of a line that passes through $P(x_1, y_1)$ and has slope m is:
> $$y - y_1 = m(x - x_1)$$

Example 1 | Graphing a Line Given Its Equation in Slope-Point Form

a) Write the slope and the coordinates of a point on the line $y + 3 = -\frac{3}{4}(x - 2)$.

b) Graph the line.

Solution

a) Compare the given equation with the equation in slope-point form.

$$y - y_1 = m(x - x_1)$$

$$y + 3 = -\frac{3}{4}(x - 2)$$

Rewrite the given equation to match the slope-point form, which involves subtraction.

$$y - (-3) = -\frac{3}{4}(x - 2)$$

Remember integer subtraction: $-(-3) = +3$

$$y - y_1 = m(x - x_1)$$

Compare the equations: $y_1 = -3$; $m = -\frac{3}{4}$, and $x_1 = 2$

The line passes through $(2, -3)$ and has slope $-\frac{3}{4}$.

Watch the signs. A common mistake is to say the coordinates are $(-2, 3)$ instead of $(2, -3)$. Verify by substituting $x = 2$ and $y = -3$ in the equation $y + 3 = -\frac{3}{4}(x - 2)$.

b) Plot the point $P(2, -3)$.

Write the slope $-\frac{3}{4}$ as $\frac{3}{-4}$.

So, the rise is 3 and the run is -4.

From P, move 3 units up and 4 units left. Plot another point. Draw a line through the points.

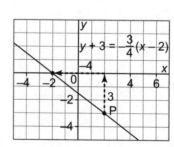

Check

1. a) Circle the number below that is the slope of the line $y - 1 = -2(x + 4)$.

i) -1 **ii)** -2 **iii)** 4 **iv)** 2

Watch the signs.

b) Circle the coordinates of one point on the line $y - 1 = -2(x + 4)$.

i) $(-4, -1)$ **ii)** $(4, -1)$ **iii)** $(4, 1)$ **iv)** $(-4, 1)$

2. a) Write the slope and the coordinates of a point on the line $y + 1 = 3(x - 2)$.

Rewrite the equation to match the slope-point form using subtraction:

$y - \underline{\hspace{1cm}} = 3(x - 2)$

Compare this equation with:

$y - y_1 = m(x - x_1)$

$y_1 = \underline{\hspace{1cm}}$, $m = \underline{\hspace{1cm}}$, and $x_1 = \underline{\hspace{1cm}}$

So, the slope is _____ and the coordinates of a point are _____.

b) Graph the line $y + 1 = 3(x - 2)$.

Plot the point P_____.
The slope is _____.

Write the slope as _____.
So, the rise is _____ and the run is _____.
From P, move _____ units _____ and _____ unit _____.
Plot a point. Draw a line through the points.

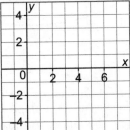

Example 2 | **Writing an Equation in Slope-Point Form**

a) Write an equation for this line.

b) Write the equation in slope-intercept form.

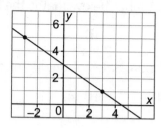

Solution

a) Identify the coordinates of two points on the line, then calculate its slope.

Two points are: A(-3, 5) and B(3, 1)

To calculate the slope, m, use:

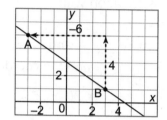

$$m = \frac{\text{rise}}{\text{run}}$$

$$m = \frac{4}{-6}$$

$$m = -\frac{2}{3}$$

Use the slope-point form of the equation: $y - y_1 = m(x - x_1)$

Substitute the coordinates of A(-3, 5),

and the slope: $x_1 = -3$, $y_1 = 5$, and $m = -\frac{2}{3}$

$y - 5 = -\frac{2}{3}[x - (-3)]$ Simplify.

$y - 5 = -\frac{2}{3}(x + 3)$ This is the slope-point form.

> You could substitute the coordinates of B to get the slope-point equation $y - 1 = -\frac{2}{3}(x - 3)$. Both equations represent the same line.

b) To write the equation in slope-intercept form:

$y - 5 = -\frac{2}{3}(x + 3)$ Expand.

$y - 5 = -\frac{2}{3}x - \frac{2}{3}(3)$ Simplify.

$y - 5 = -\frac{2}{3}x - 2$ Solve for y. Add 5 to each side.

$y = -\frac{2}{3}x - 2 + 5$

$y = -\frac{2}{3}x + 3$ This is the slope-intercept form.

> A line can be represented by many slope-point equations, but only one slope-intercept equation.

Check

1. a) Write an equation for this line.

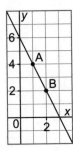

Two points are: _____ and _____

$m = \dfrac{\text{rise}}{\text{run}}$

$m =$

_____

$m =$ _____

Use the slope-point form of the equation:

_____

Substitute the coordinates of point _____
and the slope:

$x_1 =$ _____, $y_1 =$ _____, and $m =$ _____

$y -$ _____ $=$ _____$(x -$ _____$)$

In slope-point form, an equation is: _____

b) Write the equation in slope-intercept form.

$y -$ _____ $=$ _____$(x -$ _____$)$ Expand.

$y -$ _____ $=$ _____   Solve for y.

$y =$ _____

$y =$ _____

Example 3 — Writing an Equation of a Line That Is Parallel to a Given Line

The graph of $y = -\frac{1}{2}x + 2$ is given.

Write an equation for the line that passes through A(4, 3) and is parallel to the line $y = -\frac{1}{2}x + 2$.

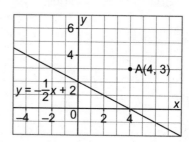

Solution

Compare the equation: $y = -\frac{1}{2}x + 2$

with the equation: $\quad\quad y = mx + b$

The slope of the line is: $m = -\frac{1}{2}$

Parallel lines have the same slope,

so any line parallel to $y = -\frac{1}{2}x + 2$ has slope $-\frac{1}{2}$.

The required line passes through A(4, 3).
Use the slope-point form of the equation.

Substitute: $x_1 = 4$, $y_1 = 3$, and $m = -\frac{1}{2}$

$y - y_1 = m(x - x_1)$

$y - 3 = -\frac{1}{2}(x - 4)$

An equation of the line is: $y - 3 = -\frac{1}{2}(x - 4)$

Check

1. The graph of $y = \frac{2}{3}x + 6$ is given.

Write an equation for the line that passes through A(−4, 1) and is perpendicular to the line $y = \frac{2}{3}x + 6$.

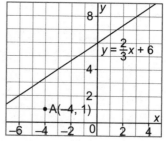

Perpendicular lines have slopes that are negative reciprocals.

Compare the equation: $y = \frac{2}{3}x + 6$

with the equation: $\quad\quad y = mx + b$

The slope of the line is: $m = $ _____

Any line perpendicular to $y = \frac{2}{3}x + 6$ has a slope that is the negative

reciprocal of _____; that is, its slope is _____.

The required line passes through A(−4, 1).

Use the slope-point form of the equation: _____

Substitute:

_____

An equation of the line is: _____

Practice

1. a) Write the slope and the coordinates of a point on the line $y - 4 = \frac{1}{2}(x + 2)$.

Rewrite the equation to match the slope-point form using subtraction:

$y - 4 = \frac{1}{2}(x - \underline{\hspace{1cm}})$

Compare this equation with:

$y - y_1 = m(x - x_1)$

$y_1 = \underline{\hspace{1cm}}$, $m = \underline{\hspace{1cm}}$, and $x_1 = \underline{\hspace{1cm}}$

So, the slope is _____, and the coordinates of a point are _____.

b) Graph the line.

Plot the point P_____.

The slope is _____.

So, the rise is _____ and the run is _____.

From P, move _____ unit _____ and

_____ units _____.

Plot a point. Draw a line through the points.

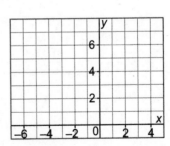

2. A line passes through F(-1, 8) and has slope -3. Write an equation for the line.

Use the slope-point form of the equation: _____

Substitute: _____

An equation is: _____

3. a) Graph the line that passes through U(2, -1), and has slope $\dfrac{5}{3}$.

The slope is _____.
So, the rise is _____ and the run is _____.
On the grid, from the point _____,
move _____ and _____.
Mark a point.
Join the points.

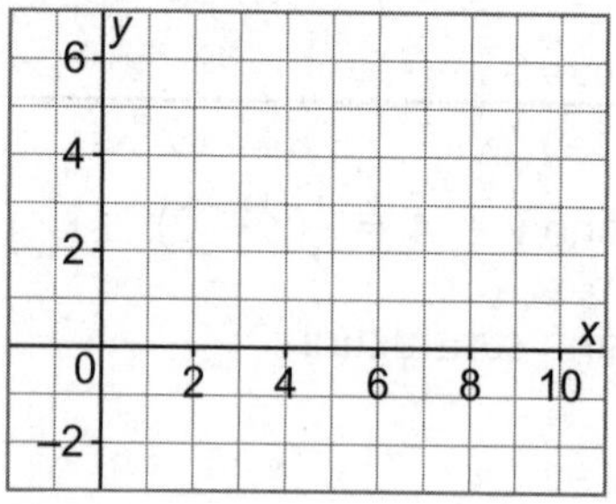

b) Write an equation for the line in part a.

Use the slope-point form of the equation: _____

Substitute: _____

An equation is: _____

4. Write this equation in slope-intercept form: $y + 5 = -4(x - 3)$

$y + 5 = -4(x - 3)$ Expand.

$y + 5 =$ _____   Solve for y.

$\quad\quad y =$ _____

$\quad\quad y =$ _____

The equation is: _____

5. A line passes through $P(-3, 4)$ and $Q(3, -6)$. Write an equation for the line.

Plot the points on a grid, then draw a line through the points.

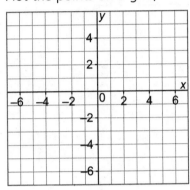

Use the formula: $\text{Slope} = \dfrac{y_2 - y_1}{x_2 - x_1}$

Let P be _____ and Q be _____.

$\text{Slope of PQ} = \dfrac{y_2 - y_1}{x_2 - x_1}$

Substitute: $x_1 =$ _____, $y_1 =$ _____, $x_2 =$ _____, and $y_2 =$ _____

$\text{Slope of PQ} =$

_____

$\quad\quad\quad = $

_____

The slope is _____.

Use the slope-point form of the equation: _____

Use the coordinates of _____ to write the equation.

Substitute:

_____

In slope-point form, an equation is:

_____

6. An equation of a line is $y = -\frac{3}{8}x + 4$.

    a) Write an equation for the line that passes
        through R(1, −3) and is perpendicular to $y = -\frac{3}{8}x + 4$.

        The slope of the line is _____.

        The slope of a perpendicular line is _____.

        Use the slope-point form of the equation: _____

        Substitute: _____

        An equation of the line is: _____

    b) Write an equation for the line that passes
        through R(1, −3) and is parallel to $y = -\frac{3}{8}x + 4$.

        An equation of the line is: _____

CHECKPOINT 2

Can you...

- use technology to graph a line?
- write an equation for a line given its slope and *y*-intercept?
- graph an equation in slope-intercept form and in slope-point form?
- write an equation for a line given its slope and a point on the line?
- write an equation for a line given two points on the line?

6.3 **1.** Use a graphing calculator or a computer.
Graph $y = -3x + 5$.
Copy the graph on the grid below.

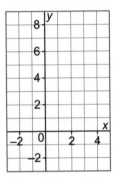

Compare $y = -3x + 5$ with
$$y = mx + b$$

a) What is the slope of the line? _____

b) What is the *y*-intercept? _____

c) Write an equation of a line that has the same slope as $y = -3x + 5$,
but has a different *y*-intercept. _____

d) Write an equation of a line that has the same *y*-intercept as $y = -3x + 5$,
but has a different slope. _____

6.4 **2.** Write an equation of a line with:

a) slope 4 and *y*-intercept 8

Use: $y = mx + b$

Substitute: $m =$ _____ and $b =$ _____

An equation is: $y =$ _____

b) slope $\dfrac{3}{2}$ and *y*-intercept −1

Use: _____

Substitute: _____

An equation is: _____

3. Graph the line $y = \frac{1}{3}x - 2$.

Compare the given equation with:

$y = mx + b$

$y = \frac{1}{3}x - 2$

The slope of the line, m, is _____.
The y-intercept, b, is _____.
The rise is _____; the run is _____.
From a point at _____ on the _____-axis,
move _____ unit _____ and _____ units _____.
Mark a point. Join the points.

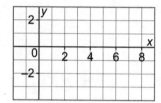

6.5   **4.** For the line $y + 4 = 3(x - 5)$:

a) Write the coordinates of a point on the line, and the slope of the line.

Rewrite the equation to match the slope-point form using subtraction:
$y - (\underline{\quad}) = 3(x - \underline{\quad})$
Compare: $y - (\underline{\quad}) = 3(x - \underline{\quad})$
with: $y - y_1 = m(x - x_1)$
$y_1 = \underline{\quad}$, $m = \underline{\quad}$, and $x_1 = \underline{\quad}$
Coordinates are: $(\underline{\quad})$
Slope is: _____

b) Graph the line.

Plot the point $(\underline{\quad})$, then
move: _____
Mark a point. Draw a line through the points.

5. a) Write an equation for the line that passes through C(3, −5), and has slope 2.

Use the slope-point form of the equation:

$y - y_1 = m(x - x_1)$

Substitute: $x_1 =$ _____ , $y_1 =$ _____ , and $m =$ _____

An equation is: _____

b) Write the equation in part a in slope-intercept form.

An equation is: _____

6. Write an equation for the line that passes through D(4, −1) and E(6, 3).

Use the formula: Slope $= \dfrac{y_2 - y_1}{x_2 - x_1}$

Let D be _____ and E be _____ .

Slope of DE $= \dfrac{y_2 - y_1}{x_2 - x_1}$

Substitute: $x_1 =$ _____ , $y_1 =$ _____ , $x_2 =$ _____ , and $y_2 =$ _____

Slope of DE $=$

The slope is _____ .
Use the slope-point form of the equation:

_____

Use the coordinates of _____ to write the equation.

Substitute: _____

_____ $=$ _____

In slope-point form, an equation is:

_____

6.6 General Form of the Equation for a Linear Relation

FOCUS Relate the graph of a line to its equation in general form.

We can write an equation in different forms.

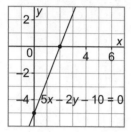

An equation for this graph is $5x - 2y - 10 = 0$.

We can write this equation in slope-intercept form.

$5x - 2y - 10 = 0$ Add 10 to each side.

    $5x - 2y = 10$ Subtract $5x$ from each side.

       $-2y = -5x + 10$ Divide each side by -2.

          $y = \dfrac{5}{2}x - 5$

> *When the equations are equivalent, they represent the same line.*

The equation $5x - 2y - 10 = 0$ is in **general form**.
All the terms are on the left side of the equation.
The coefficients are integers, and the coefficient of
x is a positive integer.

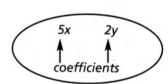

> ## General Form of the Equation of a Line
> $Ax + By + C = 0$ is the general form of the equation of a line, where A, B, and C are integers and A is positive.

Example 1 | **Rewriting an Equation in General Form**

Write each equation in general form.

a) $y = -3x + 5$

b) $y = -\frac{1}{2}x + 3$

Solution

a)

$y = -3x + 5$	Move all terms to the left side.
$y + 3x - 5 = 0$	Rearrange the terms so the x-term is first.
$3x + y - 5 = 0$	This equation is in general form.

> *Remember to change the sign of a term when you move it to the other side of the equation.*

b)

$y = -\frac{1}{2}x + 3$	Remove the fraction. Multiply each term by 2.
$2y = 2\left(-\frac{1}{2}x\right) + 2(3)$	Simplify.
$2y = -x + 6$	Move all terms to the left side.
$2y + x - 6 = 0$	Rearrange the terms so the x-term is first.
$x + 2y - 6 = 0$	This equation is in general form.

Check

1. Write this equation in general form: $y + 5 = \frac{2}{3}(x - 4)$

$y + 5 = \frac{2}{3}(x - 4)$	Remove the fraction. Multiply each side by ____.
____$(y + 5) = $ ____$\left[\frac{2}{3}(x - 4)\right]$	
$3(\underline{\hspace{1cm}}) = 2(\underline{\hspace{1cm}})$	Expand.
____$y + $ ____ $= $ ____$x - $ ____	Move all terms to the left side.
____$y + $ ____ $- $ ____$x + $ ____ $= 0$	Collect like terms.
____$y - $ ____$x + $ ____ $= 0$	Rearrange so the ____-term is first.
____$x + $ ____$y + $ ____ $= 0$	Multiply each term by -1 so the x-term is positive.
$-1(\underline{\hspace{0.5cm}}x + \underline{\hspace{0.5cm}}y + \underline{\hspace{0.5cm}}) = 0$	
$\underline{\hspace{5cm}}$	This equation is in general form.

Find the slope of the line with equation $4x - 3y - 12 = 0$.

Solution

Write the equation in slope-intercept form.

$4x - 3y - 12 = 0$	Solve for y. Subtract $4x$ from each side.
$-3y - 12 = -4x$	Add 12 to each side.
$-3y = -4x + 12$	Divide each term by -3.
$\dfrac{-3y}{-3} = \dfrac{-4x}{-3} + \dfrac{12}{-3}$	Simplify.
$y = \dfrac{4}{3}x - 4$	

Compare this equation with $y = mx + b$.

$m = \dfrac{4}{3}$

So, the slope of the line is $\dfrac{4}{3}$.

Check

1. Find the slope of the line with equation $6x + 4y - 5 = 0$.

Write the equation in slope-intercept form.

$6x + 4y - 5 = 0$	Subtract _____ from each side.
$4y - 5 = $ _____	Add _____ to each side.
$4y = $ _____ $+$ _____	Divide each term by _____.
$\dfrac{4y}{4} = \dfrac{}{\rule{2em}{0.4pt}} + \dfrac{}{\rule{2em}{0.4pt}}$	Simplify.
$y = \dfrac{}{\rule{2em}{0.4pt}} + \dfrac{}{\rule{2em}{0.4pt}}$	

The slope of the line is _____.

When you are given the equation of a line in general form, using intercepts may be the fastest way to graph the line.

Example 3 | Using Intercepts to Graph a Line Given in General Form

a) Find the x- and y-intercepts of the line $4x + y - 8 = 0$.

b) Use the intercepts to graph the line.

Solution

a) $4x + y - 8 = 0$

To find the x-intercept, substitute $y = 0$.

$4x + (0) - 8 = 0$ Solve for x.

$4x - 8 = 0$ Add 8 to each side.

$4x = 8$ Divide each term by 4.

$\dfrac{4x}{4} = \dfrac{8}{4}$

$x = 2$

With practice, you can find the intercepts using mental math.

The x-intercept is 2.

To find the y-intercept, substitute $x = 0$.

$4(0) + y - 8 = 0$ Solve for y.

$y - 8 = 0$

$y = 8$

The y-intercept is 8.

b) On a grid, mark a point at 2 on the x-axis and a point at 8 on the y-axis.

Draw a line through the points.

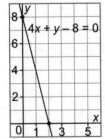

Check

1. a) Find the *x*- and *y*-intercepts of the line $3x - 4y - 24 = 0$.

$3x - 4y - 24 = 0$

To find the *x*-intercept, substitute: _____

$3x - 4(\underline{\hspace{1cm}}) - 24 = 0$ Solve for _____.

$3x \underline{\hspace{1cm}} = 0$ Add _____ to each side.

$3x = \underline{\hspace{1cm}}$ Divide each term by _____.

$$\frac{3x}{\underline{\hspace{1cm}}} = \frac{\underline{\hspace{1cm}}}{\underline{\hspace{1cm}}}$$

$x = \underline{\hspace{1cm}}$

The *x*-intercept is: _____

To find the *y*-intercept, substitute: _____

$3(\underline{\hspace{1cm}}) - 4y - 24 = 0$ Solve for _____.

$-4y \underline{\hspace{1cm}} = 0$ Add _____ to each side.

$-4y = \underline{\hspace{1cm}}$ Divide each term by _____.

$$\frac{-4y}{\underline{\hspace{1cm}}} = \frac{\underline{\hspace{1cm}}}{\underline{\hspace{1cm}}}$$

$y = \underline{\hspace{1cm}}$

The *y*-intercept is: _____

b) Use the intercepts to graph the line.

On a grid, mark a point at _____ on the _____-axis and a point
at _____ on the _____-axis.
Draw a line through the points.

1. Write each equation in general form.

a) $\qquad$ $y = 2x - 1$

$y - \underline{\hspace{1cm}} + \underline{\hspace{1cm}} = 0$

$\underline{\hspace{1cm}} + y + \underline{\hspace{1cm}} = 0$

$\underline{\hspace{1cm}} - y - \underline{\hspace{1cm}} = 0$

In general form, the equation is: $\underline{\hspace{3cm}}$

Move all terms to the $\underline{\hspace{1cm}}$ side.

Put the $\underline{\hspace{1cm}}$-term first.

Multiply by $\underline{\hspace{1cm}}$ so the $\underline{\hspace{1cm}}$-term is positive.

b) $\qquad$ $y = -\dfrac{1}{3}x + 4$

$\underline{\hspace{1cm}}(\underline{\hspace{1cm}}) = \underline{\hspace{1cm}}\left(-\dfrac{1}{3}x\right) + \underline{\hspace{1cm}}(4)$

$\underline{\hspace{1cm}} = -x + \underline{\hspace{1cm}}$

$\underline{\hspace{1cm}} + x - \underline{\hspace{1cm}} = 0$

$x + \underline{\hspace{1cm}} - \underline{\hspace{1cm}} = 0$

In general form, the equation is: $\underline{\hspace{3cm}}$

Multiply each term by $\underline{\hspace{1cm}}$.

Simplify.

Move all terms $\underline{\hspace{2cm}}$.

Put the $\underline{\hspace{2cm}}$ first.

c) $\qquad$ $y + 1 = -\dfrac{2}{5}(x - 2)$

$5(\underline{\hspace{1cm}}) = -2(\underline{\hspace{1cm}})$

$\underline{\hspace{1cm}} + \underline{\hspace{1cm}} = \underline{\hspace{1cm}} + \underline{\hspace{1cm}}$

$\underline{\hspace{1cm}} + \underline{\hspace{1cm}} + \underline{\hspace{1cm}} - \underline{\hspace{1cm}} = \underline{\hspace{1cm}}$

$\underline{\hspace{1cm}} + \underline{\hspace{1cm}} + \underline{\hspace{1cm}} = \underline{\hspace{1cm}}$

$\underline{\hspace{1cm}} + \underline{\hspace{1cm}} + \underline{\hspace{1cm}} = \underline{\hspace{1cm}}$

In general form, the equation is: $\underline{\hspace{3cm}}$

Multiply each side by $\underline{\hspace{1cm}}$.

Expand.

Move all terms $\underline{\hspace{2cm}}$.

Collect $\underline{\hspace{1cm}}$ terms.

Put the $\underline{\hspace{2cm}}$ first.

2. Find the slope of each line.

a) $4x + y - 1 = 0$

Write the equation in slope-intercept form.

$4x + y - 1 = 0$

$y - 1 = \underline{\hspace{1cm}}$

$y = \underline{\hspace{1cm}} + \underline{\hspace{1cm}}$

Compare this equation with $y = mx + b$.

The slope of the line is: $\underline{\hspace{1cm}}$

Subtract $\underline{\hspace{1cm}}$ from each side.

Add $\underline{\hspace{1cm}}$ to each side.

b) $3x - 2y + 2 = 0$

Write the equation in _____ form.

$3x - 2y + 2 = 0$

_____ $+$ _____ $=$ _____   Subtract _____ from each side.

_____ $=$ _____ $-$ _____   Subtract _____ from each side.

$\dfrac{}{} = \dfrac{}{} - \dfrac{}{}$ Divide each term by _____.

_____ $=$ _____

The slope of the line is: _____

3. Find the x- and y-intercepts of each line.

   a) $4x + 5y + 20 = 0$

To find the x-intercept, substitute: _____

$4x + 5(\_\_\_\_) + 20 = 0$

$4x + \_\_\_\_ = 0$

$4x = \_\_\_\_$

$\dfrac{4x}{} = \dfrac{}{}$

$x = \_\_\_\_$

The x-intercept is: _____

To find the y-intercept, substitute: _____

$4(\_\_\_\_) + 5y + 20 = 0$

$5y + \_\_\_\_ = 0$

$5y = \_\_\_\_$

$\dfrac{5y}{} = \dfrac{}{}$

$y = \_\_\_\_$

The y-intercept is: _____

   b) $3x - 6y - 18 = 0$

To find the x-intercept, substitute: _____   To find the y-intercept, substitute: _____

The x-intercept is: _____   The y-intercept is: _____

 978-0-321-61066-9

4. Use intercepts to graph $3x - 2y + 12 = 0$.

To find the *x*-intercept, substitute: _____

To find the *y*-intercept, substitute: _____

The *x*-intercept is: _____

The *y*-intercept is: _____

To graph the line:
On the grid, mark a point at _____ on the _____-axis and a point at _____ on the _____-axis.
Draw a line through the points.

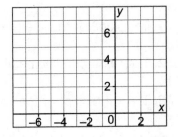

5. Write this equation in slope-intercept form, then graph it: $3x + 4y - 16 = 0$

$3x + 4y - 16 = 0$ Solve for *y*.

In slope-intercept form,

the equation is: _____

The slope is _____.
The *y*-intercept is _____.
To graph the line:
Plot a point at _____ on the _____-axis, then move _____ units _____ and _____ units _____.
Mark a point. Draw a line through the points.

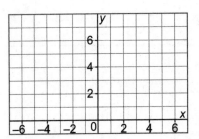

Pushups

Canadian athlete Doug Prudent took a pushup challenge.
How many pushups on fists did he do in just over 18 min?

To find out, answer each question in the space provided.
Then, in the array below, cross out any number that is in your answers.
The remaining number is the number of Doug's pushups.

1. The slope of the line through A(1, 6) and B(0, 2): _____

2. The slope of a line parallel to the line $6x - y - 2 = 0$: _____

3. The x-intercept of the line $y = 2x - 4$: _____

4. The slope of a line perpendicular to the line through A(−2, 4) and B(−8, 6): _____

5. The y-intercept of the line $x - 2y + 10 = 0$: _____

6. The graph of $y + 2 = -\frac{2}{3}(x - 8)$ passes through P(a, −2). The value of a is: _____

7. The y-intercept of the line through A(1, 5) and B(2, 3): _____

8. The y-intercept of the line $x - 2y + 18 = 0$: _____

3	4	6	9	2
2	8	5	7	3
9	5	6	9	5
4	3	2	4	7
7	1	0	0	0

Answer: _____ pushups

Skill	Description	Example
Find the slope of a line.	Slope $= \dfrac{\text{rise}}{\text{run}}$ The slope of a line through $A(x_1, y_1)$ and $B(x_2, y_2)$ is: $\dfrac{y_2 - y_1}{x_2 - x_1}$	For $A(2, -4)$ and $B(-1, 3)$: Rise: $3 - (-4) = 7$ Run: $-1 - 2 = -3$ Slope: $\dfrac{7}{-3}$, or $-\dfrac{7}{3}$
Identify parallel lines and perpendicular lines.	Parallel lines have equal slopes. Perpendicular lines have slopes that are negative reciprocals.	Line AB has slope $-\dfrac{7}{3}$. Line CD has slope $-\dfrac{7}{3}$. Line EF has slope $\dfrac{3}{7}$. Lines AB and CD are parallel. Lines AB and EF are perpendicular. Lines CD and EF are perpendicular.
Write the equation of a line in slope-intercept form.	A line with slope, m, and y-intercept, b, has equation: $y = mx + b$	For a line with slope 3 and y-intercept -2, an equation is: $y = 3x - 2$
Write the equation of a line in slope-point form.	A line with slope, m, that passes through $P(x_1, y_1)$, has equation: $y - y_1 = m(x - x_1)$	A line with slope -4 that passes through $P(-1, 3)$ has equation: $y - 3 = -4(x - (-1))$, or $y - 3 = -4(x + 1)$
Find the intercepts of a line when its equation is in general form.	The general form of an equation is: $Ax + By + C = 0$, where A, B, and C are integers, and A is positive	A line has equation: $3x - 2y + 6 = 0$ For the y-intercept, substitute $x = 0$: $3(0) - 2y + 6 = 0$ $\qquad -2y = -6$ $\qquad\quad y = 3$ For the x-intercept, substitute $y = 0$: $3x - 2(0) + 6 = 0$ $\qquad 3x + 6 = 0$ $\qquad\quad 3x = -6$ $\qquad\quad\; x = -2$

6.1 **1.** Find the slope of this line segment.

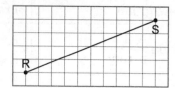

Count units for the rise and run.

Rise = _____

Run = _____

Slope = _____

2. Find the slope of the line through A(−4, 3) and B(1, 6).

Use the formula:

Slope $= \dfrac{y_2 - y_1}{x_2 - x_1}$

Let A be (x_1, y_1) and B be (x_2, y_2).
Substitute: $x_1 =$ _____, $y_1 =$ _____, $x_2 =$ _____, and $y_2 =$ _____

Slope of AB = _____

Slope of AB = _____

The slope of the line is: _____

3. Draw line CD that passes through C(−3, −2), and has slope −3.

Write the slope −3 as the fraction _____.
So, the rise is _____ and the run is _____.
Plot point C(−3, −2).
From C, move: _____
Mark point D. Draw a line through CD.

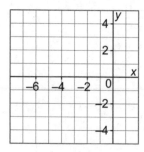

4. a) Find the slope of the line through each pair of points:

    i) A(0, 5) and B(4, 2)

$$\text{Slope of AB} = \frac{2 - \underline{}}{4 - \underline{}}$$

    Slope of AB = _____

    ii) C(−1, 3) and D(2, 7)

    Slope of CD = _____

    Slope of CD = _____

    iii) E(−2, −3) and F(4, 5)

    Slope of EF = _____

    Slope of EF = _____

Remember to write the fractions in simplest form.

b) Which lines in part a are parallel?

_____

Which lines in part a are perpendicular?

_____

5. Graph $y = \frac{1}{2}x - 3$.

The *y*-intercept is ____;
so, mark a point at ____ on the *y*-axis.

The slope is _____; so, from the plotted point,
move ____ unit ____ and ____ units _____.

Mark a point.
Draw a line through the points.

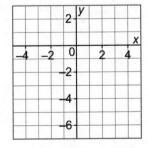

6. For each line:
- Write its slope and *y*-intercept.
- Write an equation in slope-intercept form.

a)

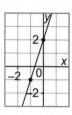

Choose two points.

Rise = _____

Run = _____

Slope = _____

The *y*-intercept is _____.

For the equation, use:

$y = mx + b$

Substitute: $m =$ _____ and $b =$ _____

_____ = _____

An equation is: _____

b)

Choose two points.

Rise = _____

Run = _____

Slope = _____

The *y*-intercept is _____.

For the equation, use:

_____

Substitute: _____

_____

An equation is: _____

7. For the line $y - 4 = \frac{1}{2}(x + 3)$

a) Write the slope of the line: _____

b) Write the coordinates of a point on the line: _____

c) Graph the line:

Plot point P_____.

The slope is _____; so, from P, move:

_____

Mark a point. Draw a line through the points.

8. a) Write an equation for this line.

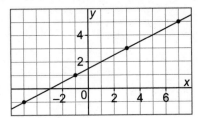

Find the slope.
Two points have coordinates:

_____ and _____

$$m = \frac{rise}{run}$$

$m =$ _____

$m =$ _____

Use the slope-point form of the equation:

_____

Substitute the coordinates _____
and the slope: $x_1 =$ _____, $y_1 =$ _____, and $m =$ _____

$y -$ _____ $=$ _____$(x -$ _____$)$

In slope-point form, an equation is: _____

b) Write the equation in part a in slope-intercept form.

In slope-intercept form, the equation is: _____

9. Graph each line.

a) $3x + 6y - 12 = 0$

Use intercepts.
To find the x-intercept, substitute: _____

$x =$ _____

To find the y-intercept, substitute: _____

$y =$ _____

On the grid, mark a point at _____ on the _____-axis
and a point at _____ on the _____-axis.
Draw a line through the points.

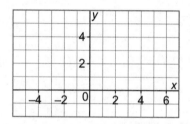

b) $2x - 3y - 9 = 0$

Write the equation in slope-intercept form.

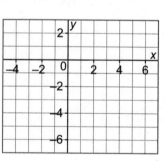

$y =$
_____

For the graph:
From a point at _____ on the _____-axis,
move: _____
Mark a point. Join the points.

Systems of Linear Equations

What You'll Learn

- Use different strategies to solve a system of linear equations in two variables.

- Use a linear system to model and solve a problem.

- Find the number of solutions of a linear system.

Why It's Important

Systems of linear equations are used by:

- electricians, to find the current flowing through an electrical circuit and the voltage across the circuit

- economists, to assess supply and demand in an economy

- geneticists, to study the transmission of genes from one generation to another

Key Words

system of linear equations
linear system
solve by substitution

solve by elimination
infinite solutions

7.1 Developing Systems of Linear Equations

FOCUS Model a situation using a system of linear equations.

We can use equations to model a situation.

Tickets are sold for the school play.
Felix buys 3 adult tickets and 2 student tickets. He pays $31.
Ellen buys 1 adult ticket and 1 student ticket. She pays $12.

Let a represent the cost of an adult ticket.
Let s represent the cost of a student ticket.

The cost of 3 adult tickets and 2 student tickets is equal to $31.
So, $3a$ + $2s$ $= 31$
The cost of 1 adult ticket and 1 student ticket is equal to $12.
So, a + s $= 12$

The equations that model the situation are:
$3a + 2s = 31$
$a + s = 12$

> These two equations form a **system of linear equations** in 2 variables, or a **linear system**.

The solution of the system of equations is: $a = 7$ and $s = 5$
1 adult ticket costs $7 and 1 student ticket costs $5.

To verify the solution, substitute the values of a and s into the equations.
In each equation, substitute: $a = 7$ and $s = 5$

$3a + 2s = 31$ $a + s = 12$
L.S. $= 3a + 2s$ R.S. $= 31$ L.S. $= a + s$ R.S. $= 12$
    $= 3(7) + 2(5)$ $= 7 + 5$
    $= 21 + 10$ $= 12$
    $= 31$

For each equation, L.S. $=$ R.S., so $a = 7$ and $s = 5$
is the solution of the linear system.

> A solution of a linear system is a pair of values that satisfy both equations.

Example 1 | Identifying the Correct Solution of a Linear System

Which pair of values is a solution for this linear system?
$c = 2d + 2$
$c + 2d = -6$
Solution A: $c = 4$ and $d = 1$

Solution B: $c = -2$ and $d = -2$

Solution

Check Solution A:

In each equation, substitute: $c = 4$ and $d = 1$

$c = 2d + 2$

L.S. $= c$ R.S. $= 2d + 2$

     $= 4$ $= 2(1) + 2$

                            $= 2 + 2$

                            $= 4$

$c + 2d = -6$

L.S. $= c + 2d$ R.S. $= -6$

     $= 4 + 2(1)$

     $= 4 + 2$

     $= 6$

For the equation $c + 2d = -6$, L.S. $\neq$ R.S.

So, $c = 4$ and $d = 1$ is not the solution.

Since Solution A is not correct, we might expect Solution B is. We need to check to be sure.

Check Solution B:

In each equation, substitute: $c = -2$ and $d = -2$

$c = 2d + 2$

L.S. $= c$ R.S. $= 2d + 2$

     $= -2$ $= 2(-2) + 2$

                          $= -4 + 2$

                          $= -2$

$c + 2d = -6$

L.S. $= c + 2d$ R.S. $= -6$

     $= -2 + 2(-2)$

     $= -2 - 4$

     $= -6$

For each equation, L.S. $=$ R.S.

So, $c = -2$ and $d = -2$ is the solution.

Check

1. Which pair of values is a solution for this linear system?

$m + n = -3$

$m = 3n + 5$

Solution A: $m = -4$ and $n = 1$

Solution B: $m = -1$ and $n = -2$

Check Solution A:

In each equation, substitute: $m =$ _____ and $n =$ _____

$m + n = -3$

L.S. $= m + n$ R.S. $=$ _____

    $=$ _____

    $=$ _____

$m = 3n + 5$

L.S. $= m$ R.S. $= 3n + 5$

    $=$ _____ $=$ _____

                          $=$ _____

                          $=$ _____

For the equation $m + n = -3$, L.S. _____ R.S.

For the equation $m = 3n + 5$, L.S. _____ R.S.

So, $m = -4$ and $n = 1$ _____ the solution.

Check Solution B:

In each equation, substitute: $m = $ _____ and $n = $ _____

$m + n = -3$ $m = 3n + 5$

L.S. = _____   R.S. = _____   L.S. = _____   R.S. = _____

= _____   = _____   = _____

= _____   = _____

                                                                    = _____

For the equation $m + n = -3$, L.S. _____ R.S.

For the equation $m = 3n + 5$, L.S. _____ R.S.

So, $m = -1$ and $n = -2$ _____ the solution.

Example 2   Using a Diagram to Create a Linear System

a) Use a diagram to create a linear system to model this situation:
Eight-passenger vans and 6-passenger vans carried 110 people.
There were 15 vans in all.

b) There were 10 eight-passenger vans and 5 six-passenger vans.
Use the linear system from part a to verify these numbers.

Solution

a) Draw a diagram to represent each type of van.

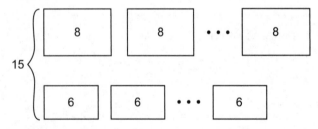

The number of each type of van is unknown.

Let the number of 8-passenger vans be e.
Let the number of 6-passenger vans be s.

Each eight-passenger van carries 8 people.
So, the number of people carried by the 8-passenger vans is: $8e$
Each six-passenger van carries 6 people.
So, the number of people carried by the 6-passenger vans is: $6s$
There were 110 people.
So, $8e + 6s = 110$

The total number of vans is 15.
So, $e + s = 15$

A linear system that models the situation is:
$8e + 6s = 110$
$e + s = 15$

b) There were 10 eight-passenger vans and 5 six-passenger vans.

To verify this solution:

Substitute $e = 10$ and $s = 5$ in each equation..

$8e + 6s = 110$

L.S. = $8e + 6s$ R.S. = 110
    = $8(10) + 6(5)$
    = $80 + 30$
    = 110

$e + s = 15$

L.S. = $e + s$ R.S. = 15
    = $10 + 5$
    = 15

For each equation, L.S. = R.S.

So, the solution is correct.

Check

1. a) Use a diagram to create a linear system to model this situation:

A gardener bought carrot seeds for $2 a packet and squash seeds for $5 a packet.
He spent $38 and bought 13 packets of seeds.

Draw a diagram to represent each type of packet.

> The number of each type of packet is unknown.

Let the number of packets of carrot seeds be c.
Let the number of packets of squash seeds be s.

Each packet of carrot seeds costs _____.
So, the cost of c packets in dollars is: _____
Each packet of squash seeds costs _____.
So, the cost of s packets in dollars is: _____
The total cost is _____.
So, _____ + _____ = _____

The total number of packets is _____.
So, _____ + _____ = _____

A linear system that models the situation is:

_____

_____

b) The gardener bought 9 packets of carrot seeds and 4 packets of squash seeds.
Use the linear system from part a to verify these numbers.

To verify this solution:
Substitute $c =$ _____ and $s =$ _____ in each equation.

_____

L.S. = _____   R.S. = _____   L.S. = _____   R.S. = _____

  = _____   = _____

  = _____   = _____

  = _____

For each equation, L.S. _____ R.S.
So, the solution _____ correct.

Example 3 | Using a Table to Create a Linear System

a) Use a table to create a linear system to model this situation:
A school sold 175 smoothies to raise money for charity.
A banana smoothie cost $3 and a peach mango smoothie cost $5.
The school raised $625.

b) The school sold 125 banana smoothies and 50 peach mango smoothies.
Use the data in the problem to verify these numbers.

Solution

a) Let the number of banana smoothies sold be b.
Let the number of peach mango smoothies sold be p.
Create a table.

	Price of smoothie ($)	Number sold	Money raised ($)
Banana	3	b	$3b$
Peach mango	5	p	$5p$
Total		175	625

This column shows that the total
number of smoothies sold is
represented by the equation:
$b + p = 175$

This column shows that the
money raised is represented
by the equation:
$3b + 5p = 625$

A linear system that models the situation is:
$b + p = 175$
$3b + 5p = 625$

b) The school sold 125 banana smoothies and 50 peach mango smoothies.

125 banana smoothies at $3 each is: $125 \times \$3 = \$375$
+ 50 mango smoothies at $5 each is: $50 \times \$5 = \$250$

175 smoothies for a total of $\$625$

The total number of smoothies and the money raised match the data in the problem. So, the solution is correct.

Check

1. a) Use a table to create a linear system to model this situation:
One afternoon, the Winnipeg Art Gallery sold 300 adult and student tickets.
An adult ticket cost $8 and a student ticket cost $6.
The total money collected was $2000.

Let the number of adult tickets sold be a.
Let the number of student tickets sold be _____.
Create a table.

	Price of ticket ($)	Number sold	Money collected ($)
Adult	8	a	$8a$
Student			
Total			

The total number of tickets sold is represented by the equation:

$a +$ _____ $=$ _____

The money collected is represented by the equation:

$8a +$ _____ $=$ _____

A linear system that models the situation is:

_____

_____

b) The gallery sold 100 adult tickets and 200 student tickets.
Use the data in the problem to verify these numbers.

_____ adult tickets at _____ each is: _____ $\times$ \$_____ $=$ _____
+_____ student tickets at _____ each is: _____ $\times$ \$_____ $=$ _____

_____ tickets for a total of _____

The total number of tickets sold and the money collected _____ the data in the problem.
So, the solution _____ correct.

1. Verify that the solution for this linear system is: $x = 3$ and $y = 2$

$4x - y = 10$

$-2x + y = -4$

In each equation, substitute: $x =$ _____ and $y =$ _____

$4x - y = 10$ $-2x + y = -4$

L.S. = _____   R.S. = _____   L.S. = _____   R.S. = _____

      = _____   = _____

      = _____   = _____

      = _____   = _____

For the equation $4x - y = 10$, L.S. _____ R.S.

For the equation $-2x + y = -4$, L.S. _____ R.S.

So, $x = 3$ and $y = 2$ _____ the correct solution.

2. Which pair of values is a solution for this linear system?

$a + b = -5$

$2b - 8 = a$

Solution A: $a = -7$ and $b = 2$

Solution B: $a = -6$ and $b = 1$

Check Solution A:

In each equation, substitute: $a =$ _____ and $b =$ _____

$a + b = -5$ $2b - 8 = a$

L.S. = _____   R.S. = _____   L.S. = _____   R.S. = _____

      = _____   = _____   = _____

      = _____   = _____

                                                = _____

For the equation $a + b = -5$, L.S. _____ R.S.

For the equation $2b - 8 = a$, L.S. _____ R.S.

So, $a = -7$ and $b = 2$ _____ the solution.

Check Solution B:

In each equation, substitute: $a =$ _____ and $b =$ _____

_____   _____

L.S. = _____   R.S. = _____   L.S. = _____   R.S. = _____

      = _____   = _____   = _____

      = _____   = _____

                                                = _____

For the equation $a + b = -5$, L.S. _____ R.S.

For the equation $2b - 8 = a$, L.S. _____ R.S.

So, $a = -6$ and $b = 1$ _____ the solution.

3. a) Use a diagram to create a linear system to model this situation:
The total number of wheels on the bicycles and tricycles in a store is 45.
There are 10 more bicycles than tricycles.

Draw a diagram to represent each type of bike.

Let the number of bicycles be _____.
Let the number of tricycles be _____.

Each bicycle has _____ wheels.
So, the number of wheels on _____ bicycles is: _____
Each tricycle has _____ wheels.
So, the number of wheels on _____ tricycles is: _____
The total number of wheels is _____.
So, _____ + _____ = _____

There are 10 more bicycles than tricycles.
So, _____ = _____ + 10

A linear system that models the situation is:

_____

_____

b) There are 15 bicycles and 5 tricycles in the store.
Use the linear system from part a to verify these numbers.

To verify this solution:
Substitute _____ = _____ and _____ = _____ in each equation.

_____
L.S. = _____   R.S. = _____   L.S. = _____   R.S. = _____
    = _____   = _____   = _____
    = _____   = _____
    = _____

For each equation, L.S. _____ R.S.
So, the solution _____ correct.

4. a) Use a table to create a linear system to model this situation:

Dalton has $5 and $10 bills in his wallet.

He has 12 bills in total with a value of $75.

Let the number of $5 bills be _____.

Let the number of $10 bills be _____.

Create a table.

	Value of bill ($)	Number of bills	Total value ($)
$5 bill			
$10 bill			
Total			

The total number of bills is represented by the equation:

_____ + _____ = _____

The total value of the bills is represented by the equation:

_____ + _____ = _____

A linear system that models the situation is:

_____

_____

b) Dalton has nine $5 bills and three $10 bills.

Use the data in the problem to verify these numbers.

So, the solution _____ correct.

7.2 Solving a System of Linear Equations Graphically

FOCUS Use the graphs of the equations of a linear system to estimate its solution.

The solution of a linear system can be found by graphing both equations on the same grid. If the two lines intersect, the coordinates of the point of intersection are the solution of the linear system.

Example 1 | Solving a Linear System by Graphing

Solve this linear system by graphing.

$x - y = 3$
$4x + 5y = 30$

Solution

Use intercepts to graph each line.
To find the x-intercepts: substitute $y = 0$

$x - y = 3$ $\qquad\qquad$ $4x + 5y = 30$
$x - 0 = 3$ $\qquad\qquad$ $4x + 5(0) = 30$
$\quad x = 3$ $\qquad\qquad$ $\quad 4x = 30$
$\qquad\qquad\qquad\qquad\qquad x = \dfrac{30}{4}$, or $7\dfrac{1}{2}$

To find the y-intercepts: substitute $x = 0$

$x - y = 3$ $\qquad\qquad$ $4x + 5y = 30$
$0 - y = 3$ $\qquad\qquad$ $4(0) + 5y = 30$
$\quad y = -3$ $\qquad\qquad$ $\quad 5y = 30$
$\qquad\qquad\qquad\qquad\qquad y = 6$

Mark a point at 3 on the x-axis and at -3 on the y-axis. Draw a line through the points.

Mark a point at $7\dfrac{1}{2}$ on the x-axis and at 6 on the y-axis. Draw a line through the points.

The point of intersection appears to be (5, 2).

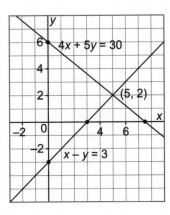

We verify the solution to check.

Verify the solution.

In each equation, substitute: $x = 5$ and $y = 2$

$x - y = 3$ $4x + 5y = 30$

L.S. $= x - y$ R.S. $= 3$ L.S. $= 4x + 5y$ R.S. $= 30$

    $= 5 - 2$ $= 4(5) + 5(2)$

    $= 3$ $= 20 + 10$

                                                        $= 30$

For each equation, L.S. $=$ R.S.

So, the solution of the linear system is $x = 5$ and $y = 2$.

Check

1. Solve this linear system by graphing.

$x - y = 5$

$3x + 2y = 10$

Use intercepts to graph each line.

To find the x-intercepts: substitute _____ $= 0$

$x - y = 5$ $3x + 2y = 10$

_____ $-$ _____ $= 5$ _____ $+$ _____ $= 10$

        $x =$ _____   _____ $= 10$

                                                        $x =$ _____ , or

                                                            _____
                                                            _____

To find the y-intercepts: substitute _____ $= 0$

$x - y = 5$ $3x + 2y = 10$

_____ $-$ _____ $= 5$ _____ $+$ _____ $= 10$

        $y =$ _____   _____ $= 10$

                                                        $y =$ _____

Mark a point at _____ on the   Mark a point at _____ on the
x-axis and at _____ on the y-axis. x-axis and at _____ on the y-axis.
Draw a line through the points.   Draw a line through the points.

                            The point of intersection appears to be (_____ , _____).

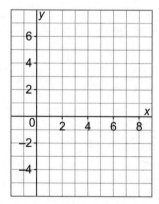

Verify the solution.

In each equation, substitute: $x =$ _____ and $y =$ _____

$x - y = 5$ $3x + 2y = 10$

L.S. $= x - y$ R.S. $=$ _____   L.S. $= 3x + 2y$ R.S. $=$ _____

    $=$ _____ $=$ _____

    $=$ _____ $=$ _____

    $=$ _____ $=$ _____

For each equation, L.S. _____ R.S.

So, the solution of the linear system is $x =$ _____ and $y =$ _____.

Example 2 | Solving a Problem by Graphing a Linear System

Cassie has a grass-cutting business. She charges $12 to cut a small lawn and $20 to cut a large lawn. One weekend, Cassie earned $180 by cutting 11 lawns.

A linear system that models this situation is:

$s + L = 11$

$12s + 20L = 180$

where s is the number of small lawns cut and L is the number of large lawns cut

a) Graph the linear system above.

b) Use the graph to solve this problem: How many small lawns and how many large lawns did Cassie cut?

Solution

----

a) Use intercepts to graph each line.

Equation	s-intercept (let $L = 0$)	L-intercept (let $s = 0$)
$s + L = 11$	$s + 0 = 11$ $s = 11$	$0 + L = 11$ $L = 11$
$12s + 20L = 180$	$12s + 20(0) = 180$ $12s = 180$ $s = 15$	$12(0) + 20L = 180$ $20L = 180$ $L = 9$

Plot s on the horizontal axis and L on the vertical axis.

For each graph, plot points at the s-intercept and L-intercept, then join the points with a broken line.

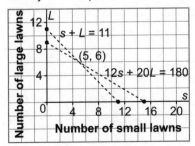

We use a broken line because Cassie cuts a whole number of lawns, so decimal values for s and L are not possible.

b) The point of intersection appears to be (5, 6).
To verify this solution:

5 small lawns at $12 each = $60
+ 6 large lawns at $20 each = $120
_____
11 lawns for $180

We could have graphed s on the vertical axis and L on the horizontal axis.

The total number of lawns is 11 and the money earned is $180.
So, the solution is correct.
Cassie cut 5 small lawns and 6 large lawns.

Check

1. Jerome purchased small and large multipacks of yogurt for a Grade 10 breakfast. Each small multipack contains 4 yogurt cups and each large multipack contains 12 yogurt cups. Jerome purchased 9 multipacks for a total of 60 yogurt cups.
A linear system that models this situation is:

$s + L = 9$

$4s + 12L = 60$

where s is the number of small multipacks purchased and L is the number of large multipacks purchased

a) Graph the linear system above.

Use intercepts to graph each line.

Equation	s-intercept (let ____ = 0)	L-intercept (let ____ = 0)

Plot s on the horizontal axis and L on the vertical axis.
For each graph, plot points at the s-intercept and L-intercept,
then join the points with a broken line.

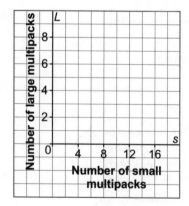

b) Use the graph to solve this problem: How many small multipacks and how many large multipacks did Jerome purchase?

The point of intersection appears to be (_____, _____).
To verify this solution:

_____ small multipacks containing _____ cups each = _____ cups
+_____ large multipacks containing _____ cups each = _____ cups
_____

_____ multipacks for a total of   _____ cups

The total number of multipacks is _____ and the total number of cups is _____.
So, the solution is correct.
Jerome purchased _____ small multipacks and _____ large multipacks.

Practice

1. Find the solution of each linear system.

a)

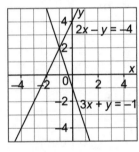

Point of intersection: (_____, _____)
Solution: $x =$ _____ and $y =$ _____

Verify the solution.
In each equation, substitute: $x =$ _____ and $y =$ _____

$2x - y = -4$ $3x + y = -1$
L.S. = _____   R.S. = _____   L.S. = _____   R.S. = _____
   = _____   = _____
   = _____   = _____
   = _____   = _____

For each equation, L.S. _____ R.S.
So, $x =$ _____ and $y =$ _____ is the solution of the linear system.

b)

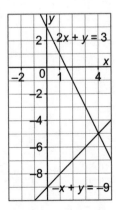

Point of intersection: (_____, _____)
Solution: $x =$ _____ and $y =$ _____

Verify the solution.

In each equation, substitute: $x =$ _____ and $y =$ _____

$2x + y = 3$ $-x + y = -9$

L.S. = _____   R.S. = _____   L.S. = _____   R.S. = _____

     = _____   = _____

     = _____   = _____

     = _____   = _____

For each equation, L.S. _____ R.S.

So, $x =$ _____ and $y =$ _____ is the solution of the linear system.

2. Solve this linear system by graphing.

$x + y = 4$
$2x + y = 6$

Use intercepts to graph each line.

To find the x-intercepts: substitute _____ = 0

$x + y = 4$ $2x + y = 6$

_____ + _____ = 4   _____ + _____ = 6

       _____ = _____   _____ = 6

                                                   _____ = _____

To find the y-intercepts: substitute _____ = 0

$x + y = 4$ $2x + y = 6$

_____ + _____ = 4   _____ + _____ = 6

       _____ = _____   _____ = _____

Mark a point at _____ on the _____-axis and at _____ on the _____-axis. Draw a line through the points.

Mark a point at _____ on the _____-axis and at _____ on the _____-axis. Draw a line through the points.

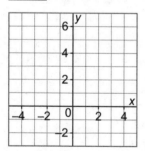

The point of intersection appears to be (_____, _____).

Verify the solution.

In each equation, substitute: $x =$ _____ and $y =$ _____

$x + y = 4$ $2x + y = 6$

L.S. = _____   R.S. = _____   L.S. = _____   R.S. = _____

    = _____   = _____

    = _____   = _____

                                                     = _____

For each equation, L.S. _____ R.S.

So, the solution of the linear system is $x =$ _____ and $y =$ _____.

3. Solve this linear system by graphing.

$x + y = 3$

$2x + y = 5$

Use intercepts to graph each line.

Equation	x-intercept (let _____ = 0)	y-intercept (let _____ = 0)
$x + y = 3$		
$2x + y = 5$		

For each graph, plot points at the x-intercept and y-intercept, then draw a line through them.

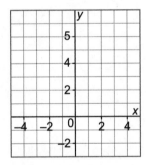

The point of intersection appears to be (_____, _____).

Verify the solution.

In each equation, substitute: $x =$ _____ and $y =$ _____

$x + y = 3$ $2x + y = 5$

L.S. = _____   R.S. = _____   L.S. = _____   R.S. = _____

    = _____   = _____

    = _____   = _____

                                                     = _____

For each equation, L.S. _____ R.S.

So, the solution of the linear system is $x =$ _____ and $y =$ _____.

4. Anika purchased sleeves and boxes of golf balls. Each sleeve contained 3 golf balls and each box contained 12 golf balls. Anika purchased 7 packages for a total of 48 golf balls. A linear system that models this situation is:

$s + b = 7$

$3s + 12b = 48$

where s is the number of sleeves purchased and b is the number of boxes purchased

a) Graph the linear system above.

Use intercepts to graph each line.

Equation	s-intercept (let _____ = 0)	b-intercept (let _____ = 0)

Plot s on the horizontal axis and b on the vertical axis.

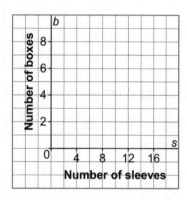

b) Use the graph to solve this problem: How many sleeves and how many boxes did Anika purchase?

The point of intersection appears to be (_____, _____).
To verify this solution:

_____ sleeves containing _____ golf balls each = _____ golf balls
+_____ boxes containing _____ golf balls each = _____ golf balls
_____

_____ packages for a total of   _____ golf balls

The total number of packages is _____ and the total number of golf balls is _____.
So, the solution is correct.
Anika purchased _____ sleeves and _____ boxes of golf balls.

▶ 7.3 Skill Builder

Using Technology to Graph a Line

To graph the equation $y = 3x - 7$ on a TI-83 or TI-84 calculator: Press $\boxed{Y=}$.

If there is an expression in the first line, press $\boxed{CLEAR}$.

To enter the equation, press: $\boxed{3}\ \boxed{X,T,\Theta,n}\ \boxed{-}\ \boxed{7}$

Press: $\boxed{ZOOM}\ \boxed{6}$

To find the coordinates of points on the line, press $\boxed{TRACE}$, then use the $\boxed{\blacktriangleleft}$ and $\boxed{\blacktriangleright}$ arrows to move the cursor along the line.

The coordinates are displayed at the bottom of the screen.

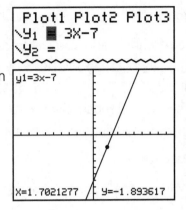

The equation is shown at the top of the screen.
Press $\boxed{TRACE}$ $\boxed{2}$ $\boxed{ENTER}$ to find
the value of y when x = 2.

We can graph more than one equation on the same screen.

To graph $2x + y = 5$, rewrite the equation in the form $y = mx + b$:

$y = -2x + 5$

Press $\boxed{Y=}$ and move the cursor to the second line.

To enter the equation $y = -2x + 5$,

press: $\boxed{(-)}\ \boxed{2}\ \boxed{X,T,\Theta,n}\ \boxed{+}\ \boxed{5}$

To graph the equation, press: $\boxed{GRAPH}$

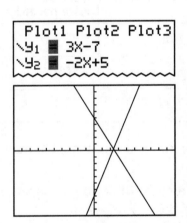

Check

1. Graph the equations $y = 5x + 3$ and $2x - y = 3$.

Write $2x - y = 3$ in the form $y = mx + b$.

$2x - y = 3$

$-y = $ _____

$y = $ _____

Enter the equations in the calculator.

Graph the equations. Sketch the lines.

Press $\boxed{TRACE}$. Use $\boxed{\blacktriangle}$ or $\boxed{\blacktriangledown}$ to move from one line to the other.

Write the coordinates of a point on $y = 5x + 3$: _____

Write the coordinates of a point on $2x - y = 3$: _____

▶ 7.3 Math Lab: Using Graphing Technology to Solve a System of Linear Equations

FOCUS Find and verify the solution of a linear system.

Work with a partner.
You will need a graphing calculator.

Léa's school had a carnival to celebrate *Festival du Voyageur*.
The school raised $1518.75 by charging
an adult $3.75 and a student $2.50.
The total attendance was 520.
How many adults and how many students attended?

Part A

Write a linear system to model this situation.

Let the number of adults be *x*.
Let the number of students be *y*.

	Price per ticket ($)	Number in attendance	Amount raised ($)
Adult	3.75	x	$3.75x$
Student	2.50	y	$2.50y$
Total		_____	_____

From the 3rd column, the number in attendance is represented by:
$x + y =$ _____
From the 4th column, the amount raised in dollars is represented by:
$3.75x + 2.50y =$ _____

A linear system that models the situation is:
$x + y =$ _____
$3.75x + 2.50y =$ _____

Part B

Write each equation in the form $y = mx + b$.

$x + y =$ _____

$\quad y =$ _____

$3.75x + 2.50y =$ _____   Subtract $3.75x$ from each side.

$\quad\quad 2.50y = -3.75x +$ _____   Divide each side by 2.50.

$\quad\quad\quad y = \dfrac{-3.75}{2.50}x +$ _____

Enter $\dfrac{-3.75}{2.50}x$ in the calculator as (−3.75/2.5)x. Remember to use [(-)] to enter a negative number.

Enter the equations in your graphing calculator.

Press [WINDOW] and use the arrow keys to enter these settings:

```
WINDOW
 Xmin=0
 Xmax=550
 Xscl=50
 Ymin=0
 Ymax=650
 Yscl=50
 Xres=1
```

These data will not show in the standard window, so we have to change the window settings.

Press [GRAPH].

Part C

To find the point of intersection, press [2nd] [TRACE] for CALC, then press [5] [ENTER] [ENTER] [ENTER].

Sketch the lines.

```
Intersection
X=       Y=
```

The point of intersection is (_____ , _____).

Part D

Verify this solution:

_____ adults at _____ per ticket   = _____

+_____ students at _____ per ticket = _____

_____ people attended for a total of _____

The total attendance is _____ and the total amount raised is _____.

So, the solution is correct.

_____ adults and _____ students attended the carnival.

1. A student used a graphing calculator
to solve this linear system:
$2x - y = 15$
$7x + 6y = 24$
Verify the solution shown.

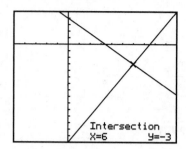

To verify the solution:
In each equation, substitute: $x =$ _____ and $y =$ _____

$2x - y = 15$

L.S. = _____   R.S. = _____

  = _____

  = _____

  = _____

$7x + 6y = 24$

L.S. = _____   R.S. = _____

  = _____

  = _____

  = _____

For each equation, L.S. _____ R.S.
So, the solution of the linear system is $x =$ _____ and $y =$ _____.

2. Use graphing technology to find the solution of this linear system.
$y = 2x - 5$
$y = 3x - 8$

Enter the equations in a calculator, then graph them.
Sketch the lines.
To find the point of intersection,
press [2nd] [TRACE] [5], then press [ENTER] 3 times.

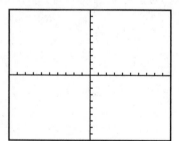

The point of intersection is: (_____, _____)
To verify the solution, substitute $x =$ _____ and $y =$ _____ in each equation.

$y = 2x - 5$

L.S. = _____   R.S. = _____

  = _____

$y = 3x - 8$

L.S. = _____   R.S. = _____

  = _____

  = _____

  = _____

  = _____

  = _____

  = _____

For each equation, L.S. _____ R.S.
So, the solution of the linear system is $x =$ _____ and $y =$ _____.

 978-0-321-61066-9

3. Use graphing technology to find the solution of this linear system.

$2x + y = 10$

$2x + 3y = 14$

Write each equation in the form $y = mx + b$.

$2x + y = 10$

$y = \underline{\qquad} + \underline{\qquad}$

$2x + 3y = 14$

$3y = -2x + \underline{\qquad}$

$y = \dfrac{}{\underline{\qquad}} + \dfrac{}{\underline{\qquad}}$

Enter the equations in your calculator, then graph them.

Sketch the lines.

Find the point of intersection.

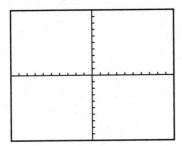

The point of intersection is: (\underline{\qquad} , \underline{\qquad})

To verify the solution, substitute $x = $ \underline{\qquad} and $y = $ \underline{\qquad} in each equation.

$2x + y = 10$

L.S. = \underline{\qquad}   R.S. = \underline{\qquad}

= \underline{\qquad}

= \underline{\qquad}

= \underline{\qquad}

$2x + 3y = 14$

L.S. = \underline{\qquad}   R.S. = \underline{\qquad}

= \underline{\qquad}

= \underline{\qquad}

= \underline{\qquad}

For each equation, L.S. \underline{\qquad} R.S.

So, the solution of the linear system is $x = $ \underline{\qquad} and $y = $ \underline{\qquad} .

Can you...

- create a linear system to model a situation?
- verify the solution of a linear system?
- graph the equations of a linear system and find the point of intersection?
- use graphing technology to find the solution of a linear system?

7.1 **1. a)** Create a linear system to model this situation:

Jacob rented 3 movies and 2 video games. He paid $29.

Kaylee rented 5 movies and 1 video game. She paid $32.

Draw a diagram.

Let the cost of a movie rental be _____ dollars.

Let the cost of a video game rental be _____ dollars.

From the diagram, a linear system that models the situation is:

_____

_____

b) The cost of a movie rental is $5 and the cost of a video game rental is $7.

Use the data in the problem to verify these numbers.

2. Solve this linear system by graphing.

$x + y = 2$

$2x - y = 7$

Use intercepts to graph each line.

To find the x-intercepts: substitute _____ = 0

$x + y = 2$ $2x - y = 7$

_____ + _____ = 2   _____ - _____ = 7

$x =$ _____   _____ = 7

$x =$ _____ , or _____

To find the y-intercepts: substitute _____ = 0

$x + y = 2$ $2x - y = 7$

_____ + _____ = 2   _____ - _____ = 7

$y =$ _____   _____ = 7

$y =$ _____

Mark a point at _____ on the   Mark a point at _____ on the

x-axis and at _____ on the y-axis. x-axis and at _____ on the y-axis.

Draw a line through the points.   Draw a line through the points.

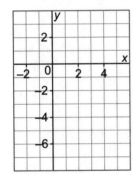

The point of intersection appears to be (_____, _____).

Verify the solution.

For each equation, L.S. _____ R.S.

So, the solution of the linear system is $x =$ _____ and $y =$ _____.

978-0-321-61066-9 Copyright © 2011 Pearson Canada Inc.

3. Regis scored 18 points in a football game by kicking field goals and singles.
Each field goal scored 3 points and each single scored 1 point.
The total number of kicks was 8.
A linear system that models this situation is:

$f + s = 8$

$3f + s = 18$

where f is the number of field goals kicked and s is the number of singles kicked

a) Graph the linear system above.

Use intercepts to graph each line.

Equation	f-intercept (let ___ = 0)	s-intercept (let ___ = 0)

Plot f on the horizontal axis and s on the vertical axis.

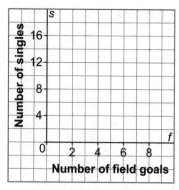

b) Use the graph to solve this problem:
How many field goals and how many singles did Regis make?

The point of intersection appears to be (____, ____).
Use the data in the problem to verify the solution.

Regis made _____ field goals and _____ singles.

4. Use graphing technology to find the solution of this linear system.

$-3x + 4y = -28$
$2x + y = 4$

Write each equation in the form $y = mx + b$.

$-3x + 4y = -28$ $2x + y = 4$
$\qquad 4y = $ _____ $-$ _____ $\qquad y = $ _____ $+$ _____

$\qquad y = \dfrac{\text{_____}}{\text{_____}} - \dfrac{\text{_____}}{\text{_____}}$

$\qquad y = $ _____ $-$ _____

Enter the equations in a calculator, then graph them.
Sketch the lines.
Find the point of intersection.

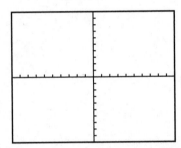

The point of intersection is: (_____, _____)
Use the equations to verify the solution.

For each equation, L.S. _____ R.S.
So, the solution of the linear system is $x = $ _____ and $y = $ _____

7.4 Using a Substitution Strategy to Solve a System of Linear Equations

FOCUS Use substitution to solve a linear system.

One algebraic strategy is to **solve by substitution**. We use this strategy when one variable has coefficient 1.

| **Example 1** | Solving a Linear System by Substitution |

Solve this linear system.

$2x + y = 3$ ①

$4x + 3y = 5$ ②

> We number the equations in a linear system to be able to refer to them easily.

Solution

$2x + y = 3$ ①

$4x + 3y = 5$ ②

In equation ①, the coefficient of y is 1.

So, solve equation ① for y.

$2x + y = 3$ Subtract $2x$ from each side.

$y = 3 - 2x$

Substitute $y = 3 - 2x$ in equation ②.

$4x + 3\mathbf{y} = 5$ ②

$4x + 3(\mathbf{3 - 2x}) = 5$ Multiply to remove the brackets.

$4x + 9 - 6x = 5$ Combine like terms.

$-2x + 9 = 5$ Isolate $-2x$. Subtract 9 from each side.

$-2x = 5 - 9$

$-2x = -4$ Solve for x. Divide each side by -2.

$x = 2$

To find the value of y when $x = 2$, substitute in one of the given equations.

Choose equation ①.

$2x + y = 3$ ①   Substitute: $x = 2$

$2(2) + y = 3$ Solve for y.

$4 + y = 3$

$y = 3 - 4$

$y = -1$

The solution is: $x = 2$ and $y = -1$

Verify the solution.

In each equation, substitute: $x = 2$ and $y = -1$

$2x + y = 3$ $4x + 3y = 5$

L.S. $= 2x + y$ R.S. $= 3$ L.S. $= 4x + 3y$ R.S. $= 5$

$\quad = 2(2) + (-1)$ $\quad = 4(2) + 3(-1)$

$\quad = 4 - 1$ $\quad = 8 - 3$

$\quad = 3$ $\quad = 5$

For each equation, L.S. $=$ R.S.

So, the solution of the linear system is $x = 2$ and $y = -1$.

Check

1. Solve this linear system.

$x + 3y = -2$ ①

$-3x + 5y = 6$ ②

In equation ①, the coefficient of x is 1.

So, solve the equation for x.

$x + 3y = -2$

$\quad x =$ _____

Substitute $x =$ _____ in equation ②.

$-3x + 5y = 6$ ②

$-3($_____$) + 5y = 6$ Multiply to remove the brackets.

$\qquad\qquad y =$ _____

To find the value of x when $y =$ _____, substitute in equation ①.

$\quad x + 3y = -2$ ①

$x + 3($_____$) = -2$

$\quad$ _____ $=$ _____

$\qquad x =$ _____

The solution is: $x =$ _____ and $y =$ _____

Verify the solution.

In each equation, substitute: $x =$ _____ and $y =$ _____

$x + 3y = -2$ $-3x + 5y = 6$

L.S. $=$ _____   R.S. $=$ _____   L.S. $=$ _____   R.S. $=$ _____

$\quad =$ _____ $\quad =$ _____

$\quad =$ _____ $\quad =$ _____

$\quad =$ _____ $\quad =$ _____

For each equation, L.S. _____ R.S.

So, the solution of the linear system is $x =$ _____ and $y =$ _____.

Example 2 | Using a Linear System to Solve a Problem

a) Create a linear system to model this situation:

Tickets are sold for the Senior Safari Day at the Greater Vancouver Zoo.

Meryl buys 5 admission tickets and 3 train tickets. She pays $65.

Howard buys 2 admission tickets and 1 train ticket. He pays $25.

b) Solve this problem: What is the price of each type of ticket?

Solution

a) Cost of 5 admission tickets + cost of 3 train tickets = $65

Cost of 2 admission tickets + cost of 1 train ticket = $25

Let the cost of an admission ticket be a dollars and the cost of a train ticket be t dollars.

A linear system that models the situation is:

$5a + 3t = 65$ ①

$2a + t = 25$ ②

b) Solve the linear system.

In equation ②, the coefficient of t is 1. So, solve equation ② for t.

$2a + t = 25$ ②

$t = 25 - 2a$

Substitute $t = 25 - 2a$ in equation ①.

$5a + 3\boldsymbol{t} = 65$ ①

$5a + 3(\boldsymbol{25 - 2a}) = 65$	Multiply to remove the brackets.
$5a + 75 - 6a = 65$	Combine like terms.
$-a + 75 = 65$	Isolate $-a$. Subtract 75 from each side.
$-a = 65 - 75$	
$-a = -10$	Solve for a. Multiply each side by -1.
$a = 10$	

To find the value of t when $a = 10$, substitute in equation ②.

$2a + t = 25$ ②

$2(10) + t = 25$

$20 + t = 25$

$t = 5$

It's a good idea when checking the solution to a problem to use the original problem, not the equations.

The solution is: $a = 10$ and $t = 5$

Use the data in the problem to verify these numbers.

Cost of 5 admission tickets at $10 each and 3 train tickets at $5 each: $50 + $15 = $65

Cost of 2 admission tickets at $10 each and 1 train ticket at $5: $20 + $5 = $25

The total costs match the data in the problem.

So, the solution is correct.

An admission ticket costs $10 and a train ticket costs $5.

Check

1. a) Create a linear system to model this situation:

A math test has short-answer questions and word problems.

A short-answer question is worth 2 marks and a word problem is worth 4 marks.

There are 11 questions for a total of 30 marks.

Let the number of short-answer questions be s, and the number of word problems be w.

	Marks per question	Number of questions	Number of marks
Short answer			
Word problem			
Total			

The number of questions is represented by equation ①: _____ + _____ = _____

The total number of marks is represented by equation ②: _____ + _____ = _____

A linear system that models the situation is:

_____ ①

_____ ②

b) Solve this problem: How many short-answer questions and how many word problems are on the test?

In equation ①, the coefficients of both s and w are _____.

Solve equation ① for w.

> Since the coefficient of s is also 1, we could have solved for s.

$w =$ _____

Substitute $w =$ _____ in equation ②.

$$2s + 4w = 30 \qquad ②$$

$$2s + 4(\underline{\qquad}) = 30$$

$$s = \underline{\quad}$$

To find the value of w when $s =$ _____, substitute in equation ①.

$$w = \underline{\quad}$$

The solution is: $s =$ _____ and $w =$ _____

Use the data in the problem to verify the solution.

_____ short-answer questions worth _____ marks each = _____ marks

\+ _____ word problems worth _____ marks each = _____ marks

_____ questions for a total of _____ marks

This matches the data in the problem, so the solution is correct.

There are _____ short-answer questions and _____ word problems on the test.

1. For each linear system, the value of one variable in the solution is given.
Find the value of the other variable.

a) $-x + 2y = 1$ ①
$3x + 3y = -12$ ②
Given: $y = -1$

Substitute $y =$ _____ in equation ①.
$-x + 2y = 1$
$-x + 2(\_\_\_\_) = 1$

$x =$ _____

b) $-3x + y = 17$ ①
$2x + y = -8$ ②
Given: $x = -5$

Substitute $x =$ _____ in equation ②.
$2x + y = -8$

$y =$ _____

2. Solve this linear system.
$y = x + 6$ ①
$3x - 2y = -13$ ②

Substitute $y = x + 6$ in equation ②.
$3x - 2y = -13$ ②
$3x - 2(_____) = -13$

$x =$ _____

To find the value of y when $x =$ _____, substitute in equation ①.
$y = x + 6$ ①
$y =$ _____ $+ 6$
$y =$ _____
The solution is: $x =$ _____ and $y =$ _____

Verify the solution. In each equation, substitute: $x =$ _____ and $y =$ _____
$y = x + 6$ $3x - 2y = -13$
L.S. = _____   R.S. = _____   L.S. = _____   R.S. = _____
    = _____   = _____   = _____
                  = _____   = _____

For each equation, L.S. _____ R.S.
So, the solution of the linear system is $x =$ _____ and $y =$ _____.

3. Solve this linear system.

$3x + 2y = 25$ ①
$x - 2y = -5$ ②

In equation ②, the coefficient of x is 1.
So, solve equation ② for x.

$x - 2y = -5$ ②

    $x = $ _____

Substitute $x = $ _____ in equation ①.

        $3x + 2y = 25$ ①

$3($_____$) + 2y = 25$

            $y = $ _____

To find the value of x when $y = $ _____, substitute in equation ②.

    $x - 2y = -5$ ②

$x - 2($____$) = -5$

      $x = $ ____

The solution is: $x = $ ____ and $y = $ ____

Verify the solution.

In each equation, substitute: $x = $ ____ and $y = $ ____

$3x + 2y = 25$ $x - 2y = -5$

L.S. = _____   R.S. = _____   L.S. = _____   R.S. = _____

L.S. = _____   L.S. = _____

For each equation, L.S. ____ R.S.
So, the solution of the linear system is $x = $ ____ and $y = $ ____.

4. a) Create a linear system to model this situation:

Michelle and Marty spend the afternoon at the local fair. Michelle rides the roller coaster 3 times and the super swing 5 times. She pays $25. Marty rides the roller coaster 5 times and the super swing once. He pays $27.

Cost of _____ roller coasters + cost of _____ super swings = _____
Cost of _____ roller coasters + cost of _____ super swing = _____

Let the cost of a roller coaster ride be _____ dollars.
Let the cost of a super swing ride be _____ dollars.

A linear system that models the situation is:

_____   ①

_____   ②

b) Solve this problem: What is the cost of each type of ride?

The solution is: _____ = _____ and _____ = _____
Use the data in the problem to verify the solution.

A roller coaster ride costs _____ and a super swing ride costs _____.

 978-0-321-61066-9 Copyright © 2011 Pearson Canada Inc.

7.5 Using an Elimination Strategy to Solve a System of Linear Equations

FOCUS Use elimination to solve a linear system.

The solution of this linear system is:

$x = 2$ and $y = 1$

We can add the equations:

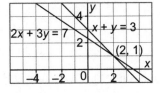

$$\begin{array}{rcl} 2x + 3y &=& 7 \\ + x + \ y &=& 3 \\ \hline 3x + 4y &=& 10 \end{array}$$

When we graph the new equation on the same grid, we see it also passes through (2, 1).

We can use this property to solve a linear system.

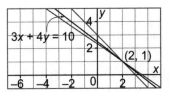

| **Example 1** | **Solving a Linear System by Adding to Eliminate a Variable** |

Solve this linear system.

$4x - 2y = 10$ ①
$5x + 2y = 26$ ②

Solution

$4x - 2y = 10$ ①
$5x + 2y = 26$ ②

The coefficients of y in both equations are opposite integers: -2 and 2
So, use elimination.
Add the equations to eliminate y.

> When we add equations to eliminate one variable, we **solve by elimination**.

$$\begin{array}{rcl} 4x - 2y &=& 10 \quad ① \\ +(5x + 2y &=& 26) \quad ② \\ \hline 9x \ \ \ \ &=& 36 \\ x \ \ \ \ &=& 4 \end{array}$$

> $-2y + 2y = 0$

Solve for x. Divide each side by 9.

To find the value of y when $x = 4$, substitute in one of the original equations.
Choose equation ①.

$4x - 2y = 10$ ①
$4(4) - 2y = 10$
$16 - 2y = 10$ Isolate $-2y$. Subtract 16 from each side.
$-2y = 10 - 16$
$-2y = -6$ Solve for y. Divide each side by -2.
$y = 3$

The solution is: $x = 4$ and $y = 3$

Verify the solution.

In each equation, substitute: $x = 4$ and $y = 3$

$4x - 2y = 10$

L.S. = $4x - 2y$	R.S. = 10
$= 4(4) - 2(3)$	
$= 16 - 6$	
$= 10$	

$5x + 2y = 26$

L.S. = $5x + 2y$	R.S. = 26
$= 5(4) + 2(3)$	
$= 20 + 6$	
$= 26$	

For each equation, L.S. = R.S.

So, the solution of the linear system is $x = 4$ and $y = 3$.

Check

1. Solve this linear system.

$$2x - 8y = -18 \qquad ①$$
$$-2x + 3y = 8 \qquad ②$$

The coefficients of x in both equations are opposite integers. So, use elimination.

Add the equations to eliminate x.

$$2x - 8y = -18 \qquad ①$$
$$+(-2x + 3y = \quad 8) \qquad ②$$

_____ = _____   Divide each side by _____.

$y = $ _____

To find the value of x when $y = $ _____, substitute in equation ②.

$$-2x + 3y = 8 \qquad ②$$
$$-2x + 3(\text{\_\_\_\_\_}) = 8$$
$$-2x + \text{\_\_\_\_\_} = 8$$

$x = $ _____

The solution is: $x = $ _____ and $y = $ _____

Verify the solution.

In each equation, substitute: $x = $ _____ and $y = $ _____

$2x - 8y = -18$

L.S. = _____	R.S. = _____
= _____	
= _____	
= _____	

$-2x + 3y = 8$

L.S. = _____	R.S. = _____
= _____	
= _____	
= _____	

For each equation, L.S. _____ R.S.

So, the solution of the linear system is $x = $ _____ and $y = $ _____.

Sometimes we have to multiply one or both equations by a number before we can eliminate a variable by adding.

| Example 2 | Solving a Linear System by Multiplying then Eliminating |

Solve this linear system.

$4x - 2y = 2$ ①
$3x + y = -6$ ②

Solution

$4x - 2y = 2$ ①
$3x + y = -6$ ②

Use elimination.

No coefficients of like terms are opposite integers.

Look at the y-terms: $-2y$ and y

To make the coefficients opposite integers, multiply equation ② by 2.

$2 \times$ equation ②:

$2(3x + y = -6) \longrightarrow 6x + 2y = -12$ ③

Add equations ① and ③ to eliminate y.

$$\begin{array}{rl} 4x - 2y = & 2 \quad ① \\ +(6x + 2y = & -12) \quad ③ \\ \hline 10x \quad\;\; = & -10 \\ x \quad\;\; = & -1 \end{array}$$

Solve for x. Divide each side by 10.

To find the value of y when $x = -1$, substitute in equation ①.

$$\begin{array}{rl} 4x - 2y = 2 & \quad ① \\ 4(-1) - 2y = 2 & \\ -4 - 2y = 2 & \quad \text{Isolate } -2y. \text{ Add 4 to each side.} \\ -2y = 2 + 4 & \\ -2y = 6 & \quad \text{Solve for } y. \text{ Divide each side by } -2. \\ y = -3 & \end{array}$$

The solution is: $x = -1$ and $y = -3$

Like terms have the same variable.

*When we multiply an equation by a number, we produce an **equivalent** equation.*

We could substitute $x = -1$ in either equation to find y.

Verify the solution.

In the original equations, substitute: $x = -1$ and $y = -3$

$4x - 2y = 2$		$3x + y = -6$	
L.S. $= 4x - 2y$	R.S. $= 2$	L.S. $= 3x + y$	R.S. $= -6$
$= 4(-1) - 2(-3)$		$= 3(-1) + (-3)$	
$= -4 + 6$		$= -3 - 3$	
$= 2$		$= -6$	

For each equation, L.S. = R.S.

So, the solution of the linear system is $x = -1$ and $y = -3$.

Check

1. Solve this linear system.

$3x - 10y = 16$ ①

$2x + y = 3$ ②

Scan the equations, and look for numbers that are easiest to work with.

Use elimination.

No coefficients of like terms are opposite integers.

Look at the y-terms: $-10y$ and y

To make the coefficients opposite integers, multiply equation ② by _____.

_____ × equation ②: _____$(2x + y = 3)$ ⟶ _____ + _____ = _____   ③

Add equations ① and ③ to eliminate y.

$3x - 10y = 16$ ①

_____   ③

_____ = _____   Divide each side by _____.

x = _____

To find the value of y when $x =$ _____, substitute in equation ②.

$2x + y = 3$ ②

$2($_____$) + y = 3$

$y =$ _____

The solution is: $x =$ _____ and $y =$ _____

Verify the solution.

In the original equations, substitute: $x =$ _____ and $y =$ _____

$3x - 10y = 16$ $2x + y = 3$

L.S. = _____   R.S. = _____   L.S. = _____   R.S. = _____

L.S. = _____   L.S. = _____

For each equation, L.S. _____ R.S.

So, the solution of the linear system is $x =$ _____ and $y =$ _____.

| Example 3 | **Using a Linear System to Solve a Problem** |

a) Create a linear system to model this situation:

Ava and Ethan sold flower bulbs for a school fundraiser. Ava sold 5 bags of tulip bulbs and 2 bags of daffodil bulbs. She raised $80. Ethan sold 1 bag of tulip bulbs and 4 bags of daffodil bulbs. He raised $70.

b) Solve this problem: What is the cost of a bag of each type of bulb?

Solution

a) Cost of 5 bags of tulip bulbs + cost of 2 bags of daffodil bulbs = $80

Cost of 1 bag of tulip bulbs + cost of 4 bags of daffodil bulbs = $70

Let the cost of a bag of tulip bulbs be t dollars.
Let the cost of a bag of daffodil bulbs be d dollars.

A linear system that models the situation is:

$$5t + 2d = 80 \quad ①$$
$$t + 4d = 70 \quad ②$$

b) Use elimination. No coefficients of like terms have opposite integers.

Look at the t-terms: $5t$ and t

To make the coefficients opposite integers, multiply equation ② by −5.

$(-5) \times$ equation ②: $-5(t + 4d = 70) \longrightarrow -5t - 20d = -350 \quad ③$

Add equations ① and ③ to eliminate t.

$$\begin{array}{r} 5t + 2d = 80 \quad ① \\ +(-5t - 20d = -350) \quad ③ \\ \hline -18d = -270 \end{array}$$
Solve for d. Divide each side by -18.
$$d = 15$$

To find the value of t when $d = 15$, substitute in equation ②.

$$t + 4d = 70 \quad ②$$
$$t + 4(15) = 70$$
$$t + 60 = 70 \qquad \text{Solve for } t. \text{ Subtract 60 from each side.}$$
$$t = 70 - 60$$
$$t = 10$$

The solution is: $t = 10$ and $d = 15$

We could substitute $d = 15$ in either equation to find t.

Use the data in the problem to verify the solution.

Cost of 5 bags of tulip bulbs at $10 each and 2 bags of daffodil bulbs at $15 each is:
$50 + $30 = $80

Cost of 1 bag of tulip bulbs at $10 and 4 bags of daffodil bulbs at $15 each is:
$10 + $60 = $70

The total costs match the data in the problem. So, the solution is correct.

A bag of tulip bulbs costs $10 and a bag of daffodil bulbs costs $15.

Check

1. a) Create a linear system to model this situation:

A store sells running shoes and hiking boots. The store makes $25 profit from the sale of a pair of running shoes and $50 profit from the sale of a pair of hiking boots. One afternoon, the company sold 14 pairs of footwear for a total profit of $450.

Let the number of pairs of running shoes sold be r.
Let the number of pairs of hiking boots sold be h.

	Profit per pair ($)	Number sold	Total profit ($)
Running shoes			
Hiking boots			
Total			

The number of pairs sold is represented by equation ①:

_____ + _____ = _____

The total profit in dollars is represented by equation ②:

_____ + _____ = _____

A linear system that models the situation is:

_____ ①

_____ ②

b) Solve this problem: How many pairs of running shoes and how many pairs of hiking boots were sold?

Use elimination. No coefficients of like terms have opposite integers.
Look at the r-terms: _____ and _____
To make the coefficients opposite integers, multiply equation ① by _____.

_____ × equation ①: _____(_____) ⟶ _____ ③

Add equations ② and ③ to eliminate r.

> *We could have multiplied equation ① by −50, then added to eliminate h.*

$$h = \_\_\_\_\_$$

To find the value of r when $h =$ _____, substitute in equation ①.

$$r = \_\_\_\_\_$$

The solution is: $r =$ _____ and $h =$ _____

Use the data in the problem to verify the solution.

_____ pairs of running shoes at a profit of _____ each = _____
_____ pairs of hiking boots at a profit of _____ each = _____

_____ pairs for a total profit of _____

The totals match the data in the problem.

So, the solution is correct.

_____ pairs of running shoes and _____ pairs of hiking boots were sold.

Practice

1. To solve each linear system by elimination, what would you multiply equation ① by?

a) $x + 2y = 2$ ①
$4x - 6y = 8$ ②

In equation ②, the coefficient
of x is: _____
Its opposite is: _____
So, multiply equation ① by _____.

b) $2x + y = 6$ ①
$3x - 5y = 9$ ②

In equation ②, the coefficient
of y is: _____
Its opposite is: _____
So, multiply equation ① by _____.

2. Solve this linear system using elimination.
$5x - 7y = 24$ ①
$3x + 7y = -8$ ②

The coefficients of y in both equations are opposite integers.
So, add the equations to eliminate y.

$5x - 7y = 24$ ①
$+(3x + 7y = -8)$ ②
————————————
_____ = _____
x = _____

To find the value of y when $x =$ _____, substitute in equation ②.

$3x + 7y = -8$ ②
$3(\underline{\quad}) + 7y = -8$
$\underline{\quad} + 7y = -8$

$y =$ _____

The solution is: $x =$ _____ and $y =$ _____

Verify the solution. In each equation, substitute: $x =$ _____ and $y =$ _____

$5x - 7y = 24$ $3x + 7y = -8$

L.S. = _____   R.S. = _____   L.S. = _____   R.S. = _____

= _____   = _____

For each equation, L.S. _____ R.S.

So, the solution of the linear system is $x =$ _____ and $y =$ _____ .

3. Solve this linear system using elimination.

$-3x + 2y = 2$ ①

$2x - 5y = -16$ ②

Sometimes, we have to multiply both equations by numbers to get opposite coefficients.

No coefficients of like terms are opposite integers.

Look at the y-terms: $2y$ and $-5y$

To make the coefficients opposite integers,

multiply equation ① by _____ and equation ② by _____ .

_____ × equation ①: _____ $(-3x + 2y = 2)$ ⟶ _____ ③

_____ × equation ②: _____ $(2x - 5y = -16)$ ⟶ _____ ④

Add equations ③ and ④ to eliminate y.

_____

_____ = _____

x =   _____

To find the value of y when $x =$ _____ , substitute in equation ①.

$-3x + 2y = 2$ ①

$-3(\underline{\hspace{1cm}}) + 2y = 2$

$y =$ _____

The solution is: $x =$ _____ and $y =$ _____

Verify the solution.

In the original equations, substitute: $x =$ _____ and $y =$ _____

$-3x + 2y = 2$ $2x - 5y = -16$

L.S. = _____   R.S. = _____   L.S. = _____   R.S. = _____

L.S. = _____   L.S. = _____

For each equation, L.S. _____ R.S.

So, the solution of the linear system is $x =$ _____ and $y =$ _____ .

4. a) Create a linear system to model this situation:

A dog groomer charges $50 to groom a small dog and $75 to groom a large dog.
One Saturday, the groomer groomed 9 dogs for a total income of $500.

Let the number of small dogs groomed be s.
Let the number of large dogs groomed be L.

	Cost per grooming ($)	Number groomed	Total income ($)
Small dog			
Large dog			
Total			

Let the number of dogs groomed be represented by equation ①:

_____

Let the total income in dollars be represented by equation ②:

_____

A linear system that models the situation is:

_____ ①

_____ ②

b) Solve this problem: How many small dogs and how many large dogs were groomed?

The solution is: $s =$ _____ and $L =$ _____
Use the data in the problem to verify these numbers.

_____ small dogs and _____ large dogs were groomed.

Can you...

- solve a linear system using substitution?
- solve a linear system using elimination?

7.4 **1.** Solve this linear system by substitution.

$x - y = 7$ ①

$3x - 5y = 27$ ②

In equation ①, the coefficient of x is 1.

So, solve equation ① for x.

$x - y = 7$

$x = $ _____

Substitute $x = $ _____ in equation ②.

     $3x - 5y = 27$ ②

$3(\underline{\hspace{1.5cm}}) - 5y = 27$

     $y = $ _____

To find the value of x, substitute $y = $ _____ in equation ①.

     $x - y = 7$ ①

$x - (\underline{\hspace{1cm}}) = 7$

     $x = $ _____

The solution is: $x = $ _____ and $y = $ _____

Verify the solution.

In each equation, substitute: $x = $ _____ and $y = $ _____

$x - y = 7$ $3x - 5y = 27$

L.S. = _____   R.S. = _____   L.S. = _____   R.S. = _____

L.S. = _____   L.S. = _____

For each equation, L.S. _____ R.S.

So, the solution of the linear system is $x = $ _____ and $y = $ _____.

7.5 **2.** Solve this linear system by elimination.

$6x + 7y = 10$ ①

$2x - 3y = 14$ ②

No coefficients of like terms are opposite integers.

Look at the x-terms: $6x$ and $2x$

To make the coefficients opposite integers, multiply equation ② by _____.

_____ × equation ②: _____$(2x - 3y = 14) \longrightarrow$ _____ + _____ = _____ ③

Add equations ① and ③ to eliminate x.

$6x + 7y = 10$ ①

_____ ③

_____ = _____

$y =$ _____

To find the value of x, substitute $y =$ _____ in equation ②.

$2x - 3y = 14$ ②

$2x - 3($_____$) = 14$

$x =$ _____

The solution is: $x =$ _____ and $y =$ _____

Verify the solution.

In the original equations, substitute: $x =$ _____ and $y =$ _____

$6x + 7y = 10$ $2x - 3y = 14$

L.S. = _____   R.S. = _____   L.S. = _____   R.S. = _____

L.S. = _____   L.S. = _____

For each equation, L.S. _____ R.S.

So, the solution of the linear system is $x =$ _____ and $y =$ _____.

3. a) Create a linear system to model this situation:

The coach of a lacrosse team bought ice cream cones to celebrate a tournament victory. A single-scoop cone was $3 and a double-scoop cone was $5. The coach bought 15 cones and paid $57.

Let the number of single-scoop cones be s.
Let the number of double-scoop cones be d.

	Cost per cone ($)	Number bought	Total cost ($)
Single scoop			
Double scoop			
Total			

Let the number of cones bought be represented by equation ①:

_____

Let the cost in dollars be represented by equation ②:

_____

A linear system that models the situation is:

_____   ①

_____   ②

b) Solve this problem: How many single-scoop cones and how many double-scoop cones did the coach buy?

i) Use substitution.

In equation ①, the coefficient of s is 1.
So, solve equation ① for s.

Since the coefficient of d is also 1, we could have solved for d.

$s = $ _____

Substitute $s = $ _____ in equation ②.

$d = $ _____

To find the value of s, substitute $d = $ _____ in equation ①.

$s = $ _____

The solution is: $s = $ _____ and $d = $ _____

Use the data in the problem to verify these numbers.

The coach bought _____ single-scoop cones and _____ double-scoop cones.

ii) Use elimination to solve the problem in part b.

_____ ①

_____ ②

The solution is: $s =$ _____ and $d =$ _____

The coach bought _____ single-scoop cones and _____ double-scoop cones.

c) Which method did you prefer? Explain.

_____

_____

▶ 7.6 Properties of Systems of Linear Equations

FOCUS Find the numbers of solutions of different types of linear systems.

All linear systems you have studied so far have had exactly one solution.

For example:

$4x - y = 8$

$-2x + y = -3$

The graphs of the equations have different slopes;
the lines intersect at one point.

This linear system has exactly one solution.

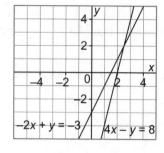

Some linear systems have no solution.

For example:

$-4x + 2y = -10$

$2x - y = 3$

The graphs of the equations are parallel;
the lines never intersect.

So, this linear system has no solution.

The lines have the same slope and different y-intercepts.

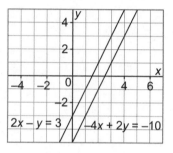

Other linear systems have **infinite solutions**.

For example:

$2x + y = -1$

$6x + 3y = -3$

The graphs of the equations are the same line.

Every point on one line is also a point on the other line.

So, this linear system has infinite solutions.

The lines have the same slope and the same y-intercept.

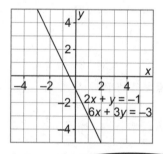

When two graphs are the same line, the graphs coincide.

One solution	No solution	Infinite solutions
Lines intersect at one point.	Lines are parallel.	Lines coincide.
• different slopes	• same slope	• same slope
	• different y-intercepts	• same y-intercept

Example 1 | Finding the Number of Solutions of a Linear System

Without solving, find the number of solutions of each linear system.

a) $2x + y = 8$

$4x + 2y = 16$

b) $3x + y = 9$

$6x + 2y = 12$

c) $x + y = 8$

$-5x + y = 1$

Solution

Write each equation in the form $y = mx + b$ to find the slope and
y-intercept of its graph.

a) $2x + y = 8$ ①

$4x + 2y = 16$ ②

> *In $y = mx + b$, m is the slope and b is the y-intercept.*

For equation ①:

$2x + y = 8$

$y = -2x + 8$

The slope is -2 and the y-intercept is 8.

For equation ②:

$4x + 2y = 16$

$2y = -4x + 16$

$y = -2x + 8$

> *Rewriting each equation in slope-intercept form shows that the equations represent the same line.*

The slope is -2 and the y-intercept is 8.

The slopes are the same and the y-intercepts are the same.

So, the lines coincide.

The linear system has infinite solutions.

b) $3x + y = 9$ ①

$6x + 2y = 12$ ②

For equation ①:

$3x + y = 9$

$y = -3x + 9$

The slope is -3 and the y-intercept is 9.

For equation ②:

$6x + 2y = 12$

$2y = -6x + 12$

$y = -3x + 6$

The slope is -3 and the y-intercept is 6.

The slopes are the same and the y-intercepts are different.

So, the lines are parallel.

The linear system has no solution.

c) $x + y = 8$ ①
    $-5x + y = 1$ ②

For equation ①:

$x + y = 8$

     $y = -x + 8$

The slope is -1 and the y-intercept is 8.

For equation ②:

$-5x + y = 1$

       $y = 5x + 1$

The slope is 5 and the y-intercept is 1.

The slopes are different.
So, the lines intersect at exactly one point.
The linear system has one solution.

Check

1. Without solving, find the number of solutions of each linear system.

a) $4x - 2y = -2$ ①
   $-5x + y = -2$ ②

Write each equation in the form $y = mx + b$.

For equation ①:

$4x - 2y = -2$

       $y =$ _____

The slope is ____; the y-intercept is ____.

For equation ②:

$-5x + y = -2$

       $y =$ _____

The slope is ____; the y-intercept is ____.

The slopes are _____.
So, the lines _____.
The linear system has _____.

b) $3x + y = 7$ ①
   $12x + 4y = -8$ ②

Write each equation in the form $y = mx + b$.

For equation ①:

$3x + y = 7$

       $y =$ _____

The slope is ____; the y-intercept is ____.

For equation ②:

$12x + 4y = -8$

       $y =$ _____

The slope is ____; the y-intercept is ____.

The slopes are _____.
The y-intercepts are _____.
So, the lines _____; the lines _____ intersect.
The linear system has _____.

c) $12x - 4y = -8$ ①
$\quad -3x + y = 2$ ②

Write each equation in the form $y = mx + b$.

For equation ①: For equation ②:

$12x - 4y = -8$ $-3x + y = 2$

$\qquad\qquad\qquad\qquad\qquad\qquad\qquad y = \underline{\hspace{2cm}}$

$\qquad\quad y = \underline{\hspace{2cm}}$

The slope is ____; the y-intercept is ____.   The slope is ____; the y-intercept is ____.

The slopes are _____.

The y-intercepts are _____.

So, the lines _____.

The linear system has _____.

Practice

1. The graphs of the two equations in 3 different linear systems are shown.

System A   **System B**   **System C**

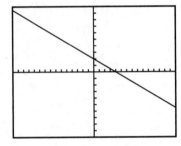   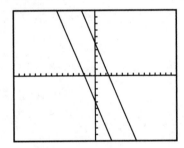   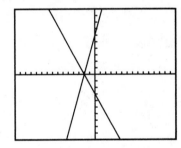

In which linear system do the lines intersect at exactly one point? _____

How many solutions does the system have? _____

In which linear system are the lines parallel? _____

How many solutions does the system have? _____

In which linear system do the lines coincide? _____

How many solutions does the system have? _____

2. The slope-intercept form of each equation in a linear system is given. How many solutions does each system have?

a) $y = -2x + 4$ ①

   Slope: _____ ; y-intercept: _____

   $y = -2x - 1$ ②

   Slope: _____ ; y-intercept: _____

   The slopes are _____.

   The y-intercepts are _____.

   So, there is _____.

b) $y = -3x + 4$ ①

   Slope: _____ ; y-intercept: _____

   $y = -2x + 4$ ②

   Slope: _____ ; y-intercept: _____

   The slopes are _____.

   So, there is _____.

3. Without solving, find the number of solutions of each linear system.

a) $2x + 2y = 6$ ①

   $x + y = -2$ ②

For equation ①:

$2x + 2y = 6$

$y =$ _____

The slope is _____ ; the y-intercept is _____.

For equation ②:

$x + y = -2$

$y =$ _____

The slope is _____ ; the y-intercept is _____.

The slopes are _____ and the y-intercepts are _____.

So, the system has _____.

b) $3x - y = 5$ ①

   $-6x + 2y = -10$ ②

For equation ①:

$3x - y = 5$

$y =$ _____

The slope is _____ ; the y-intercept is _____.

For equation ②:

$-6x + 2y = -10$

$y =$ _____

The slope is _____ ; the y-intercept is _____.

The slopes are _____ and the y-intercepts are _____.

So, the system has _____.

c) $x + y = 4$ ①

   $-4x + 2y = 8$ ②

For equation ①:

$x + y = 4$

$y =$ _____

The slope is _____ ;

the y-intercept is _____.

For equation ②:

$-4x + 2y = 8$

$y =$ _____

The slope is _____ ;

the y-intercept is _____.

The slopes are _____.

So, the system has _____.

Dancing Variables

Contestants *x* and *y* entered a dance contest.
Why was *y* disappointed with his results?

To find out:

On a separate sheet of paper, determine the solution of each linear system.
Match each system to its solution at the right. Write the corresponding letter
above the question number in the answer below.

Question	System
1	$x + y = 3$ $x - y = 1$
2	$3x + y = 1$ $6x - 2y = -2$
3	$2x - y = -3$ $x + y = 0$
4	$2x + y = -6$ $x + y = -4$
5	$2x + y = 4$ $x + y = 4$
6	$2x - y = 6$ $-x - y = -12$
7	$8x - 4y = 4$ $-5x + y = 2$
8	$-x - y = -3$ $2x + y = 6$
9	$-2x - y = 9$ $x + y = -5$
10	$-5x + y = -4$ $6x - 2y = 4$
11	$-4x + y = -10$ $-x + y = -1$

Solution	Letter
$x = -2; y = -2$	M
$x = 6; y = 6$	W
$x = -1; y = -3$	A
$x = 0; y = 4$	E
$x = 0; y = 1$	L
$x = -4; y = -1$	I
$x = 2; y = 1$	H
$x = -1; y = 1$	N
$x = 1; y = 1$	T
$x = 3; y = 2$	D
$x = 3; y = 0$	S

Answer:

1	5		6	7	8		5	2	9	4	9	3	7	10	5	11

Chapter 7 Study Guide

Skill	Description	Example
Solve a linear system by graphing.	To solve a linear system, graph both equations on the same grid or enter the equations in a graphing calculator. The coordinates of the point of intersection are the solution of the linear system.	For this linear system: $2x - y = -1$ $x + y = 4$ The solution of the system is: $x = 1$ and $y = 3$
Solve a linear system using algebra.	To solve a linear system, use substitution or elimination. Then verify that the solution is correct by substituting the x- and y-values into both equations.	For this linear system: $2x + y = 3$　　① $3x - y = 7$　　② The coefficients of y are opposite integers, so use elimination. $2x + y = 3$　　① $\underline{+(3x - y = 7)}$　　② 　$5x\quad = 10$ 　$x\quad = 2$ Substitute $x = 2$ in equation ①. $2(2) + y = 3$ 　　　$y = -1$ The solution is: $x = 2$ and $y = -1$
Find the number of solutions of a linear system.	To find the number of solutions of a linear system: • compare the graphs of the equations, or • compare the slopes and y-intercepts of the lines	These lines have different slopes, so the system has exactly one solution: $y = 3x + 4$ $y = -2x + 1$ These lines have the same slope and different y-intercepts, so the system has no solution: $y = 3x + 4$ $y = 3x + 2$ These lines have the same slope and the same y-intercept, so the system has infinite solutions: $y = 3x + 4$ $2y = 6x + 8$

7.1 **1. a)** Use a table to create a linear system to model this situation:

A family recently moved to Calgary and each member registered at the library.
It costs $12 for an adult registration and $6 for a young adult registration.
The family registered 8 people and paid $66.

Let the number of adults be a.
Let the number of young adults be y.

	Cost per registration ($)	Number	Total cost ($)
Adult			
Young adult			
Total			

The number of registrations is represented by: _____ + _____ = _____

The total cost in dollars is represented by: _____ + _____ = _____

A linear system that models the situation is:

_____

_____

b) The family registered 3 adults and 5 young adults.
Use the data in the problem to verify these numbers.

_____ adults at _____ each   = _____
+ _____ young adults at _____ each = _____
_____ registrations for a total of   _____

The total number of registrations and the total cost _____ the data in the problem.
So, the solution _____ correct.

7.2 **2.** Solve this linear system by graphing.

$x + y = 6$
$x + 2y = 7$

Use intercepts to graph each line.

Equation	x-intercept (let _____ = 0)	y-intercept (let _____ = 0)
$x + y = 6$	$x =$_____	$y =$_____
$x + 2y = 7$	$x =$_____	$y =$_____

For each graph, plot points at the x-intercept and y-intercept, then draw a line through them.

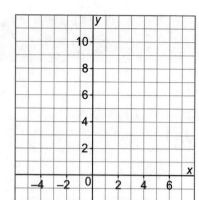

The point of intersection appears to be (_____, _____).

Verify the solution.

In each equation, substitute: $x =$ _____ and $y =$ _____

$x + y = 6$ $x + 2y = 7$

L.S. = _____   R.S. = _____   L.S. = _____   R.S. = _____

   = _____   = _____

   = _____   = _____

                                              = _____

For each equation, L.S. ____ R.S.

So, the solution of the linear system is $x =$ _____ and $y =$ _____.

7.3   **3.** Use graphing technology to find the solution of this linear system.

$3x + 4y = 5$

$5x - 2y = 4$

Write each equation in the form $y = mx + b$.

$3x + 4y = 5$ $5x - 2y = 4$

$4y =$ _____ + _____ $-2y =$ _____ + _____

$y = $ _____ + _____ $y = $ _____ + _____

$y = $ _____ $y = $ _____

Enter the equations in a calculator, then graph them.

Sketch the lines.

Find the point of intersection.

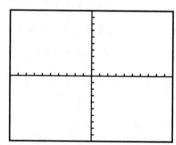

The point of intersection is: (_____, _____)

To verify the solution, substitute: $x =$ _____ and $y =$ _____ in each equation.

$3x + 4y = 5$ $5x - 2y = 4$

L.S. = _____   R.S. = _____   L.S. = _____   R.S. = _____

   = _____   = _____

   = _____   = _____

   = _____   = _____

For each equation, L.S. _____ R.S.

So, the solution of the linear system is $x =$ _____ and $y =$ _____.

4. Solve this linear system by substitution.

$2x - 3y = -2$ ①

$4x + y = 24$ ②

In equation ②, the coefficient of y is 1. So, solve equation ② for y.

$4x + y = 24$

$y = $ _____

Substitute $y = $ _____ in equation ①.

         $2x - 3y = -2$ ①

$2x - 3($_____$) = -2$

            $x = $ ____

To find the value of y when $x = $ ____, substitute in equation ②.

     $4x + y = 24$ ②

$4($___$) + y = 24$

        $y = $ _____

The solution is: $x = $ _____ and $y = $ _____

Verify the solution.

In each equation, substitute: $x = $ _____ and $y = $ _____

$2x - 3y = -2$ $4x + y = 24$

L.S. = _____   R.S. = _____   L.S. = _____   R.S. = _____

L.S. = _____   L.S. = _____

For each equation, L.S. _____ R.S.

So, the solution of the linear system is $x = $ _____ and $y = $ _____.

5. Solve this linear system by elimination.

$2x - y = 9$ ①

$3x + 4y = -14$ ②

No coefficients of like terms are opposite integers.

Look at the y-terms: $4y$ and $-y$

To make the coefficients opposite integers, multiply equation ① by _____.

_____ $\times$ equation ①: _____$(2x - y = 9)$ $\longrightarrow$ _____   ③

Add equations ② and ③ to eliminate y.

        $x = $ _____

To find the value of y when $x =$ _____, substitute in equation ①.

      $2x - y = 9$ ①

  $2($_____$) - y = 9$

           $y =$ _____

The solution is: $x =$ _____ and $y =$ _____

Verify the solution.

In the original equations, substitute: $x =$ _____ and $y =$ _____

$2x - y = 9$ $3x + 4y = -14$

L.S. = _____   R.S. = _____   L.S. = _____   R.S. = _____

L.S. = _____   L.S. = _____

For each equation, L.S. _____ R.S.

So, the solution of the linear system is $x =$ _____ and $y =$ _____.

7.6   **6.** Find the number of solutions of each linear system.

    a) $-x + y = 8$ ①

        $2x - 2y = -16$ ②

      For equation ①: For equation ②:

      $-x + y = 8$ $2x - 2y = -16$

          $y =$ _____

      The slope is ____;

      the y-intercept is ____. $y =$ _____

                                   The slope is ____;

                                   the y-intercept is ____.

      The slopes are _____ and the y-intercepts are _____.

      So, the system has _____.

    b) $4x + y = 2$ ①

        $8x + 2y = 8$ ②

      For equation ①: For equation ②:

      The slope is ____;

      the y-intercept is ____.   The slope is ____;

                                   the y-intercept is ____.

      The slopes are _____ and the y-intercepts are _____.

      So, the system has _____.

ANSWERS

Chapter 1 Measurement

1.1 Skill Builder, Check, page 2

1. a) $\frac{9}{2}$ b) $\frac{31}{4}$ c) $\frac{67}{12}$

2. a) $2\frac{3}{5}$ b) $4\frac{5}{8}$ c) $6\frac{11}{12}$

1.1 Imperial Measures of Length, page 3

Example 1, Check, page 3
1. The yard; my arm span

Example 2, Check, page 4
1. a) 168 in.   b) 4 yd. 2 ft.

Example 3, Check, page 5
1. 3520 steps

Practice, page 6
1. a) The yard   b) My arm span
2. a) The inch
   b) The length of my thumb to the first knuckle
3. a) The foot   b) My foot
4. a) 3 ft.; 6 ft.; 9 ft.; 12 ft.; 15 ft.
   b) 12 in.; 24 in.; 36 in.; 48 in.; 60 in.
5. a) 96 in.   b) 705 ft.   c) 10 560 yd.
6. a) 6 ft.   b) 29 yd.   c) 8 yd.
7. a) 5 ft. 7 in.   b) 139 yd. 1 ft.   c) 59 yd. 2 ft.
8. a) 89 in.   b) 28 ft.   c) 420 in.   d) 16 224 ft.
9. 132 ft.   10. 156 in.   11. 8 sections

1.2 Math Lab: Measuring Length and Distance, page 9

Practice, page 11
1. a) Calipers or ruler   b) Ruler
   c) Measuring tape   d) String, then ruler
2. a) The inch   b) The inch
   c) The yard or foot   d) The inch

1.3 Skill Builder, Check, page 12
1. a) 700 cm   b) 3300 cm   c) 4.5 cm   d) 0.6 cm
2. a) 90 mm   b) 890 mm
   c) 3000 mm   d) 38 000 mm
3. a) 8 m   b) 0.27 m   c) 9 m   d) 0.235 m

1.3 Relating SI and Imperial Units, page 13

Example 1, Check, page 13
1. a) 180 cm   b) 120 cm   c) 32.5 cm   d) 78.3 m

Example 2, Check, page 15
1. a) 3666 in.   b) $109\frac{4}{5}$ mi.

Example 3, Check, page 16
1. Yes; the height of the shed is 3.45 m.

Practice, page 16
1. a) 2160 cm   b) 12.5 cm   c) 2.4 m   d) 11.2 km
2. a) 468 in.   b) $4\frac{1}{5}$ mi.   c) $11\frac{1}{25}$ in.   d) $34\frac{4}{10}$ in.
3. a) 1425 mm   b) 330 cm
4. Tammy   5. No   6. Ben

Checkpoint 1, page 19
1. a) i) The foot or the yard
      ii) The length of my stride
   b) i) The inch
      ii) The length of my thumb to the first knuckle
2. a) A yard; my stride
   b) An inch; the length of my thumb to the first knuckle
3. a) 8 ft. 3 in.   b) 168 in.
4. Yes
5. a) i) Foot or yard   ii) Inch
   b) i) Kilometre or metre   ii) Millimetre
6. Centimetre; string or ruler
7. a) 4.8 m   b) 43.2 km   c) $1\frac{19}{25}$ in.   d) 9 yd. 1 ft.
8. 4 mi. 1408 yd.

1.4 Skill Builder, Check, page 22
1. 15.8 cm

1.4 Surface Areas of Right Pyramids and Right Cones, page 23

Example 1, Check, page 24
1. 312 cm²

Example 2, Check, page 25
1. 84.8 cm²

Example 3, Check, page 26
1. 718 square yards

Example 4, Check, page 27
1. 820 square feet

Practice, page 28
1. a) 96 square inches   b) 63 m²   c) 696 cm²
2. 249.6 cm²   3. $12\frac{1}{5}$ yd.
4. 179 cm²   5. 204 square inches

6. $10\frac{2}{5}$ in.

1.5 Skill Builder, Check, page 31
1. 585 cubic inches   **2.** 1890 cubic yards

1.5 Skill Builder, Check, page 32
1. a) 8482.3 cm³   **b)** 5343.8 mm³

1.5 Volumes of Right Pyramids and Right Cones, page 33

Example 1, Check, page 33
1. 49 cubic feet

Example 2, Check, page 34
1. 12.6 m³

Example 3, Check, page 35
1. 342 cubic yards

Example 4, Check, page 36
1. 10.3 cm

Practice, page 37
1. a) 15 cm³   **b)** 280 m³
2. 1866 cubic feet   **3.** 241 cubic inches
4. 1097 cubic inches
5. The pyramid; prism: 768 cm³; pyramid: 816 cm³
6. Cylinder: $9\frac{9}{10}$ in.; cone: $29\frac{7}{10}$ in.

1.6 Surface Area and Volume of a Sphere, page 40

Example 1, Check, page 40
1. a) 2463 square feet   **b)** 6871 cm²

Example 2, Check, page 41
1. a) 17 157 cubic inches   **b)** 718 mm³

Example 3, Check, page 42
1. 16.8 m

Practice, page 43
1. a) 50 square feet   **b)** 908 cm²
    c) 1140 square inches   **d)** 59 m²
2. a) 34 cubic feet   **b)** 2572 cm³
    c) 2788 cubic inches   **d)** 33 m³
3. a) 615.8 cm²   **b)** 1437 cm³
4. $1\frac{1}{2}$ in.   **5.** 20 in.

Checkpoint 2, page 46
1. a) 39 cm²   **b)** 632.7 m²
2. 52 square feet
3. 670 cubic inches   **4.** 11 cubic inches
5. a) 907.9 cm²   **b)** $150\frac{4}{5}$ square inches
6. a) 2572 cm³   **b)** 134 cubic inches

1.7 Skill Builder, Check, page 50
1. 150 cm²

1.7 Skill Builder, Check, page 51
1. a) 170 square feet   **b)** 12 215 cm²

1.7 Solving Problems Involving Objects, page 52

Example 1, Check, page 53
1. 3315 cubic feet

Example 2, Check, page 54
1. 188 cm²

Practice, page 55
1. 373.2 m²
2. a) 3266 m³   **b)** 15 787 mm³
3. 226 cm³   **4.** 261 square feet

Chapter 1 Puzzle, page 59
A. 283 units²; 339 units³
B. 113 units²; 113 units³
C. 59 units²; 27 units³
D. 211 units²; 171 units³
E. 283 units²; 314 units³
D, E, C, B, A; 1001

Chapter 1 Review, page 61
1. a) The yard   **b)** The foot or yard
    c) The inch
2. a) 28 yd.   **b)** 115 in.
3. a) The inch; the centimetre; measuring tape
    b) The foot and inch; the metre; measuring tape
4. a) 15.3 m   **b)** 108.8 km
5. Ryan
6. a) 2771 m²   **b)** 95 square inches
7. 160.1 cm²   **8.** No; 518 square inches
9. 147 cm³   **10.** 75 cm³
11. a) 616 mm²; 1437 mm³
    b) 1140 square inches; 2788 cubic inches
12. a) 272 square feet   **b)** 448 cubic feet

Chapter 2 Trigonometry

2.1 Skill Builder, Check, page 68
1. **a)** No **b)** Yes

2.1 The Tangent Ratio, page 69

Example 1, Check, page 70
1. **a)** 1.25 **b)** 0.8

Example 2, Check, page 71
1. **a)** 52° **b)** 29°

Example 3, Check, page 72
1. 69°

Practice, page 73
1. **a)** GH: hypotenuse; FH: adjacent; FG: opposite
   b) PN: hypotenuse; MP: adjacent; MN: opposite
2. **a)** $\frac{7}{3}$ **b)** $\frac{16}{15}$
3. **a)** 27° **b)** 40°
4. 43° **5.** 66° **6.** 3°

2.2 Skill Builder, Check, page 75
1. **a)** $a = 35$ **b)** $c = 72$ **c)** $f = 12$ **d)** $b = 2.5$

2.2 Using the Tangent Ratio to Calculate Lengths, page 76

Example 1, Check, page 77
1. **a)** 13.3 cm **b)** 8.8 cm

Example 2, Check, page 79
1. 4.9 cm

Example 3, Check, page 80
1. 3.5 m

Practice, page 81
1. **a)** 3.6 cm **b)** 7.7 cm
2. 16.6 cm **3. a)** 13.1 cm **b)** 18.5 cm
4. 2.6 m **5.** 2.0 m

2.3 Math Lab: Measuring an Inaccessible Height, page 84

Practice, page 85
1. **a)** 35° **b)** 10° **2.** 3.6 m **3.** 4.4 m

Checkpoint 1, page 87
1. **a)** $\frac{11}{7}$ **b)** $\frac{15}{22}$
2. **a)** 25° **b)** 72°
3. **a)** 16.4 cm **b)** 9.7 cm **4.** 1.3 m

2.4 Skill Builder, Check, page 89
1. **a)** 104° **b)** 45° **2. a)** 34° **b)** 41°

2.4 The Sine and Cosine Ratios, page 90

Example 1, Check, page 91
1. 0.47; 0.88

Example 2, Check, page 92
1. **a)** $\angle U \doteq 56°$; $\angle W \doteq 34°$ **b)** $\angle U \doteq 37°$; $\angle S \doteq 53°$

Example 3, Check, page 93
1. 76° **2.** 68°

Practice, page 94
1. **a)** CD; BC; BD **b)** FG; BF; GB
2. **a)** sin B = 0.8; cos B = 0.6
   b) sin B = 0.96; cos B = 0.28
3. **a)** 53° **b)** 32°
4. 57° **5.** 21°

2.5 Using the Sine and Cosine Ratios to Calculate Lengths, page 97

Example 1, Check, page 98
1. **a)** 10.0 cm **b)** 11.2 cm

Example 2, Check, page 100
1. **a)** 27.6 cm **b)** 13.6 cm

Example 3, Check, page 102
1. 5.4 m

Practice, page 102
1. **a)** Cosine **b)** Sine
2. **a)** 11.1 cm **b)** 6.2 cm
3. 15.1 m
4. **a)** 17.3 cm **b)** 25.8 cm
5. 5.1 m **6.** 7.9 m

Checkpoint 2, page 106
1. sin A $\doteq$ 0.78; cos A $\doteq$ 0.63
2. **a)** 42° **b)** 26°
3. **a)** 2.4 cm **b)** 4.7 cm
4. 9.4 cm

2.6 Applying the Trigonometric Ratios, page 108

Example 1, Check, page 109
1. **a** $\angle G \doteq 31°$; $\angle J \doteq 59°$ **b)** $\angle K \doteq 67°$; $\angle N \doteq 23°$

Example 2, Check, page 111
1. ST $\doteq$ 27.0 m; SU $\doteq$ 19.7 m

Example 3, Check, page 113
1. DF $\doteq$ 8.1 cm; DE $\doteq$ 15.3 cm

Practice, page 113
1. a) Tangent   b) Cosine
2. a) Sine   b) Tangent
3. a) $\angle U \doteq 50°$; $\angle W \doteq 40°$ b) $\angle Q \doteq 37°$; $\angle R \doteq 53°$
4. QS $\doteq$ 11.7 cm; RS $\doteq$ 7.8 cm
5. $\angle E \doteq 50°$; $\angle C \doteq 40°$; CD $\doteq$ 16.5 cm
6. a) 4.1 m   b) 4.5 m

2.7 Solving Problems Involving More than One Right Triangle, page 117

Example 1, Check, page 118
1. 40°

Example 2, Check, page 120
1. 23.2 m

Example 3, Check, page 122
1. 6.7 m

Practice, page 123
1. 25°   2. 9.3 m   3. 1701 m

Chapter 2 Puzzle, page 126
A. PJ: 11°, PH: 14°, PG: 18°, PF: 27°,
PA: 45°, PB: 63°, PC: 72°, PD: 76°, PE: 79°
B. 80°: 6 squares; 88°: 29 squares; 85°: 12 squares;
89°: 58 squares
C. 10°: 6 squares; 5°: 12 squares; 2°: 29 squares;
1°: 58 squares

Chapter 2 Review, page 128
1. 54°   2. 11.5 cm
3. 21 m   4. 50.6 m
5. a) 39°   b) 61°   6. 28°
7. a) 14.4 cm   b) 9.6 cm
8. 6.6 m
9. $\angle G = 39°$; FG $\doteq$ 10.5 cm; EG $\doteq$ 13.5 cm
10. 43 m

Chapter 3 Factors and Products

3.1 Skill Builder, Check, page 134
1. a) No; no   b) 12; yes
   c) No; no   d) 12; yes; yes
   e) Yes; 18; yes; yes   f) 064; yes; yes

3.1 Factors and Multiples of Whole Numbers, page 135

Example 1, Check, page 136
1. $2 \times 2 \times 2 \times 3 \times 5$, or $2^3 \times 3 \times 5$
2. $2 \times 2 \times 2 \times 5 \times 7$ or $2^3 \times 5 \times 7$

Example 2, Check, page 137
1. a) 8   b) 9

Example 3, Check, page 138
1. 100   2. 90

Example 4, Check, page 139
1. 16 m

Practice, page 140
1. a) $2 \times 2 \times 2 \times 2 \times 3 \times 3$ b) $2 \times 2 \times 2 \times 3 \times 5 \times 5$
2. a) $2^4 \times 3^2$ b) $2^3 \times 3 \times 5^2$
3. a) $2^2 \times 3^2 \times 7$ b) $2^2 \times 3^2 \times 5^2$
4. a) 2   b) 12
5. a) 7, 14, 21, 28, 35, 42, 49, 56, 63, 70;
     10, 20, 30, 40, 50, 60, 70, 80, 90, 100
   b) 70
6. a) 60   b) 144   7. 24 hamburgers

3.2 Perfect Squares, Perfect Cubes, and Their Roots, page 142

Example 1, Check, page 143
1. 24

Example 2, Check, page 144
1. 6

Example 3, Check, page 145
1. 4 in.

Practice, page 146
1. a) 15   b) 14   c) 35
2. a) 9   b) 15   c) 21
3. 18 cm

Checkpoint 1, page 148
1. a) $5^2 \times 7$ b) $2 \times 3^2 \times 5^2$
2. 2   3. a) 63   b) 154
4. a) 22   b) 42   5. a) 7   b) 20

3.3 Skill Builder, Check, page 151
1. $12b + 6$ 2. $3r^2 + 2r$

3.3 Skill Builder, Check, page 153
1. $12b^2 + 6b$ 2. $3a + 4$

3.3 Common Factors of a Polynomial, page 154

Example 1, Check, page 156
1. **a)** $5(c+2)$ **b)** $2n(2n+7)$

Example 2, Check, page 157
1. **a)** $4(n-8)$ **b)** $6r(-3r+2)$

Example 3, Check, page 159
1. **a)** $3(2n^2+n+3)$ **b)** $-4(3v^2-2v+4)$

Practice, page 160
1. **a)** $6x+12$ **b)** $6(x+2)$
2. **a)** $4(2w+3)$ **b)** $3x(2x+5)$
3. **a)** $9(-z+4)$ **b)** $5t(5t-2)$
4. **a)** $2(2x^2+4x+1)$ **b)** $-5(3a^2-2a+6)$
    c) $8(3n^2-2n-1)$

3.4 Math Lab: Modelling Trinomials as Binomial Products, page 162

Practice, page 165
1. **a)** $x^2+7x+10=(x+2)(x+5)$
    b) $2x^2+11x+12=(2x+3)(x+4)$
    c) $3x^2+10x+8=(3x+4)(x+2)$
2. **b)** x^2+6x+8 **c)** $(x+4)(x+2)$

3.5 Skill Builder, Check, page 166
1. **a)** $9x+3$ **b)** $4n+3$ **c)** $-3x-1$ **d)** $-s-6$
2. **a)** $m+2$ **b)** $3+h$ **c)** $3t-2$ **d)** $5r+1$

3.5 Polynomials of the Form x^2+bx+c, page 167

Example 1, Check, page 168
1. **a)** $x^2+9x+14$ **b)** n^2-n-12

Example 2, Check, page 169
1. **a)** $x^2-8x+15$ **b)** $v^2-4v-21$

Example 3, Check, page 170
1. $(x+3)(x+4)$

Example 4, Check, page 172
1. **a)** $(x-2)(x-4)$ **b)** $(c-3)(c+5)$

Practice, page 172
1. **a)** $x^2+8x+15$ **b)** $n^2+2n-35$
2. **a)** $x^2-6x-40$ **b)** $n^2+3n-54$
    c) $h^2-11h+28$
3. **a)** $(x+9)(x+1)$ **b)** $(x-1)(x-12)$
    c) $(n+2)(n-10)$ **d)** $(c-2)(c+9)$

3.6 Polynomials of the Form ax^2+bx+c, page 175

Example 1, Check, page 176
1. **a)** $8x^2+16x+6$ **b)** $15n^2+29n-14$

Example 2, Check, page 177
1. **a)** $6f^2+10f-24$ **b)** $-20m^2-53m-18$

Example 3, Check, page 178
1. **a)** $(2x+1)(x+4)$ **b)** $(7n+2)(n+2)$

Example 4, Check, page 181
1. $(2m+1)(4m-3)$

Practice, page 182
1. **a)** $3x^2+8x+5$ **b)** $20w^2-51w+27$
2. **a)** $-10v^2+36v-18$ **b)** $-28c^2+39c-8$
3. **a)** $(2x+1)(x+7)$ **b)** $(5m+1)(m+3)$
4. **a)** $(x-2)(3x+1)$ **b)** $(x-5)(2x-3)$

Checkpoint 2, page 185
1. **a)** $5(3q+5)$ **b)** $6(3s^2-4s-1)$
2. $t^2-4t-45$ 3. $(x+1)(x-6)$
4. $-6a^2+28a-30$ 5. $(u-3)(3u-2)$

3.7 Multiplying Polynomials, page 187

Example 1, Check, page 188
1. $6z^3+20z^2+37z+28$

Example 2, Check, page 189
1. $12n^3-22n^2+2$

Practice, page 189
1. **a)** $15n^3+10n^2+5n$ **b)** $8b^3+22b^2+24b+9$
2. **a)** $-4n^3+8n^2-10n$ **b)** $4b^3-33b^2+67b-40$
    c) $-16y^3+37y-21$

3.8 Factoring Special Polynomials, page 191

Example 1, Check, page 192
1. **a)** $(r+3)^2$ **b)** $(3m-2)^2$

Example 2, Check, page 193
1. **a)** $(x+10)(x-10)$ **b)** $(5h+9)(5h-9)$

Practice, page 193
1. **a)** $(r-9)^2$ **b)** $(5b+4)^2$
2. **a)** $(x+6)(x-6)$ **b)** $(3w+1)(3w-1)$
3. **a)** $(10c+7)(10c-7)$ **b)** $(8m-1)^2$

Hum Happy Birthday

Chapter 3 Review, page 196

1. **b)** 2×5^3
2. 5   **3.** 80   **4.** 45   **5.** 14
6. $6(2p+3)$
7. **a)** $3x(3x-4)$ **b)** $-5(2m^2+3m-1)$
8. **a)** $c^2-11c+30$ **b)** $h^2+3h-28$
9. **a)** $(x+8)(x+1)$ **b)** $(x-3)(x-5)$
10. $6x^2-3x-30$ **11.** $(2x+1)(x+5)$
12. **a)** $(7n+1)(n+1)$ **b)** $(v-2)(3v-2)$
13. **a)** $6m^3+7m^2+17m+10$
    b) $3z^3-11z^2-6z+8$
14. **a)** $(2c+5)^2$ **b)** $(4m+9)(4m-9)$

Chapter 4 Roots and Powers

4.1 Skill Builder, Check, page 202

1. **a)** 2.8   **b)** 7.2

4.1 Skill Builder, Check, page 203

1. **a)** 2.7   **b)** 8.4

4.1 Math Lab: Estimating Roots, page 204

Practice, page 205

1. **a)** 5   **b)** 7   **c)** 8   **d)** 10
2. **a)** 12   **b)** 100   **c)** –3   **d)** 4
3. Exact: $\sqrt{100}$, $\sqrt{49}$, $\sqrt[3]{-1}$, $\sqrt[3]{1000}$;
approximate: $\sqrt{3}$, $\sqrt{10}$, $\sqrt{15}$, $\sqrt[3]{100}$
4. **a)** 3 and 4   **b)** 3 and 4   **c)** 1 and 2

4.2 Irrational Numbers, page 206

Example 1, Check, page 207

1. **a)** Irrational   **b)** Irrational   **c)** Rational

Example 2, Check, page 208

1. $\sqrt[3]{-30}$, $\sqrt[3]{27}$, $\sqrt{18}$

Practice, page 208

1. **a)** Rational   **b)** Irrational **c)** Rational   **d)** Rational
2. Rational number: 4, $1.\overline{6}$, $\sqrt[3]{-1}$, $1\frac{3}{4}$, –16;
irrational number: $\sqrt{1.1}$, $\sqrt[3]{10}$
3. **a)** Rational   **b)** Rational
4. **a)** $\sqrt{5}$; 2, 2.236 067 978..., 3, 10
    b) $\sqrt[3]{100}$; –6, 4, 1, 4.641 588 834...
5. **a)** >   **b)** <   **c)** <   **d)** >

6. $\sqrt[3]{60}$: A, $\sqrt{9}$: D, $\sqrt[3]{-9}$: B, $\sqrt{3}$: C   **7.** False

4.3 Skill Builder, Check, page 211

1. **a)** $7^3 \times 11^3$ **b)** $8^4 \times 13^4$
2. **a)** =   **b)** =   **c)** ≠   **d)** =

4.3 Mixed and Entire Radicals, page 212

Example 1, Check, page 213

1. **a)** $4\sqrt{2}$ **b)** $2\sqrt[3]{7}$

Example 2, Check, page 214

1. $6\sqrt{35}$

Example 3, Check, page 215

1. **a)** $\sqrt{98}$ **b)** $\sqrt[3]{3000}$

Practice, page 215

1. **a)** 9   **b)** 4   **c)** 4, 16   **d)** 49
2. **a)** 8   **b)** 8   **c)** 27   **d)** 27
3. **a)** $\sqrt{4 \cdot 6}$ **b)** $\sqrt{3 \cdot 36}$ **c)** $\sqrt[3]{5 \cdot 8}$ **d)** $\sqrt[3]{6 \cdot 27}$
4. **a)** $8\sqrt{5}$ **b)** $7\sqrt{15}$ **c)** $3\sqrt[3]{7}$ **d)** $4\sqrt[3]{9}$
5. **a) i)** $2 \cdot 2 \cdot 2 \cdot 2 \cdot 2 \cdot 3$ **ii)** $2 \cdot 2 \cdot 2 \cdot 5 \cdot 5$
    b) i) $4\sqrt{6}$ **ii)** $2\sqrt[3]{25}$
6. **a)** $\sqrt{99}$ **b)** $\sqrt{52}$ **c)** $\sqrt[3]{108}$ **d)** $\sqrt[3]{120}$

Checkpoint 1, page 217

1. **a)** 3.3   **b)** 3.9
2. **a)** Irrational **b)** Rational   **c)** Rational
3. **b)** $\sqrt[3]{-7}$, $\sqrt{5}$, $\sqrt{30}$
4. **a)** $2\sqrt{31}$ **b)** $2\sqrt[3]{50}$
5. **a)** $\sqrt{90}$ **b)** $\sqrt{125}$ **c)** $\sqrt[3]{320}$ **d)** $\sqrt[3]{875}$

4.4 Fractional Exponents and Radicals, page 219

Example 1, Check, page 220

1. **a)** 9   **b)** –5   **c)** 10
2. **a)** 3.16   **b)** 4.22   **c)** 2.22   **d)** 2.24

Example 2, Check, page 221

1. **a)** $\sqrt{82^5}$ or $\left(\sqrt{82}\right)^5$ **b)** $\sqrt[3]{9^2}$ or $\left(\sqrt[3]{9}\right)^2$

Example 3, Check, page 222

1. **a)** $57^{\frac{5}{2}}$ **b)** $3^{\frac{4}{3}}$ **c)** $6^{\frac{5}{4}}$ **d)** $10^{\frac{7}{2}}$

Example 4, Check, page 222

1. **a)** 32   **b)** 81   **c)** 100

Practice, page 223

1. **a)** $\sqrt{8}$ **b)** $\sqrt[3]{32}$ **c)** $\sqrt[4]{12}$

2. a) $35^{\frac{1}{2}}$ **b)** $11^{\frac{1}{3}}$ **c)** $6^{\frac{1}{4}}$

3. a) 10   **b)** 5   **c)** 3

4. a) 4.69   **b)** 3.11   **c)** 3.98

5. 2   **6.** $\left(\sqrt[4]{52}\right)^3$

7. a) $\sqrt{114^3}$, or $\left(\sqrt{114}\right)^3$ **b)** $\sqrt[3]{92^2}$, or $\left(\sqrt[3]{92}\right)^2$

8. a) $537^{\frac{3}{2}}$ **b)** $15^{\frac{4}{3}}$ **c)** $63^{\frac{5}{4}}$

9. a) 125   **b)** 16   **c)** 8

4.5 Negative Exponents and Reciprocals, page 224

Example 1, Check, page 224

1. a) $\dfrac{1}{49}$ **b)** $\dfrac{1}{10\ 000}$ **c)** 64

Example 2, Check, page 225

1. a) $\dfrac{1}{4}$ **b)** $-\dfrac{1}{2}$

Example 3, Check, page 226

1. a) $\dfrac{1}{10^{\frac{3}{2}}}$ **b)** $\dfrac{1}{120^{\frac{2}{3}}}$

2. a) $\dfrac{1}{343}$ **b)** $\dfrac{1}{1000}$

Example 4, Check, page 227

1. a) $\left(\dfrac{5}{3}\right)^2$ **b)** $\left(\dfrac{7}{6}\right)^4$ **c)** $\left(\dfrac{4}{9}\right)^3$

2. a) $\dfrac{27}{64}$ **b)** $\dfrac{25}{49}$ **c)** 1.953 125

Practice, page 228

1. a) $\dfrac{1}{36}$ **b)** $\dfrac{1}{5}$ **c)** $\dfrac{1}{32}$ **d)** 16

    e) 27   **f)** 10   **2.** $\dfrac{1}{64}$

3. a) $\dfrac{1}{\sqrt{3}}$ **b)** $\dfrac{1}{\sqrt[3]{2}}$ **c)** $\dfrac{1}{\sqrt[4]{8}}$

4. a) $\dfrac{1}{3^{\frac{2}{3}}}$ **b)** $\dfrac{1}{2^{\frac{3}{2}}}$ **c)** $\left(\dfrac{6}{5}\right)^4$

5. a) $\dfrac{1}{10}$ **b)** $-\dfrac{1}{5}$ **c)** $\dfrac{1}{2}$

6. a) $\dfrac{1}{1000}$ **b)** $\dfrac{1}{625}$ **c)** $\dfrac{1}{32}$

7. a) $\dfrac{36}{25}$ **b)** $\dfrac{343}{8}$

    c) 0.014 138 652...

Checkpoint 2, page 230

1. a) $\sqrt{13}$ **b)** $\sqrt[3]{-2}$ **c)** $\sqrt[4]{15}$

2. a) 5   **b)** -10 **c)** 1

3. a) 33 mm   **b)** 107 mm

4. a) $5^{\frac{3}{2}}$ **b)** $27^{\frac{5}{2}}$ **c)** $25^{\frac{4}{3}}$ **d)** $11^{\frac{3}{4}}$

5. a) 4   **b)** 8   **c)** 16   **d)** 243

6. a) $\dfrac{1}{7^3}$ **b)** 2^3 **c)** $\dfrac{1}{5^{\frac{3}{2}}}$ **d)** $\left(\dfrac{9}{4}\right)^5$

7. a) $\dfrac{1}{6}$ **b)** $\dfrac{1}{2}$ **c)** $\dfrac{1}{9}$

4.6 Skill Builder, Check, page 232

1. a) 2^{10} **b)** 3^4 **c)** 2^6 **d)** 3

4.6 Skill Builder, Check, page 232

1. a) 2^{27} **b)** 3^{12}

4.6 Applying the Exponent Laws, page 233

Example 1, Check, page 234

1. a) $\dfrac{1}{2^7}$ **b)** $\dfrac{1}{3^4}$ **c)** 11^7

Example 2, Check, page 236

1. a) $4^{\frac{3}{4}}$ **b)** $\dfrac{1}{2^{\frac{1}{3}}}$ **c)** $\dfrac{1}{5^{11}}$

Example 3, Check, page 238

1. a) $\dfrac{2}{x^2}$ **b)** $36a^8$ **c)** $\dfrac{y^6}{2}$

Example 4, Check, page 240

1. a) x **b)** $\dfrac{4}{3}a^{\frac{5}{3}}$

Practice, page 240

1. a) 5^4 **b)** 11^5 **c)** $\dfrac{1}{3^8}$ **d)** 8^4

2. a) 49   **b)** $\dfrac{1}{5}$ **c)** $\dfrac{1}{256}$

3. a) $5^{\frac{1}{2}}$ **b)** $\dfrac{1}{7^4}$ **c)** $\dfrac{1}{3^{\frac{2}{3}}}$ **d)** $\dfrac{1}{2^{4.5}}$

4. Parts a, b, d   **5.** ab

6. a) $3y^3$ **b)** $\dfrac{144}{x^2}$ **c)** $\dfrac{5}{2}b^5$ **d)** $\dfrac{49}{a^2}$

7. a) $\dfrac{1}{x^{\frac{7}{2}}}$ **b)** $\dfrac{2}{3}a^{\frac{4}{3}}$

Chapter 4 Puzzle, page 243
They are under eighteen.

Chapter 4 Review, page 245
1. a) 11   b) 20   c) 4   d) −5
2. 3.6
3. a) Irrational   b) Rational
4. $\sqrt[3]{64}$: A, $\sqrt[3]{-3}$: B, $\sqrt{14}$: C, $\sqrt{8}$: D
5. b) $\sqrt[3]{-9}$, $\sqrt{5}$, $\sqrt[3]{35}$
6. a) i) 4, 16; 16   ii) 9   iii) 9
      b) i) $4\sqrt{2}$ ii) $3\sqrt{7}$ iii) $3\sqrt{10}$
      c) i) 27   ii) 1   iii) 8
      d) i) $3\sqrt[3]{2}$ ii) $\sqrt[3]{60}$ iii) $2\sqrt[3]{9}$
7. a) $2\sqrt{13}$ b) $3\sqrt[3]{15}$
8. a) $2 \cdot 2 \cdot 2 \cdot 3 \cdot 3 \cdot 3 \cdot 5$
      b) i) $6\sqrt{30}$ ii) $6\sqrt[3]{5}$
9. a) $\sqrt{126}$ b) $\sqrt[3]{250}$
10. a) 6   b) 5   c) 27
11. a) i) 3.18   ii) 9.81   b) i) 73.10   ii) 5.62
12. a) $\dfrac{1}{8^5}$ b) $\dfrac{1}{6^{\frac{2}{3}}}$ c) 3^{10} d) $\left(\dfrac{2}{9}\right)^3$
13. a) $\dfrac{1}{27}$ b) $\dfrac{1000}{27}$ c) $\dfrac{1}{8}$
14. a) 81   b) $\dfrac{1}{16}$
15. a) $\dfrac{1}{x^{\frac{4}{3}}}$ b) $\dfrac{3}{4}x^2$

Chapter 5 Relations and Functions

5.1 Representing Relations, page 250

Example 1, Check, page 251
1. a) The relation shows the association "is located in" from a set of tourist attractions to a set of provinces.
   b) {(Butchart Gardens, British Columbia), (Icefields Parkway, Alberta), (Royal Canadian Mint, Manitoba), (Stanley Park, British Columbia)}

Example 2, Check, page 252
1. a 1st column: 1988, 1992, 1996, 2000, 2004, 2008;
     2nd column: 10, 18, 22, 14, 12, 18
   b) The association is: "was a year when Canada's medal count was"

Practice, page 253
1. a) The relation associates a set of capital cities with a set of provinces and territories.
   b) Part ii   c) Part iv

2. a) The relation shows the association "is coloured" from a set of properties to a set of colours.
   b) {(Atlantic Avenue, yellow), (Baltic Avenue, purple), (Boardwalk, dark blue), (Marvin Gardens, yellow), (Pacific Avenue, green)}
3. a) 1st column: Aquarium, Audio, Banana, Evacuate, Oodles; 2nd column: 5, 4, 3, 5, 3
   b) The relation shows the association "has this number of vowels" from a set of words to a set of numbers.
4. a) 1st column: Robert Borden, John Diefenbaker, John A. MacDonald; Lester B. Pearson, Pierre Trudeau; 2nd column: 1937, 1979, 1891, 1972, 2000
   c) Yes; the order of the ovals may not be reversed.

5.2 Skill Builder, Check, page 257
1. a) 13   b) 8

5.2 Skill Builder, Check, page 257
1. a) 9   b) 7

5.2 Properties of Functions, page 258

Example 1, Check, page 259
1. a) Domain: {3, 4, 6, 7}; range: {Cosmo's Space Derby, Galaxy Twister, Mindbender, Galaxyland Raceway, Balloon Race}; not a function
   b) Domain: {alto saxophone, clarinet, French horn, piano, trombone}; range: {B♭, C, E♭, F}; function

Example 2, Check, page 260
1. b) Dependent variable: C; independent variable: n
   c) Domain: {5, 10, 15, 20, 25, ...}; range: {0.67, 1.34, 2.01, 2.68, 3.35, ...}

Example 3, Check, page 262
1. a) $E(n) = 50n + 150$ b) $600   c) 14

Practice, page 262
1. a) Not a function   b) Not a function   c) Function
2. a) Domain: {4, 6, 8, 9}; range: {cube, pentagon, rectangle, square, triangle}
   b) Domain: {Winnipeg, Vancouver, Calgary, Regina}; range: {Chantal Kreviazuk, Michael J. Fox, Stephen Harper, Steve Nash, Pamela Anderson}
   c) Domain: {1, 2, 3, 4, 5}; range: {2, 4, 6, 8, 10}
3. b) Dependent variable: f; independent variable: s
   c) Domain: {75, 80, 85, 90, 100, 110}; range: {89, 124, 150, 177, 264, 351}
4. a) $P(s) = 2s + 15$ b) $f(x) = -3x + 5$
5. a) $d = 4t - 7$ b) $y = -2x - 3$
6. a) 3   b) 38
7. a) $M(n) = 5n + 2.5$ b) 32.5 kg   c) 8

Checkpoint 1, page 265

1. a) 1st column: Calgary Flames, Edmonton Oilers, Montreal Canadiens, Ottawa Senators, Toronto Maple Leafs;
   2nd column: 1, 5, 23, 4, 13

   b) The relation shows the association "has this number of Stanley Cup wins" from a set of hockey teams to a set of numbers.

2. a) Domain: {Apples to Apples, Life, Twister, Yahtzee};
   range: {cards, dice, spinner}; not a function

   b) Domain: {Lord of the Flies, Romeo and Juliet, Harry Potter, Catcher in the Rye, Of Mice and Men}; range: {Golding, Shakespeare, Rawlings, Salinger, Steinbeck}; function

3. b) Dependent variable: r; independent variable: a

   c) Domain: {49, 54, 59, 64, 69, 74, 79, 84, 85};
   range: {2.88, 2.95, 2.98, 3.04, 3.91, 4.88, 7.73, 13.34, 19.32}

4. a) $A(n) = 5n + 32$ b) $f(x) = -7x + 12$

5. a) $P = 8n - 5$ b) $y = 4x - 1$

6. a) 19   b) 12

5.3 Skill Builder, Check, page 268

1. a) Jodie's height from 5 to 20 years of age

   b) Jodie grew taller. The line segments go up to the right.

   c) Jodie stopped growing. The line segments are horizontal.

   d) About 170 cm

5.3 Interpreting and Sketching Graphs, page 269

Example 1, Check, page 270

1. a) D; $10   b) F; 16
   c) C and E; $8   d) B and C; 4

Example 2, Check, page 271

1. The graph shows how the volume of gas in Winston's motorcycle tank changes over time.

Practice, page 272

1. a) F; 28°C   b) E; 95%
   c) D and E; 26°C   d) D and F; 65%

2. a) False   b) True   c) True   d) True

3. The graph shows how Troy's distance from home changes on his hike.

5.4 Skill Builder, Check, page 275

1. D(-2, -4); E(0, 2); F(6, 0); G(4, -4)

5.4 Math Lab: Graphing Data, page 276

Practice, page 277

1. a) Yes   b) No   c) Yes
   d) Yes   e) No

2. d) Domain: {7 A.M., 8 A.M., 9 A.M., 10 A.M., 11 A.M., 12 noon, 1 P.M., 2 P.M., 3 P.M., 4 P.M.};
   range: {0, 5, 10, 20, 25, 30, 35}

5.5 Skill Builder, Check, page 279

1. a) <   b) ≥   c) >   d) ≤

2. a) $2 < g < 10$ b) $-5 < h \le 6$

5.5 Graphs of Relations and Functions, page 280

Example 1, Check, page 281

1. a) No; function   b) Yes; not a function

Example 2, Check, page 282

1. a) Domain: $-2 \le x \le 3$; range: $1 \le y \le 5$

   b) Domain: $x \le 1$; range: $y \ge -2$

Example 3, Check, page 284

1. a) 6   b) 8

Practice, page 284

1. a) Yes; not a function   b) No; function

2. a) Domain: {-3, -2, -1, 0, 1, 2};
   range: {-1, 0, 1, 2}

   b) Domain: {-3, -2, -1, 0, 1, 2};
   range: {-1, 0, 1, 2, 3, 4}

3. a) Function   b) Not a function   c) Function

4. a) Domain: $-4 \le x \le 1$; range: $-3 \le y \le 3$

   b) Domain: $x \ge -2$; range: $y \ge -1$

5. a) Graph A   b) Graph B

6. a) -5   b) -2

7. a) About 5   b) About -2

Checkpoint 2, page 287

1. a) The graph shows how the volume of water in Marty's kitchen sink changes over time.

2. b) No, because there is no such thing as a fraction of a prize.

   c) Yes, because no two numbers in the *Number of prizes* column are the same.

   d) Domain: {1, 2, 6, 12, 20}; range: {6, 12, 24, 42, 60}

3. Graph A: function; Graph B: not a function;
   Graph C: not a function

4. Domain: $x \le 3$; range: $y \le 3$

5. a) -2   b) About -3

5.6 Skill Builder, Check, page 290

1. a) 3rd column: -2, 1, 4, 7, 10

   b) 1st column: 0, 1, 2; 2nd column: 9, 7, 5, 3, 1

5.6 Properties of Linear Relations, page 291

Example 1, Check, page 292

1. a) The same; the same; linear

   b) The same; different; not linear

Example 2, Check, page 293

1. **a)** 3rd column: 3, 0, –1, 0, 3; No; No
   b) 3rd column: 0, 1, 2, 3, 4; Yes; Yes

Example 3, Check, page 295

1. **a)** Dependent variable: A; independent variable: t
   b) –3 m/s

Practice, page 296

1. **a)** The same; different; not linear
   b) The same; the same; linear

2. **a)** Linear   **b)** Not linear   **c)** Linear

3. Part b   **4. a)** No   **b)** Yes

5. **a)** Dependent variable: d; independent variable: t
   b) –60 km/h

6. **a)** Dependent variable: A; independent variable: n
   b) $20/pledge

5.7 Interpreting Graphs of Linear Functions, page 299

Example 1, Check, page 300

1. **a)** Vertical intercept: 100; horizontal intercept: 5
   b) Domain: $0 \leq t \leq 5$; range: $0 \leq d \leq 100$

Example 2, Check, page 301

1. y-intercept: 6; x-intercept: 3

Example 3, Check, page 303

1. Graph B

Practice, page 303

1. Vertical intercept: 12; horizontal intercept: 3
2. Domain: $0 \leq t \leq 12$; range: $-3 \leq C \leq 6$
3. y-intercept: 6; x-intercept: –2

5. **a)** Graph C   **b)** Graph A   **c)** Graph B

Chapter 5 Puzzle, page 306

1. 100   2. 4   3. 200   4. 120
5. –12   6. –2   7. –4   8. 50
9. 3   10. 0   11. 5   12. 20

Giraffe passing a window

Chapter 5 Review, page 308

1. **a)** 1st column: iPod Touch; iPod Touch; iPod Nano; iPod
   Nano; iPod Shuffle; 2nd column: 8, 32, 8, 16, 4
   b) The relation shows the association "has a memory of"
   from a set of iPods to a set of numbers of gigabytes.
2. **a)** Function   **b)** Not a function
3. **a)** $f(x) = 7x - 2$ **b)** $C(n) = 15n + 50$
4. **a)** 4   **b)** –3
5. The graph shows how the volume of Toby's television
   changes over time.

6. **b)** No, because there is no such thing as a fraction of a
   student.
   d) Domain: {1, 2, 3, 4, 5, 6}; range: {10, 15, 20, 25}
7. **a)** Function   **b)** Not a function
8. **a)** 6   **b)** 4
9. **a)** Linear   **b)** Linear   **c)** Not linear
10. **a)** Yes   **b)** No
12. **a)** Vertical intercept: 18; horizontal intercept: 6
    b) Domain: $0 \leq t \leq 8$; range: $-6 \leq C \leq 18$
    c) –3°C/h

Chapter 6 Linear Functions

6.1 Slope of a Line, page 314

Example 1, Check, page 316

1. **a)** $\dfrac{3}{4}$ **b)** $-\dfrac{1}{2}$ **c)** –2   **d)** $\dfrac{1}{5}$

2. **a)** –4   **b)** $\dfrac{4}{7}$

Example 3, Check, page 319

1. $-\dfrac{2}{5}$

Example 4, Check, page 321

1. $\dfrac{15}{7}$

Practice, page 321

2. $-\dfrac{4}{7}$

3. AB: $-\dfrac{3}{5}$; CD: $\dfrac{1}{4}$; EF: $\dfrac{1}{2}$; GH: –2   **5.** 2

6.2 Slopes of Parallel and Perpendicular Lines, page 324

Example 1, Check, page 325

1. AB and GH   2. Lines AB and CD

Example 2, Check, page 328

1. AB and CD
2. Lines RS and TU are perpendicular.

Example 3, Check, page 329

1. Yes

Practice, page 330

1. Parts a and c   2. Parts a and c
3. **a)** $\dfrac{1}{3}$ **b)** $-\dfrac{4}{3}$ **c)** $\dfrac{8}{7}$ **d)** –1
4. **a)** Neither   **b)** Perpendicular   **c)** Parallel
5. Yes   6. Yes   7. Yes

Checkpoint 1, page 333

1. AB: rise = 1; run = 6; slope = $\frac{1}{6}$;

   DE: rise = 2; run = –6; slope = $-\frac{1}{3}$

2. $\frac{1}{2}$

4. **a)** The slopes are equal.

   b) The slopes are negative reciprocals.

5. No

6.3 Math Lab: Investigating Graphs of Linear Functions, page 335

Practice, page 338

1. **a)** AB: 2; CD: 0; EF: –1   **b)** AB: 3; CD: 3; EF: 3

2. **a)** The graph is a line that goes up to the left.

   Slope = –4; y-intercept: 2

   b) The graphs have the same slope: –4

   The graphs have different y-intercepts: 4 and 2

4. **a)** The slopes of the graphs are negative reciprocals.

6.4 Slope-Intercept Form of the Equation for a Linear Function, page 340

Example 1, Check, page 340

1. Part c

2. $y = \frac{1}{4}x - 6$

Example 3, Check, page 343

1. $y = \frac{2}{3}x + 4$

Practice, page 343

1. Part b

2. **a)** Slope = 2; y-intercept = 6

   b) Slope = $-\frac{1}{2}$; y-intercept = $\frac{3}{2}$

   c) Slope = $\frac{1}{4}$; y-intercept = 0

   d) Slope = –1; y-intercept = 1

3. **a)** $y = -2x + 3$ **b)** $y = \frac{1}{4}x - 2$

   c) $y = 4x - 3$ **d)** $y = -\frac{3}{4}x$

4. $y = -\frac{2}{3}x - 4$ 5. **a)** $y = -\frac{3}{2}x + 1$ **b)** $y = \frac{7}{4}x - 3$

6.5 Slope-Point Form of the Equation for a Linear Function, page 346

Example 1, Check, page 347

1. **a)** Part ii   **b)** Part iv

2. **a)** Slope: 3; coordinates: (2, –1)

Example 2, Check, page 349

1. **a)** $y - 4 = -2(x - 1)$ **b)** $y = -2x + 6$

Example 3, Check, page 350

1. $y - 1 = -\frac{3}{2}(x + 4)$

Practice, page 350

1. **a)** Slope: $\frac{1}{2}$; coordinates: (–2, 4)

2. $y - 8 = -3(x + 1)$ 3. **b)** $y + 1 = \frac{5}{3}(x - 2)$

4. $y = -4x + 7$ 5. $y - 4 = -\frac{5}{3}(x + 3)$

6. **a)** $y + 3 = \frac{8}{3}(x - 1)$ **b)** $y + 3 = -\frac{3}{8}(x - 1)$

Checkpoint 2, page 355

1. **a)** –3   **b)** 5

2. **a)** $y = 4x + 8$ **b)** $y = \frac{3}{2}x - 1$

4. **a)** Coordinates: (5, –4); slope: 3

5. **a)** $y + 5 = 2(x - 3)$ **b)** $y = 2x - 11$

6. Sample response: $y - 3 = 2(x - 6)$

6.6 General Form of the Equation for a Linear Relation, page 358

Example 1, Check, page 359

1. $2x - 3y - 23 = 0$

Example 2, Check, page 360

1. $-\frac{3}{2}$

Example 3, Check, page 363

1. **a)** x-intercept: 8; y-intercept: –6

Practice, page 363

1. **a)** $2x - y - 1 = 0$ **b)** $x + 3y - 12 = 0$ **c)** $2x + 5y + 1 = 0$

2. **a)** –4   **b)** $\frac{3}{2}$

3. **a)** x-intercept: –5; y-intercept: –4

   b) x-intercept: 6; y-intercept: –3

4. x-intercept: –4; y-intercept: 6 **5.** $y = -\frac{3}{4}x + 4$

Chapter 6 Puzzle, page 366

1. 4   2. 6   3. 2   4. 3
5. 5   6. 8   7. 7   8. 9
1000 pushups

Chapter 6 Review, page 368

1. $\frac{2}{5}$ 2. $\frac{3}{5}$

4. a) i) $-\dfrac{3}{4}$ **ii)** $\dfrac{4}{3}$ **iii)** $\dfrac{4}{3}$

b) Parallel: CD and EF
    Perpendicular: AB and CD; AB and EF

6. a) Slope: 3; y-intercept: 2; $y = 3x + 2$
b) Slope: –4; y-intercept: –3; $y = -4x - 3$

7. a) $\dfrac{1}{2}$ **b)** $(-3, 4)$

Chapter 7 Systems of Linear Equations

7.1 Developing Systems of Linear Equations, page 374

Example 1, Check, page 375
1. Solution B: $m = -1$ and $n = -2$

Example 2, Check, page 377
1. a) $2c + 5s = 38; c + s = 13$

Example 3, Check, page 379
1. a) $a + s = 300; 8a + 6s = 2000$

Practice, page 380
2. Solution B: $a = -6$ and $b = 1$
3. a) Variables may differ: $2b + 3t = 45; b = t + 10$
4. a) Variables may differ: $f + t = 12; 5f + 10t = 75$

7.2 Solving a System of Linear Equations Graphically, page 383

Example 1, Check, page 384
1. $x = 4; y = -1$

Example 2, Check, page 386
1. b) 6 small multipacks; 3 large multipacks

Practice, page 387
1. a) $x = -1; y = 2$ **b)** $x = 4; y = -5$
2. $x = 2; y = 2$ **3.** $x = 2; y = 1$
4. b) 4 sleeves; 3 boxes

7.3 Math Lab: Using Graphing Technology to Solve a System of Linear Equations, page 392

Practice, page 394
1. $x = 6; y = -3$ **2.** $x = 3; y = 1$ **3.** $x = 4; y = 2$

Checkpoint 1, page 396
1. a) Variables may differ: $3m + 2g = 29; 5m + g = 32$
2. $x = 3; y = -1$
3. b) 5 field goals; 3 singles   **4.** $x = 4; y = -4$

7.4 Using a Substitution Strategy to Solve a System of Linear Equations, page 400

Example 1, Check, page 401
1. $x = -2; y = 0$

Example 2, Check, page 403
1. a) $s + w = 11; 2s + 4w = 30$
b) 7 short-answer questions; 4 word problems

Practice, page 404
1. a) $x = -3$ **b)** $y = 2$
2. $x = 1; y = 5$ **3.** $x = 5; y = 5$
4. a) Variables may differ: $3r + 5s = 25; 5r + s = 27$
b) Roller coaster ride: \$5; super swing ride: \$2

7.5 Using an Elimination Strategy to Solve a System of Linear Equations, page 407

Example 1, Check, page 408
1. $x = -1; y = 2$

Example 2, Check, page 410
1. $x = 2; y = -1$

Example 3, Check, page 412
1. a) $r + h = 14; 25r + 50h = 450$
b) 10 pairs of running shoes; 4 pairs of hiking boots

Practice, page 413
1. a) Multiply by –4.   **b)** Multiply by 5.
2. $x = 2; y = -2$ **3.** $x = 2; y = 4$
4. a) $s + L = 9; 50s + 75L = 500$ **b)** 7 small dogs; 2 large dogs

Checkpoint 2, page 416
1. $x = 4; y = -3$ **2.** $x = 4; y = -2$
3. a) $s + d = 15; 3s + 5d = 57$
b) 9 single-scoop cones; 6 double-scoop cones

7.6 Properties of Systems of Linear Equations, page 420

Example 1, Check, page 422
1. a) One solution   **b)** No solution   **c)** Infinite solutions

Practice, page 423
1. System A: infinite solutions; System B: no solution; System C: one solution
2. a) No solution   **b)** One solution
3. a) No solution   **b)** Infinite solutions **c)** One solution

Chapter 7 Puzzle, page 425
He was eliminated.

Chapter 7 Review, page 427
1. a) $a + y = 8; 12a + 6y = 66$
2. $x = 5; y = 1$ **3.** $x = 1; y = 0.5$
4. $x = 5; y = 4$ **5.** $x = 2; y = -5$
6. a) Infinite solutions   **b)** No solution